ROYAL BOOKS AND HOLY BONES

Essays in Medieval Christianity

ROYAL BOOKS AND HOLY BONES

Essays in Medieval Christianity

EAMON DUFFY

BLOOMSBURY CONTINUUM
LONDON • NEW YORK • OXFORD • NEW DELHI • SYDNEY

BLOOMSBURY CONTINUUM
Bloomsbury Publishing Plc
50 Bedford Square, London, WC1B 3DP, UK

BLOOMSBURY, BLOOMSBURY CONTINUUM and the Diana logo are trademarks of
Bloomsbury Publishing Plc

First published in Great Britain 2018

Copyright © Eamon Duffy

Eamon Duffy has asserted his right under the Copyright, Designs and Patents Act, 1988, to be
identified as Author of this work

For legal purposes the Acknowledgements on p. 319
constitute an extension of this copyright page

All rights reserved. No part of this publication may be reproduced or transmitted
in any form or by any means, electronic or mechanical, including photocopying,
recording, or any information storage or retrieval system, without prior permission
in writing from the publishers.

Bloomsbury Publishing Plc does not have any control over, or responsibility for,
any third-party websites referred to or in this book. All internet addresses given in this
book were correct at the time of going to press. The author and publisher regret any
inconvenience caused if addresses have changed or sites have ceased to exist, but can
accept no responsibility for any such changes.

A catalogue record for this book is available from the British Library.

Library of Congress Cataloguing-in-Publication data has been applied for.

ISBN: HB: 978-1-4729-5323-0
EPDF: 978-1-4729-5321-6
EPUB: 978-1-4729-5322-3

2 4 6 8 10 9 7 5 3 1

Typeset by Newgen KnowledgeWorks Pvt. Ltd., Chennai, India
Printed and bound in Great Britain by CPI Group (UK) Ltd, Croydon CR0 4YY

To find out more about our authors and books visit www.bloomsbury.com
and sign up for our newsletters.

Contents

List of illustrations vii

Introduction: Royal Books and Holy Bones 1

BOOKS 5

1. Early Christian Impresarios 7
2. Books Held by Kings 19
3. The *Golden Legend* 29
4. Secret Knowledge – or a Hoax? 43
5. The Psalms and Lay Piety 53

CRISES AND MOVEMENTS 71

6. Plague and Historical Memory 73
7. The Rise of Sacred Song 87
8. Holy Terror 97
9. The Cradle Will Rock: Histories of Childhood 111

SAINTS 123

10. Blood Libel: The Murder of William of Norwich 125
11. Sacred Bones and Blood 137

12	Treasures of Heaven: Saints and their Relics	149
13	St Erkenwald	165
14	The Cult of 'St' Henry VI	187
15	The Dynamics of Pilgrimage in the Late Middle Ages	205
16	'Lady, Pray Thy Son for Me': Prayer to the Virgin in the Late Middle Ages	221

ON THE EVE OF THE REFORMATION 237

17	Provision Against Purgatory: Wingfield College, Suffolk	239
18	Monasticism and the Religion of the People: Crowland Abbey	255
19	The Four Latin Doctors in the Late Middle Ages	275
20	The Reformation and the Alabastermen	289
21	Brush for Hire: Lucas Cranach the Elder	301

Acknowledgements	319
Notes	321
Index	355

List of Illustrations

1. John Talbot, 1st Earl of Shrewsbury, presents a collection of chivalric romances to Margaret of Anjou and Henry VI, her husband. Illuminated in Rouen in the mid-1440s, at the height of the Hundred Years War, Shrewsbury's book, which contains a genealogy tracing Henry VI's pedigree back to St Louis of France, is one of the most splendid manuscripts in the Old Royal Library. (Chapter 2) © British Library Board. All rights reserved / Bridgeman Images

2. One of the many impossible plants illustrated in the mysterious – and probably fraudulent – 15th century Voynich Manuscript. (Chapter 4) Beinecke Rare Book and Manuscript Library, Yale University

3. Arm reliquaries, like this 11th century example from France, might contain any relic of the saint, and not necessarily bones from their arm: cast in the dynamic form of an arm raised in blessing, such reliquaries vividly symbolised the benign presence and power to heal and bless of the saint or saints whose relics were enshrined within. (Chapters 11 & 12) Saint Louis Art Museum, Missouri, USA / Bridgeman Images

4. The late 15th century figure of King Henry VI on the south aisle screen at Barton Turf in the Norfolk Broads, though painted in an unsubtle 'folk' idiom, reflects the standard iconography of the royal 'saint' – crowned, clean-shaven, ermine robed and carrying orb and sceptre. (Chapter 14) Mike Dixon

5. The alabaster images of John De la Pole, Duke of Suffolk (d. 1491) and his wife Elizabeth Plantagenet (d. 1503), sister of Edward IV and Richard III, once highly coloured, dominate the chancel at Wingfield and back on to the De la Pole chantry chapel of the Holy Trinity (now the vestry), serving both as a reminder of the family's greatness, and a call to prayer for the repose of their souls. (Chapter 17) Peter Bloore

6. The power of Mary's prayers: this 15th century Nottingham alabaster (Chapter 20) shows the Archangel Michael weighing souls. Demons seek to load the scales against the soul undergoing judgement, to drag it down to hell: the Virgin Mary, sheltering another supplicant beneath her mantle, lays her rosary on the scales, tipping the balance in favour of the sinner being weighed – a vivid illustration of medieval confidence in the power of her intercession, as in the final words of the Hail Mary – 'pray for us sinners, now, and at the hour of our death'. (Chapter 16) Master and Fellows of Pembroke College, Cambridge

7. Roundel 8 of the late 12th century Guthlac Roll depicts Guthlac at the gates of hell, being given a scourge to curb the demons by his patron saint, Bartholomew. The seventeen illustrations on the Roll were perhaps designs for stained glass roundels in the shrine church illustrating Saint Guthlac's

LIST OF ILLUSTRATIONS IX

legend. (Chapter 18) © British Library Board. All Rights Reserved / Bridgeman Images

8. Representations of wealthy parishioner John Baymunt or Baymonde (d. 1485) and his wife Agnes kneel before St Ambrose and St Jerome on the doors of the rood screen at Foxley in Norfolk, which they had paid for. The Latin inscriptions on the white banderoles appeal for prayers for their souls, while the depictions of the Four Latin Doctors – Pope, Cardinal, Archbishop and Bishop – present a strong image of ecclesiastical hierarchy. (Chapter 19) Mike Dixon

9. This panel, now in the German National Museum, is one of Cranach's many schematic representations of the contrast between Law and Grace, proclaiming the Lutheran gospel of the centrality of faith in Christ's Cross as the only means of salvation: such images established an iconography taken up by other reformation artists, like Hans Holbein the Younger. (Chapter 21) German National Museum

10. The late 15th century 'Swansea Altarpiece' has four panels depicting the 'Joys of the Virgin' (Annunciation, Adoration of the Magi, Ascension of Christ and Assumption of the Virgin) flanking the central image of the Trinity, in which Father and Holy Spirit support Christ on the cross. Thousands such altarpieces were smashed by English reformation iconoclasts, but Nottingham alabaster altarpieces had been a major pre-Reformation export, and many, like this one, survived in Catholic Europe. (Chapter 20) V&A Museum

Introduction: Royal Books and Holy Bones

In a hugely influential discussion of the end of the pagan classical world and 'the triumph of Christianity and Barbarism', Edward Gibbon characterized the Christianity of the Middle Ages as having been deliberately distorted by a 'pernicious innovation', the superstitious veneration of the material remains of the holy dead. 'In the long period of twelve hundred years which elapsed between the reign of Constantine and the reformation of Luther', he wrote, 'the worship of saints and relics corrupted the pure and perfect simplicity of the Christian model.' That process, he thought, had begun almost as soon as Christianity became a tolerated religion, when the clergy secured the conformity of the credulous Roman populace by metaphorically baptizing the materialistic pagan beliefs they ostensibly sought to destroy. As a result, 'the minute particles of those relics, a drop of blood or the scrapings of a bone, were acknowledged, in almost every province of the Roman world, to possess a divine and miraculous virtue.'[1] The scathing contempt which pervades that discussion in the twenty-eighth chapter of Gibbon's *Decline and Fall of the Roman Empire* had twin sources, in the rationalism of Enlightenment thought, and in an older tradition of specifically Protestant historiography, which saw the history of medieval Catholicism as one long sad tale of decline into gross idolatry.

To most historians of Christianity till the late nineteenth century it seemed axiomatic that there were 'true' and 'false' versions of Gibbon's 'pure and perfect simplicity of the Christian model', however ironically he may have deployed the phrase. The history of the Church was the story of the unfolding of a single movement, founded by Christ and his Apostles, whose salient teachings distilled over time into the Creeds: there were 'right' and 'wrong' developments of Christianity's characteristic beliefs and institutions. For both Catholics and Protestants, true Christianity was marked above all by doctrinal orthodoxy, and stood sharply defined against deviant and erroneous forms of teaching, 'heresy'. In a culture decisively shaped both by Protestantism and by the Enlightenment, medieval Christianity seemed quite clearly a decline from earlier purity, and such assumptions shaped even the terminology used to characterize immense and multifaceted tracts of time. So the term 'medieval', and its English equivalent, 'the Middle Ages', reflected the tacit conviction that almost a millennium of Western civilization was essentially a transitional period between one great age – antiquity or the classical world – and another – the modern or proto-modern age of 'Renaissance' (rebirth) and Reformation. The hierarchy of value that thereby privileged one 'period' over another was even plainer in the term 'the Dark Ages', used to characterize the five centuries after the decline of the Roman Empire, centuries during which the distinctive institutions and identities of Europe had emerged.

Over the last couple of generations, most of those assumptions have crumbled. In a relativistic culture increasingly detached from the organized churches, historians are less inclined to privilege a particular story-line, and more prepared to view 'mainstream' accounts of Christianity as the version of the foundation myth that happened to win out. Sober historians nowadays are prone to speak of 'Christianities' in the plural, and to interest themselves in the rise of 'micro-Christendoms': the radically different and sometimes seemingly incompatible forms in which the Christian impulse, if it ever had been one impulse, metamorphosed and diversified as it adapted to changing times and new and disparate cultures.[2]

Unsurprisingly, that more pluralistic way of thinking has led medieval scholarship away from institutional concern with the

INTRODUCTION: ROYAL BOOKS AND HOLY BONES

doings of popes, kings and bishops, or theological debate over the niceties of Christian doctrine, crucial as such things have been in Christian history. Interest has shifted towards the study of Christianity – perhaps we should say Christianities – first and foremost as a set of practices, the religious strategies adopted by the people of the past to make sense of their daily existence.

And with growing interest in the history of religion as *practice* has come the realization that Gibbon's 'pure and perfect simplicity of the Christian model' is a mirage – specifically, that Christianity is and has been, first and foremost, a materialistic religion. It is rooted in the belief that in the Incarnation the eternal Godhead took on human flesh – in Wesley's words

> Our God contracted to a span,
> Incomprehensibly made man.

So any attempt to understand Christianity must engage with the multifarious temporal practices and material artifacts by which it has expressed that central incarnational conviction.

Christianity is one of the three so-called 'Abrahamic' religions – Judaism, Christianity and Islam – the great monotheisms that trace their origins to the religion of ancient Israel. All three can justly be characterized as 'religions of the book', because all three have at their heart reverence for a corpus of sacred scripture. But Christianity, for most of its history, has also been a religion in which the divine has been understood as immanent in and accessible through created matter: in the material elements of the sacraments (bread and wine, oil and water); in the painted or carved images of Christ and the saints; in the music and ceremonies of the liturgy; in the landscapes, routes and journeyings in which the shrines of the saints were located; and in the very flesh and bones of the holy dead themselves.

Most of the essays in this book reflect that growing historical interest in the material culture of Christianity, and in the practices by which the Christians of the past articulated their deepest convictions. The topics dealt with stretch over more than a thousand years, and range from the emergence in late antiquity of the Codex as the distinctive physical form of the Christian holy book, through medieval preoccupation with the bones, hair, teeth and blood of the saints, to the vehement Protestant rejection of the 'idolatrous' millennium-old cult of holy images. Some of the chapters originated from engagement with the work of other scholars in extended review essays, others as attempts to explore and explain some of the distinctive expressions of the faith of medieval Christians – the meaning for them of pilgrimage and holy place, the books which shaped their praying, the ebb and flow of fashion in the saints to whom they turned for help and healing, the strategies by which they mastered the universal human fear of death. For all their diversity, I hope that these essays have a common focus in a concern to understand the people of the past through the objects, places, beliefs and practices in which their deepest hopes and fears found expression.

Eamon Duffy
Feast of St Laurence, 2017

Books

I

Early Christian Impresarios

Early Christianity was more than a new religion: it brought with it a revolutionary shift in the information technology of the ancient world. That shift was to have implications for the cultural history of the world over the next two millennia at least as momentous as the invention of the Internet seems likely to have for the future. Like Judaism before it and Islam after it, Christianity is often described as 'a religion of the Book'. The phrase asserts both an abstraction – the centrality of authoritative sacred texts and their interpretation within the three Abrahamic religions – and also a simple concrete fact: the importance of a material object, the book, in the history and practice of all three traditions.

To modern readers, the phrase is bound to evoke images of the 'book' as we know it – the family Bible, say: something printed (or, if ancient, written) on both sides of folded sheets of paper (or parchment), stitched in bundles between protective covers of a thicker and tougher material. But for ancient Israel, as for pagan Greece and Rome, the 'book' implied no such thing. Instead, the word first and foremost denoted a literary unit inscribed on a long scroll or roll, formed from glued- or stitched-together membranes (initially of papyrus, later the tougher and more flexible parchment), whose contents were written in parallel columns at right angles to the length of the roll, normally on one side only. And this is the form in which the books of the Hebrew Bible are still read in synagogue worship.

The book roll, which had to be deliberately unfurled to be read, symbolized formality, permanence and, in general, cultural, literary or scientific worth. (And would long continue to do so: until 1849 the official file copies of British Acts of Parliament were inscribed on parchment rolls.) By contrast, for the people of the ancient world, writing on flat pages was essentially ephemeral. Students, lawyers and administrators might jot notes on such pages or bundles of pages, and writers often composed their first drafts on them, but anything of enduring value, and all completed works of literature or science, anything that might be stored in a library, would be copied into a roll. Suetonius thought it an oddity worth recording that Julius Caesar sent his campaign dispatches to the Senate in the form of sheets of papyrus rather than rolls.

None of this is hard to understand. Our modern book form, the codex, in fact evolved from the ancient equivalent of the stenographer's pad: bundles of wooden tablets linked with string hinges and coated with wax, on which information could be jotted with a stylus (often in shorthand). When the information was no longer needed, the wax could be heated and smoothed, and the tablets re-used. The first papyrus and (especially) parchment books of pages were recyclable in just the same way: folded and stitched bundles written on with soluble ink that could be washed off to leave the pages blank again. To inscribe the words of Holy Scripture on such jotting pads would demean its sacred character and authority.

All the more extraordinary, therefore, that from its very first emergence Christianity deliberately chose the form of the codex rather than the roll for its sacred writings. The earliest surviving texts of the gospels and of the Epistles of Saint Paul are, without exception, copied into codices. The Gospel of Saint Mark, usually thought to be the earliest of the four canonical gospels, lacks its original ending, a fact hard to account for except by wear and tear on the final page of the master copy of a papyrus codex, and almost inexplicable if Mark's Gospel had been first issued in the form of a roll, for in that case the missing conclusion would have been at the inner and best-protected end.

Why should the new religion have adopted this down-market and unfashionable book technology? The codex, it is true, has obvious practical advantages. Being written on both sides of the page, it is more economical than the roll; it can be readily indexed; it can be leafed through quickly to find a particular place; and it is more robustly portable. But these practical advantages, which certainly contributed to its eventual adoption as the normative form of the book, do not adequately explain the early Christians' exclusive preference for the form, even for their copies of the Jewish scriptures, which must of course have been transcribed from rolls. Historians have speculated that *difference* from Judaism may have been the point – that the codex was adopted to distance the emergent Church from its origins within the religion of Israel, or perhaps in an attempt to signal that its foundational texts were indeed a sort of sacred stenography, the living transcript of apostolic experience, taken from the mouths of the first witnesses.

However that may be, until recently surprisingly little has been made of this momentous foundational shift to a new book technology. The history of the early Church has been studied without much reference to the material culture of book production and distribution, and the impact of the physical form of the earliest Christian writings on the evolution of Christian ideas and institutions has been little explored. But in their jointly authored *Christianity and the Transformation of the Book*, Anthony Grafton and Megan Williams set about rectifying that omission, by exploring the work of two seminal figures in the history of third- and fourth-century Christianity, Origen of Alexandria and Eusebius of Caesarea.[1] The innovative form of their writings would profoundly shape the intellectual and material culture of the Roman Empire, soon to be Christianized, and, later, of medieval and early modern Europe.

Origen, born in Egypt toward the end of the second century, was the greatest biblical scholar of the early Church and, though posthumously tainted by suspicion of heresy, one of the most influential thinkers in the entire history of Christianity. The product of a persecuted Christian minority (his father was executed for his faith in AD 202), his own religious ardour found expression in awesome ascetical feats of fasting and self-denial that earned him the nickname Adamantius, 'man of steel'. Notoriously, he took literally the New Testament's praise of those who became 'eunuchs for the kingdom of heaven' and castrated himself.

Origen's religious zeal was matched by profound learning, not only in the Jewish and Christian scriptures, but in classical philosophy. Origen cannot be fully understood against the narrow background of official Church institutions, which were still in flux in his lifetime, but as belonging to the cultivated world of the late-classical philosopher. The practice of 'philosophy' was a way of life, involving immersion in the composition and copying of texts, and in detailed philosophical, grammatical and philological commentary on them. Libraries were vital to this process, and were accumulated by the gift, loan and copying of texts. The scholar was necessarily part of a network of like-minded users and producers of texts, and needed the backing of a wealthy patron to finance the huge costs involved in acquiring and copying them.

Origen taught philosophy as well as Christian doctrine for a time in Alexandria (if we are to believe his biographer Eusebius, he was the official catechist of the diocese). Eventually, however, he settled at Caesarea in Palestine, a town with vigorous Jewish and pagan communities, under the patronage of a rich Roman, Ambrose. There they built up an extensive working library, and established a scriptorium and a staff of scribes, some of whom must have been competent in Hebrew as well as Greek. Origen devoted himself to teaching and commenting on his basic texts, not now primarily the Neoplatonic philosophers in whose works he had been grounded and in which he continued to school his students, but above all the Jewish and Christian scriptures, the fundamental sources for a new Christian 'philosophy'. In the religious mixing pot of third-century Palestine, pagan, Jewish and Christian ideas jostled and clashed, and Origen's life's work was to make Christianity, rooted as it was in the 'barbarian' world of the Hebrew scriptures, intelligible to itself and to others within the sophisticated third-century

Greek intellectual world. He was the pioneering Christian translator between cultures, systematically striving to bring together the apparently incompatible thought-worlds of Moses and Plato, Jerusalem and Athens, and in the process to vindicate Christian teaching against enemies within and without.

Like most Christians of his time, and like Orthodox Christians even today, Origen read the Old Testament in a Greek translation known as the Septuagint, completed long before the Christian era, and before the normative Hebrew text had been stabilized. The Septuagint, therefore, often differed, sometimes significantly, from the Hebrew versions used by third-century (and modern) Jews. In Isa. 7:14, for example, the Septuagint translated the Hebrew word *almah*, young woman, with the Greek *parthenos*, virgin, and in that form the text was crucial for Christian belief in and defence of the Virgin Birth. Inevitably, Christians suspected Jews of deliberately corrupting such texts to discredit Christian teaching.

Origen believed passionately in the inspired authority of the Septuagint, but he recognized that Jewish–Christian debate was hampered by the lack of an agreed-upon authoritative text. He set about remedying the situation in an awe-inspiring scholarly project which could only have been conceived in the light of Christian deployment of the codex. Having taught himself Hebrew with the help of local rabbis (the extent of his knowledge is debated), Origen compiled the most famous multi-volume book of antiquity, the Hexapla ('Sixfold'). This was a complete edition of the Old Testament in six separate versions, set out in parallel columns across each double opening of a codex, three columns to each single page.[2] On the extreme left was the Hebrew; next to that a phonetic rendering of the Hebrew in Greek letters; next to that a hyperliteral translation of the text into Greek by the Jewish convert Aquila; next to that a more idiomatic version by another Greek Jew, Symmachus; then the Septuagint; and finally, on the extreme right, another modern Jewish-Greek version by Theodotion.

For poetic books like the Psalms, Origen added still other Greek versions (including an anonymous one he had found buried in a jar, like the Dead Sea Scrolls), the object of the whole exercise being to provide as many interpretative tools for a correct reading of the Septuagint as possible. He also edited the Septuagint text itself, adding symbols to indicate where it differed from the Hebrew, and supplying 'missing' material from the best of the other versions. This corrected Septuagint text circulated separately, and was to prove immensely influential for centuries. The Hexapla dealt with a single Hebrew word or short phrase and its Greek cognates, one Hebrew word to a line, thereby inviting a microscopic comparison between the various texts. By Grafton and Williams's computation, the complete text probably occupied up to forty large codices.

It would be hard to exaggerate the revolutionary nature of Origen's project. No other ancient book had looked like this, no other ancient text had been edited with such immense elaboration, and for the first time all the sophistication of Greek philological and grammatical methods were applied to a 'barbarian' book. But more than that, Origen's gigantic labours were simultaneously an ardent expression of his religious reverence for every shade of meaning in the words of the sacred text and a standing refutation of fundamentalism. The many-columned Hexapla was a visual monument to the elusiveness of meaning and the impossibility of fixing a single infallible text, and it physically embodied the endless labour of cross- and intercultural translation and interpretation. Origen's own practice as a commentator on scripture followed suit: though he took the Septuagint to be the divinely inspired scripture, he routinely employed what Grafton and Williams, following the scholar Adam Kamesar, call 'an exegetical maximalism': commenting on other, differing versions, Hebrew and Greek, as if they too conveyed divine meaning.

We know the Hexapla mainly from contemporary descriptions of it. Though considered one of the wonders of the scholarly world, it was probably just too big to be copied in its entirety, and although hexaplic texts of individual books of the Bible probably circulated, it and they have perished almost without trace. So far only fragments of two much later versions have been found, the most revealing of them, now in Cambridge, a single opening containing part of the text of Psalm 32, which was rescued in the nineteenth century from the wastepaper storage room of a medieval Cairo synagogue. Most of Origen's own immense output of biblical commentary and doctrinal exposition has similarly perished, the victim of later suspicions of his orthodoxy. But not before they had been endlessly quarried and plagiarized by every other early Christian commentator on scripture: he had established patterns of thought and interpretation that would continue to have an effect for more than a millennium.

Origen's work was perpetuated in Caesarea. Though his books appear to have been dispersed after his death, the Beirut-born priest Pamphilius re-established a theological school there, and devoted his ample personal fortune to creating a truly great library, the pride of which was the complete Hexapla and a complete collection of Origen's original writings. With the help of one of his own pupils, the Church historian Eusebius, Pamphilius wrote an elaborate defence of Origen's teaching (now mostly lost). After Pamphilius's death by martyrdom in 310, Eusebius, who eventually became bishop of the city, continued to expand the library, and launched a series of scholarly projects in which Origen's intellectual legacy was consolidated and developed.

Eusebius is one of the most remarkable figures in the fourth-century Church: far from heroic (he probably survived the persecution in which his master Pamphilius died by flight, or by even more ignoble conformity), he was the first theorist of the Christianization of the *Pax Romana*. Within two years of Pamphilius's death a Christian fellow-traveller, Constantine, seized control of the empire, and Christianity became Rome's 'most favoured religion'. Eusebius, a highly successful client of the powerful, would eventually become Constantine's official biographer and panegyrist. He saw in the emergence of a Christian emperor God's providential action: the gospel would march along the roads that imperial power had made. Though a clumsy writer, he was a tireless compiler and editor, and his great *Church History* is a treasure house of otherwise lost documents, not all of which Eusebius himself fully understood. Book Six of the *Church History* contains our fullest information about the life of Origen.

Eusebius has been described as 'a Christian impresario of the Codex',[3] not merely because of his prodigious book-collecting (he built around Pamphilius's collection one of the finest libraries of antiquity, which would remain the greatest treasure of the diocese of Caesarea), but because of his innovations in book *production*. It was to Eusebius that Constantine turned to provide the sacred texts for the great churches he was establishing in the new centre of empire at Byzantium, commissioning him to provide, from his own scriptorium or others, fifty great codices of the Bible. Two of these may in fact survive, Codex Vaticanus (now, as its name implies, in Rome) and Codex Sinaiticus (now divided between libraries in Sinai, London, Leipzig and St Petersburg), in which the Septuagint text and the Greek New Testament are laid out, three or four columns to a page, in majestically large 'Uncial' script, forming the first surviving Christian 'lectern bibles'.[4]

Eusebius himself initiated a series of remarkable projects that may well have been directly inspired by the Hexapla. The most significant of these was his universal chronicle of human history, presented in the form of a set of comparative chronological tables, laid out across successive openings of a codex in the manner of the Hexapla, and setting key events derived from the records of all the civilizations of the known world alongside the chronology derived from the Bible. Like earlier chroniclers, Eusebius wrestled with the problems that beset all attempts to reconcile the often legendary histories of the civilizations of the Middle East with a timeline derived from the narratives and genealogies of the Old Testament – for example, he disposed of the apparently immense and, in biblical terms, awkward antiquity of Egyptian civilization by suggesting that several of the dynasties of the Pharaohs had reigned contemporaneously. But where other Christian chronologists, in Eusebius's time and since, have attempted to establish around the Bible's timeline a single universal chronology of human history, Eusebius knew that this simply could not be done. The discrepancies could not all be resolved, and the best one could do was to privilege the biblical timeline, certainly, but then to set the others alongside it for comparison. Far from being a way to make the ancient past neat and familiar, Eusebius's chronology 'became a guide to the cosmopolitan variety of traditions that Christian historiography needed to take into account'. His chronological tables were thus 'a stunningly original work of scholarship', 'history made visible'.[5] They would be adapted and updated for the Latin-speaking world by another great 'impresario of the codex', Saint Jerome, and in that form would go on being used into modern times. Like the Hexapla, they embodied, a page at a glance, a living sense of the flux and uncertainty of divergent chronologies, and of the irreducible plurality of human history.

Christianity and the Book was a highly enjoyable and successful collaboration between a distinguished senior scholar (Grafton, a specialist in Renaissance cultural history, was chair of the Council of the Humanities and Henry Putnam University Professor of History at Princeton) and a very bright young historian. Drawing on a wealth of recent writing on the cultural setting of early Christianity (much of it inspired by the seminal work of Peter Brown), Grafton and Williams brought their own distinctive insistence on the centrality of innovations in book production and book distribution to the formation of momentous new patterns of thought. Their book was often speculative, and the pluralist values and objectives they attribute to their two heroes were sometimes suspiciously redolent of the twenty-first-century Western academy rather than of the ancient world. But they succeeded in placing Origen and Eusebius firmly and illuminatingly against a world in which Christianity had not yet triumphed, and conveyed vividly the intellectual daring involved in these pioneering attempts to articulate and define Christianity alongside and against the Jewish and the classical world-views, thereby completing the potent mix of cultural influences which underlie the most fundamental assumptions and directions of our inherited Western culture.

Megan Williams's first book, *The Monk and the Book*, dealt with another man of the book, the career of Saint Jerome, himself one of the defining figures of Western Christianity.[6] Born in the western Balkans a century after Origen's death and a generation after Constantine's conversion, Jerome was a brilliant intellectual grounded in Latin rhetoric. Chronically quarrelsome, and with a genius for turning friends into enemies second only to his genius as a textual critic and translator, he was one of the most vivid and influential figures of the fourth and fifth centuries. His turbulent career took him to Asia Minor, to Italy (where he served for three years as private secretary to Pope Damasus), to Gaul, to the Syrian desert, and finally to Bethlehem. There he established both a convent for women (in which he settled some of the devout and learned Roman ladies whose wealth supported his studies) and a monastery for men, where he devoted himself to a life of startling austerity and to epoch-making work on the Bible.

Jerome was an outstanding biblical commentator whose writings on the Old Testament prophets and on the gospels would shape Latin thought for centuries. But his greatest achievement was a Latin translation of the Bible based not on the Greek of the Septuagint but on profound knowledge of the Hebrew text. Though sharing contemporary Christian suspicion of the Jews, he recognized the primacy of the Hebrew text of the Old Testament, and he incurred accusations of heretical 'Judaizing' by insisting on the need for Christians to accept the 'Hebrew verities', by which he meant not only the authentic text of the Hebrew Bible but also, on occasion, rabbinic commentary and interpretation.

Enormously indebted to Origen both as an editor and exegete, he nevertheless rejected Origen's doctrinal teaching and, characteristically, campaigned for its condemnation. Jerome insisted on the primary authority of the Old Testament books recognized as canonical by Jews (the Septuagint contained apocryphal books that survive only in Greek and hence were not in the Hebrew canon). In expounding the Bible he gave priority to the literal and historical sense of the Hebrew text over allegorical or spiritual interpretation (which, however, he also valued). These emphases would help separate the thought-world of Latin Christianity from that of the Greek East, always more receptive to the 'spiritual' interpretation favored by Origen.

In Renaissance art Jerome is portrayed in two contrasting ways: the learned scholar in his book-filled study, at work on the text of the Bible, and the wild-eyed ascetic, half-naked in the desert, often beating his breast with a stone.[7] Both images capture fundamental aspects of Jerome's career: in the Middle Ages he was considered a model for monks as well as for scholars and theologians. Megan Williams took the two images as highlighting a troubling inconsistency in Jerome's own self-perception and self-presentation. Placing him, like Origen and Eusebius, whose work he quarried and translated extensively, in the world of the leisured scholar of late antiquity, she argued that Jerome had trouble reconciling the call to monasticism with the scholarly work of editor and translator. The monastic heroes of the desert whom Jerome aspired to imitate renounced all possessions, including books, and worked with their hands. He therefore needed a rhetorical frame, even a smokescreen, in which the enormously costly activities of the scholar, with his precious library and his staff of scribes and servants, were presented as a form of painful asceticism, akin to the weaving of rush baskets by which many of the desert monks earned their living.

In one of the most famous of his letters Jerome recounted a terrifying dream, in which he was hauled before the Judgment seat of Christ, and in which the Judge rejected him because he was not a Christian but 'a Ciceronian'. In the wake of the dream, Jerome claimed to have renounced all his classical learning and his study of literature, and resolved to devote himself purely to work for the gospel. Accordingly, the older Jerome would present his labours on the text of the Bible not as literary delight (when younger he had praised the style of the biblical writers) but as backbreaking and uncongenial work, wrestling with the truth, in which style and enjoyment were irrelevancies or distractions.

This divide between Jerome the monk and Jerome the scholar, at root an opposition between profane culture and the demands of discipleship, would not be resolved until later Benedictine monasticism established the congruence of learning and monastic discipline. Since monks repudiated property and luxury, Williams traces the roots of Jerome's dilemma to the contrast between the asceticism demanded of the monk, and the lavish comprehensiveness of

Jerome's library at Bethlehem, claiming that he must have owned a copy of the Hexapla (which is in fact extremely unlikely), and implying that he must have possessed copies of every book he can be shown to have used.

Jerome had Jewish teachers, he dictated most of his writings and, as his eyesight deteriorated, he needed secretaries even to read to him. Williams suggests that all this, too, places him in a world of moneyed scholarship at odds with his monastic vocation, since all of these people would have had to be paid. There is clearly something in this, and we know that Jerome did in fact pay monks from other communities for copying work: he certainly must have had a significant income from somewhere. But it would be a mistake to make too much of this point. Jerome himself, as she herself shows, complained of his dependence on (presumably unpaid) monk-secretaries, whose other duties prevented them from giving him the time he needed. Friends and admirers who sought copies of his works were expected to supply scribes and materials themselves. This suggests a less than lavish establishment at Bethlehem, and accordingly a less stark contrast between Jerome's two vocations than she implies. Great ideas, like great people, have particular origins, and their own complex settings. But whatever the circumstances of its production, not always recoverable after the lapse of centuries, Jerome's Latin Bible would become the foundational text for the intellectual development of the West, providing words for the deepest aspirations and most intensely held convictions of an entire civilization.

2

Books Held by Kings

A reader climbing the great staircase of the British Library's modern premises near St Pancras Station in London is confronted suddenly by that wonderful building's most wonderful feature. Behind the glass walls of an internal tower six stories high, more than 60,000 sumptuously bound books stretch upward, shelf upon shelf, a cliff-face of leather and gilt lettering gleaming softly through the tinted glass. In that architectural *coup de théâtre*, a world of learning serves as the visible core of a building created to contain all the learning of the world.

In its day that display, the so-called King's Collection, made up one of the greatest of Enlightenment libraries, assembled over a lifetime of dedicated book-buying by the bookish King George III. It rests now at St Pancras because within ten years of the old king's death in 1820, his books were presented to the nation by his son, King George IV. 'Prinny', as his subjects liked to call him (half affectionately, half contemptuously), was a lavish patron of the visual arts, but not much of a reader. More to the point, perhaps, he was eager to clear the site of the run-down royal residence at the western end of the Mall where his father's library was stored, in order to build Buckingham Palace, a lavish setting for his own overblown notions of royal grandeur.

George III had created a great library for himself in part because the monarchy he inherited in 1760 from his grandfather had disposed of all its books just three years earlier. The Old Royal Library had been a magnificent collection of more than 2,000 medieval manuscripts and 9,000 printed books. Begun in the 1470s by King Edward IV, though incorporating many older books, it had been expanded over the centuries, not least by an influx of loot from the monastic libraries dissolved during the English Reformation. But the entire collection was signed away to the nation in 1757 by King George II.

His motives are far from clear, but he almost certainly felt no pang at the parting, for he cared nothing about books. '*Rex illiteratus est quasi asinus coronatus*,' declared the twelfth-century scholar John of Salisbury: 'A king without learning is like a donkey with a crown.' If so, George II was to father a long line of donkeys, for, his grandson George III apart, the monarchs of the House of Hanover were more noted for their devotion to horses and the hunting field than to the pursuit or patronage of libraries. Alan Bennett playfully exploited the persisting reputation of royal philistinism in the House of Windsor in his 2007 comic novella *The Uncommon Reader*. In it, Queen Elizabeth II happens upon a van containing a circulating library, intended for the use of the palace servants, and discovers in herself a compulsive love of reading. There follows a sharp decline in her attention to duty, with disturbing consequences for the constitutional position of the Crown.

Bennett's fable depended for its humour on the wild improbability of a bookish monarch. But it was not ever thus. For earlier English royal dynasties, as for their European counterparts back into late antiquity, the creation of lavish royal libraries had been one of the pillars of royal reputation and display. The Yorkist King Edward IV, the Tudor Henry VIII and the Stuart Charles II, as well as the Merry Monarch's uncle, the young Prince Henry Frederick, who had died while heir apparent to James I in 1612, were all avid book collectors. Between them they assembled the superb collection that George II parted with so lightly in 1757.

Allowing for items mislaid or misappropriated during the many mishaps and migrations of the collection before and after 1757, that collection, the Old Royal Library, remains one of the glories of

Britain's national book collection. Unlike George III's books, however, on spectacular permanent display in their new tower of glass, no one for centuries has seen the Old Royal Library assembled in a single place. Its 2,000 manuscripts have been absorbed into the library's general holdings, and lie hidden from view in the air-conditioned obscurity of the stacks.

In 2011 the British Library put on show 111 of the Old Royal Library's 1,200 illuminated books, together with thirty-seven complementary manuscripts with royal associations, drawn from other collections.[1] Though fewer than a tenth of the royal collection's illuminated books were included, the show was a concentration of pictorial glory surviving with an intensity and opulence that exists in almost no other medium. Most medieval art objects – wall paintings, panel paintings, jewellery or carved statuary – have fallen casualty to time in one way or another. The majority have been lost, and what remains is often dilapidated, faded, incomplete. Medieval paintings and statues were mostly religious, and myriads of images were therefore scraped, hammered or burned into oblivion by zealous Protestant iconoclasts in the sixteenth century. And most of the precious metalwork into which so much medieval craftsmanship and wealth were poured has long since been broken up and melted down for its bullion and gemstone value.

Most medieval manuscripts, too, have perished. But where they survive, they are often in better condition than any other kind of medieval artifact. The splendour of an illuminated manuscript constituted a form of conspicuous consumption valuable only for itself. A book, however costly, is a book: it cannot be melted down for bullion. Pages might be removed for the sake of the individual miniatures they contained; whole volumes might be ripped up or burned as the superstitious rags of popery; texts considered redundant might be carelessly dismembered to wrap cheese, or to do humbler duty still in the privy. In the course of the Reformation, whole libraries were lost in this way.

But for all that, medieval books endure still in their thousands. The sheep- or calfskin on which they were written is remarkably durable, and a closed book protects bright colours from the bleaching light. So that British Library exhibition was, among other things, a heart-stopping display of some of the most perfect surviving medieval works of art, pictures and text created for monarchs, centuries old, yet as fresh as the day they were completed. Their bright pages offered window upon window into the medieval world as it imagined itself, gloriously frozen in vermilion and lapis lazuli and burnished gold.

Not all these royal books, though, were to be treasured for the splendour of their pictures. One of the earliest and most evocative items in the Old Royal Library is a worn and rather dowdy early eighth-century Latin gospel book, with few illuminations and no pictures, though it was probably written in the same scriptorium as the more famous and far more spectacular Lindisfarne Gospels, the illuminated Latin manuscript now in the British Museum. But the Old Royal Library gospel book is remarkable all the same, for it contains an added note in Anglo-Saxon, recording the manumission of a slave by King Athelstan, immediately on his accession in 925. This moving record of the king's magnanimity (the earliest such manumission to survive) suggests that the book was being used for services in Athelstan's own chapel royal at Winchester.[2]

The Lindisfarne book is exceptional in the Old Royal Library because it is a liturgical book, designed for weekly use at Mass. It is not in itself surprising that altar and choir books, however sumptuous, rarely feature in the catalogues of aristocratic or royal libraries, for they were kept where they were needed, in the vestry or the chapel book chest. But in any case, the religious upheavals of the sixteenth century took their toll on these kinds of books in particular. In 1550, Edward VI's Protestant government decreed the systematic destruction of every medieval liturgical book in England, and in 1551 the Privy Council specifically ordered 'the purging of his Highnes Librarie at Westminster of all superstitiouse bookes'.

As a result, the Old Royal Library contains not a single missal, and only eight other liturgical manuscripts of any kind. It is equally thin in medieval books of personal devotion, with only eight books of hours and eighteen illuminated psalters, half of which entered the Royal Library only in the seventeenth century. These absences are truly remarkable, for psalters and books of hours are the most common of all medieval manuscripts, and every other comparable library contains multiple examples of them. The great eighteenth-century library of the Earls of Oxford, for example, whose manuscript collections are similar in scale and opulence to those of the Old Royal Library, and which are also in the British Library, has sixty-one psalters and 103 books of hours.

But the religious upheavals of mid-Tudor England brought gain as well as loss. Two of the psalters that do survive in the collection were presented to Queen Mary I, as part of the restoration of Catholicism after 1553. And one of those two, the so-called Queen Mary Psalter, has a fair claim to be one of the most beautiful books produced anywhere in the whole of the Middle Ages.[3] The work of a single anonymous early-fourteenth-century English master, its 319 leaves contain no fewer than 223 prefatory tinted drawings, recapitulating the Old Testament from the creation of the world to the death of Solomon; twenty-four calendar pages with signs of the zodiac and labours of the months; 104 whole- or half-page miniatures; twenty-three historiated initials (i.e., enlarged and containing a figure or scene); and 464 marginal drawings.

No one knows for whom this sublime and lavish book was made, but in 1553 the manuscript, with its parade of delicate, curly-headed holy figures and its furred and feathered marginal bestiary, belonged to Henry Manners, Earl of Rutland. An ardent Protestant, Manners had made the huge mistake of supporting the Duke of Northumberland's attempt to prevent Queen Mary's accession, long after it was clear that this *coup* had failed. Imprisoned in the Fleet in July 1553, Manners's goods were forfeit: his psalter, that miraculous and exquisite survivor of the Edwardine holocaust of 'superstitious books', entered the comparative safety of the royal collection.

As that suggests, English monarchs might acquire books by many means – by gift, by marriage, by spoil of war and by confiscation. But some of them at least set out to buy them. In this they were self-consciously following the pattern set by fabled European royal book collectors like Alfonso the Wise of Castile or Robert the Wise of Anjou, king of Naples. Looted and dispersed in the 1340s, much of Robert's magnificent library found its way to the royal library of France, and from there a few of his books, including a lavishly illustrated history of Troy, even found their way to England.

But in the 1470s, Edward IV, who presided over what foreign visitors considered 'the most splendid court in all Christendome', determined to outdo all such royal predecessors and contemporaries by commissioning a series of deluxe manuscripts from the best workshops in the centre of such production, the southern Netherlands. Edward seems especially to have favoured sumptuously illustrated chronicles and world histories. These enormous (and enormously costly) books obviously mattered greatly to him. Despite their bulk, they may have accompanied him on his progresses from palace to palace, in specially constructed 'cofyns of fyrre' (coffins of fir), though eventually they seem to have been settled in his favourite residence at Eltham, under the care of a yeoman employed specially 'to kepe the kinges bookes'.[4]

Edward IV almost certainly commissioned more new illuminated books than any other English monarch, and the fifty or so of his manuscripts remaining in the Old Royal Library form a distinctive and homogeneous group. The four hundred surviving manuscripts added to the Old Royal Library by Henry VIII represent fewer than half the 908 books we know him to have owned and kept in his 'upper Library' at Whitehall alone, and Whitehall, though his main residence, was just one among the sixty royal residences Henry used.

We know in detail what books he kept at Whitehall, many of which have survived in the Old Royal Library, because a detailed Whitehall inventory not only lists all the manuscripts and printed books there, but even preserves their probable shelf order and physical arrangement. By contrast, the content of Henry's libraries at Greenwich and at Hampton Court is entirely lost to us. The only inventory for the palace at Greenwich reveals that there were 329 books in 'the highest library', but says nothing about what they might have been, while the post-mortem inventory for Hampton Court dismisses the large library there with the maddeningly imprecise 'item, a greate nombre of bookes'.

Even so, Henry's remaining books constitute 20 per cent of the surviving Old Royal Library, making him by far the single most important royal contributor. Some of these books were specially commissioned, like the collections of motets copied and decorated in the Netherlands with Henry's Tudor rose and the pomegranate of his queen Catherine of Aragon, or the magnificent Renaissance psalter illuminated by Jean Mallard for the king's personal use, in which the bear-like figure so familiar from Holbein's portraits appears both as the 'blessed man' of Psalm I and as the royal psalmist, David, himself. But well over half Henry's manuscripts were made for someone else, the majority confiscated from the monastic libraries he himself had dissolved, a staggering hundred of them from the single cathedral priory at Rochester alone.

These, however, were no random acquisitions: in the later 1530s, Henry's book collecting was 'issue-driven', and he dispatched the antiquary and bookman John Leland to scour monastic and college libraries all over England for legal, historical and theological texts that might provide backing for his divorce from Catherine of Aragon, and an intellectual pedigree for the novel doctrine of the Royal Supremacy. Relatively few of these working texts were lavishly illustrated, and it is one of history's ironies that so high a proportion of the monastic libraries of England should have been preserved to help the man who had destroyed those libraries divorce his wife and renounce the pope.[5]

Later royal bibliophiles, like Prince Henry Frederick and Charles II, built their libraries more serendipitously, by acquiring other people's collections. Prince Henry, who modelled his collecting on European royal connoisseurs like the Emperor Rudolf II, was fortunate in acquiring (perhaps as a gift) one of the greatest of Elizabethan libraries, that of John, Lord Lumley. Lumley's library in turn incorporated the books of his Catholic father-in-law Henry Fitzalan, Earl of Arundel. Arundel had been a key figure in Mary

Tudor's regime and, in addition to many former monastic books, he had acquired about a hundred manuscripts from the library of Archbishop Thomas Cranmer, executed by Mary's Catholic regime in 1556. Perhaps unsurprisingly, most of the surviving liturgical books in the Old Royal Library came from this Arundel–Lumley collection.

Charles II, the last great benefactor of the Old Royal Library, collected in a deliberate effort to replace the royal books lost in the depredations of the Civil War. Like his uncle Prince Henry, he benefited from the discriminating eye of another great collector, the Gloucester antiquary John Theyer, from whose estate he acquired, among much else, 334 manuscripts, the spoil of more than twenty West Country monastic houses. In 1678 Theyer's manuscripts were valued at £841, a significant expenditure even for a Restoration king. Charles's love of learning is, however, put in its proper setting by the fact that a few years before he bought Thayer's books, he had given his mistress Nell Gwynn a present of £2,265, to buy silver ornaments for her bed![6]

Kings needed books for a host of reasons: to pray with, to play or sing with, to codify laws, or to map the realm's coastline. Princes bought encyclopedias to master facts, they bought chivalric romances to while away long winter evenings, they bought illuminated bibles to symbolize (and feed) their piety. An array of costly books in the king's chamber proclaimed his wisdom, learning, civilization. Books on etiquette, morals or the arts of war were needed to educate his heirs. These royal requirements did not change much over the course of the Middle Ages, and the books made to meet them often passed from hand to hand. The results could be poignant. One of the manuscripts from outside the Royal Library which was included in the 2011 exhibition was a lavish psalter illuminated in a London stationer's shop for Prince Alphonso, son of Edward I and Eleanor of Castile, and heir apparent to the English throne. In 1284 the ten-year-old prince was betrothed to Margaret, daughter of the Count of Holland and Zeeland. The psalter, which was to be a wedding gift, was duly emblazoned with their arms.

But while work on the manuscript was still in progress, Alphonso died, the book lost its point, and the scribe put down his pen. Thirteen years later, however, Alphonso's sister Elizabeth married John, Count of Holland, brother of Alphonso's intended bride. Thriftily, and with the heraldry of the two royal houses once more apposite, the abandoned book was dusted down for completion in an East Anglian scriptorium. New calendars and illuminations were added, and the updated book assumed its interrupted role as the visible token of a royal alliance designed to straddle the North Sea. The manuscript remains, a monument to the fragility of even royal lives, and to the persistence of dynastic imperatives that transcended the mere individuals who served them.[7]

A similar pathos surrounds several of the manuscripts associated with the tragic figure of Henry VI, who died in 1471. England's claims to the throne of France in the age of Crécy and Agincourt brought many French manuscripts to England. John, Duke of Bedford, Henry IV's third son, was an especially lavish patron, and the magnificent book of hours he and his Duchess Anne presented at Christmas 1430 to the young Henry VI is one of the glories of late medieval manuscript production, though it never formed part of the Old Royal Library. Several other surviving books were intended to educate Henry in piety and kingcraft: in one of them, another psalter given to him in his coronation year, the young king is portrayed being presented to the Virgin and her Son by Saint Louis, robed in *Fleurs de Lys*. Henry's court will have seen this jewelled image as a fitting affirmation of English claims to the throne of France. In fact, however, the portrait was painted before Henry was born, and originally represented Louis of Guyenne, dauphin of France, for whom the book was first intended, but who had died while still a minor in 1415. The transferred image, charged with doomed territorial aspirations, is all the more poignant because Henry VI was to prove ardently pious but hopelessly inept, and in his disastrous reign the legacy of Agincourt would be frittered away.

Most of the manuscripts in the Old Royal Library have passed through many hands, and that very fact can make for ambiguity in describing a manuscript as 'royal'. A manuscript now in the British

Library with a royal provenance, but which was never part of the Old Royal Library, illustrates the point. It is a parchment roll, eleven feet long and only five inches wide, decorated with prayers, rubrics and religious emblems such as the crucifix, the instruments of the Passion or the wounds of Christ. Such rolls were intended for use in prayer, but also as a talisman, the mere possession of which could bring good luck, and which could be wrapped around the belly of a woman in labour for blessing and protection.[8] Such rolls are rare – only sixteen are known to have survived – and this example is a recent arrival in the British Library, having been acquired from the library of the former Roman Catholic seminary at Ushaw. Though commissioned in the late fifteenth century by an anonymous English bishop, who is portrayed on it in prayer, this roll was later customized by the addition of the badges of the future King Henry VIII, and the sheaf of arrows of his wife Catherine. Inserted between emblems of the Passion, the young Henry himself wrote a dedication to one of the gentlemen of the Privy Chamber, William Thomas: 'I pray yow pray for me your lovyng master Prynce Henry.' The inscription was treated in the catalogue of the 2011 exhibition as evidence that, despite his future break with Rome, the young prince Henry practised an entirely traditional Catholic piety: the distinguished Tudor historian David Starkey used this roll to make the same point in his biography of the young Henry.[9]

In fact, however, the badges may well indicate only that the roll belonged to someone in Henry's household, and the inscription makes it clear that it was William Thomas, not Henry, who routinely prayed with it. Pious royal inscriptions of this kind were common in the prayer books of courtiers in early Tudor England – an affectionate royal autograph in one's book, produced in chapel, was a public token of royal favour. Henry may well have given William Thomas this second-hand (and by the early sixteenth century decidedly old-fashioned) prayer roll: there is nothing whatever to suggest that he himself ever prayed with it.

3

The *Golden Legend*

The *Legenda Aurea*, or *Golden Legend*, of Jacobus de Voragine was one of the most influential books of the later Middle Ages.[1] It is a compendium of saints' lives and of liturgical and doctrinal instruction, culled in the 1260s from a wide range of patristic and medieval sources. Its compiler, Blessed Jacobus de Voragine (the Latin form of Jacopo or Giacomo de Varrazze, ca. 1229–98), intended his book as an aid for busy priests and preachers in need of a handy source of vivid anecdote, instruction and edification to bulk out their sermons and catecheses.[2] Many such compilations were produced in thirteenth-century Europe, as the Church sought both to promote more active religious engagement among parish clergy and laypeople, and to police the orthodoxy of popular belief and practice. The new orders of mendicant friars were in the forefront of this campaign to instruct and enthuse ordinary Christians, and Jacobus, an Italian Dominican Friar who became Prior of the Lombard Province in 1267, was working in a tradition established earlier in the same century by members of his own relatively new order. Jean de Mailly began work on his *Abbreviatio in gestis et miraculis sanctorum* in the late 1220s, within ten years of the foundation of the Order of Preachers, and his fellow Dominican Bartholomew of Trent produced his *Epilogus in gesta sanctorum* in the mid-1240s.[3] Jacobus drew freely on both these collections, but those books, popular as they were, survive now in just a couple of dozen manuscripts apiece. Jacobus's *Legenda Aurea*, by contrast, has survived in almost a thousand manuscript copies of the Latin text alone, with another five hundred or so manuscripts containing translations of all or part of the *Legenda* into one or another of the great European vernaculars. His own order seems not at first to have considered Jacobus's *Legenda* definitive, and other Dominicans went on compiling similar hagiographical works well into the fourteenth century. But even in Jacobus's own lifetime his book, doubtless transmitted across Europe through Dominican networks initially, had moved well beyond the confines of the order, and was establishing itself as the most widely used compendium of its kind. As early as the 1280s it was already one of the shaping influences on local hagiographical projects far removed from Italy, such as the vernacular *South English Legendary*.[4] Within two generations, hagiographical compilers all over Europe were adopting Jacobus's framework and lifting material wholesale from his book. Its popularity earned it the nickname the *Golden Legend*, with the implication that it was worth its weight in gold: the word 'legenda' then meant simply a text to be read aloud, with none of the associations with fiction or fancy that the word 'legend' has since acquired. In the two centuries after its composition, Jacobus's *Legenda* was translated and retranslated into most of the major languages of Western Europe. There were seven versions in French alone, and two in English. And with the advent of printing, Jacobus's text became as big a bestseller in the new medium as it had been in the old. Between 1470 and 1500, at least eighty-seven Latin editions of the *Legenda* were printed, as well as sixty-nine editions in various vernaculars, including four editions in English, considerably more than all the known printings of the Bible in any language during the same period.[5]

At first sight modern readers may find this remarkable medieval popularity a bit of a puzzle. The *Legenda Aurea* is not an easy book to use. For convenience of reference, any modern encyclopedia of religion would be likely to present its subject matter alphabetically. Jacobus organized his book on quite different principles. A brief and rather confusing prologue claims that its contents are arranged under 'four distinct periods' corresponding simultaneously to epochs in the world's history, to phases of human life, and to the representation of those phases within the cycle of the liturgy. Jacobus characterizes these four periods as the times of deviation, of renovation, of reconciliation and of pilgrimage. In practice, however, his book actually falls into five unequal sections, corresponding to the main divisions of the liturgical year: namely, the periods from Advent to Christmas (covered in chapters 1–5); from Christmas to Septuagesima (i.e., the Sunday nominally seventy days before Easter) (chapters 6–30); from Septuagesima to Easter (chapters 31–53); from Easter Day to Pentecost (chapters 54–76); and from the octave of Pentecost to Advent again (chapters 77–180). The lives of the saints occupy just 153 of the 182 chapters in the standard modern edition of Jacobus's book, and are clustered chronologically, as their feast days fall within these larger liturgical seasons. Twenty-three non-hagiographical chapters mark off the larger divisions of the book, and these are devoted to the systematic exposition of the medieval Church's understanding of salvation, arranged according to the main liturgical seasons and feasts. The feast days covered include the Annunciation, Advent, Nativity of Christ (i.e., Christmas Day), Circumcision, Epiphany, the Sundays leading up to Lent – Septuagesima, Sexagesima, and Quinquagesima–Quadragesima (i.e., the first Sunday of Lent), the Ember Day fasts, the Passion, Resurrection, the Rogation days, Ascension, Pentecost, and the Invention (i.e., Discovery) and Exaltation of the Holy Cross. To these, Jacobus added a cycle of Marian feasts (the Birth, Purification, and Assumption of the Virgin), which he used to set forth an elaborate and ardent theology of the Virgin Mary, the feasts of All Saints, All Souls (in the course of which he expounds the doctrine of purgatory), and the Dedication of a Church.

Most of these expository chapters differ markedly from the chapters devoted to the lives of the saints. Instead of the eventful narratives enlivened by miracle stories and other sensational happenings that characterize most of the 'sanctorale' entries, in these 'temporale' chapters Jacobus offers a dense doctrinal and symbolic analysis of the main features of the Christian faith as the medieval Church understood it. In effect, these sections of the *Legenda* form an encyclopedic handbook of doctrine, clearly designed to provide material for instruction and preaching. Though presented in highly compressed form, these parts of the book are also self-consciously learned, and abundant citations of sources and authorities are mustered to underpin Jacobus's teaching. Although these chapters occupy less than one-sixth of the book's total bulk, they contain at least half of Jacobus's thousand-plus citations from the writings of early Christian Fathers and theologians like Saint Augustine, Saint John Chrysostom, Saint Bede and Saint Bernard, as well as from the standard medieval theological reference books like Peter Comestor's *Historia Scholastica* and Cassiodorus's *Historia Tripartita*. The scholastic urge to order, systematize, tabulate and analyse is especially in evidence here, reminding the reader that Jacobus was an exact contemporary of Saint Thomas Aquinas (they entered the Dominican order in the same year, 1244). But Jacobus was essentially deploying here an intensive form of a characteristic medieval version of catechesis, which was routinely organized and structured into numbered categories – the Ten Commandments, Seven Deadly Sins, four cardinal and three theological virtues, seven corporal works of mercy, and so on. In this mode, Jacobus's chapter on the Passion of Christ[6] is structured around a dense series of numerical lists, themselves divided into sub-clauses and lesser lists – the five pains of the Passion, the four prerogatives of Christ's nature, the four modes of mockery to which he was subjected, the three reasons for his silence before his judges, the three special fruits of his passion, and the fourfold benefits flowing from his death by crucifixion. That dense and at times dauntingly numerical framework for doctrinal and devotional exposition is especially characteristic of Jacobus's 'temporale' chapters, but it spills over also into some of the lives of the saints – for example, in his account of the preaching of Saint Andrew, or the whole chapter on the birth of John the Baptist. The complexity of this expository material reminds us that the *Legenda* was never intended as straightforward devotional reading for the ordinary layman, although it would eventually be adapted for just such use. It was essentially a handbook for preachers, a quarry from which material could be extracted, to be presented more palatably and discursively in the pulpit. Many vernacular sermon collections drew very heavily on the *Legenda*, such as the late-fourteenth-century English *Festial* compiled by the Augustinian Canon John Mirk, for whom Jacobus's text was the invariable and in many cases the sole source of sermon material. It is notable, though, that Mirk, like many other homilists normally dependent on Jacobus, often modified or set aside altogether these formidable doctrinal sections, in favour of greater simplicity and more entertaining anecdotage.[7]

But important as these 'temporale' chapters are for the structure of his book, Jacobus's coverage of the greater feasts and seasons is highly selective. The whole forty days and six Sundays of Lent are dealt with in a single short and scrappy entry (chapter 34), and he provides no coverage for the major liturgical celebrations of either Palm Sunday or Maundy Thursday. By the same token, Jacobus ignores the brand-new feast of Corpus Christi (established by Pope Urban IV in 1264). Despite its recent institution, this seems a surprising omission, given Thomas Aquinas's authorship of the texts for the feast, and the wider Dominican investment in the propagation of orthodox Eucharistic teaching. Because he also omits any treatment of Maundy Thursday, there is no extended discussion of the Mass in Jacobus's book, a striking omission in an age increasingly concerned about heresy.

The omission of Corpus Christi gives Jacobus's *Legenda* an old-fashioned look, and that impression of old-fashionedness deepens into positive archaism when we come to consider the list of saints whose lives he does include. The early thirteenth century had been momentous for the development of notions of sanctity, and in the actual process of saint-making. The popes had only recently established their monopoly over the canonization of saints, formerly a general Episcopal prerogative, and the Roman introduction of more rigorous (and more expensive) forms of scrutiny of the lives and miracles of candidates for sanctity would lead to a marked reduction in the numbers of canonizations.[8] But in the seventy years before Jacobus wrote the *Legenda*, successive popes had nevertheless carried out more than twenty canonizations, and these new papal saints embodied a wide spectrum of holiness and states of life – from Homobonus of Cremona, a married layman revered for his goodness to the poor, to holy queens and empresses like Margaret of Scotland, Cunegund of Bamberg, or Elisabeth of Hungary. There had been saintly bishops like Hugh of Lincoln, Richard of Chichester and the Irishman Laurence O'Toole, clerical martyrs like Stanislas of Cracow, and the founders and early heroes and heroines of the mendicant orders, Francis and Claire of Assisi, Anthony of Padua and, among the Dominicans, Saint Dominic and Saint Peter Martyr.[9] As a mendicant friar himself, Jacobus predictably included long chapters on the lives of the two great founders, Francis and Dominic, as well as a similarly extended treatment of the Dominican order's great martyr, Peter of Verona, who had been murdered by heretics in Jacobus's native Lombardy in 1252.[10] He also fairly unsurprisingly included a life of the English martyr-archbishop Thomas Becket, an icon for the authority and independence of the Church whose shrine was one of the great pilgrimage venues of Europe. But there Jacobus's interest in modern sanctity appears to have ended: he ignored not only all the other papal canonizations of the preceding hundred years, but all saints of whatever kind from the preceding five centuries. The standard text of the *Legenda* does admittedly include a life of Elisabeth of Hungary, canonized in 1235, but that life is so very different in tone and style from virtually every other life in the *Legenda* that it may very well be an interpolation by another hand.

Jacobus's saints, therefore, are overwhelmingly drawn from a traditional list of those who had been venerated for centuries. They include the major figures of the New Testament (the Apostles, Evangelists, Saint John the Baptist, Saint Mary Magdalene, Saint Stephen), the Fathers, Doctors, popes, monks, and hermits of the early Church (Saint Silvester, Saint Augustine, Saint Gregory the Great, Saint Anthony, Saint Benedict), and above all, the martyr saints of the first four Christian centuries. These lives of the martyr saints, filled as they are with lurid detail of gruesome sufferings, with defiance and rejection of the world, and larded with spectacular miracles, undoubtedly appeal to a medieval taste for romance, excitement and pious entertainment. These qualities gave the *Legenda Aurea* much of its distinctive character, and its huge popularity. But they were also precisely the qualities against which sober sixteenth-century religious reformers, both Catholic and Protestant, would react, which would lead to the widespread repudiation of Jacobus's book as a tissue of unedifying tall tales, and would help to give the word 'legend' its negative connotations.

The entry for the martyr Saint Agnes[11] can be taken as representative of Jacobus's handling of the lives of such saints. The historical Saint Agnes was a young girl (twelve years old, according to Saint Ambrose, whose treatise *De Virginitate* is the earliest source) executed for her Christian faith in the Diocletian persecution circa 305. She was buried outside Rome on the Via Nomentana, where in the later fourth century a basilica was erected over her grave. She became one of Rome's most important saints, and her name is one of those recited during the canon of the Mass. She was celebrated by Ambrose, Jerome, Augustine and other fourth- and fifth-century writers as an exemplar of heroic virginity, and the scant details of her martyrdom were soon elaborated. According to Ambrose, she was killed by burning; according to her shrine inscription by Pope Damasus, at her execution Agnes's hair grew miraculously to cover her naked body; and according to the hymn writer Prudentius, her chastity was tested by exposure in a brothel. These and many other details were elaborated in the highly coloured fifth-century *Acts of the Martyrdom of Saint Agnes*, which was Jacobus's main source. He also used and quoted extensively from Saint Ambrose's panegyric on Agnes in *De Virginitate*.[12]

Jacobus's account of Saint Agnes opens, as is his custom, with a fanciful etymological paragraph, offering three different explanations of Agnes's name. It may have come from *agnus*, the Latin for 'lamb', reflecting her lamb-like meekness. Alternatively, it might derive from the Greek word *agnos*, 'pious', because she was pious and compassionate. Or yet again, it might derive from the Latin participle *agnoscendo*, 'knowing', because 'she knew the way of truth'. In fact, however, there is nothing remotely meek about Jacobus's portrait of Agnes. In his account, she is a defiant, even an aggressive paragon of chastity, the vowed bride of Christ, 'a child in body but already aged in spirit'. As she returns from school one day, the son of the 'prefect' of Rome sees her in the street and is smitten by her beauty. She repudiates the hapless young man's tentative advances immediately and ferociously, calling him 'the spark that lights the fire of sin, you fuel of wickedness, you food of death', and taunting him that 'The one I love is far nobler than you. ... His mother is a virgin, his father ... is served by angels.' Agnes then goes on to enumerate the five transcendent virtues of Christ as a heavenly lover. The lovesick youth, unable to compete, takes to his sickbed, and his worried father attempts to persuade Agnes to yield to his son, first by wheedling and then with threats. When she persists in defiant fidelity to her heavenly husband, the prefect charges her with being a Christian, has her stripped naked, and sends her to a brothel. En route, however, her hair grows to preserve her modesty. Once in the brothel, an angel surrounds her in an even more glorious garment of blinding light, and the brothel itself becomes a place of prayer and spiritual healing. The lovesick young man now shows his true colours by inciting his companions to gang-rape Agnes, and is punished by being throttled by the Devil. At the bereaved father's request, Agnes raises the bad lad from the dead, but is then accused of being a witch by jealous pagan priests. The now chastened prefect seeks to release her, but out of cowardice hands the case over to his deputy, who condemns Agnes to be burned. The flames part around her and consume the hostile bystanders. The irrepressible Agnes is finally dispatched when a soldier thrusts a dagger into her throat. Jacobus adds a brief account of the martyrdom by stoning of Agnes's mythical foster sister, Emerentiana, complete with an appearance of the glorified Agnes, clad in gold and attended by angels and a snow-white lamb. He also provides two post-mortem miracle stories, both of which relate directly to Agnes's shrine church on the Via Nomentana. In the first of these, the Emperor Constantine's daughter, Constance, a leper, makes a pilgrimage to Agnes's grave and sleeps there, in search of a cure. Agnes appears to her in a dream and heals her, and the grateful Constance builds the basilica over Agnes's grave and vows to live a virginal life there with her maidens. In the second miracle, a priest assailed by lust is cured of temptation when he betroths himself to Agnes by placing a jewelled ring on the finger of the statue of her 'that stood in her church'. Jacobus provides two quite different versions of this story but assures the reader that 'it is said the ring is still to be seen on the finger of the statue.' The entry concludes with a paragraph of extended quotation from Saint Ambrose's eulogy of Saint Agnes in his *De Virginitate*.

This is a lot of colour to crowd into fewer than 1,500 words (in the Latin). Such a torrent of incident leaves no room for religious subtlety or refined psychologizing. Jacobus's Agnes is less a holy human being than a cipher for a drastically two-dimensional representation of the virtue of chastity. The saint's monotone angry defiance is in play from the very opening of the account, and the saturation of the story in the miraculous moves it closer to folk or fairy tale than to any kind of biographical study. The story exemplifies Jacobus's apparent fascination with the multiple forms of torture and execution undergone by the martyrs: one modern analysis has identified eighty-one different forms of suffering, mutilation and death in Jacobus's narrative.[13] The medieval reader or listener, as well as being entertained, would doubtless have found plenty to relate to, not least the easily recognizable features of contemporary religious practice reflected in the miracles, which feature pilgrimages, shrine images, vows and ex-voto gifts. He or she would have found in the stories vivid, even lurid, assurances of God's power and providence. But there would not have been much here to emulate – no template, apart from ritual matters, for ordinary Christian living. This was holiness presented not so much as a pattern to be imitated, but as a power to be harnessed, and a source of intercession to be supplicated.

The miraculous elements in such stories were eventually to earn Jacobus the contempt of humanist and Protestant scholars as a peddler of fable to the gullible. But it is worth noting that in his account of the miracle of the lustful priest, Jacobus in fact offered his readers two different and incompatible versions of the episode, leaving them to choose which, if either, they accepted, just as in the etymology he offers three quite different explanations of Agnes's name. Jacobus's etymologies were in a long tradition of medieval learning derived from Isidore of Seville's vast *Etymologiae*, the most widely used encyclopedia of the Middle Ages. The first users of the *Legenda* would have recognized both the genre itself and the element of intellectual playfulness implicit in it. And however marvellous the stories he relates, Jacobus can also display both scepticism and some sophistication in his handling of the incidents and evidence that form the body of his narrative. Famously, in his account of Saint Margaret he repeated the story of how the saint had allegedly been swallowed alive by the devil in the form of a dragon, but burst from his stomach by making the sign of the cross. Jacobus commented, 'What is said here, however … is considered apocryphal, and not to be taken seriously.' This is not an isolated case. In his account of Saint Andrew he reports Andrew's alleged rescue of the Apostle Matthew from kidnappers, but adds, '[S]o we are told but I find the story very hard to believe.' Reporting a revenge miracle in which a servant who slapped Saint Thomas was devoured by lions and dogs, Jacobus cites a long passage from Saint Augustine that casts doubt on the story. 'St Augustine in his book against Faustus will have none of this act of vengeance, and declares that the incident is apocryphal.' In the same way, in his section on the Passion of Christ Jacobus compares accounts of the horrible end of Pontius Pilate from an apocryphal Gospel and from the *Historia Scholastica*, and comments, '[L]et the reader judge whether the story is worth the telling.' In his life of Saint Hilary he expresses disbelief about the story of Hilary's triumph over a heretical 'Pope Leo'. These expressions of scepticism are often underpinned by appeal to contradictions or disagreements between authorities and evidences: in his life of Saint Matthew he raises a doubt about the morality of casting lots in the making of decisions, citing varying opinions from Saint Jerome, Saint Bede and Pseudo-Dionysius.

Jacobus, then, was clearly aware that even revered patristic authorities might contradict one another, and he often leaves it to the reader to choose between conflicting accounts. But we are certainly not dealing here with the kind of critical approach to historical evidence that was ushered in by the Renaissance, and by whose standards the *Legenda* was found lamentably wanting. The contradictions and doubts that trouble Jacobus do so as inconsistencies within a doctrinal system. He doubts the story of the heretical pope defeated by Saint Hilary because a priori popes cannot be heretical, not because the source is suspect. The debate about the casting of lots interests him not because ancient authorities contradict one another about it, but because the legitimacy of lots was a theological question still unresolved in his own day, with a direct bearing on practical morality. He is concerned to guard the internal coherence of Catholicism, not the authenticity of historical evidence.[14]

The range of Jacobus's sources has been quantified by Alain Boureau, and subjected to a more detailed if essentially unsympathetic analysis by Sherry Reames.[15] The breadth of the material he drew on is impressive: the Gospels, the book of Psalms, the book of Isaiah, the Pauline epistles and the Acts of the Apostles head the list of biblical authorities, and Jacobus also made use of apocryphal writings such as the Gospel of Nicodemus. But he also drew heavily on patristic writers, above all Saint Augustine, Saint Gregory the Great, Saint Jerome, Saint John Chrysostom and Saint Ambrose (in that order). Among his medieval contemporaries or near-contemporaries, Saint Bernard equals Saint Augustine in the number of citations. A cluster of lives of hermit saints grouped at the end of the book was extracted from the accounts of the desert fathers in the Latin *Vitae Patrum*, Jacobus's account of Saint Anthony was abbreviated from the life by Saint Athanasius, and the story of Barlaam and Josaphat, a Christianized version of the life of the Buddha, was taken from a Latin version of a seventh-century Syrian monastic text, attributed in Jacobus's day to Saint John Chrysostom.

Given the scaling-down inevitable in a compilation, all of these materials are paraphrased and drastically reduced, even when Jacobus is following his original's narrative framework very closely. There are exceptions: more than half his long chapter on Saint Paul consists of an immense extended quotation from Chrysostom's sermon '*De laudibus Pauli*'. His life of the fourth-century Roman widow Saint Paula is a shortened version of Jerome's magnificent eulogy in Epistola 108, recognizably Jerome's in emphasis and rhetoric, despite the abbreviation. His life of 'A Virgin of Antioch' is lifted entire from Ambrose's *De Virginitate*. His life of Saint Augustine, one of the longest in the *Legenda*, abbreviates the contemporary life by Possidius but supplements it extensively from Augustine's own autobiographical writings, especially the *Confessions* and the *Soliloquies*.

Modern commentators have been uncomplimentary about Jacobus's use of his early Christian materials, seeing in his abbreviations not merely the inevitable problems of reduction, but an invariable coarsening and externalization of religious motive and feeling, which reflected a similar hardening in the religious culture of his own time.[16] On this account the *Legenda*'s focus on sanctity as heroic virtue in conflict with the world, and the typology of the saint as normally a martyr, a cleric or a monk, deliberately turns away from some of the most vital and inclusive religious energies of his own time, in favour of an unimaginative clericalization of the concept of the holy. None of Jacobus's saints were ordinary men and women living ordinary lives. His saints are uncomfortable people, insofar as they can be said to be people at all, often at odds with the world around them. Their virtues are those of absolute world-renunciation and denial, and they themselves are often beset by enemies – demonic forces, unbelieving parents and family, heretics and hostile secular rulers. In his handling not merely of a contemporary figure like his confrère Peter Martyr, but of remoter exemplars like Saint Ambrose, Jacobus certainly reflected anxieties about some of the most pressing preoccupations of the Church of his own day – in the case of Ambrose, the struggle between papacy and Empire; in the case of Peter Martyr, the campaign to obliterate heresy, in which the Dominican Order was so heavily involved.

Jacobus was indeed a man of his own times. A patriotic Lombard, he included under the pretext of a life of Pope Pelagius a chronicle of Christian history that focused predominantly on the events and notables of his own region, and which earned his book the nickname 'The Lombardic History'. He was a man immersed in affairs, as administrator of a great religious order, as a papal diplomat, and finally as an outstanding and much-loved Bishop of Genoa. But Jacobus can hardly be blamed for being of his own times. If he did not transcend the limitations of institutional Christianity in the thirteenth century, he embodied some of its most distinctive energies, as well as some of its tensions and contradictions. His book quite evidently touched a contemporary nerve, and was seen and seized on for three centuries as an indispensable pastoral resource, as well as a vademecum of entertainment and of inspiration and source material for poets, dramatists and painters.

It was inevitable that the Protestant reformers would see in the *Golden Legend* a magazine and embodiment of superstition and idolatry – everything they despised and rejected in medieval Christianity. But even before and beyond the Reformation, it had come to seem old-fashioned and passé to reform-minded Catholics. In the mid-fifteenth century the great Catholic reformer Nicholas of Cusa forbade his clergy to teach their people the fables of the *Legenda Aurea*, and to successive generations of Catholic humanists, trained by Erasmus to look back to the pure sources of early Christianity, and to ground their religion on sound historical truth and solid moral worth, Jacobus's book, with its far-fetched miracles and martyrdoms, came to seem anathema. The lives of the saints should be sober and credible, exemplars of virtue rather than chronicles of wonders. The Spanish humanist Luis de Vives articulated this new mentality when he declared,

> [H]ow unworthy of the saints, and of all Christians, is that history of the saints called the Golden Legend. I cannot imagine why they call it Golden, when it is written by a man with a mouth of iron and a heart of lead. What can be more abominable than this book? What a disgrace to us Christians that the pre-eminent deeds of our saints have not been more truly and accurately preserved, so that we may know or imitate such virtue, when the Greek and Roman authors have written with such care about their generals, philosophers and sages. [17]

Counter-Reformation Catholicism would reform the cult of the saints accordingly, purging the breviary lections of the more bizarre episodes culled from Jacobus, and in the hands of the seventeenth-century Jesuit scholar Jean Boland hagiography became an exact science. In this new climate, though Jacobus's book remained in many clerical libraries, it fell into relative eclipse. It would not fully emerge again from obscurity until the nineteenth century, when Romantic admiration for the Middle Ages and an interest in the sources of medieval and Renaissance art would send readers back to the *Golden Legend*, as a repository of ancient lore, and as the distillation of both the imagination and the soul of the Christian Middle Ages.

4
Secret Knowledge – or a Hoax?

In 1969 America's most significant dealer in medieval manuscripts, the Viennese-born bibliophile Hans Peter Kraus, donated a celebrated volume to Yale University's Beinecke Library. Measuring 10 inches by 7 and bound in limp white vellum (the Renaissance bookbinder's equivalent of paperback, and definitely not the original cover), Kraus's gift was catalogued as Beinecke MS 408.

The manuscript's celebrity is at first sight puzzling, since it is an unglamorous, even somewhat shabby object: 234 pages gathered in eighteen 'quires', or foldings, each consisting of between one and six double pages, or 'bifolia'. Very unusually for a medieval manuscript, Beinecke MS 408 also includes eleven larger 'fold-out' pages, containing what appear to be astronomical or astrological diagrams. At some date after the book's compilation, each folio was numbered in ink on the right-hand opening (technically known as the recto).[1]

The first 130 pages of the volume are taken up with what appears to be a herbal, each page containing a large if somewhat sloppily executed drawing of a plant, depicting root, stem, flowers and leaves, around which extensive text, in no recognizable language but written in a fluent cursive hand, has been carefully arranged so as to avoid encroaching on any part of the picture. This 'herbal' section is followed by a cluster of large fold-out pages decorated with circular zodiacal or astrological diagrams, and this in turn gives way to a section of ten folios containing yet more unrecognizable text, interspersed with decidedly unerotic drawings of groups of plump, naked women, bathing in pools and conduits of blue or green water, which some students of the manuscript have suggested might be symbolic representations of bodily functions such as reproduction.

After a further group of large fold-out pages with more astronomical images, there follows another cluster of 'herbal' images. These consist of multiple small drawings embedded in the text of each page, alongside objects in the margin that resemble pharmacological jars, perhaps suggesting that this part of the manuscript refers back to the opening herbal, and was intended as a collection of medical recipes. The book's closing section consists of twenty-three pages of closely written text without illustration, made up of short paragraphs of just a few lines apiece, each paragraph prefaced by a star or asterisk.

Kraus had bought this baffling manuscript as a commercial speculation in 1961, for $24,500 plus a half share in any future profit. The vendor was Anne Nill, secretary, professional collaborator and ultimate heir of the manuscript's first discoverer, a remarkable Polish-Lithuanian bookdealer and adventurer, Wilfrid Michael Voynich.[2] Born in 1864 and a graduate in law and chemistry from the University of Moscow, Voynich had been arrested in 1885 as a revolutionary Polish nationalist and had spent five years in exile in Siberia. Escaping via Mongolia on a forged passport, he had ultimately arrived penniless in England, having bartered even his spectacles and waistcoat to pay for his passage. Initially drawn again into revolutionary circles in London around the Ukrainian political agitator Sergei 'Stepniak' Kravchinsky, Voynich was befriended by Richard Garnett, keeper of the British Museum Reading Room, the regular haunt of late-nineteenth-century Russian and other Eastern European exiles.

It was at Garnett's suggestion that Voynich put his omnivorously eclectic learning, his cosmopolitan personal connections and his gifts as a linguist to use as a buyer and seller of rare books, a field in which he rapidly established himself as a piratical and successful entrepreneur. A flamboyant personality regarded with hostility or condescension by less successful dealers and more orthodox bibliophiles, Voynich packed his catalogues with arcane bibliographical detail, which established his reputation for near-omniscience: he was soon making money. Specializing at first in incunabula – books printed before 1501 – he sold to prestigious collectors and libraries, including the British Museum, which bought the entire contents of his eighth catalogue. The books from that purchase, now shelved together in the British Library, provide a snapshot of the rich contents of Voynich's shop in Soho Square, later moved to the grander purlieus of Piccadilly.

The precise circumstances surrounding Voynich's acquisition of Beinecke MS 408 are obscure, but it had certainly been one of a group of manuscripts and books from the library of Athanasius Kircher, the seventeenth-century Jesuit polymath and scientist.[3] Kircher's books were rescued from confiscation by the new state of Italy during its stand-off with the Church in the years after unification in 1871, along with other rarities from the library of the Jesuit university in Rome, the Collegio Romano, where Kircher had been a professor for forty years. More than 300 of these hidden Jesuit treasures ultimately ended up in the Vatican Library, but in 1912 Voynich, who regularly toured Italy in search of incunabula and manuscripts, managed to buy a few. One of these, described by Voynich as the 'ugly duckling' of the former Collegio Romano collection, was the future Beinecke MS 408.

If Voynich labelled his acquisition an ugly duckling, he was nevertheless convinced that he had acquired an exceptional swan in the making, for he believed its baffling text concealed a scientific treatise of major importance by one of the greatest minds of the high Middle Ages. In this belief, he was following a letter from the Prague physician Johannes Marcus Marci to Kircher, dated 19 August 1665, which had been tucked inside the manuscript. Marci's letter claimed that the manuscript was the work of the thirteenth-century English Franciscan scientist and alchemist Roger Bacon, and that more recently it had been acquired for the library of the emperor Rudolf II for the very large sum of 600 golden ducats.[4]

The alleged connection to Bacon would prove to be illusory, but Rudolf's avid interest in alchemy, astrology, magic and all manner of occult studies, together with the presence on the first leaf of the manuscript of the signature (now invisible to the naked eye) of Jacobus Hořcický de Tepenec (circa 1575–1622), court pharmacist to the emperor, ennobled by Rudolf in 1608, lends plausibility to the alleged imperial provenance. Marci's motive for presenting Kircher with the manuscript was to induce him to decipher the text.

This was not the first such appeal. Marci had acquired the book from the library of another Bohemian alchemist, Georgius Barschius. In 1637 Barschius himself had copied extracts from the manuscript and sent them to Kircher, who, among much else, was an expert on Oriental languages and whose *Lingua Aegyptiaca Restituta* (1643) would be regarded as a foundational text for the study of Egyptian hieroglyphics. So Barschius hoped that this all-knowing 'Oedipus of Egypt' was just the man to decipher his enigmatic manuscript, 'a certain riddle of the Sphinx', which he believed must have been written in a code or cipher, as alchemical and magical treatises often were. Kircher told another Prague-based Jesuit mathematician, Theodor Moretus, that he had indeed tried unsuccessfully to decipher the text: marginal traces of an early effort to supply equivalents from the Latin alphabet for the mysterious letters in the manuscript itself may be relics of these attempts at decryption.

Voynich was immensely excited by all this. His knowledge of the court of Rudolf II was not very deep, and largely derived from a popular history of scientific and alchemical studies at the Prague court published in 1904 by Henry Carrington Bolton, an American chemist, bibliographer and historian of science. Bolton's book, *The Follies of Science at the Court of Rudolf II, 1576–1612*, gave a prominent place to the English magician and alchemist John Dee, who with his assistant and 'scryer' Edward Kelley spent years attempting to communicate with angels, in order to learn the universal language spoken by Adam in Paradise before the Fall.[5]

Dee's journals contained passages in an arcane alphabet purporting to be written in this language. To Voynich, here was the obvious background for his mysterious new acquisition, and Dee's presence in Rudolfian Prague seemed to provide a plausible conduit for the transmission of a mysteriously encrypted text by Roger Bacon to the court of the alchemist emperor.

Voynich eagerly set about publicizing his manuscript, which he valued at the huge sum of $100,000, and which he invariably referred to as 'the Roger Bacon Cipher Manuscript'. Especially after the outbreak of war in 1914, his business was increasingly in the United States, and on his many trips to America he did everything he could to talk up the importance of his find. He told the *New York Times* that 'when the time comes, I will prove to the world that the black magic of the Middle Ages consisted in discoveries far in advance of twentieth-century science.'

To supplement his own attempts to decrypt the manuscript, he made photographs of individual pages available to inquirers. In a time of war, Voynich's endless harping on decryption prompted suspicions that he might be a spy attempting to penetrate American security, but the decipherment of the so-called Roger Bacon manuscript aroused considerable scholarly interest. It was enthusiastically embraced by distinguished medievalists, including the Chicago-based textual scholar John Matthews Manly, who publicized Voynich's find in an article in *Harper's Magazine* in 1921 as 'The Most Mysterious Manuscript in the World'.[6]

Even more sensationally, William Romaine Newbold, a distinguished medievalist and historian of medicine at the University of Pennsylvania, toured academic and popular lecture halls with the announcement that he had cracked the code in which this mysterious manuscript was written, and that it did indeed contain amazing revelations. These included the claim that Bacon, in the thirteenth century, had understood and made use of both the compound microscope and the telescope, and with their aid had anticipated the discoveries of twentieth-century scientists about germ cells, spermatozoa and other mechanisms of organic life.

Newbold's supposed decryption of the Voynich manuscript was taken at face value by world-class scholars like the French medievalist Étienne Gilson, but it was in fact based on an elaborate set of misunderstandings and unfounded hypotheses. Newbold's entire scheme was mercilessly demolished in 1931 in a devastating article in the medieval journal *Speculum* by none other than J. M. Manly, now disillusioned about all claims to have cracked the Voynich manuscript code. Voynich himself had died of cancer the previous year, but despite the disproof of Newbold's theories and the inaccessibility of the manuscript itself (now locked away in a bank vault by Voynich's widow, Ethel), interest in its mysteries grew. Although he rejected Newbold's claims, Manly remained intrigued by Voynich's manuscript. During the First World War he himself had worked as a US Army cryptographer. In 1916 he had been befriended by William F. Friedman, America's most talented maker and breaker of codes, and reputedly the world's greatest cryptologist.

At that time Friedman was based in the department of ciphers at the private research institute funded by the textile magnate George Fabyan at Riverbank, near Chicago. Fabyan was an ardent believer in the theory that Shakespeare's works had in fact been written by Francis Bacon (no relation to Roger Bacon), and the chief code-breaker at Riverbank, Elizabeth Wells Gallup, was the principal advocate of the theory that Bacon had written not only all of Shakespeare, but also the plays of Christopher Marlowe, as well as Richard Burton's immense *Anatomy of Melancholy*. Convinced that all these pseudonymous works were dense with encrypted secret messages, she devoted manic ingenuity to decoding them. Friedman and his wife Elizabeth, initially employed as Gallup's assistants, came to reject her bizarre theories, but the world of American cryptology in the aftermath of the war was saturated with conspiracy theories and fascination with the idea of hidden mysteries in ancient texts.

Friedman, who ultimately became head of cryptology at the National Security Agency, was one of those who applied to Voynich for photographs of his manuscript. He remained intrigued to the end of his life by the attempt to decipher it, and built up what is probably the largest private archive of material relating to it. During the Second World War, Friedman's team was at the centre of the successful cracking of the Japanese secret code 'Purple' by

US intelligence; but from 1944 onward he found time to establish a special study group devoted to decrypting the Voynich manuscript, which met regularly at Arlington Hall, America's equivalent of Britain's code-breaking centre at Bletchley Park.

After the end of the Second World War, Friedman convened prestigious scholarly seminars devoted to the manuscript. He involved, among many others, Brigadier John Tiltman, the noted British cryptographer and assistant director of the British Intelligence Headquarters (GCHQ), in attempts to decode the manuscript. At Tiltman's suggestion a young NSA cryptologist, Mary D'Imperio, was appointed to continue the ailing Friedman's work on it, and in 1978 she would eventually publish, under the auspices of the National Security Agency, what is still considered the best introduction to its mysteries, *The Voynich Manuscript: An Elegant Enigma.*

But all to no avail. Voynich's find retained its secrets, and by the time of Friedman's death in 1969, the year Kraus donated the manuscript to Yale, Friedman himself had concluded that, rather than being an encrypted text written in cipher, the Voynich manuscript was an early-sixteenth-century attempt to create an artificial universal language.

This steady expansion of interest in the Voynich manuscript was the background to Kraus's speculative purchase in 1961. Like Voynich, Kraus believed this 'ugly duckling' might one day lay a golden egg. To preserve its commercial value, he rejected all requests for scholarly access to it, and refused to lend it to exhibitions. He put it on the market for $160,000, but despite the escalating scholarly and cryptological fascination, there were no buyers. So in 1969 he decided to cut his losses gracefully and donated Voynich's ugly duckling to Yale.

The deposit of the Voynich manuscript in a great university library at last made sustained scholarly analysis possible, and over the four and a half decades of Yale's custodianship some certainties have been established, and some myths laid to rest. Exhaustive scientific and conservational analysis of the parchment on which the manuscript is written, the stitching of the binding in which it is contained, and the inks and paints with which it was written and illuminated, have disposed of the notion that the manuscript dates from the thirteenth century, or that it is the work of Roger Bacon. Radiocarbon dating of slivers from a range of pages has firmly dated the book's materials to the years around 1430. The vellum pages are made of good-quality (and therefore expensive) calfskin, commonly used in book production all over medieval Europe. (Goatskin vellum, by contrast, would have strengthened the case for a southern German or Italian origin, a provenance favoured by many students of the manuscript.)

Equally, all this effectively rules out any possibility that the manuscript is a post-medieval forgery – it is inconceivable that the huge quantities of blank parchment needed for such a forgery could have survived from the early fifteenth century. The book's pages, whose consistency suggests that they derived from a single source, would have required at least fourteen or fifteen entire calfskins. It is therefore overwhelmingly likely that the manuscript was written and illustrated soon after the parchment was prepared, in the first third of the fifteenth century. Its fluent cursive handwriting, without emendation of any kind, seems incompatible with the notion that it might nevertheless be a careful scribal copy of an earlier medieval text. The dating of its materials to the early fifteenth century rules out the suggestion, credited by art historians like Erwin Panofsky, but never very convincing, that the manuscript contains illustrations of plants such as capsicum or the sunflower, unknown before the discovery of the New World.

Scientific study has gone alongside steadily growing public interest. More than 10 per cent of the visits to the Beinecke Library website relate to the Voynich manuscript, as do almost 50 per cent of visits to the website's zoom-viewer, which enables close-up examination of single pages. When Umberto Eco, the semiologist, medievalist and author of the bestselling medieval puzzle-novel *The Name of the Rose*, lectured at Yale to celebrate the Beinecke Library's fiftieth anniversary, the only one of its many treasures he asked to see was the Voynich manuscript. In an era when the fictions of Dan Brown can be imagined to have lifted the lid on ancient conspiracies, none of this is perhaps surprising. The publication by Yale University Press of an actual-size coloured facsimile, with an informative set of specialist essays on the manuscript's history, materials, cryptological puzzles, and public impact, will no doubt encourage wider engagement with its enigmas and set off a multitude of amateur as well as professional attempts to decipher it.

But if we can be fairly sure that the manuscript is not a modern forgery, it by no means follows that it is not in fact a medieval hoax. Four centuries of attempts to decode, decipher or translate the text have all ended in bafflement. The finest cryptological minds of the twentieth century and sustained computer analysis alike have drawn a blank: the text refuses to yield meaning. Attempts to find parallels to the text in cabbalistical, hermetic or alchemical code systems have all thrown up more disparities than resemblances. What if the book's mysteries are in fact pure mystification, specious appearance that never had any real meaning?

This is a possibility strongly suggested by the manuscript's single largest component, the herbal, with its crudely coloured images of plants. No student of the herbal illustrations has ever succeeded in identifying convincingly a single image as any known plant. Medieval herbals were rarely based on exact observation from nature, but even by the conventions of medieval botanical representation, the Voynich images are, collectively and singly, biological impossibilities. Roots and branches bifurcate and then rejoin again to form a single stem (folios 5v, 22, 23, 40, 52), two separate stalks are joined by a single lateral branch or end in the same single leaf (23), slender stalks emerge from holes in the thick flat surfaces of roots that have been cut across like sawn tree trunks (14, 16, 16v, 19, 39v, 45v), and spiky leaves exactly mirror the forms of the same plant's improbable roots (54).

In other words, the 'plants' represented in the book's herbal section never did and never could exist in nature: they are pure fantasy. And if the images are, then possibly the text is too. Even an uninformed observer examining any random pages of Beinecke MS 408 will be struck by the highly repetitive character of the text, with the same symbols and clusters of 'letters' occurring in consecutive words and lines. This is a feature of the Voynich manuscript that has often been noted. It is one of the reasons for suspecting that the text is not in fact a real language at all, cunningly concealed, but an elegantly scripted but meaningless babble, deploying a limited number of forms over and over again.

Why might such a hoax have been perpetrated? The sheer scale, expense and complexity of the Voynich manuscript would seem to preclude the notion that it was assembled as some kind of joke: it's hard to imagine a punchline that required so elaborate a build-up. That leaves lunacy or lucre as possible motives. Madness can't entirely be ruled out: mania takes many forms, and a well-to-do obsessive convinced he (or she) held the key to great secrets might drive the production of such a compilation.

But the likeliest motive surely must be money. The modern history of the Voynich manuscript, and the huge investment of time and effort by some of the most ingenious intelligences of the twentieth century in its decipherment, amply testify to human fascination with the possibility of uncovering secret knowledge. Back in the sixteenth century Rudolf II paid some persuasive soul 600 gold ducats for Beinecke MS 408. It may well be that somewhere in early-fifteenth-century Europe another wealthy seeker after hidden truths was swindled by an equally enterprising purveyor of plausible nonsense. We shall probably never know. But maybe from the pages of Voynich's 'ugly duckling', a long quack of derisive laughter echoes down the centuries.

5
The Psalms and Lay Piety

My topic in this essay is the Psalms, but not the Psalter, and this essay addresses some very simple questions, in what may strike the reader as a rather elementary way: I'll come to those questions in a moment. In the course of the late fourteenth and fifteenth centuries the Psalter, the text of the 150 psalms in Latin, often prefaced by a Calendar for the church year, gave way to the *Horae* or Book of Hours as the most commonly owned book of devotion among lay people. The replacement of the one by the other was never total, and Psalter-Hours incorporating both types of book went on being produced and used into the age of print, though in far smaller numbers than in the high Middle Ages. But it's worth considering for a moment this transition. The reasons for the move from Psalter to Hours as the most favoured devotional aide for the laity are readily enough understood. The Psalter must always have been a difficult book for lay people to find their way around, and there is a good deal of obscurity about the ways in which lay people might have used it. For a start, in the later Middle Ages the Psalter itself, considered purely as a text, physically resembled no other book of the Bible, and presented unique problems of navigation for the lay (and indeed clerical) user.

The Bible had been divided into our modern chapter divisions in Paris at the start of the thirteenth century, to enable easy reference. But the Psalter, which was often excluded from otherwise complete bibles, was not numbered in this way, whether in the context of a whole bible or when it circulated as a separate book.[1] Though the 150 psalms of course occurred in the Psalters in their numerical sequence, the psalms themselves were almost never individually numbered, and the layout of medieval psalters, geared towards liturgical recitation, militated against easy reference to individual psalms other than those which headed the traditional eightfold or ten-fold divisions of the Psalter.[2] Separate books containing the psalms were presumably first produced for monks and clergy obliged to recite the daily office in choir. Such a book provided the owner with the core non-seasonal elements of the office. Psalms in these books were identified and distinguished from each other by the decoration, initial miniatures and often larger-scale script used in the *incipit* or opening verse of the psalm. The verse divisions, which of course were necessary for alternate recitation in choir, might be marked by points in the text or by the use of alternating red and blue letters for the opening words of each verse.

The body of the text as a whole was further divided with illuminated initials or miniatures at the opening of each liturgical division; that is, marking the opening of each block of psalms recited daily in the office of Matins: psalms 1–20 on Monday, where conventionally David was depicted playing his harp at the start of Psalm 1, *Beatus Vir* (Blessed is the man), 26–37 on Tuesday, pointing to his eyes at the start of psalm 26, *Dominus Illuminatio mea* (The Lord is my light), 38–51 on Wednesday, where he fights Goliath at the start of *Dixi Custodiam* (I said I will be careful), and so on. A few other psalms were singled out with special decoration in the same way – for example, psalm 109, *Dixit Dominus* (The Lord declared), the first psalm of Sunday vespers, and Psalm 50 , *Miserere mei* (Have mercy on me), recited every weekday in the ferial office of Lauds, and Psalms 117, *Confitemini Domino* (Praise the Lord), and 118, *Beati immaculati* (Blessed are the undefiled), which formed the text for the Little Hours of *Prime, Terce, Sext* and *None*. These pictorial markers would therefore enable the owner to find their place at the recitation of Matins and Vespers, though the antiphons, hymns and other seasonal elements would have to be supplied from elsewhere. There was no straightforward way of locating the psalms at

Lauds since, unlike those at Matins, Vespers and the other hours, the Lauds psalms were not arranged in their numerical sequence. The liturgical function of the Psalter was signalled in the fact that most psalters included a calendar, the Old and New Testament Canticles used at Lauds and Vespers, and the Litany.

The utility of all this for priests and religious is obvious. Just how lay people employed them, however, is quite another matter. The likeliest use of the Psalter by lay people, where it was not straightforwardly talismanic, must have been to follow the office as it was recited or sung either in their parish or monastic church, or, in the case of specially wealthy patrons, by their domestic clergy: a few psalters included parallel verse psalters in French or English, as a crib to enable the lay user, *non literatus* in Latin, to understand what was being said. Additional devotional material, in the form of prayers and, in the more luxurious manuscripts, miniatures depicting biblical scenes, the Passion or the images and miracles of the Virgin and the saints, augmented the devotional value of the Psalter, and it seems clear that, for many owners, the pictorial decoration must have been a good deal more important than the text. Certainly lay participation in the full round of the daily office must have been rare, and a book in which it was so difficult to locate the text of favourite individual psalms, supposing that more than a tiny handful of lay people did have favourite psalms, clearly presented problems.

As lay literacy grew, there was an obvious need for shorter and more user-friendly devotions better adapted to a lay lifestyle, and to lay reading capacities. In the fourteenth and fifteenth centuries more and more psalters were produced, which included, in addition to the psalms in numerical sequence, the Office of the Dead and the Little Office of the Blessed Virgin. Older psalters often had these items added, enabling the owner to recite these shorter and less demanding offices without the need for slow and confusing thumbing through the unnumbered psalms to find the right place. And as the market for cheaper devotional books for lay people widened and moved down the social scale in the course of the fifteenth century, for most prospective purchasers the *Horae* or Book of Hours came to supplant the Psalter altogether.

The Book of Hours, this comparative newcomer, was essentially an amplified anthology of psalms, built round the core texts of the Little Hours of the Blessed Virgin Mary, the Litany of the Saints with the seven Penitential Psalms and the Gradual Psalms, the Commendations (i.e. the immensely long alphabetic psalm 118/119) and the Office of the Dead, consisting of first Vespers (that is, Vespers of the preceding evening), Matins and Lauds only.[3] By the end of the Middle Ages most Books of Hours contained a good deal else as well, but these are the texts which will be my main concern here.

The Book of Hours emerged as an independent text in the first decades of the thirteenth century, and most of the surviving examples from that time are luxury items made for wealthy owners. Luxurious manuscript Books of Hours continued to be produced well into the sixteenth century, but the production history of these books is one of widening appeal and availability. One or more copies of the Book of Hours were to be found in most aristocratic and gentry households by the later fifteenth century, and, with the spread of production-line cheap manuscripts especially from Flemish scriptoria, and emphatically with the invention of printing, they became familiar objects in many merchant and professional households too, and cheap examples were to be found even in the hands of artisans and small shopkeepers. Women formed a very high proportion of the owners and therefore presumably the users of books of Hours.[4]

And that brings me at last to one of my simple questions: like the Psalter, the Book of Hours was a Latin book and, despite its importance in lay piety, there appear to have been very few English versions of it produced in the Middle Ages. The users of Books of Hours must be presumed to have been in *some* sense literate in Latin, but it is not at all clear how many women, or for that matter lay men, would have had a sufficient grip even of the relatively simple and repetitious Latin of the Psalter to have read the psalms with any degree of ease or real comprehension. In what sense, therefore, did the users of these books *know* the psalms: how did they read them, and what devotional sense did they make of them?

There are two prior questions here, which are fortunately much easier to answer: what psalms might lay people know? And which and how many psalms were there in the Book of Hours? I shall concentrate here on Books of Hours for England, and in fact on *Sarum* Books of Hours – books giving the Office of the Blessed Virgin as performed in Salisbury Cathedral, the liturgical use which became the model for churches throughout much of late medieval England and indeed Scotland. These formed the bulk of those produced, here or abroad, for the English market.

The description that follows is necessarily complex, for which the reader's patience is required. The Sarum Office of the Blessed Virgin differed significantly from that of the Roman rite, and included six fewer psalms. Its basic components included three psalms for Matins (in theory there were nine, but usually only the first nocturne was included in at any rate the cheaper manuscript books: the six psalms of the other two nocturnes were sometimes provided as supplements for use on alternate days in Advent). Then followed four psalms and an Old Testament canticle, *Benedicite opera omnia* (Bless the Lord all his works), for Lauds (the psalms for this hour being identical to Sunday Lauds in the Roman breviary), three apiece for *Terce*, *Sext* and *None*, five for Vespers (in the Sarum rite, for some reason, this hour contained the five breviary psalms for Vespers on Tuesdays, rather than those for Sunday, as in the Roman and most other uses), and four for Compline.

If you are good at arithmetic, and have followed so far, you'll have grasped that this arrangement ought to have made a total of twenty-five in the Little Office of the Virgin. But because of the oddity of using the Tuesday Vespers psalms, instead of the Sunday Vesper psalms, for the evening office, there was an overlap of five with the psalms in *Terce, Sext* and *None*, some of which were duplicated in the Tuesday evening psalms, so there were in fact only a total of twenty separate psalms in that part of the book. The Office for the Dead had five psalms for first Vespers (Sunday and feast-day prayers began officially with the evening service of Vespers recited after sundown the previous day). There was a full complement of nine psalms for the three nocturnes of Matins, though the second and third nocturnes weren't always said, and four psalms and a canticle were provided for Lauds: *Terce, Sext, None*, second Vespers and Compline were not provided in the Office for the Dead. That should have given eighteen psalms in all, but six of the psalms provided overlapped with parts of the Office of the Virgin, so there were just twelve additional psalms there in all.

In addition, almost all Books of Hours included the seven Penitential psalms (i.e. Psalms 6, 31, 37, 50, 101, 129 and 142, Vulgate numbering) and fifteen Gradual Psalms (119–133), to be recited after the Litany, and towards the end of the Middle Ages many included the ten psalms of the Passion (21–30): but here again there were many overlaps. Finally, the Commendations included the whole of the very long psalm 118.

In all, therefore, and excluding these duplications, the Book of Hours included on average fifty-five psalms, or just over a third of the Psalter.[5] These included many of the most beautiful psalms in the Psalter, and much of what was left out was no great loss, and in some cases very tiresome indeed – for example, the long and frankly tedious historical psalms used in the Matins office in the breviary, banging on for a hundred verses or so about smashing the Amalekites or wandering endlessly in the wilderness. But there were also a great many notable exclusions. Numbers alone don't convey the issue here – but the psalms left out included 1, *Beatus Vir* (Happy is the man), 46, *Omnes gentes plaudite* (O clap your hands, all ye nations), 69, *Deus in adiutorium* (O God come to my aid), 88, *Quam dilecta tabernacula* (How lovely are your dwellings), 89, *Domine refugiam factus* (The Lord is my refuge), 90, *Qui habitat in adjutorio altissimi* (He who dwells in the shade of the almighty), 109, *Dixit Dominus* (The Lord Declared), 110, *Confitebor tibi Domine in toto corde meo* (I will confess the Lord with my whole heart), 112, *Laudate pueri* (Praise God, children), 113a, *In Exitu Israel* (When Israel went out of Egypt), 113b, *Non nobis, domine* (Not to us, Lord), 136, *Super flumina Babylonis* (By the rivers of Babylon), and many other psalms which were and would remain staples of Christian prayer.

These were notable omissions, not least because the devotional guides sometimes included even in liturgical psalters listing the benefits of reciting the psalms and directing the devout reader to the appropriate texts for specific religious needs or moods, frequently specified psalms which were simply not to be found in the Sarum *Horae*. One such guide, attributed to Jerome under the title *De laude dei super psalterium*, for example, directs the soul seeking true penitence to the two *Domine exaudi* psalms, and the soul seeking to express joy and hope to psalms 16, *Exaudi Domine*, 69, *Deus in adiutorium*, and 89, *Domine refugium factus*, none of which occurs in the Horae.[6] And this may well be one of the reasons for the proliferation in late medieval Books of Hours of non-biblical prayers for special needs and occasions, as devotional creativity moved in to supply what was lacking from the limited range of psalms texts available.

In any case, locating individual psalms in a Book of Hours can never have been much easier than in the full Psalter. As we've seen, the psalms in Psalters were arranged in numerical order, though without numbers, and were subdivided into smaller blocks marked by a larger and more elaborate initial or illumination. The divisions within the Book of Hours were of course into the eight liturgical hours themselves (*Matins, Lauds, Prime, Terce, Sext, None, Vespers, Compline*), and so the user of these books must invariably have read the psalms in the clustered sequences provided by the liturgical hours, rather than as discrete items. Indeed, although the earliest surviving set of vernacular directions for the use of the Book of Hours by laywomen, *Ancrene Wisse*, insisted on the desirability of reciting each of the hours as near as possible to its correct liturgical timing, in practice many lay people, like most priests, will have read several hours, and in some cases the whole of the Little Office, as a single daily recitation. So John Sheppey, Bishop of Rochester, preaching at the funeral of Lady Cobham in 1344, told his hearers that 'on no day would she willingly come down from her chamber to speak with any stranger, until she had said Matins and the Hours of Our Lady, the Seven Psalms and the Litany, almost every day'.[7] Lady Margaret Beaufort similarly recited the whole of the Office of the Dead and the Commendation psalm 118 as a single devotional act every day, but, in contrast to Lady Cobham, she recited *Matins* and *Lauds* of the Virgin at the proper time in the morning after her chaplain had recited these offices in full from the breviary, and in the same way *Vespers* of Our Lady at the appropriate time in the evening, after *Vespers* of the day had been recited.

Lady Margaret had unusual leisure for such devotional refinements, and it seems likely that most users of Books of Hours used the psalms as Lady Cobham did, in large conglomerated recitations of more than one of the liturgical Hours at a time, a practice which left little opportunity for the ruminative absorption of the full meaning of individual psalms. So the treatise on 'The Maner to live well' which features as a catechetical item in many printed Books of Hours in the 1530s advises the reader each morning, 'When you have arrayed you, say in your chamber or lodging, Matins, Prime and Hours if ye may. Then go to the church...'[8] And even Lady Margaret must have cut corners: to turn the daily recitation of the Dirige and Commendations together into a manageable part of an already crowded devotional schedule she and her chaplains must have galloped through the verses.

And in any case, we cannot remind ourselves too often that these were Latin texts being used for the most part by people who were literate in Latin only in the sense that they could pronounce the words written before them, but who must only rarely have had a detailed grip on their meanings. John Fisher tells us that Lady Margaret's Latin was hazy: 'Ful often she complained that in her youth she had not given her to the understanding of latyn wherin she had a lyttell perceyvynge specially of the rubbryshe of the ordynall for the saying of her service whiche she dyde wel understande.'[9] What Lady Margaret 'did well understand' here, note, is not the psalms, for more than a 'little perceiving' would be needed for that, but the rubrics for the recitation of the psalms in proper order. And that search for the ability to steer round a Latin book so as to be able to use it properly without penetration of the word-by-word meaning of the individual psalms confronts us everywhere in the meagre sources we possess for assessing lay comprehension: the detailed instructions for the recitation of the Little Office in *Ancrene Wisse* is entirely devoted to instructing the ladies concerned in the appropriate bodily gestures and posture which accompany each text, keyed to untranslated tags and cues from the beginning of the psalms and hours.[10]

Two centuries on, a monk of Syon compiled the English *Myrroure of our Lady*, an explanation of the Briggetine breviary for the benefit of the aristocratic ladies from whom were drawn the choir nuns of the Briggetine order. The author explained that

> Forasmuche as many of you, though ye can synge and rede, yet ye cannot se what the meaning therof ys: therefore to the only worschyp and praysyng of oure lorde Iesu cryst and hys moste mercyfull mother our lady and to the ghostly comfort and profit of your soules I have drawen youre legende and all your service in to Englysche, that ye shulde se by the understandynge therof, how worthy and holy praysyng of our gloryouse lady is contente therin, and the more devoutly and knowingly synge yt and rede yt and say yt to her worship.[11]

The author of the *Myrroure* did not translate the psalms for his nuns, referring them instead either to the translation made in the early fourteenth century by Richard Rolle for the recluse Margaret Kyrkby, an anchoress who had no Latin, or to the book of psalms in the so-called Wycliffite English Bible 'if ye have lysence therto'.

But it was not of course intended that the sisters should recite the psalms in English. English translations of scripture, as Christopher de Hamel has argued, were never thought of by medieval Catholics as being in themselves holy scripture. Holy Scripture *was* the Latin text of the Vulgate, its words a divine given, sanctified by use in the liturgy, and having a power and virtue in the very sound and shape of the words which no vernacular rendering could fully transmit or rival.[12] Medieval celebrations of the virtues of the psalms, like the *De Laude Psalmorum* attributed to Augustine and often included at the beginning of Psalters, understood the power of the words of the psalms objectively, almost, we might be tempted to say, magically:

> *Canticus psalmorum corpus sanctificat, animam decorat, invocat angelos in adiutorium, effugat demones, expellet tenebras, efficit sanitatem homini peccatori ... delet pecata ... sicut sol illuminat, sicut aqua mundificat ... Deum ostendit, diabollum offendit, iocundatem illicitatem extinguit ... os purificat, cor laetificat, turrem in caelo aedificat, hominem clarificat, omne malum occidit.*
>
> (The singing of psalms sanctifies the body, adorns the soul, calls angels to our aid, drives out demons, scatters the darkness, brings healing to sinful man, washes sin away, illuminates like the sun, washes like water ... points towards God, affronts the devil, extinguishes unseemly levity, cleanses the mouth, gladdens the heart, builds a tower into heaven, enlightens a person, slays all evil.)

And so on.[13] It was the *ipsissima verba* of the psalmist – as it were, his original Latin – which worked these transformations and purifications, *ex opere operato*. The function of biblical translations, therefore, was to enlighten the layperson to the riches embedded in the Latin text, so that they might return to that text with an enhanced perception of its worth and wealth. As Rolle had said in the prologue to his translation, his intention was not to substitute English for Latin, but so 'that thei that knawes noght Latyn, by the Inglis may cum tille many Latyne wordes'.[14]

Rolle too believed that the very sound of the psalms brought objective good: he takes up the very wording of *De Laude Psalmorum* to insist that 'the sange of psalmes chaces fendes, excites aungels tille our help, it dose away synne, it qwemes [pleases] God, ... it dose away and destroys noy and angere of saule and makes pees bytwix body and saule.' But he envisaged all this as effected by the elevation of the minds and hearts of the holy women for whom he wrote, who should come to the psalter with a heightened devotional awareness of their content, so that the singing of psalms 'rayses tham to contemplative lyf and ofte syth in to soun and myrth of heven'.[15]

There was therefore a tension in the use of the psalms by lay people in the late Middle Ages, a tension which appears not to have troubled them, but which is troubling to modern perceptions. On the one hand, there was the practice of the recitation of sequences of half-understood Latin psalms in emulation of the monastic choir offices. This form of recitation approximated to other ascetical or devotional practices, such as the making of pilgrimage journeys, or the recitation of the rosary or other pious formulae, where conscious meaning was not the primary consideration, but rather the sanctification of time and the offering of the self to God by the lengthy repetition of words of power or, as medieval English men and women would have said, of *vertu*. That way of thinking about the psalms, as a continuous text to be recited for calculable spiritual benefit, was embodied in another psalm text almost invariably found in late medieval Books of Hours, the so-called 'Psalter of Saint Jerome', a catena of verses drawn from the whole Psalter, though not from every individual psalm, and not in numerical sequence. Jerome's psalter, which probably originated as a substitute for the bulky office-books or breviary for priests or religious travelling, or otherwise impeded from fulfilling the canonical requirement of reciting the office, was largely penitential and supplicatory in character. In the form normally included in the Book of Hours, it carried a rubric promising salvation for those who recited it, and it is notably lacking in passages from the historical or doxological psalms. Its tone is urgent, and the psalm verses which make it up are reduced to an incantatory appeal for divine favour.[16] And of course a major part of the point of Jerome's psalter was not simply that it distilled the essence of the Psalter, and formed an adequate substitute for the whole. In that respect it resembled another routine but much shorter inclusion in the Book of Hours, the so called 'St Bernard's Verses', a catena of seven verses from the psalms, beginning *Illumina occulos meos ne unquam obdormiam in morte* (Enlighten my eyes lest at any time I should fall asleep in death) and, as that suggests, of a similar supplicatory character to St Jerome's Psalter. St Bernard's verses often carried a legend explaining that St Bernard had learned from a devil that there were seven verses in the psalms which if recited daily would ensure salvation.[17] The devil refused to disclose which verses, till

Bernard threatened to recite the entire psalter every day: and to prevent this greater good, the devil told all. The recitation of these seven verses therefore recapitulated the entire Psalter, another indication of a way of thinking about the recitation of the psalms as a task to be got through to bring about a specific good.

Yet this form of pious recitation, for all its mechanistic overtones, was increasingly located within a devotional ethos which valued affectivity and understanding interiority over the fulfilment of ritual requirements. Fifteenth-century writing about the psalms draws on the body of writing and thinking about the *vertu* of the recitation of the psalms which I have discussed, recognizing the objective power of the pronunciation of the words, yet emphasizing even more their ability to elevate and sanctify the understanding. As the author of the *Myrroure* wrote, once again directly paraphrasing *De Laude Psalmorum*,

> for in few wordes they conteyne moche mystery & grete sentence more then other scrypture. For as saynt Austyn sayeth. All that the olde lawe. All that the prophetes / & all that the gospel & the new lawe bydde & ordeyne is conteyned in these holy psalmes / & therfore he sayeth the syngyng of them pleasyth god moche / for al that is in them / longeth to hys worshyp / ... what degre or age or condycyon that he be of Eche man & woman and childe yonge & olde / may fynde in these psalmes that shall teche hym / & that shall delyte hym. For psalmes he sayth comforteth the heuy / & tempereth them that ar mery / they appese them that ar wrothe / & they refreshe the pore / they warne the riche to knowe themself and not to be prowde / & so they gyue able medycyne to all that receyue them.[18]

This exalted view of the effects of praying the psalms was of course being expounded to women vowed to contemplative life. So my next simple question is: is there any sign that this is how ordinary users of Books of Hours in late medieval England thought about and used the psalms? I think the answer to that question is, yes and no. I want to suggest that there are signs of growing lay engagement with an attentive focus on the detailed meaning of the psalms, but that this engagement was highly selective, focusing on a small number of psalms of a particular type, and therefore bypassing the bulk of those recited in the course of saying the little office. This was a perception which was borne in on me a couple of years ago when I examined the printed Sarum Book of Hours and Psalter, bound as one book, which Thomas More had with him in the Tower in the months before his death, and in which, famously, he made many annotations.[19] I imagined that I was familiar with the book from using the excellent Yale University Press facsimile. What the facsimile had not prepared me for was the very noticeable staining and wear on the pages of More's *Horae* containing the Litany of the saints, suffrages and the seven penitential psalms: it was clear that More (or a later owner) had turned these pages far more heavily than any others in the book.

In this, of course, he was characteristically at one with the devotional fashions of his age. The bestselling religious book of Henry VIII's reign was John Fisher's exposition of the seven penitential psalms, published at the behest of Margaret Beaufort, who 'much delighted' in the sermons from which the book derived, and other expositions of one or other of the penitential psalms, for example that by Savonarola on the *Miserere*, retained popularity into and beyond the Reformation. The growth of a prosperous lay readership for pious literature, focused as their devotional life in general was on penitence and supplication, provided an interpretative framework for the penitential psalms. The extraordinary popularity of Fisher's book, which first appeared in 1509 and ran through seven editions till the break with Rome, demonstrates the appetite among the Tudor laity for just this sort of exposition.[20]

It is no great surprise, therefore, to find that the seven penitential psalms were almost certainly those most often resorted to, and presumably reflected on, by More in his last months.[21] There are no annotations of the psalms occurring in More's *Horae*. He did make marginal additions in the day hours, but these form an original prayer and are unrelated to the psalms alongside which they occur.

Scrutiny of the copious annotations in his Psalter, bound at the back of his Book of Hours, however, yields some striking results. Here More had evidently worked his way through his Psalter, pen in hand, annotating verses as they struck him, sometimes with a mere word or two of interpretation – *spes et fiducia, contra demones* (hope and trust, against demons), and the like – sometimes with more substantial glosses, some of them intensely moving, in the light of the circumstances in which they were made, as in his annotation against the first verses of psalm 83, *Quam dilecta tabernacula* (How lovely are your dwellings): 'The prayer either of a man who is shut away in prison, or of one lying sick in bed, yearning to go to the church, or of any faithful man who hopes for heaven'.

More did not make it through the whole Psalter, and the annotations cease altogether after psalm 105. In all, he placed some sort of annotation against 177 verses. What is striking is that overwhelmingly he chose to annotate psalms which do not occur at all in the Book of Hours, or which, if they do, do so either in the penitential Office of the Dead, and express corresponding sentiments, or occur in the book as part of the two popular penitential gatherings of psalms – the penitential psalms proper, or the psalms of the Passion. More comments on only nineteen psalms which also occur somewhere in his Book of Hours, in contrast to the fifty-nine he annotated which are *not* represented there at all. He also consistently commented more copiously on this latter category than on the annotated psalms which also occur in the office, and, strikingly, only seven of the verses he annotated occur in psalms found in the Little Office of the Virgin. The overwhelming majority of the annotations therefore are on psalms of a penitential and supplicatory character, which More would not have encountered in reciting the hours, and in general he shows a striking lack of interest in psalms primarily devoted to celebration and praise.

I'm aware, of course, that More was a theological sophisticate who read and wrote Latin as easily as he did English. In that sense he can hardly be considered a representative Tudor devotee. But if More was atypical in his intelligence and education, his devotional outlook and his practice of piety strike me as close in most respects to those of the professional classes from which he and his father came. So the evidence of More's Hours and Psalter suggests to me that there were at the end of the Middle Ages two very different ways of using the psalms. The first of these was liturgical, in the ordinary course of recitation within the office, where the interpretation of the psalm was not personal but ecclesial and Christological, and governed by the framework of the other texts in the Hours. The second was a more interiorized, reflective reading of psalms which fell outside that context. In fact, many of More's annotations follow traditional Christological or ecclesial lines of interpretation, and I have commented elsewhere on the strikingly small number of his annotations which can be convincingly related directly to his own personal circumstances as a man imprisoned and under threat of death for treason – most of what he wrote could have come from any standard Tudor devotional treatise.[22]

There is no room here to flesh this argument out in detail, but if what I am suggesting is correct, it provides further reason for rejecting the suggestion of John Bossy, Jonathan Hughes, Colin Richmond and others that the praying of the psalms in the Book of Hours in the late Middle Ages was both the sign and in some sense the cause of a spiritual individualism, which eroded communal and parish religion, and encouraged, in Hughes's words, 'the egocentric and abrasive expression of social hostility'.[23] Most people will have prayed the psalms rapidly, without close comprehension of the precise meaning of the Latin. A growing devout minority did focus on the sense of the words they recited, but they did so primarily in relation to small groups of psalms understood as lamentations for the passion of Christ, or as expressions of the devotee's own penitence and longing for forgiveness. They read these psalms in a culture which related penitence and forgiveness directly and powerfully to the ascetical and sacramental discipline of the Church – as any reader of Fisher's bestselling devotional exposition of these psalms can see: that is, personally but precisely *not* individualistically.[24] There is not the slightest support in More's annotations, for example, for Jonathan Hughes's claim that the late medieval devotee read the penitential psalms as 'egocentric confessions of a worshipper who confesses to God a sense of isolation and being at odds with the world, persecuted by his enemies': this is simply not the mood encountered in More's comments on the words of the persecuted man in psalm 37: 'A meek man ought to behave like this in tribulation, neither speaking proudly nor responding in kind when spoken ill of, but blessing those who curse him, and suffering gladly, for the sake of justice if he has deserved it, or for God's sake if he has deserved no evil.'[25]

The case of More is, I repeat, atypical of lay users of the psalms. There can have been few other early Tudor Englishmen who wrote as fluently and idiomatically in Latin as they did in English, and More's comprehension of the Latin text of the psalms was certainly superior to that of the vast majority of the clergy. But his devotional taste is another matter, and seems fairly representative of the literate laity at large. And for them, the majority of lay users of the Psalter, comprehension was a matter of a sliding scale of familiarity with imperfectly understood texts, whose words had power not because of their power to convey sense *precisely*, to express emotion *directly*, to edify or instruct *persuasively*, but because they were words of power, sanctified by their revealed status and perhaps even more by their mysterious deployment in the liturgy. For many lay people, therefore, the use of the psalms was as an exercise of piety which had as much or even more in common with penitential exercises like fasting and pilgrimage, or rote devotional activities like saying the Rosary, than with the considered absorption of a piece of vernacular text in the hands of a modern reader. By the mid-1530s in England, after the break with Rome, Books of Hours, themselves entirely Catholic in content, were appearing with full English translations. The Latin text quickly moved from centre-page with translations in the margin, to the main text presented in English, with the Latin now consigned to the margins. There was to be no reversal of this trend, even under the Catholic Mary, when the restored Catholic regime issued official Books of Hours in which full English translations dominated or even entirely replaced the traditional Latin text.

Within a generation, of course, lay experience of the Psalter for all but a handful of English men and women would be transformed by the singing of metrical English psalms. The bilingual psalms in the Books of Hours of the 1530s therefore straddle the tectonic plates of a huge and seismic rift in Christian piety. They represent the divide between two devotional worlds, two radically different understandings of Christianity, and two vastly different experiences of prayer.

Crises and Movements

6

Plague and Historical Memory

I

In the spring of 2003, on a visit to Toronto, I was startled by the sight of passersby in the streets with mouths and noses hidden under medical face masks. My trip, it emerged, had coincided with an outbreak of severe acute respiratory syndrome (SARS). Those nervous Torontonians were reacting to speculation in the mass media that this might be the start of a pandemic which could wipe out entire populations, send world financial markets crashing, and form the prelude to the imminent collapse of civilization.

These apocalyptic terrors were, happily, unrealized, but from time to time the fears of plague recur. In Britain during the winter of 2016–17, alarm in the press and on television focused on long-distance migratory wildfowl arriving to winter here in salt marshes, estuaries and wetlands. Commentators have emphasized the possibility that these migrants from the East might infect domestic chickens and turkeys in intensive farms with the virulent H5N1 strain of avian flu, and so set off a lethal pandemic. The H5N1 virus is in fact not easily transmitted among humans, but in these doom scenarios it mutates into a strain lethal to human beings. Consequently, government intervened to force poultry farmers to keep their birds under cover, threatening the livelihood of free-range poultry and egg producers. And in general, we have become more conscious than ever that there is a price to the dense network of communication which has given us almost instant access to even the remotest parts of the world. In the global village, bird flu in the shanties of rural China may well turn out to be very bad news indeed for London, Los Angeles or New York.

Pandemic disease is not, of course, a twenty-first-century novelty. Everyone has heard of the Black Death, which decimated the populations of Europe and Asia in the fourteenth and following centuries. Yet the actual historical consequences of such nightmare mortality rates are hard to nail down, and have proved curiously resistant to integration into wider frames of historical explanation and analysis. The worldwide flu epidemic of 1918–19 was responsible for between 20 and 50 million deaths, a death toll far greater than that caused by all the guns and bombs of the First World War put together. Yet while the impact of the war is endlessly explored, flu seldom features as one of the determining forces shaping the problems and character of the early twentieth century.

In 2001 a group of specialists in history, archaeology, epidemiology and molecular biology gathered at the American Academy in Rome to see what light the pooling of their very different kinds of expertise might cast on one of the most significant of history's forgotten pandemics. The Academy's director, Lester K. Little, subsequently edited the colloquium proceedings as *Plague and the End of Antiquity*.[1] The focus of the colloquium was the recurrent waves of plague which ravaged Europe and Asia for two centuries, appearing suddenly in the Egyptian port of Pelusium in 541 AD. It spread from there to Alexandria, probably from an incubation centre somewhere in central Africa, then moved rapidly through Syria, north and east into Greek Asia Minor, Mesopotamia, and Persia, and west into Europe. By 542 the plague had reached Constantinople. The emperor Justinian was the renewer of the greatness of Rome's empire and patron of the world's greatest religious building, Hagia Sophia, but the disease was no respecter of persons, and he himself contracted it. Justinian recovered to rule for another twenty years, unlike his enemy the king of Persia, who perished from plague the same winter.

The death toll from this 'Justinianic plague' was terrible. Eyewitnesses speak of the depopulation of entire regions, a third of the people of Palestine dead, whole villages and towns utterly deserted. When the disease reached the capital of the empire, deaths climbed from 5,000, to 7,000, to 12,000, until as many as 16,000, mostly of the poor, were being removed every single day.[2]

At first the authorities stationed officials at the city gates and the harbours to count the bodies, but when the count reached 230,000 it was abandoned. To begin with, a combination of hygiene and piety had prompted the city authorities to provide free burial and religious rites for the corpses of the poor, who lay where they had died in streets and houses. But as the mortality rates mounted, the dwindling numbers of clergy could not cope, and the overwhelming priority anyway became simply to rid the beleaguered living of the murderous presence of the dead. Panic stashing of corpses in the guard towers around the city walls filled Constantinople with the stench of death. Every available form of transport was mobilized to get the mountains of dead out of the city. The corpses were heaped along the seashore in piles of up to 5,000, then loaded onto ships and dumped at sea or on unpopulated shores as far away as possible. The emperor sent the commander of his palace guard to oversee the disposal.

Contract labourers from outlying regions were hired (for a king's ransom) to dig vast plague pits, some of which were said to hold as many as 70,000 bodies. Successive layers of corpses were trodden down like grapes to make room for the next, gaps were plugged with the bodies of children, and the chroniclers offer harrowing descriptions of corpses whose putrid bellies burst open when they landed in the pits, of new batches of the dead sinking into a queasy sea of corruption.

The early waves of this plague 'by which the whole human race came near to being annihilated' – as the gossipy Greek historian Procopius put it – were vividly documented by a cluster of eyewitnesses. Procopius, recently returned from a spell on the staff of Justinian's great General Belisarius during his reconquest of Italy, was probably in Constantinople when the disease arrived there in 542: to him we owe many of the details of the imperial administration's handling of the crisis.[3] Outside the capital, Evagrius

Scholasticus, a Syrian lawyer and historian, contracted the plague while still a schoolboy during the first outbreak at Antioch.[4] He recovered, but his life was to be dogged by recurrence of the disease. His own childhood infection had apparently immunized him, but the rest of his family were not so lucky. In one epidemic after another he lost his wife, several of his children, and many more distant relatives, as well as an assortment of domestic servants and farm staff whose loss greatly impoverished him. Fifty years after his own first brush with plague, and just before he commenced work on his great *Ecclesiastical History*, a fresh outbreak at Antioch carried off two more much-loved children 'besides those who had died previously'.[5]

The fullest eyewitness account of all comes from the Syriac writings of a Monophysite Christian bishop, John of Ephesus, who happened to be in Alexandria on business when the plague arrived there in 541. John, whose account is analysed in an essay by Michael G. Morony, journeyed back to Constantinople, more or less keeping pace with the spread of the disease north through Syria and on into Thrace, where, he wrote, 'day after day we ... used to knock at the door of the grave'. His haunting evocations of abandoned villages, domestic herds turning feral, and whitening crops standing unharvested in an eerily empty landscape, burned themselves into the literary imagination of late antiquity, and would resurface in many later accounts of epidemics.[6]

For the plague persisted for two centuries, hectically and chronically, turning back on itself to revisit earlier hotspots, but also to devastate regions which until then had escaped, all the time spreading inexorably. It may not have penetrated the newly Islamicized Arab world until the late 630s, but it then took hold and recurred frequently, though tracing its progress is complicated by the fact that the earliest Arabic accounts survive for the most part embedded and recast in much later compilations. Its progress north and west was probably more rapid, though here too the literary sources are fragmentary and require a good deal of interpretation. The plague may have reached Gaul as early as 543: certainly by the 570s it was rampant there, its inroads chronicled in Gregory of Tours's contemporary *History of the Franks*. The plague was also sweeping through northern Italy in the 570s and 580s; the Lombard historian Paul the Deacon recorded, 'You might see the world brought back to its ancient silence: no voice in the field; no whistling of shepherds ... human habitations become places of refuge for wild beasts.'[7]

The plague was virulently present in Rome by 589, when its victims included Pope Pelagius II. More than eighty citizens are said to have dropped dead during the first of the great supplicatory processions ordered by Pelagius's successor, Pope Gregory the Great. Gregory's processions were an attempt to turn aside the wrath of God, and would be imitated all over Christian Europe for the rest of the Middle Ages, but the summoning of such large crowds almost certainly helped instead to spread the infection.

By the mid-seventh century the plague had arrived at the western fringes of the known world: it was in England by 14 July 664, in Ireland by August the same year. Saint Cuthbert of Lindisfarne, at that time a monk of Melrose in the Scottish borders, contracted the disease, but recovered. His abbot, Boisil, succumbed, along with many other monks. The monasteries were by now the largest concentrations of population in England, since most vestiges of Roman urban civilization had faded, and it is by the disease's impact on the monasteries that we can trace its progress. The historian Bede records that at the great community of Jarrow only the abbot and one small boy survived to recite the daily office: the boy may well have been Bede himself.[8]

From its first appearance in Egypt the chroniclers had commented on the devastating psychological effects of plague: dissolving social convention and established morality, numbing the feelings of survivors so that mothers might watch with passive indifference the sufferings of their children. In Britain, mass mortality on an unprecedented scale struck at the still-precarious Christianity of a nation only recently converted. The apparent powerlessness of the new religion in the face of this devastating visitation turned many back to the ancient gods. The king of the East Saxons, Sighere, came from a line of Christian kings which included his uncle Redwald, probably the grandee commemorated by the famous ship burial at Sutton Hoo. But Sighere now took his whole kingdom back to paganism, and the work of conversion would have to begin all over again in the following generation.

Given the fragmentary nature of the literary evidence, a host of unanswered questions hang over the nature, progress and persistence of this, the first great pandemic in history. Even the identity and continuity of the disease over two centuries and two continents can be questioned. Many of those who left descriptions of the Black Death of the fourteenth century were qualified medical observers, unable to cure the disease but practised in precise description. On the basis of their accounts, historians can be reasonably sure that the Black Death was in fact bubonic plague, carried by fleas from infested rats (though even this conclusion has been contested).

As it happens, none of the surviving accounts of the Justinianic plague was written by an observer with medical training, and though all the contributors to the symposium are convinced that this plague was also bubonic, they are frank about the difficulties of the diagnosis. The early Syriac sources do include unmistakable descriptions of victims suffering with swellings – the 'buboes' from which bubonic plague takes its name – in the groin, armpit or neck. A century later, Bede described a similar swelling in the groin as one of Cuthbert's plague symptoms. But literary descriptions of many outbreaks of the disease lack any such tell-tale indicators, or include details less obviously consistent with bubonic plague – the 'yellowness' of the plague mentioned in Irish sources, or the sudden death of apparently healthy victims, stricken in mid-breath with no external symptoms, or the marking of sufferers not with buboes but with black or purple spots on abdomen, limbs, or even the palms of the hands. In some sources the great speed of the spread of the disease seems inconsistent with bubonic plague, which spreads relatively slowly through the bite of infected rat fleas.

These are not insuperable difficulties: bubonic plague may develop into pneumonic plague, which kills with few external warning symptoms, and which is far more virulent than the bubonic form, being spread not by fleabites but by airborne water droplets from the lungs of the infected. Nevertheless, the deficiencies of the documentary sources make recourse to other types of evidence very desirable: hence the centrality in this symposium of archaeology, epidemiology and molecular biology.

Archaeology, it has to be said, is of only rather limited help. As John Maddicott observes in a wonderfully wide-ranging essay on plague in seventh-century England, 'archaeology cannot tell us much about the progress of epidemic disease in any period. If we relied on it alone, we would hardly be able to detect the Black Death.'[9] Maddicott does his best, assembling a list of nine archaeological sites from Anglo-Saxon England which may have been settlements abandoned suddenly at the end of the seventh century. These sites may therefore provide evidence for the decline of the rural population one would expect in the wake of epidemic, but Maddicott concedes that this remains no more than 'an open possibility'.

The impact of the disease in seventh- and eighth-century Britain has to be deduced from scattered references to it in Bede, and from ambiguous material evidence such as the few burial sites containing disordered corpses and shoddy or shallow burials indicating some sort of crisis, which may or may not have been the plague. Negative evidence of a sort is perhaps provided by the comparatively small number of English settlements discovered so far which can be firmly dated to the eighth or ninth centuries, suggesting a reduced population.

Archaeological absences, however, can be double-edged assets. An archaeological obstacle to firmly identifying the seventh-century British epidemic as bubonic plague, for example, is the fact that though rats are known to have existed in Roman Britain, and again in early medieval England, 'no rat bones have been recovered from any early Anglo-Saxon site'. There may well, therefore, have been no rats in Bede's England to spread the disease, perhaps because they had died out with the fading of the Romano-British towns, and the consequent disappearance of concentrations of population large enough to support rodent colonies.

Rats, of course, are fine-boned animals, and the damp English climate is not particularly conducive to the preservation of the fragile remains of small mammals. It seems likely, nevertheless, that the experts at the American Academy colloquium would heave a collective sigh of relief if a rat bone or two were to turn up in a datable English seventh-century site. The situation is even worse for Ireland, where there is no pertinent archaeological evidence at all, and the progress of the disease has to be inferred from what might or might not be thought suspiciously high levels of mortality among the ruling caste of the late seventh century, as recorded in later succession lists and dynastic poetry.

In Spain, according to another contributor to the Rome colloquium, Michael Kulikowski, tracing the Justinianic plague 'is a matter of guesswork and extrapolation from a very small body of evidence'.[10] This includes a puzzling group of plague sermons, so badly written that the likeliest explanation for their preservation in a much more sophisticated collection of sermon texts might be that plague sermons were often needed. More concretely, Kulikowski offers the suggestive evidence of two burial sites within the ancient city walls of Valencia, where thirty or so bodies deposited on more than one occasion, jumbled ignominiously into a ditch and hastily covered over, may date from the sixth century, and so may be from a plague pit.

Even relatively firm archaeological evidence, however, may seem to the layman to require an act of faith in its interpretation. The sole evidence for the spread of the first outbreak of the epidemic to Sicily, for example, consists of a single tombstone recording the deaths there of three young boys, perhaps brothers, in December 542. The presence of the disease in Rome the following year is inferred from the survival there of nine epitaph inscriptions datable to a period of four months from November 543 to February 544. This cluster may seem to the non-specialist a shaky enough basis on which to deduce the presence of a devastating epidemic, but in fact this is the densest surviving concentration of such epitaphs in the whole of the very rich corpus of sixth-century Roman inscriptions. As Dionysios Stathakopoulos, another contributor to the collection, writes, the cluster of deaths probably does therefore establish (though not of course explain) an unusually high mortality rate in Rome in the winter and spring of 543–4.[11]

Advances in the biological sciences may one day perhaps come to the aid of both historians and archaeologists. In 1998 a team of molecular biologists based in Marseille collaborated with archaeologists and historians on a mass burial site associated with the quarantine hospitals operating during outbreaks of bubonic plague there in 1590 and 1720. Analysis of the DNA in dental pulp from unerupted teeth in these burial pits allegedly identified traces of the *Y. pestis* bacterium, which causes bubonic plague. The Marseille findings did not go unchallenged, but the group subsequently extended their analysis to three skulls taken from a fourteenth-century plague pit, and once again claimed to have identified traces of *Yersina pestis* DNA. In 2005 scholars at Munich, using the same techniques on a burial in Upper Bavaria dated by archaeologists to the sixth century, claimed to have detected *Y. pestis* DNA there too. If their findings are sound, this would constitute the sole evidence for the presence of the disease in sixth-century Germany.

A generation accustomed to *Jurassic Park* fantasies of dinosaur DNA recovered from the bloodstream of mosquitoes preserved in amber may have no imaginative difficulty in accepting that diseases might be diagnosed from fragments of DNA a millennium and a half old. But it is far too soon to start the cheering. An Oxford laboratory specializing in the analysis of ancient biomolecules and using a far larger sample of more than sixty victims from five suspected plague pits has failed to replicate the Marseille and Munich findings. While this failure does not in itself invalidate the results from Marseille and Munich, it does underline the precarious nature of such analysis, and suggests the need for caution in theorizing from the alleged results.

The molecular biologists support the historians and archaeologists in thinking that Justinian's plague was probably humanity's first bubonic pandemic. Analysis of the structure of *Y. pestis* DNA suggests that the disease was a very late arrival in the history of evolution, and that it mutated from a far less virulent gastrointestinal pathogen somewhere between 20,000 and 1,500 years ago. It may be that refinements in the ability of scientists to read the time by the 'molecular clock' will supply a more precise date for the first emergence of the disease. Whether or not this becomes possible, the historians still have to set themselves to explain what it was about the mid-sixth century that provided the conditions for the eruption and spread of the pandemic on so vast a scale.[12]

They will also have to work harder to provide a convincing account of the impact which such overwhelming mortality may have had on the subsequent course of human history. Lester Little announced boldly in his preface to the colloquium's published proceedings that 'plague helped carry out Antiquity and usher in the Middle Ages,' but his experts were hard pressed to say exactly how. There was plenty of speculation, of varying degrees of plausibility, about how the disappearance of a third or more of the population might have shaped the course of the next few centuries. Did the Justinianic plague make possible the spread of Islam, by fatally undermining the armed force of Byzantium? Did it trigger the great flowering of monastic culture in England and Ireland which produced the Lindisfarne Gospels and the Book of Kells, by stimulating a more anxious and interiorized spirituality, wiping out small scattered monastic houses, and concentrating the survivors and their talents in larger and more vigorous communities?

Did the plague inaugurate a new and positive work ethic in the Latin West? Was the emergence of a new and intense Christian devotion to the Virgin Mary in sixth- and seventh-century Byzantium the direct consequence of a desperate search for consolation in the face of an angry God? Or was even so devastating a depopulation no more than a blip on the demographic scale, as John Maddicott says of its impact in England: 'a brief and temporary intermission in an upward trend'? It is all so elusive. If the Justinianic pandemic did indeed strike on the scale that some of these essayists suggest, it must have felt to those who endured it a catastrophe on a par with the sinking of Atlantis. It speaks volumes about the fragility of human knowledge and the shortness of human collective memory that so vast a calamity has left so little trace, and must be reconstructed with so much effort and uncertainty. That's a thought to season our anxious watch for signs of sickness among the migrating wildfowl.

II

The Black Death
Late in the year 1347 a new and terrible disease arrived in Europe from the Tartar regions north of Constantinople, carried first by Genoese merchants vainly fleeing from a pestilence that raced faster than war horses. It was said to have been introduced into the Genoese trading community at Caffa in the Crimea by a besieging Tartar army, who deliberately catapulted the infected corpses of their own dead across the city walls. Originating ten years or more before in the steppes of Asia, the plague had already decimated the populations of China, India, Transoxiana, Persia and southern Russia. By the spring of 1348 it had galloped through Italy and had reached the papal court in exile in the south of France at Avignon (where it was thought that as many as 62,000 died, and where Pope Clement VI ordered huge new graveyards to be consecrated to hold the mounting piles of dead). By June it was in Paris, by November in southern Austria. That autumn the plague entered England simultaneously though the West Country sea ports and through London. From there it spread at once to Ireland, by November it had reached Bergen, and so on to the rest of north-west Europe, Scandinavia, even remote Iceland.[13]

Sufferers from the disease developed flu symptoms such as fever and shivering; blackened buboes or swellings appeared in the groin, neck, and armpits, charged with dark and vile-smelling pus. Many also suffered purple or red discolorations under the skin, internal bleeding, and bloody urine, diarrhoea or vomiting. Death seems often to have come from a pneumonia-like flooding of the lungs, and though sometimes delayed as much as eight days, could also occur very soon after the first appearance of infection – stories were told of doctors or priests ministering to the victims in the morning and being dead themselves by nightfall.

Historians are undecided about the precise scale of mortality. Until recently the consensus suggested something between one third and one half of the population of Europe. More recent studies, including those under review, are inclined to push the numbers higher. Medieval observers were in no doubt that this was the worst Visitation of God since the Flood, feared the imminent end of the world, and offered terrifyingly large estimates of the dead. The poet Boccaccio thought that 100,000 had succumbed in his native Florence alone (unlikely, since the city's fourteenth-century population was almost certainly nearer 80,000!). But at the height of the infection as many as 200 corpses a day were being collected for burial from the streets of London. In this, as in so much else, England is the best-documented country in late-medieval Europe, and calculations based on sources such as manorial rent rolls, or statistics of clerics who took over livings vacated by death, suggest that at least half the population there may have died in the eighteen months after the arrival of the disease.

From the eye of the storm, it seemed possible that no one would be left to tell the tale. Brother John Clynn, the Franciscan chronicler of the disease in the Irish cathedral town of Kilkenny, who himself fell victim, 'waiting among the dead for death to come', noted that he was leaving blank pages in his book 'in case anyone should still be alive in the future and any son of Adam can escape this pestilence and continue the work'. All over Europe, the living were barely able to keep up with the disposal of the dead, stacked one above the other in deep plague pits like logs in a woodpile or, as one Italian observer noted, like the layers in lasagna.

The nature of this horrifying disease itself is obscure. The title by which it is generally known, the Black Death, is a modern coinage based on one of the more striking symptoms. Medieval science could describe the plague, but not diagnose it. The medical faculty of the University of Paris, consulted by the King of France, attributed the outbreak to the malign conjunction of the planets Saturn, Jupiter and Mars at 1 p.m. on 20 March 1345. Preventative measures included sniffing sponges soaked in vinegar, or posies of flowers and aromatic spices, or, in total contrast, the accumulated and fetid contents of chamber pots and privies. Remedies included the lancing of blisters and buboes, the administration of laxatives, vomits and bleeds, or the drinking of treacles made from boiled and fermented ingredients such as snakeskin.

Twentieth-century historians, struck by similarities with modern epidemics in India, have overwhelmingly concluded that the Black Death was a combination of bubonic and pneumonic plague, caused by the bacteria *Y. pestis* or *Pasteurella pestis*, and spread by the bite of the rat flea, *Xenopsylla chepsis*. The intestine of fleas infected with bubonic plague fills with congealed blood. The flea becomes voraciously hungry, and so more than usually aggressive. Because of its full gut, it regurgitates infected matter into its victims at every bite, and so the plague spreads.

But there are problems with this explanation. Bubonic plague slows down in the winter, when rat populations dwindle or become torpid or die, but the Black Death showed no such slackening. Pneumonic plague can flourish in cold weather, but the plague appeared in places like Iceland, where there were few or no rats. The suggestion that the famished fleas had transferred themselves to human hosts, or into woollen goods in peddlers' packs, or into bales of imported cloth, helps, but does not quite account for the astonishing race of the disease across Europe. These difficulties convinced the British zoologist Graham Twigg that suggestions that the plague was actually a form of anthrax or some similar cattle murrain should be taken seriously. There is a real issue here, but the difficulty with these alternatives is that though observers in Constantinople claimed that flocks of birds had died from the disease (raising the possibility that it was spread by airborne carriers), there is not much evidence of widespread mortality among livestock. More recently, a team of specialists in historical epidemiology at the University of Liverpool argued persuasively that the plague was not a bacterial disease at all, but a viral infection similar to the devastating haemorrhagic fever spread by the Ebola virus in late-twentieth-century Africa.

The Black Death was without question the greatest calamity in Medieval European history, inspiring hysterical processions of penitents scourging themselves with spiked whips to avert the anger of God, and setting off murderous pogroms against the Jews of Europe, who, despite attempts to protect them by Pope Clement VI, were widely blamed for poisoning their Gentile neighbours. But like the Justinianic plague, it has left historians with a sheaf of unanswered and perhaps unanswerable questions. What happens to a panic-stricken civilization brought to the brink of oblivion by death on this sudden, vast and uncontrollable scale? How do people who have lost entire families or helped bury half their neighbours cope with such losses? How do institutions – the manor, the courts, the Church – faced with the disappearance of more than half their personnel, change? What happens to agriculture when there are not enough peasants to till the fields, or to sexual morality when it seems that there will be no tomorrow, or to political and social subservience when Death the Leveller sweeps the rich and powerful away along with the poor and weak, or to religious faith when horror so vast and undiscriminating is sent, as everyone then believed, from the hand of God?

In the recurrent cycles of pandemic disease, we must hope that these remain purely historical conundrums, and that we don't discover the answers to such questions existentially, at first hand.

7

The Rise of Sacred Song

Some time in the late 1020s, a choirmaster from Arezzo secured an audience in Rome with Pope John XIX. It can't have been an entirely comfortable meeting. Guido of Arezzo was no mere musician, but an austere and dedicated monk, committed to the purification of the Catholic Church from the prevailing sin of simony, the buying and selling of holy things. Pope John, by contrast, embodied everything Guido disapproved of. Romanus of Tusculum, as he had been before he became pope, was the brother of his predecessor Benedict VIII, and the younger son of a family of Roman robber barons who had kept the papacy in their pocket for generations. John had been elevated from layman to pope in a single day, and had probably bought his election. If Guido had misgivings about all that, however, he buried them, for he needed the Pope's endorsement for what was to prove one of the epochal inventions of Western civilization.

As the Cambridge musicologist and literary scholar Christopher Page has shown, for almost a thousand years before that meeting in Rome, singing had been integral to Christian worship and hence to Christian identity.[1] But Christian song existed only in the memories and mouths of its singers. With many local variations, the Church in the West had long since evolved a common core of prescribed Bible readings, antiphons, psalms and hymns specific to the time of day, the passage of the liturgical seasons, and the feasts of the saints. But the books that transmitted this daily, weekly and annual cycle contained only words. Since there was no reliable system of notation to record the sound of singing, the music of these ancient chants was passed from singer to singer as it had always been, painfully acquired by endless repetition, liable to be lost, and subject always to the vagaries of happenstance, the lapse of memory, and the tastes and idiosyncrasies of individual choirmasters.

As one medieval treatise, *De Musica*, complained, 'rarely ... do three men agree about one chant,' for there were 'as many variations in chanting as there are teachers in the world'. In the ninth century a system of neumes, or marks above the lines of text, had evolved as a primitive kind of *aide-mémoire*, recording the rise and fall of the singing voice. But these marks indicated only the upward or downward movement of the voice on a given syllable; as Page comments, 'the singer knows that a step must be made, but he does not know how large it should be.' The precise pitch and movement of a melody could be discovered only by hearing it sung.[2]

Guido of Arezzo, however, had brought to Rome an invention that was to change all that. Like other earlier musical theorists, he allocated a series of letters to the rising notes of the singing voice. Guido then prolonged these letters above the text to be sung by tracing a series of four horizontal lines across the page. The 'mode' of the melody — in modern equivalents, and very roughly indeed, the key signature and starting pitch — was indicated by a clef sign on one line coloured red or yellow. The other lines were often simply scratched with a point into the parchment of the book, but the sequence of notes or neumes strung out along these lines enabled the singer to repeat the identical sequence at the right pitch on every reading, even though he had never heard them sung by anyone else.

Guido had prepared an antiphoner, using his system of lines and neumes to record the prescribed chants for the liturgy of the hours as they were sung at Arezzo. And John was duly impressed, 'turning the pages ... as if it were a marvel and studying the prefatory rules'; the excited pope prolonged the audience till he had mastered Guido's revolutionary new technique, and 'had learned one versicle he had never heard'.[3]

Even with the Pope's endorsement, Guido's system would take generations to become universally accepted: in some places singers were still acquiring their repertoire by memory as late as the fifteenth century. But slowly, monastery by monastery, cathedral by cathedral, the potential of the new notation was grasped. The late-eleventh-century chronicle of the Belgian monastery of Sint Truiden recalls the electrifying impact of Guido's new technique, brought there by Rudolf of Moutier-sur-Sambre, a stranger who spoke neither Walloon nor German, so that the choirboys could barely understand him, yet 'to the amazement of the senior monks he made them sing straight away, only by looking ... what they had never learned by hearing.'[4]

Children still learn to sing using Guido's sequence of letters – ut (do), re, mi, fa, sol, la – and in a slightly modified form his system of lines, the stave, provides the fundamental framework for the composition and transmission of most Western music. The stave not only facilitated the acquisition of tunes without tears; in the longer run, it made possible the creation of elaborate polyphony. Tallis's forty-part motet *Spem in Alium*, Bach's B-Minor Mass, the symphonies of Beethoven, Mahler's Ninth – all would have been inconceivable without the pious ingenuity of Guido of Arezzo.

Christopher Page's magnificent survey of the first thousand years of Western Christian music set out to reconstruct the evolutionary processes that culminated in Guido's breakthrough. Page is a medievalist teaching in the Faculty of English at Cambridge, but he is also a gifted musician, founder and one-time director of Gothic Voices, one of Britain's most prestigious and pioneering early music choral ensembles. Paradoxically, however, the first three-quarters of his book had almost nothing to say about music itself, for, as he observes, there are 'no systematic or consolidated records of Western musical notation' for about nine tenths of his period. Centuries of song are therefore lost in irrecoverable silence. It may be that some of the chants of the liturgy of Easter night do indeed take us back to 'the origin of liturgical chant in late antiquity', but the arguments that might establish that continuity are too technical and uncertain to become a secure part of his story.

What Page offered instead was breathtakingly ambitious even so: nothing less than a social history of the ministry and ministers of music in Western Christendom, from the New Testament to the age of the Crusades, and from the Vandal churches of North Africa to the monasteries of Carolingian and Capetian Europe. Drawing on an astonishing range of material – catacomb inscriptions, magical amulets, letters, saints' lives, charters and monastic chronicles–making especially effective use of Latin etymology and the neglected corpus of both Greek and Latin epigraphy, Page resurrected from the dead a forgotten gallery of singers and composers, and located them in the wider setting of the Church of their times: the history of Christian chant and cantors provides a window onto the complex evolution of the churches of late antiquity and the Carolingian world.

We know little or nothing about the music of the first Christian communities, though in the early second century a writer like Ignatius of Antioch deployed metaphors of music and harmony that suggest how central music was in fostering Christian community. Page doubts, though, whether there was a distinctive early Christian music, because in the cosmopolitan mix of faiths and ethnic identities in which Christianity emerged, Christian music, like Christian visual art, almost certainly borrowed forms and themes from both Jewish and pagan sources. References to the singing of 'psalms, hymns and spiritual songs' occur in the Pauline letters in contexts that may indicate that the writer had specifically in mind the arrangements for singing in Christian households. The earliest churches were based in the houses of prosperous converts, and Page suggests that the role of the singer often developed as part of the familial structure of ministry of such communities – the wealthy paterfamilias assumed the duties of presbyter or bishop, served by a son as deacon, and by his daughters and younger children, maybe, as singers.

One of the earliest and most enigmatic of Christian texts, the *Apostolic Tradition*, allocates the singing of psalms to 'the children and the virgins', and two centuries later Saint Jerome advised 'adolescents and others charged to sing in church' against vain display or the use of throat medicines to enhance their tone. The youthfulness and sexual innocence of sacred singers and readers of scripture emerges as something of a theme in the early chapters of the book. Page's own groundbreaking exploration of the funeral epitaphs of early Christian lectors, or readers – the lowly order of ministry that, as he demonstrates, included the singers – reveals that the average age of lectors who died before reaching adulthood was just fifteen, suggesting a generally youthful constituency.[5]

The epitaph of Pope Liberius, who died in 366, related that he was a lector while still a boy possessed of *infantia simplex*, 'childish innocence'. When the clergy of Carthage were exiled in 484, the banished lectors included many *infantuli*, little children, or, perhaps more accurately, 'tiny tots'. African church legislation from the fourth century stipulated that lectors should read (and chant) the scriptures only till they reached puberty. There was more involved here than their voices breaking: ritual purity was at stake. Lectors might remain in office if they undertook a chaste (i.e. sexless) marriage. In some places, that might mean that the singing of sacred texts was limited to the clergy from deacons upward, who at least in theory were vowed to celibacy.[6]

Singers, in theory at least, occupied a marginal status of singers on the lowliest rung of the ladder of Christian ministry, alongside the gravediggers and porters. Nevertheless, by the fourth century Roman deacons, routinely equated with the biblical order of Levites, feature often in the epigraphic record as accomplished singers of liturgical psalmody. So the fourth-century deacon Redemptus, buried in the catacomb of Callistus on the Appia Antica outside Rome, is said to have 'put forth sweet honey with nectared singing, celebrating the ancient prophet with sweet music'. Pope Gregory the Great, however, thought that in a civilization threatened by barbarians and on the verge of extinction, deacons had or should have better uses for their time than cultivating a *blanda vox*, a dulcet voice, and in 595 he suppressed this musical tradition among the Roman clergy. Singing deacons would, however, continue to feature prominently in the worship of the churches of Gaul and Vandal Africa.

African Christianity was doomed by the rise of Islam. But the shift of the centre of gravity of Latin Christianity into Gaul and the rest of barbarian Europe brought profound musical changes. Early Christian congregations sang, often in the form of sometimes elaborate responsorial psalms, chanted antiphonally with the clergy, solo and chorus. But as the vocabulary and pronunciation of Latin evolved into the emergent Romance languages, and in the Germanic world where Latin had never been anyone's first language, a gulf was opening between the language of liturgy and the language of daily life: congregational singing was one of the casualties.

Though congregations in former Roman provinces might retain a passive grasp of the language of worship well into the eighth and ninth centuries, they would not be able to speak or sing it, for liturgical Latin proved doggedly conservative and resistant to change. Liturgical elaboration also played its part. By the fifth and sixth centuries everywhere the clergy were formulating set courses of psalms and readings for the liturgical seasons and feasts, and special and often elaborate melodies were emerging for these 'proper' chants. The specialist office of cantor is firmly entrenched in Latin church sources by the later fifth century.

In the centuries that followed, the training of these professional liturgical singers in cathedrals and monastic centres became increasingly demanding, requiring, among other skills, not only literacy in the Latin Bible but prodigious feats of memory. A seventh-century miracle story from southern Gaul recounts a mean trick played on Praiectus, a novice cantor in the song school at Clermont. Malicious clerics tried to humiliate the boy by demanding that he sing a long and elaborate chant that his older classmates had been taught, but that he had never heard. Invoking the miraculous aid of a local saint, Praiectus performed the chant flawlessly.[7]

In all this, the liturgy of Rome had a special prestige, and Page offers a long and fascinating exploration of the training of Rome's ritual singers up to the ninth century. The earliest history of the Roman *schola cantorum* is poorly documented, but Page persuasively argues for the long, slow emergence of the Roman song schools on Byzantine patterns, around charitable institutions like hospitals and, especially, orphanages, which eventually functioned as recruiting grounds for the clergy. He rejects the idea, proposed by the late James McKinnon, that the relatively sudden emergence of the Roman *schola cantorum* in the late seventh century produced a new sense of corporate identity among the Roman singers and set off a drastic overhaul of the texts and chants used in the liturgy, the so-called 'Advent project', which then became the core of subsequent liturgical development in the Frankish territories and beyond. Liturgy is a profoundly traditional activity, which advances by accretion rather than in revolutions engineered by professionals, and singers in any case did not have the prestige or standing necessary to push through drastic changes to traditional forms of worship: 'Ritual singing was simply too important to be left to ritual singers.'[8]

In the kingdoms of the barbarian West, too, song schools were never just academies for singers. The Latin literacy, expertise in sacred texts, and many other skills a singer needed were a good training for future service to king and Church. In Merovingian and Carolingian Europe, the singers attached to the palatine chapels of Christian kings, those 'little Constantines', provided a pool of talent and a training ground for future abbots and bishops. *Romanitas*, the sense of a link backward to the imperial past, had a profound imaginative pull – and political value – for the rulers of the new kingdoms. The Catholic liturgy itself, with its exotic materials – the antique Latin of the chants and prayers, the silk and linen of the ministerial vestments, the ivory, jewels and precious metals of the sacred vessels, the incense and wine used in the ceremonies of the mass – tied even the bleakest and most impoverished northern Christian outpost to the glamour and lavishness of the Mediterranean south.

And the tug of the Mediterranean was strongest at Rome. Though 'the city contracted in the sixth and seventh centuries around a densely impacted coop of tombs and hollowed altars where innumerable relics of the Roman saints and martyrs were kept', it continued to fascinate and elicit the imitation of the other churches of the

West. Rome was the seat of the papacy and the *limina Apostolorum*, 'threshold of the Apostles', of course. But it was also the source of what the seventh-century Northumbrian monk and scholar the Venerable Bede called 'spiritual merchandise'. Rome was where northern bishops like Wilfred or abbots like Benedict Biscop came to find the icons, silks and illuminated books needed for what Page calls 'the rich materialism of Christian rites'. And the liturgy of Rome, its saints, feast days, prayers and liturgical chanting, seemed to the increasingly confident churches of Europe the touchstone of authentic Christianity. So the Englishman Biscop would dedicate the monasteries he established at Jarrow and Monkwearmouth to Rome's patron saints, Peter and Paul, and he persuaded John, archchanter of St Peter's Basilica, to come to rain-soaked Tyneside to teach his English monks to sing the psalms in the authentic Roman manner.

Roman sacred song became the cement of emergent European Christian identities. When Pope Stephen II crossed the Alps in 753 to seek the protection of the Frankish King Pippin against the Lombards, his retinue included expert liturgical singers. When he returned to Rome, he left some of them behind to teach the Frankish clergy at Metz the texts and melodies of the liturgy as it was performed in Rome. This was the genesis of the most significant liturgical project of the Middle Ages, the creation of a Romano-Frankish liturgy by overhauling the Frankish books to bring them closer to the usages of Rome, 'for the sake of unanimity with the Apostolic See and the peaceful harmony of God's Holy Church'. Pippin the Short would mobilize this project to advance his own claims to be the heir of the Christian Imperium of late antiquity: in the longer term this new liturgical hybrid would crystallize into the Mass and office that, in its essentials, Roman Catholics continued to celebrate down to the 1960s.

But despite the glamour that Rome and its worship exerted over Pippin and his successor Charlemagne, there was a decidedly critical edge to Frankish appropriation of Roman models. The Frankish churches believed that they were improving as well as appropriating the Roman past. Frankish clergy were intensely conscious that they adorned with jewels the bones of the saints whom pagan Rome had butchered, and they did not hesitate to remind their Roman brethren that the relics of the martyrs now treasured by the Franks had been rescued from 'neglected sepulchres' in Rome. There was no question, therefore, of the simple wholesale replacement of Gallican liturgical forms and music by Roman. Local pride and a sense of the Frankish realm's divinely appointed destiny ensured that Franco-Roman chant would be significantly different from its Roman as well as from its Frankish prototypes.

Historians have tended to see Pippin's promotion of the Romanization of the Frankish liturgy as a move to consolidate the political unity of Gaul. Page dismisses this notion as anachronistic. Though both Pippin and Charlemagne certainly saw the liturgy as underpinning their claims to Imperium, there could be no question of the sudden or comprehensive imposition of a single set of liturgical norms for the whole of their realms. The new liturgy and its music spread slowly, through networks of affinity, kinship and political and religious alliance.

Bishop Remedius of Rouen, who imported the Roman singer Simeon to establish a Roman-style *schola cantorum* there, was Pippin's half-brother, and such links characterize the early spread of the Franco-Roman liturgy. Page devotes considerable attention to Simeon's work at Rouen, drawing on recent archaeological discoveries in the cathedral to suggest that Simeon's song school may even have been physically modelled on a similar building and *schola* patronized by Gregory the Great in Rome. He also speculates that this 'Roman' singer was in fact of Byzantine origin, and therefore spoke and sang in a Greek-inflected Latin that would have created special linguistic difficulties for his Frankish hearers, a fact that Page thinks might have affected both his teaching and their reception of the Roman chants.[9]

Webs of kindred and affinity, including the prayer networks of monastic families, were vital to the spread of the new liturgy and its music. The abbot of a minor monastery might write to his colleague in a more prestigious institution, begging the loan of an expert cantor to train his monks in the authentic 'Roman' chant.

The consolidation of a common liturgy across a region might therefore depend on the arrival in some outpost of a single monk musician, unpacking his saddlebags and getting down to coaching unfamiliar novices.

The attention of historians of music has tended to focus on the elaboration of the major chants of the liturgy as the key to the evolution of sacred music in this period. A trawl through the sources for named composers of chant in the centuries on either side of Guido's breakthrough in the 1020s suggests, however, that the major focus for musical innovation was in fact on the generation of local liturgies for the feasts of local saints. Page assembles an impressive list of more than fifty named medieval composers of chant, most of whom poured their creativity into the antiphons and chants for the offices of regional shrines: they were 'scholars in the service of the saints'. Given the central importance of the saints for the identity and prestige of the institutions that housed their relics, this musical focus on their cults is perhaps not so surprising. The chants created by these mainly monastic composers were often essentially, therefore, in Page's words, 'a hymn to a landowner from his tenants'. And that perception is yet another testimony to the vital importance of locality for cultural formation in the Middle Ages.[10]

8
Holy Terror

In a speech delivered in 2001 on the first Sunday after September 11, President George W. Bush pledged America to a war on terrorism, which he referred to as 'this crusade'. There was an immediate outcry across the Islamic world. Did the term 'crusade' hint at some grand confrontation between opposed civilizations, and, behind that, a hungry Western imperialism? According to a prominent European Muslim leader, the Grand Mufti of the mosque in Marseille, the President's 'most unfortunate' invocation of the Crusades recalled 'the barbarous and unjust military operations against the Muslim world', perpetrated with savagery over centuries by medieval Christian knights intent on the 'recovery' of the Holy Land, and Jerusalem in particular.

The President and the Mufti were invoking diametrically opposed sets of associations – 'crusade' as valiant and costly struggle for a supremely good cause, and 'crusade' as byword for barbarism and aggression. The contrast is no recent invention. Christian 'holy war' is by its very nature profoundly paradoxical – sanctified slaughter (but also self-sacrifice) designed to forward or protect the religion of Christ, who commanded his followers to love their enemies, to turn the other cheek to the aggressor, and who warned that all who took up the sword would perish by the sword. Yet for all its contradictions, crusading dominated the thinking and policies of Western Christendom for centuries, and shaped some of the most characteristic institutions of the Middle Ages, not least the papacy, which had invented it.

Like the Mufti, historians have found it difficult to approach the Crusades without moral outrage. In the twentieth century, the historiography of the subject was dominated for English speakers by one writer, Sir Steven Runciman, whose three-volume narrative history of the Crusades, first published in 1951, held the field for fifty years. Runciman, a devout Christian, was a civilized and vivid writer, whose view of the Crusades was coloured by Enlightenment horror of fanaticism. Famously, he ended his history with a resounding condemnation:

> The triumphs of the Crusade were the triumphs of faith. But faith without wisdom is a dangerous thing... High ideals were besmirched by cruelty and greed, enterprise and endurance by a blind and narrow self-righteousness; and the Holy War itself was nothing more than a long act of intolerance in the name of God, which is the sin against the Holy Ghost.[1]

For all his immense learning, Runciman's account of the Crusades was limited both by his materials – essentially medieval narrative sources like chronicles – and also by the narrowness of his understanding of what constituted a crusade. He was uninterested in the extensive crusades against pagans and heretics in Europe, and his consequent focus on the struggle in the East with Islam had a distorting effect. Over the last thirty years or so, a generation of British scholars led by figures like Giles Constable,[2] and especially the British doyen of crusade studies, Jonathan Riley-Smith, has transformed perceptions of the nature of crusading. They turned their attention to hitherto unexploited sources, like the records of the military orders, and the charters regulating Crusaders' property, which contain rich material on the identity and motivations of the first Crusaders. They brought the anti-pagan and anti-heretical European crusades into the story alongside the better-known crusades to the Holy Land, and called into question some of the stereotypes of the Crusaders as uniformly brutal, uncivilized and basely motivated.

It had been commonly accepted that the explosion of crusading zeal reflected the urgent need for land and wealth of a rapidly expanding European population. Some historians argued that the first crusaders were often penniless younger sons, who saw in the crusade an opportunity to grab land and get rich quick. But the new crusade history showed how ill-founded this hypothesis was, by demonstrating the immense cost of going on crusade: even penniless younger sons needed the financial backing of their families, and this often involved enormous sacrifice and the mortgaging of lands to equip and sustain them. The study of crusade preaching and crusade charters revealed the depth and force of the religious roots of crusade, and the profound appeal of the crusade indulgence, forcing historians to take more seriously the religious motivations for crusade.[3]

These and many other insights have been embodied in dozens of scholarly monographs and papers, including both single-author and collaborative histories of the crusading movement as a whole. But none of these approached the scale of Runciman's three-volume classic, until the Oxford historian Christopher Tyerman offered a massive single-volume study of the Crusades as a whole. This is a welcome synthesis for the general reader of the newer understanding of crusade which, despite self-deprecating comparisons between his own 'clunking computer keyboard' and Runciman's pen, 'at once a rapier and a paintbrush', in scale at least does invite comparison with Runciman's masterpiece.[4] Much more separated the two works than fifty years of research. Runciman was the last of the great gentleman scholar-historians, and his writing stands in a tradition which goes back through Acton and Macaulay to Gibbon, though his cast of mind was worlds away from Gibbon's sneering genius. The sweep of his narrative, the humane liberalism of his judgments, and his sometimes romanticized admiration for Byzantine civilization, are all redolent of a more leisured world, before the professionalization – and narrowing – of historical writing.[5] Tyerman's sensibility is drier, more sardonic; his perceptions and instincts are those of a working historian trained in the less leisurely ways of the modern university. His narrative, only slightly less comprehensive than Runciman's, is decidedly more businesslike, and a good deal less colourful, though Tyerman can rise to the memorable phrase when required, and he never tries to excuse the inexcusable. So he characterizes the anti-Jewish pogroms that erupted in the wake of the preaching of the First Crusade in 1096 as a 'mixture of demotic religious propaganda and material greed' which 'combined to create an obscene cocktail of butchery and bigotry'. But by and large his appraisal of both villains and heroes is more cautious than Runciman's. The great Muslim leader Saladin is not for Tyerman Runciman's wise and humane aristocrat (an appraisal that had long roots in the Enlightenment historiography which lay behind the romanticized portrait of Saladin in Sir Walter Scott's *The Talisman*). Instead, the great Muslim leader is a shrewd politician whose generosity, like his occasional savagery, was carefully calculated. And again, where Runciman saw in the sack of Constantinople in 1204 by the armies of the Fourth Crusade an unsurpassed crime against humanity, Tyerman considered it, by the standards of the time, 'an atrocity, but ... not a war-crime'.[6]

The advances in crusade history since the publication of Runciman's book are nowhere more obvious than in understanding of the evolution of Christian notions of holy war. Tyerman is as well aware as Runciman of the inner contradictions in Christian theories of holy violence, but his careful exposition of the stages by which it evolved makes for less indignation and more understanding. Both Christianity and Islam have deployed ideas of holy war: in particular, their armed confrontation over possession of the holy city of Jerusalem has shaped the thinking of both religions about the legitimacy of violence in the service of religion. But Christianity had, and has, more difficulty than Islam in accommodating the notion of holy war. Struggle – jihad – is intrinsic to Islam, enjoined on all practising Muslims, and sometimes described as the sixth pillar of Islam. This jihad takes two forms: the greater jihad, the internal or spiritual struggle with self for greater purity, the meaning dominant for most Muslims for most of Muslim history, and the lesser jihad, the military struggle against infidels in the world outside Islam – the so-called 'House of War' – until the whole human race accepts Islam (which means obedience to

God). From the beginning, Islam was propagated and protected by conquest, though in practice the drive to universal conversion was treated as a communal rather than an individual obligation, and was tempered by pragmatic considerations and political realism.

Christian justification of holy violence was an altogether more roundabout and troubled affair. The pacifism of the Beatitudes could hardly be literally sustained once Christianity became the religion of the Roman Empire. War and violence might be inherently sinful, but if Christians were to be citizens, Christianity had to give some account of the right of a state to defend itself, or to resort to force in the interests of law and order. In the writings of Saint Augustine of Hippo at the turn of the fourth and fifth centuries, the basis for a Christian theory of just war emerged. War might be legitimate where the cause was just (as in self-defence against an aggressor), where it was declared by legitimate authority (for example, by the emperor), and where the intentions of those fighting it were good (and not a pretext for grudge or gain).

But just war was still not holy war: a Christian theory of holy war would only emerge as a result of the application of Old Testament and apocalyptic models of battle in God's cause to the circumstances of barbarian Europe. European society in the early Middle Ages was ruled not by kings but by a multitude of local warlords, and the rights and liberties of the Church, indeed at times its very survival, were extremely vulnerable in the face of external threats like pagan or Islamic attack, and internally to simple violent greed. In such a world, the armed warrior who fought to secure the safety of the Church or the conversion of the heathen might take on the attributes of the heroes of the Old Testament.

The supreme example was Charlemagne, anointed emperor by Pope Leo III as a protector of the Church in general and the papacy in particular, his sword henceforth the sword of God. In the centuries that followed, this concept would be developed, as successive popes, confronted to the north by militant paganism and to the south and east by the expansion of Islam, offered spiritual privileges remitting sin, penitential 'indulgences', to Christian warriors who died defending the Church against such enemies. By the eleventh century the papacy had become the spearhead of radical reform in the Church, now confronting not paganism but violent and rebellious secular rulers, greedy for the Church's wealth, compromising her spiritual integrity, resisting her increasingly assertive spiritual claims. These reforming popes saw holy war as a way of securing the safety and independence of the Church. Summoning warriors to the banner of Saint Peter, they offered in return the indulgences of which the pope was the unique source.

The attraction of these indulgences to Christian people derived directly from the paradoxical nature of what was being offered. For all its accommodation to the world, Christianity had never wholly shaken off the conviction that armed violence was intrinsically sinful: at best a regrettable necessity, at worst an absolute bar to salvation. Since all medieval magnates maintained their authority at least in part by force, all were spiritually compromised. The Church imposed draconian and prolonged penances for all forms of homicide, and as a result upper-class laymen were likely to be excluded from communion, and hence from heaven, by their very state of life. Laymen might undertake arduous penances, especially pilgrimages, to expiate their sins, but to be sure of salvation, it seemed they must lay down their arms, even, ideally, embrace monastic life. Engagement in a holy war, however, sanctified the very activity which had before been a barrier to heaven. Here, from the highest spiritual authority on earth, was a call not merely to guiltless but to *meritorious* violence.

In the year 1095, the Byzantine emperor appealed to the Pope for help against the Islamic forces which for twenty years had been advancing through Asia Minor, and which had now almost reached the Bosphorus. Pope Urban II was himself by birth a member of the aristocratic military classes, whose spiritual aspirations he now decided to focus around the powerful symbolic issue of the recovery of the burial place of Jesus from Muslim rule. A war against Muslim forces in the Holy Land could be seen as fulfilling one of the prime conditions of a just war, counting as self-defence, since it was aimed both at recovering what had once been Christian territory and at relieving the Byzantine regime, bulwark of Christianity in the East, now under mounting military threat. A holy war to recover the Holy Sepulchre in Jerusalem could also be seen as the supreme penance for those participating – arduous, dangerous, costly in every sense, the ultimate penitential pilgrimage.

The psalms, the staple of the Church's prayer, were filled with lamentations for the loss or oppression of Jerusalem, the city in which the drama of crucifixion and resurrection had been enacted. To eleventh-century Western pieties it seemed intolerable that the very stones sanctified by God's death and resurrection should be in the hands of unbelievers; and that feeling intensified when, earlier in that century, a renegade Shiite ruler of Palestine, the Fatimid Caliph Hakim, broke with established Islamic toleration of Christian pilgrimage and ordered the destruction of the Church of the Holy Sepulchre. For Pope Urban the liberation of Jerusalem from 'abominable slavery' was the test of the resolve of Western Christendom to the cause of Christ. Here was a cause which went to the nerve centre of contemporary religious sensibilities and anxieties, sanctified employment for the arms of Europe and, because of its papal endorsement, guaranteed a means of expiation for all sins. And in case these religious incentives failed to stir the consciences of Europe, Urban, ever a realist as well as a reforming visionary, added the promise of wealth and power: 'Rescue that land from a dreadful race, and rule over it yourselves.'[7]

The response to Urban II's proclamation of what came to be known as the First Crusade was staggering. His appeal was made in a year of prodigies. Spectacular meteor showers filled the heavens, and a bumper harvest suggested that God was miraculously providing supplies for the eastward march. Apocalyptic preaching by zealots like the diminutive evangelist from Picardy, Peter the Hermit, fuelled popular excitement, and all over Europe tens of thousands flocked to take the crusade vow, whose emblem was a cross of cloth stitched on the clothing at shoulder or breast. From every country in Europe wave upon wave of armed men, some highly trained and well organized, others a rabble of poverty-stricken enthusiasts, flooded toward Constantinople, the normal route to the Holy Land.

Their arrival alarmed the Byzantine authorities almost as much as the Muslim advance, for in appealing to the Pope they had envisaged help from a few bands of professional soldiers, not this invasion of half-savage Westerners, who appeared to their sophisticated Byzantine hosts as unappetizing as the busloads of tattooed, beer-fuelled and bellicose British soccer fans who travel to Europe nowadays during World Cup competitions.

Many of the Crusaders perished on the journey, many became disheartened and returned home, and those who made it to the Middle East were plunged into three years of famine, disease and bloody and unrelenting conflict whose savagery would become legendary – notoriously, Crusaders besieging Muslim strongholds catapulted the heads of executed prisoners over the walls to demoralize the defenders. The First Crusade culminated in a spectacular and apparently miraculous victory. After a desperate siege, Jerusalem fell to the combined Western armies on 15 July 1099. The bloody aftermath would leave a permanent stain of genocide on the reputation of crusading. The victors, elated by success and agog both for loot and for vengeance after three long years of desperate danger and hardship, swarmed into the city and butchered everyone they found. Most of the Jewish population were burned alive in their synagogues. Muslim prisoners were coerced into carrying mounds of the dead outside the walls for cremation, and were then slaughtered themselves; the gutters ran with blood, and unburied corpses were still putrefying in the streets five months later. Blood was the cement for the rickety and quarrelsome federation of Crusader states, known as 'Outremer', the land overseas, which now formed around the Holy Sepulchre, its precarious symbolic centre at Jerusalem presided over (eventually) by a king, and spiritually by the Latin patriarch.

Jerusalem was eventually recovered for Islam in 1187 by the resourceful, civilized and wily Sunni Muslim warlord Saladin (a Kurd born, by one of history's little ironies, in Saddam Hussein's home town of Tikrit), for whose valour and magnanimity even contemporary Christian chroniclers admitted grudging admiration. But the dream of a Christian Holy Land would remain potent for the rest of the Middle Ages. Fresh crusades were launched in the 1140s, in 1188, in 1201, in 1217, and on into the thirteenth and fourteenth centuries. And the concept of the crusade itself was broadened – successive popes extended the crusade indulgences to warriors engaged in religiously inspired struggles against Islam in the Spanish peninsula, Tunisia, the Balkans, Eastern Europe, against northern pagans in the Baltic, and against heretics within Christendom itself, most notoriously the Cathars in southern France. Popes established a special crusade tax on Church property, and the movement generated its own new institutions, most famously the hospitaller and military orders, warriors who vowed to serve the Church whether in battle or by caring for and protecting pilgrims – the Knights of Saint John, the Teutonic Knights and, best known of all, the Templars, who have attained in modern times a posthumous fame through dubious pulp-press and cinema fantasy.

The savagery of the First Crusade would remain a recurrent feature of crusading, not merely in the confrontation with Islam (in which both sides perpetrated atrocities), but in the targeting of other victims. In the wake of Peter the Hermit's preaching in 1095 and 1096, a wave of anti-Semitism swept through Rhineland Germany, and beyond. If battle was declared on the remote Muslim enemies of Christ, what of those other age-old enemies within the gate, the Jewish communities scattered through Europe, whom preachers now declared guilty of Christ's blood? Why travel to the East to confront Islam, demanded the Crusaders at Rouen, when 'in front of our eyes are the Jews, of all races the most hostile to God'?[8] Mobs en route to the Holy Land paused to lynch Jews, desecrate cemeteries and burn synagogues in the cities through which they passed. Nothing in official Christian doctrine offered a justification for killing Jews. But in the new mood of vengeful zealotry, doctrinal niceties carried no weight. The pogroms were denounced by local bishops, and the Jews of Mainz were given refuge in the archbishop's palace. But such help was often half-hearted, and almost always ineffective. Confronted with the inflamed and murderous mob, the archbishop of Mainz fled, leaving the Jews to their fate: his palace was stormed and the entire Jewish community slaughtered. Official Church teaching might differentiate sharply between Muslim and Jew; but a new level of Christian animus toward the Jews had been established. Every successive wave of crusade enthusiasm would set off further pogroms.

This virulent anti-Semitism was not the only 'collateral damage' from crusading enthusiasm. Notoriously, the Fourth Crusade, launched by Pope Innocent III in 1201 to recover Jerusalem, never got there. Sucked into Byzantine dynastic politics, the Western armies converged on Constantinople, ostensibly to back a *coup d'état* to support Alexius Angelus as Emperor Alexius IV, in return for a guarantee of financial backing for the crusade. When Alexius was deposed in favour of an anti-Western rival, the Crusaders invaded and sacked the city, the richest and most civilized centre of Christianity on earth, and the capital of the empire which the Crusades had been called into existence to protect. For three days Westerners rampaged through the city, looting and destroying. Within weeks, a Latin emperor and a Latin patriarch had been installed, and the annexation of the Byzantine Empire had begun. Pope Innocent denounced the sack as a religious calamity – 'How is the Greek Church, so afflicted and persecuted, to return to ecclesiastical union and a devotion to the Apostolic See when she sees in the Latins only an example of perdition and the works of darkness?'[9] Nevertheless, he eventually confirmed the Latin ecclesiastical takeover, thereby cementing into place an undying Greek hatred of the treacherous imperialism of the Latin Church.

The sack of Constantinople in 1204 was one of the events that stirred Runciman's deepest sympathies as a historian. A devoted (if not practising) admirer of Byzantine Christianity, he saw the Eastern Church and empire as the principal victim of the Crusades. There was never, he declared, 'a greater crime against humanity than the Fourth Crusade', for the sack of Constantinople had given the death blow to the most civilized empire the world had ever known, and had thereby crippled Byzantium's ability to protect the beleaguered Christians of the Middle East.

By contrast, Tyerman dismisses Runciman's assessment of the disastrous consequences of the sack of Constantinople as 'clouded by a crude religious and cultural analysis'.[10] The Westerners, he points out, were drawn to Constantinople in part by the internal feuding of Byzantine factions. Byzantium, he believes, was already in decline long before 1204, and its inability to protect the Christians of the Middle East was one of the causes of the Crusades, not a consequence. And, more generally, he credits the Crusades with far more positive consequences, seeing them for example as helping to foster the inquisitive openness of Western Renaissance society toward the wider world, in marked contrast to the closed character of some other more sophisticated societies, such as medieval and early modern China.

Nevertheless, the events of 1204 were to resonate for generations in the remotest corners of Christendom. Mountains of jewels, precious metals and artworks looted from Constantinople in 1204, and the years of occupation which followed, travelled west, the best-known examples of which are the bronze horses of St Mark's in Venice, stolen from Constantinople's Hippodrome. But the greatest treasures of all were relics. Western Christianity was obsessed with relics and the sacred power they were believed to radiate – the instruments of Christ's passion, the bones of the saints. Two of the greatest trophies of the First Crusade were the Holy Lance of Antioch (believed to be the very one which pierced Christ's side on Calvary), and the Jerusalem relic of the true cross. These objects, 'discovered' during the 1090s, became the war banners and protection of the Crusaders, and the loss of the Jerusalem relic of the cross when Saladin retook the city sent shockwaves through Europe. Constantinople was the greatest repository of relics in the world, and after 1204 looted relics, some of them possibly even genuine, poured into Europe. So the Crusades became the conduit for a massive influx of sacred matter into Europe. Christ's crown of thorns, acquired by the Venetians in 1237, passed eventually to the French monarchy, and one of the most exquisite Gothic buildings of the Middle Ages, the Sainte-Chapelle in Paris, was created to house it. A jewelled relic of the true cross looted by a priest from the imperial palace in Constantinople in April 1204 found its way to England, where it revived and transformed the fortunes of the foundering Cluniac monastery of Bromholm in Norfolk, and became one of late medieval England's greatest pilgrim attractions. And on an even grander scale, Henry III's rebuilding of Westminster Abbey was to provide not merely a royal mausoleum, but a shrine for the relic of the Holy Blood of Christ presented by the Latin Patriarch of Jerusalem.[11]

As long as Islam posed any threat to Eastern Europe, crusade ideology did not entirely disappear from Western thinking. But long before its formal demise it had ceased to have any practical consequences, in a world which no longer accepted that the protection of the true faith was the principal responsibility of the secular state. For the historians of the Enlightenment, crusading was a prime example of the evils of bad religion, stirring men to atrocious acts: the figure of the Muslim Saladin, humane, wise, and above all tolerant, became a literary cudgel with which to belabour Christian fanaticism. In the Romantic era, historians, poets and novelists revived a sense of the glamour and nobility of crusade and, in the hands of conservative nationalists like the French writer J. F. Michaud, the Crusades themselves were interpreted as part of a struggle of civilizations, prefiguring the (benign) advance of the West in nineteenth-century colonialism. This anachronistic reading of the Crusades was seized and turned on its head in the late nineteenth century by Turkish leaders, as prefiguring contemporary Western aggression, though there had previously been no long-term Islamic tradition demonizing the Crusades in this way.

In the millennium year, and subsequently on a controversial visit to Greece, Pope John Paul II included the Crusades, and especially the Fourth Crusade, among the historic 'sins' perpetrated by members of the Catholic Church. Opinions will differ about the value of such apologies for the sins of the people of the past: more than one modern historian of the Crusades has viewed them as inappropriately anachronistic. In Tyerman's words, extracting 'the thread of the crusade from the weave of the Middle Ages' distorts both. That was then: this is now, and it is misleading to imagine that the Crusades, so deeply embedded in the thought-patterns and values of their own times, prefigure any sort of twenty-first-century sequence of events. But they deserve study nevertheless, because they represent an aspect of humanity at its most vivid and, at times, for all their savagery, at its most noble, 'an ideal that inspired sacrifice at times on an almost unimaginable scale and intensity'.[12]

9

The Cradle Will Rock: Histories of Childhood

I

Does childhood have a history? Are the experiences of children, and the relations between children and their elders, constants of human nature, universal through time and space, or are they social constructs, radically differing from culture to culture and from age to age? At the turn of the eighteenth and nineteenth centuries William Wordsworth wrote of childhood and youth as a uniquely privileged time of innocence and insight: 'Heaven lies about us in our infancy' – a paradisal state from which growing up was a progressive exile and disenchantment, as 'Shades of the prison-house begin to close/Upon the growing boy.' After Freud we cannot quite subscribe to so idealized an understanding of the dreaming innocence of youth. Nevertheless, the distinctiveness of childhood as a state utterly different from adulthood is deeply ingrained in our culture, and encoded in icons of childhood as different as Peter Pan and Huckleberry Finn.

In 1960 the French demographic historian Philippe Ariès published a remarkable book, *L'Enfant et la vie familiale sous l'Ancien Régime*, translated two years later as *Centuries of Childhood*,[1] in which he advanced a dramatic hypothesis. Childhood did indeed have a history, he argued, but it was a short and comparatively recent one, for the very concept of childhood was a product of modern thought. Before the seventeenth century, though children existed, childhood did not: a child was regarded as a small and inadequate adult, and the concept of the 'childish' as something distinct from adults was a creation of the modern world. Medieval children, Ariès claimed, lived in the margins of adult life, with little or no distinctive cultural identity of their own. Their clothes were miniaturized versions of adult wear, they had no special culture of play, no children's literature, there was no Wordsworthian idealization of the innocence or carelessness of childhood.

The reasons for this absence, he thought, were complex. Many children died young, and so the bonds of affection between parents and children were of necessity looser than those in the modern West, where most children can be relied on to survive into adulthood. The consequent culture of detachment manifested itself from the very beginning of infancy, for every woman who could afford it sent her infant children to wet nurses to be breast-fed, thereby depriving them, and herself, of one of the most intimate bonding experiences between mother and child. For most people the home was also the workplace, not the centre of the loving affective family, but a structure for toil, in which the immature adults we call children were part of the workforce. The children of the poor worked as soon as they were able to pick stones, glean corn, scare crows or drive a flock of geese; the children of artisans were apprenticed and went to live with their masters long before puberty; the children of the well-to-do were sent away to school, or to other households to be fostered. And because there was little or no privacy within the pre-modern house, relationships were more public and less intimate than we are accustomed to: a situation in which individuality and affection could scarcely flourish. So, Ariès argued, 'the movement of collective life carried along in a single torrent all ages and classes, leaving nobody any time for solitude and privacy. ... The family fulfilled a function; it ensured the transmission of life, property and names; but it did not penetrate very far into human sensibility.'

This changed decisively, Ariès believed, in the seventeenth century, with the arrival of a new and sentimentalized conception of family, in which the cultivation of the affections and the shaping of childish character now each had their privileged place. Alongside this went a new emphasis on education, and the multiplication of schools near the home so that children could be formed without separation: the age of the close-knit nuclear family had arrived. For this gain in privacy and affect, however, there was, he thought, a terrible price. The new emphasis on family and education recognized that the child was a distinctive being capable of formation, but the regimes devised to facilitate this all-important formation were oppressive in direct proportion to the importance newly invested in them. Family and school removed children from adult society, and dragooned them into conformity, even, in Ariès's extreme and memorable formulation, 'inflicted on [them] the birch, the prison cell – in a word, the punishments usually reserved for convicts'. The new quest for individuality, affection and privacy within the family broke up the ancient solidarities of rich and poor, heightened class barriers, and imprisoned children within suffocating family structures encircled by 'the wall of private life'. The emergence of the concepts of childhood, therefore, reduced rather than extended freedoms, and the concept of family, along with the concepts of class and race, 'appear as manifestations of the same intolerance towards variety, the same insistence on uniformity'.

On a visit to the Holy Land in January 1964, just two years after Ariès's book was translated into English, the then pope, Paul VI, celebrated in very different tones the 'austere and simple beauty', the 'sacred and inviolable character', of the paradigmatic nuclear family – Jesus, Mary and Joseph. In the Holy Family's hidden life in Nazareth the Pope saw the proof of and model for the 'irreplaceable' role of the family in the social order. Extracts from this speech were to become a permanent part of the worship of the Roman Catholic Church, being subsequently (and still) prescribed for reading in the liturgy of the Hours annually on the feast of the Holy Family (the Sunday after Christmas). But it was precisely this vision of the centrality of the affectionate nuclear family, a vision shared by most of the major religious traditions of the modern West, that Ariès's work challenged. Coming at the start of the Sixties, his bold characterization of the close-knit nuclear family not as the fundamental building block of society, but as a comparatively recently evolved structure of oppression, was eagerly taken up. In France Jean-Louis Flandrin's *Families in Former Times* (1976), in America Edward Shorter's *The Making of the Modern Family* (1975) and, for England, Lawrence Stone's *The Family, Sex and Marriage, 1500–1800* (1977), though critical of Ariès's theoretical framework, proposed variations on Ariès's theme of the evils of historic family structure, and its dramatic recent transformations.[2]

The historic family was oppressive, it de-eroticized children and women; it turned wives into baby machines, children into subordinated versions of their parents; it embodied and enforced patriarchy and hideously hurtful child-rearing practices (like swaddling). For Stone in particular, nevertheless, the story had after all a happy ending. As better nutrition, hygiene and medicine brought child mortality under control, parents could for the first time allow themselves to become truly attached to their young children; as Puritanism faded, the rigours of oppressive patriarchy softened, just as the looser and more affectionate ideas of the Enlightenment abolished swaddling, flogging and wet-nursing, and encouraged parental indulgence of children in place of coercion.

The sometimes adolescent excesses of the rebellion of the Sixties and Seventies against 'bourgeois' institutions like the family were to pass, but would give way to more radical and far-reaching concerns with the deconstruction of 'essentialist' views of human nature. In debates about the character and construction of social, gender and sexual identity, some scholarship suggested that even such apparently immemorial and fundamental human institutions and life stages as the family or childhood were in fact transient cultural artifacts, profoundly shaped – and transformed – by external factors. This could have far-reaching implications. If Ariès was right, then human nature itself was entirely in our own hands, a construct, not a given.

II

In different ways, more recent studies of the history of families and of childhood have challenged or eroded the central historical contentions of Ariès and his followers, emphasizing continuity within the institution of the family, in historical perceptions of childhood, and in the immemorial experience of being a child. These more nuanced perceptions were represented in the collection of scholarly essays edited by David Kertzer and Marzio Barbagli in 2001, *The History of the European Family: Family Life in Early Modern Times*, the first of a projected three-volume history exploring the evolution of the European family from 1500 to the present day.[3] Taking the French Revolution as their end-point, Kertzer and Barbagli's essayists explored the impact on family structure of material conditions (such as serfdom or proto-industrialization), of law and religion, of demographic forces such as fertility and mortality, in pre-Revolutionary Europe, as well as the history of family relations – parent–child relationships, marriage, widowhood, divorce, and ideas about kinship itself, in societies as different as Italy or Russia. While recognizing significant changes in family structure, such as the rise of patriarchy within the Reformation period, and its subsequent gradual decline, they were united in emphasizing the vast range and variety of the historic experience of the family in the past, a variety which militates against sweeping generalizations and dramatic monocausal historical 'turning points' and discontinuities of the kind discerned or alleged by Ariès and his school. There were huge social, regional, religious and temporal variations in such matters as the age of marriage for men and women, the location of their first domicile (in or out of one or other of the parental homes), and the numbers and frequency of childbirths. The early modern family was therefore, in a phrase of E. A. Wrigley's, a repertoire of adaptable systems rather than a single pattern.

At the same time, the essayists emphasized deep continuities within human experience, which Ariès had minimized or denied – the affection early modern parents held for their children, the recognition of the distinctiveness of children and childhood, the desire of parents to meet the special needs of their children rather than force them into adult experience. Many of the contributors explored the impact on the family of shifts in economic conditions, changes in law and legal thinking, and the revolutionary religious upheavals that divided Europe into Catholic and Protestant camps. While recognizing and charting the impact of such factors, however, they were also realistic about the limited penetration of such forces into the deep structures of family life. Though Protestants and Catholics displayed differing attitudes toward education, towards the social role and independence of women, towards divorce, and towards bastardy and illicit sexuality, their differences on such matters were in practice less striking, and less significant, for the social experience of those living under different regimes, than their fundamental similarities, which owed as much to social realism and human need as to ideology. The past was thus both more complicated and more recognizably humane than Ariès was prepared to allow. As Linda Pollock observed in her essay on 'Parent–Child Relations', we need now a more rounded view of child-rearing in the past, a past in which, as the recent historiography of childhood has argued, 'as far back as we can tell, most parents loved their children, grieved at their deaths, and conscientiously attended to the task of child-rearing.'[4]

In the same year, a much more assertive defence of the fundamental continuities of family life was represented by Steven Ozment's revealingly entitled *Ancestors: The Loving Family in Old Europe*.[5] This short survey was an unashamed polemic, robustly if not always persuasively defending the existence of the 'loving family in Old Europe', and asserting its fundamental continuity with modern family experience. Ozment was MacLean Professor of Ancient and Modern History at Harvard and a first-rate religious historian, most of whose career was devoted to various aspects of the Lutheran Reformation, not least its impact on marriage and the family. In *Ancestors*, Ozment contrasted the dogmatic simplicities of Ariès and his followers in the 1960s and 1970s with more recent and more nuanced historical work on the family, such as that represented by Kertzer and Barbagli's collection. He wanted to argue for deep continuities, from antiquity to the present, in the way the family has been written and thought about. His book was an argument for the acknowledgement of complexity and nuance in historical understanding of the family. He therefore revisited much of the evidence marshalled by Ariès, Stone and others for the absence of affection in the historic family, and explicitly challenged their claims.

Ozment's polemic was sometimes a little over-insistent. Swaddling, he argued, seems to us a cruel and unnatural restriction of the freedom of movement of children – but a swaddled infant was easier to carry, and so spent more time with its mother; swaddling made for security and calmness; even modern colicky babies benefit from light swaddling. Ozment was particularly sensitive to claims that Protestantism especially may have contributed to the harshness of early modern family life, by depressing or reducing the role and freedom of women, and by creating 'the prototype of the unconditionally patriarchal and authoritarian household'. On the contrary, he argued, with its new and positive assessment of human sexuality, Protestantism was the crucial element in facilitating the emergence of 'a new concept of marriage', and a new understanding of male–female partnership, which was embodied in Luther's own happy marriage and the extraordinary entrepreneurial career of his wife, a former nun, Katherina von Bora. Ozment's concerns about the effects of Protestantism, however, which sometimes had a whiff of special pleading about them, were subordinated to his overall argument, that the family, rather than being an oppressive modern construct, is 'the great survivor' of changing ages and cultures. Far from obstructing the modern family's future, he asserted, in a conclusion that seemed designed for the pulpit as much as the podium, 'The family of the past is an eternal spring from which present generations may draw their truest knowledge of self and the courage to soldier on.'[6]

These challenges to Ariès and his followers shared a common base in early modern evidence, and in Ozment's case the argument was clearly motivated by concern to defend a Judaeo-Christian understanding of family values. The richly illustrated *Medieval Children*, by Nicholas Orme, emeritus professor of history at Exeter University, published in 2003, mounted an even stronger critique based on much earlier sources.[7] Meticulously organized and lavishly illustrated, Orme's book presented a cascade of evidence about every aspect of childhood, drawn from an astonishing range of sources from the end of antiquity to the early sixteenth century. Orme's publishers had chosen the same detail from Brueghel's *Children's Games* for the dust jacket of his book as had been reproduced on the English edition of Ariès's *Centuries of Childhood*. But Orme, though much less overtly preachy, was as adamant as Ozment in rejecting Ariès's claims about the early modern 'invention' of childhood. There was, he insisted, 'nothing to be said for Ariès's view of childhood in the Middle Ages, nor indeed of a major shift in its history during the sixteenth and seventeenth centuries... The main difference, as one proceeds through the centuries, is the survival of evidence.'[8]

All of Ariès's central contentions about medieval children, Orme thought, were demonstrably false, from the alleged lack of affection between medieval parents and children to the absence of a distinctive culture of childhood, marked by special games, literature, clothing and toys. At one level the book was an almost overwhelming refutation of Ariès, demonstrating by the use of a very wide range of the surviving medieval material the deep continuities of the human experience of youth and growth. But, though he had a clear agenda, Orme was too good a research historian to allow that agenda to distort his deeper purpose, which was to tell us more or less everything that can be known about medieval childhood.

The abiding impression of his beautiful book was of the sheer exuberant abundance of the material, much of it visual, drawn from religious and secular paintings and manuscripts, funeral brasses, stained glass, block prints, clothing, toys, and even tableware. The surviving medieval visual material on childhood is astonishing, and demonstrates the extent to which 'childhood' was manifestly present and distinctive in medieval visual culture. So Orme's book was packed with images of medieval children being born, swaddled, fed, bathed, having their nappies changed, being baptized or confirmed, learning to walk, rocking a sibling's cradle, helping their mother in the kitchen, serving the celebrant at mass, playing hockey, riding hobbyhorses, leapfrogging, playing with pinwheels or bat and ball or hoop, watching puppet shows, whipping tops, walking on stilts, dancing and singing carols, and shooting arrows.

Orme devoted his first three chapters to a discussion of the stages of childhood, from birth (characteristically, he began with Christmas and the ubiquitous representations of and writing about the birth of Christ, moving then to explore the theme of birth more generally), through the main features of family life, to the special dangers of childhood, particularly vulnerability to disease and mortality. A series of themed chapters then explored the culture of children: words, rhymes and songs; play and games; children and the Church; learning to read; and (an especially ground-breaking section) what there was for children to read. In addition to instructive books on such matters as hunting and courtesy, there were, he wrote:

> Pure stories, divisible into *chansons de geste* like *Guy of Warwick* which centre on the deeds of knights, and romances such as Chaucer's *Troilus and Criseyde* which turn on love affairs between knights and ladies. There were also stories (often in a collected format) with a moral or message. Some of Chaucer's *Canterbury Tales* come into this category, and so does [John] Lydgate's most ambitious work, *The Falls of Princes*. One could add *The Book of the Knight of the Tower* which, though educational, makes its points through a series of tales.[9]

The book concluded with a long chapter, 'Growing Up', ranging over many topics, from work and leaving home to sexuality, betrothal and marriage, the end of childhood. The clarity, pace and economy of his treatment concealed an impressive depth of learning, and many of the individual thematic discussions were in fact ground-breaking forays into territory not adequately explored by anyone else. Orme's specialist field was the history of education, and he deployed medieval and Renaissance schoolbooks and student exercises tellingly to illuminate not only the content and character of medieval schooling, but the manner and matter of children's conversation, recreation and attitudes. He was especially good, and funny, about schoolboy scatology and sexual humour, one of his chief pieces of evidence for the fundamental continuities (no pun intended) in human experience.

Among other unexpected things here, Orme offered a fascinating account of the seven surviving medieval English nursery rhymes, and a highly original discussion of naming and godparentage, tracing the spread of Norman names among Anglo-Saxon families, as parents sought influential godparents to advance their children's careers. But almost every page contained a fascinating detail, from the keeping of birthdays to baleful grandmothers, from the administration of medicine to suckling babes by dosing the wet nurse, to the construction of sandcastles in the writings of Gerald of Wales.

Orme's book was vulnerable to the criticism that his thematic treatment, ranging over almost a thousand years of medieval history, eclipsed or obscured real historical change. Moreover, much of his material was drawn from the later Middle Ages, when the evidence becomes relatively abundant, and it might be argued that this too tended to obscure or compress longer-term evolutions. But it was part of his contention that continuity is a far more dominant feature of the surviving evidence than change. He did indeed acknowledge clear changes, for example in the Church's growing emphasis on the difference between adulthood and childhood in its sacramental theology and discipline, as it came to exclude infants and young children from reception of communion, attendance at confession, and the right to or need for extreme unction at the point of death. But this shift in ecclesiastical attitudes toward childhood, he noted, came in the twelfth and thirteenth centuries, and corresponded in its timing to none of the great watershed changes alleged by Ariès and others.

As a resolute empiricist, Orme remained suspicious of what he took to be one of Ariès's cardinal sins: sweeping conclusions drawn from slim evidence. If his book was less grandiose in its claims than those of Ariès and his followers, it was far more solidly grounded, and more benignly conceived. His book had its share of horrors, and he did not flinch, for example, from dealing with child abuse and child mortality. As he pointed out, more than a quarter of children born in Tudor England died in their first year. Characteristically, here as elsewhere he fleshed out bald statistics with vivid and unexpected detail. Orme is the historian of Exeter Cathedral, and he used the cathedral records to offer a fascinating glimpse of the landscape of death which the boys of the cathedral choir inhabited. (The churchyard in which their house stood also included a charnel house for the bones of the city's dead, while the choir provided music for the many burial and commemoration services held there.) But for all such occasional grotesqueries, the picture he offered was of a childhood in its essentials recognizably the same as our own, and the solid evidential grounding of his views carried conviction. Orme's unpretentious book offered, quite simply, the least theorized, most comprehensive, most informative and, by a long way, the most humane and enjoyable historical treatment of childhood in English.

Saints

10

Blood Libel: The Murder of William of Norwich

From the mid-twelfth century onwards, urban communities scattered across the continent of Europe persuaded themselves that each year about Easter-time the Jewish minorities living among them conspired in the systematic abduction and ritual slaughter of Christian children. That myth would be deployed to legitimate centuries of harassment, robbery and judicial murder of European Jews. Jews, it was claimed, believed that their ultimate return to the Holy Land depended on the spilling of innocent Christian blood. Alternatively, it was suggested, Jewish Passover rituals involved the baking and consumption of matzah bread which had been mixed with human blood. Jewish medicine and Jewish magical healing required the blood of children. And underpinning all other explanations was the long-standing accusation that the Jewish people collectively were guilty of deicide, God-murder, in bringing about the death of Christ, and now, maliciously and 'in contempt of the Passion', sought endlessly to renew that sin by inflicting the pains of crucifixion on the bodies of Christian children. More than a century after the Jews had been banished from medieval England, Geoffrey Chaucer would enshrine one such horrific story of Jewish murder in his Prioress's Tale, and would invoke another, the supposed killing in 1255 of 'yonge Hugh of Lincoln, slayn also/with cursed Jewes'.[1]

Nourished by a grotesque farrago of ignorance and misinformation about Jewish ritual practices, religious and racial prejudice and economic resentment, this charge of Jewish ritual murder, the so-called 'blood libel', persisted and ramified down the years.[2] An early-twentieth-century Jewish survey of historic allegations listed six cases for the twelfth century, fifteen for the thirteenth, ten for the fourteenth, sixteen for the fifteenth, thirteen for the sixteenth, and on into modern times, spread through England, France, Spain, Italy, Germany, Poland, Hungary and Russia, and increasing to almost forty cases for the nineteenth century.[3] Wherever the myth was credited, synagogues and Torah scrolls might be burned, Jews imprisoned, forcibly converted, exiled, driven to suicide, tortured or killed, and their property confiscated. Many accusations triggered horrifying mass reprisals, like the thirty-one Jewish men, women and children burned alive on the orders of Count Thibaut V of Blois in 1171, the eighteen Jews hanged in Lincoln in 1255, or the 128 Jews slaughtered by the military and by civilian mobs in Bucharest in April 1801.

The factual evidence for these blood libels was examined and exposed as worthless in the 1890s by a German Protestant Talmudic scholar, Hermann Strack, and no serious historian now credits them. But ancient animosities need no facts in order to thrive. Accusations of Jewish ritual murder are still made by ultra-nationalist and neo-fascist elements in Eastern Europe. In January 2005, 500 Russians, including twenty members of the Russian Duma, signed a petition calling for a ban on all Jewish organizations, on the grounds that Jews practised 'ceremonial murder'.[4] Similar accusations are a staple of propaganda by Hezbollah and other Islamist groups in the Middle East.

The first known example of the blood libel occurred in twelfth-century England, in the cathedral city of Norwich. The 200-strong Norwich Jewish community was one of the longest-established and wealthiest in the country, settled there for at least three generations. The city's wealthiest man was Jurnet the Jew, a moneylender with a national clientele and an international circle of associates. Wealth on this scale, generated from high-risk and high-interest moneylending, was a recurrent cause of hostility towards an already exotic-seeming minority. But the origins of the blood libel have often been discussed in more general and ahistorical terms, drawing on the disciplines of anthropology, folklore, psychology or the social sciences. It has been suggested that the charge of ritual murder was a remnant of ancient Roman attacks on Christian 'cannibalism' in the Eucharist, or arose from misunderstanding of Jewish customs such as circumcision, or kosher butchering, or Purim festivities, or even as an irrational projection of Christian self-doubt, as Christians sought to bolster their own faltering sense of religious security by demonizing the religious 'other' in the person of the Jews.

At the end of Holy Week 1144, the mutilated body of a twelve-year-old boy was discovered in Thorpe Wood, outside Norwich. England was then in the grip of bloody civil war, the so-called 'Anarchy' triggered by the struggle between two rival claimants to the English throne, the Empress Matilda (mother of Henry II, Thomas Becket's nemesis) and her cousin, Stephen of Blois. Famine and lawlessness were rife, and violent death common enough for this small corpse to seem at first unremarkable. Though noticed by a number of passers-by, the body remained exposed and unattended for several days, before being buried where it lay. William, the murdered boy, it emerged, was a local leather-worker's apprentice, identified eventually by a maternal uncle. He had been crudely gagged with a fuller's teasel, a spiked wooden tool used for carding wool, and stabbed many times: there were signs of what were later alleged to be wounds made by thorns in his shaven scalp, and holes in his hands, feet, and side, reminiscent of the marks of crucifixion, though these telling details may have been later elaborations.

William, whose services as a leather-worker had reputedly been much in demand among the Jewish community, would be presented by his biographer as a poor boy, but the skinners' trade to which he was apprenticed was a skilled one, and he was literate in Latin, and perhaps spoke Norman French, rare accomplishments for a plebeian Saxon boy. William came in fact from a respectable family whose fortunes were closely tied to the Church. His father's occupation is unknown, but his grandfather was 'Wlward [*sic*] the priest, a famous man in his time', and the uncle who identified his body, Godwin Sturt, was also a married priest, whose son Alexander was a deacon. Five years before William's murder the Second Lateran Council had declared the marriages of priests and deacons invalid, and forbidden the laity to attend services conducted by married clergy. The Norman rulers of twelfth-century England sought to enforce priestly celibacy, and promoted clergy who practised it. But in mid-twelfth-century Norwich this new discipline had made little headway. Apart from the monks who staffed the cathedral priory, almost all the clergy in William's story were married. And it was William's clericalized family who initiated the claim that he had been murdered by Jews.

Leviva, Godwin Sturt's wife and William's maternal aunt, claimed to have had a surreal dream the weekend before the murder, in which a crowd of Norwich Jews had surrounded her, broken one of her legs and carried it off, foreshadowing, as she later explained, 'that one of my friends [i.e. family] would be lost through the Jews'.[5] According to the family, William had been lured to a wealthy Jew's house by a treacherous gentile collaborator with a promise of employment: initially pampered, the boy had been seized, nailed to a door-post, tortured and bled to death, a process later alleged to have been glimpsed by a gentile maidservant, too terrified to report what she had seen. Godwin and Leviva's daughter, William's cousin, supplied a vital link in the chain of circumstantial evidence by claiming that she had followed William and seen him enter the house of a wealthy Norwich Jew from which he never emerged.

The formal charge of ritual murder against the Norwich Jews was made by Godwin Sturt himself at a diocesan synod convened by the Bishop of Norwich a few weeks after the boy's death. In his speech to the assembly Godwin appealed to apparently already current gentile prejudices about 'what by custom the Jews have been obliged to do on these days' (i.e. murder at Passover), to the suggestive nature of the wounds on the body, reminiscent of the Passion of Christ, and recounted his wife Leviva's dream. The bishop summoned the Norwich Jews before him to answer Godwin's charges, but was blocked by the intervention of the Sheriff of Norwich, John de Chesney. Jews in England came under the direct jurisdiction and protection of the Crown. Acting for the Crown and 'the king's Jews', the Sheriff rejected the bishop's right to try the case, and gave the Jewish community refuge in Norwich Castle till the furore stirred up by Godwin's accusations had subsided. The one concrete outcome of Godwin's speech was that the bishop ordered the exhumation of William's body from its grave in the woods, and had him reburied in the monastic cemetery.

But although William's family appear to have worked hard to promote their murdered boy as a saint and martyr to *odium fidei*, 'hatred of the faith', public interest soon evaporated. A few 'miracles' were reported at his tomb, like the rose that bloomed there in the depth of winter, but they failed to impress, and there was no stream of pilgrims. What changed all that, according to a recent study of the murder of William of Norwich, was another murder trial, this time before King Stephen in London, a trial in which a Jew was the victim, not the alleged perpetrator. Our information about this trial, and indeed about all the circumstances surrounding William's murder, comes from the 'Life and Passion' composed by Thomas of Monmouth, who joined the Norwich Cathedral monastery in 1150. Thomas' work is the first medieval text to spell out the charge of ritual murder against the Jews, and probably provided the matrix for all subsequent accusations.[6] And Thomas's account of the trial of Sir Simon de Novers for the murder of a wealthy Norwich Jew becomes the linchpin of Emily Rose's recent prize-winning analysis of the origin of the blood libel.[7]

Rose contends that the key to the revival of William's cult in 1150 was the failure of the Second Crusade, and the crisis of demoralization and debt which that failure created in Eastern England in 1149. The greatest magnate in the region, William de Warenne, cousin to the French King Louis VII, had 'taken the Cross' in France in 1146, and repeated the ceremony at Castle Acre priory in Norfolk the following year, immediately before setting off to crusade in the Holy Land. Rose speculates that Sir Simon de Novers, a minor East Anglian aristocrat fallen on hard times, might have been one of the men at arms who accompanied Warenne on crusade. Crusading was an expensive business, and many Crusaders borrowed heavily, from local monasteries or from gentile or Jewish moneylenders, to equip and fund their enterprise, hoping to recoup their outlay from the spoils of war. But the failure of the Crusade meant that there were no spoils, and Norwich Crusaders would have returned, Rose argues, embittered and indebted, to a region already suffering from the terrible consequences of civil war, disorder and famine. They might also have returned inflamed with anti-Jewish prejudices fomented by reactionary Crusade preachers like Radolphus the Cistercian, whose rabid sermons triggered a wave of pogroms in the Rhineland in 1146 and 1147.[8]

For Rose this was the key to the trial of Simon de Novers in 1150 before King Stephen, first in Norwich, then reconvened in London when 'the next council of clergy and barons was held'.[9] According to Thomas of Monmouth's narrative, Sir Simon was deep in debt to a wealthy Norwich moneylender, a Jew called Deus Adjuvet, usually taken as a Latinization of the Hebrew name Eleazer, but which Rose suggests was actually a version of the Norman French name 'Deulesalt'. This, Thomas claimed, was the Jew in whose house William had been murdered. Unable to repay his loans, Sir Simon arranged for the ambush and murder of Deulesalt, an event which Rose dates to 1149. The Norwich Jews appealed to the King against the assassins, and Sir Simon was defended before the king in 1150 by his feudal overlord, the new bishop of Norwich, William Turbe. Thomas admits he was not present at the trial, but offers an 'imagined' (Latin *coniecturalis*) account of Turbe's defence speech. In it, Turbe denied Sir Simon's complicity in the murder, but went on to insist that in any case, no Christian should have to defend himself for the death of the ringleader of the Norwich Jews in the murder of an innocent Christian boy (William), claiming they had only escaped punishment because of obstruction by a corrupt sheriff, John de Chesney. King Stephen deferred judgement in the case (according to Thomas because the king himself had been bribed), but for Rose the trial, which precipitated the otherwise retiring Bishop Turbe into national prominence, was the event which gave currency to the claim that Jews had murdered little William, and led the bishop and the Norwich monks to revive and promote his cult.

Unfortunately, there is not a shred of evidence that Sir Simon de Novers was ever a Crusader, and there is reason to date the murder of Deulesalt, and the subsequent murder trial, to 1147, not to 1150, and therefore two years before any East Anglian Crusaders could have returned from the Holy Land. Thomas of Monmouth gives no dates for Deulesalt's murder or Simon de Novers's trial, and the leading historian of twelfth-century Norwich, Professor Christopher Harper-Bill, dates that trial to 1147. Harper-Bill suggested that Bishop Turbe's eloquent defence of Sir Simon brought this inexperienced and hitherto obscure monk-bishop to the King's attention, and accounts for his prestigious appointment as one of the three representatives of the English episcopate at the Papal Council of Rheims in 1148.[10]

If Harper-Bill's chronology is correct, then any linkage of the revival and spread of William's cult to the financial fallout from the Second Crusade, and the transmission of the Rhineland anti-Semitism that accompanied it, looks very unlikely. Bishop Turbe certainly embraced the murdered boy's sanctity, and from 1150 undoubtedly threw his weight behind the hitherto faltering cultus. In 1150 William's body was moved from the monastic graveyard to a place of honour in the Cathedral chapter house, in 1151 it was translated to a still more public shrine near the High Altar of the cathedral, and in 1154 it was enshrined in a separate 'chapel of the martyrs' to make lay access to the tomb easier. Such 'translations' of a body were the early medieval equivalent of canonization, and would have been impossible without the bishop's support. Pilgrims began to come to William's tomb for healing and help, and 'miracles' accumulated, though the cult was never truly popular. But the key factor in this deliberate promotion of William's cultus appears to have been not the trial of Simon de Novers, but the arrival in Norwich of William's biographer, Thomas of Monmouth.

Thomas of Monmouth places the account of the trial of Sir Simon at the end of book two of his life of William. His account of the body's translation to the chapter-house and the start of popular devotion opens book three, and the break between the two books suggests that Thomas saw the revival as springing from the 'venerable and wondrous revelation' in the form of three visions granted to Thomas himself, soon after his arrival in the priory in 1150. These visions take up the opening chapter of book three: in them, the deceased founding bishop of Norwich, Herbert Losinga, appears to Thomas, emphasizing the precious treasure the monks possessed in William's body, and insistently warning that the relic would be taken away from them if not translated into the chapterhouse. Thomas duly reported these visions to the head of the monastery, Prior Elias, and claimed that Elias was 'overjoyed', because he 'saw honour of great worth coming to the church of Norwich' from the recognition of William's sanctity. The translation was decided upon, and Rose insists on the total commitment of Elias and the whole monastic community to the subsequent promotion of William's cult. Brother Thomas, she claimed, 'did not initiate the cult on his own ... there is no evidence that anyone within the cloister disavowed [his] claims ... what criticism there was came from outside'.[11]

This, unfortunately, is simply not so. Thomas consistently portrays Elias as unenthusiastic about and even opposed to the cult of the boy saint. The Prior probably was persuaded that the reburial of William's body in the chapter house was a prudent precaution against pious theft. But he appears in Thomas's narrative as a vehement opponent of any further advance of the cult of the new 'saint'. According to Thomas, Elias was 'indignant' when the slab covering William's new grave was raised above the rest of the chapter-house pavement. When Thomas took it upon himself to place a candle at the head of the grave, and covered the stone itself with an embroidered carpet, Elias 'took grave offence' and 'contemptuously' confiscated both the candle and the carpet. Subsequent 'visions' warning Elias to replace the carpet were ignored, and Thomas devoted a chapter to 'the hardening of the heart of Prior Elias', and suggested that Elias's untimely death in October 1150 was 'Saint' William's revenge for 'the injury done to him by the hard hearted prior'.[12]

Elias was not alone in his resistance to William's cult. Thomas's long and defensive 'answers to those who disparage [William's] sanctity' and warnings against those who 'disparage the miracles' or 'doubt that he was killed by the Jews' strongly suggest that he had many to persuade, both inside and beyond the monastery.[13] Certainly he himself had a decidedly proprietorial attitude to Saint William, extending beyond his official position as 'sacrist' or custodian of the shrine. He secretly removed and concealed two of the boy's teeth during the first translation of the body, and also kept 'unknown to all others' a secondary relic, a shoe, in his own cell.[14] Commissioned to chronicle the miracles, Thomas dedicated a lifetime to promoting William's cult. After the first two books outlining the 'martyrdom', Thomas appears to lose interest in the Jews. The last five books of his seven-book life of William make no mention of them; there are none of the miraculous 'conversions' of Jews common in later versions of the blood libel. Thomas seems concerned only to assert William's claims to sanctity against all rivals, including, after 1171, the newly martyred Thomas Becket. Thomas's arrival in Norwich and his alleged visions of 1150 were the true trigger for the cult's expansion: his completion twenty years later of his official account of William's life, death and miracles, with its two opening books on Jewish guilt, provided a template replicated or echoed in subsequent repetitions of the blood libel.

Exactly how, and how far, that libel was transmitted in the century or so immediately following William's murder remains unclear, and not all scholars agree that Thomas's narrative was the key source. John McCulloh has argued that Thomas's narrative remained unknown outside Norwich, and so can have played no part in the spread of the blood libel.[15] Emily Rose, by contrast, suggested four twelfth-century cases which William's story might have influenced: the recovery of a boy's body from the Severn at Gloucester in 1168, the alleged dumping of a murdered child in the Loire at Blois in 1171: the alleged crucifixion of Robert, a baby boy, at Bury St Edmunds in 1181: and the slitting of the throat of an adolescent boy, Richard of Pontoise, in Paris on Maundy Thursday 1179. Apart from the general charge that Jews ritually murdered children, however, the parallels with Norwich in none of these cases are particularly close. Most are in any case known only from fragmentary twelfth-century references lacking detail, or from late-medieval elaborations which probably drew retrospectively on Thomas's book or its derivatives. At Blois, the allegation of Jewish ritual murder originated when a Jew accidentally dropped a rolled rawhide into the water while fording the river, and a hostile observer chose to believe the object dropped was the body of a child. But no body was ever found, no one was reported missing and, unlike Norwich, the incident happened in May, long after both Passover and Holy Week. The alleged link to ritual murder by Jews at Blois was suggested by an anonymous cleric, and Rose argues that the allegation took imaginative hold mainly because the local prince, Thibaut V, was looking for an excuse to mulct local Jewish financiers, and to establish his credentials as a devout Catholic ruler by attacking an unpopular minority. She suggests nevertheless that William's story did directly influence the Blois pogrom, arguing at some length that Bishop Turbe, whose cathedral had just burned down, conducted a fund-raising tour of the Loire region in 1170, taking William's relics with him, and thus transmitted the idea of Jewish ritual murder into France.

Once again, however, evidence for this suggestion is lacking: Harper-Bill and other historians date the Norwich Cathedral fire to 1171, not 1170, and there is no evidence whatever that any such relic tour ever took place. In 1170 Bishop Turbe was in any case out of royal favour for his support of Archbishop Thomas Becket, and in all probability he was keeping his head down in Norwich. The only contemporary reference we have to his fund-raising activities after the fire militate against the notion of a French fund-raising tour, since it pictures him seated outside the cathedral begging for contributions, while the priory register records that he had vowed 'that he would not betake himself more than twelve [leagues] from his church unless driven by necessity ... [till] his church was rebuilt'.[16]

When all is said and done, if Thomas of Monmouth and his book remain the likeliest agents in the creation and propagation of William's legend, the channels by which that legend entered the imaginative mainstream of Christian Europe remain obscure. 'The Life and Passion of William of Norwich' never circulated in large numbers, and was forgotten for centuries. But too many details from it – the peeping maid, the gentile collaborator, the crucifixion wounds – surface again and again in later examples of the blood libel for the links to be merely coincidental. By whatever means, the story it told passed like a poison into the bloodstream of Christendom. Few books of piety can have unleashed so much horror.

11

Sacred Bones and Blood

Christianity is a material religion. Its central tenet is that in the man Jesus the eternal God united himself to human nature and human flesh, and thereby opened both humanity and matter itself to the possibility of divinization. So Christians place their eschatological hope not in the survival of a disembodied soul, but in the resurrection of the body, the transformation into another order of being of the whole person, flesh and spirit. In heaven Christ himself retains his body, glorified and transcendent, but bearing still the physical traces of his human suffering. 'With what rapture', says Charles Wesley's great Advent hymn, 'gaze we on those glorious scars'.

Perhaps the most unabashedly materialist form of Christianity is Catholicism, centred on the sacraments, and making material things – bread, wine, water, olive oil, the touch of human hands – vehicles of divine power. In the Mass, Catholics believe, Christ himself is made present in the elements of bread and wine, to nourish and transform those who eat and drink them. Catholics venerate the relics of the holy dead, they bless material *stuff* – water, salt, oil, wax, medals, holy pictures, palm branches – and the formulas traditionally used in such blessings more often than not implied that those objects, called sacramentals, thereby became *objectively* holy, changed in themselves, and capable of effecting change at the material as well as the spiritual level. So every year on Palm Sunday Catholics commemorate Christ's triumphant entry into Jerusalem by carrying olive, willow or palm branches that have been blessed.

Until the 1960s, the prayers used insisted on the material as well as the symbolic agency of those blessed branches. 'Bless and sanctify this creature,' ran the words, ' ... that whoever receives it may find protection of soul and body: and may it become, Lord, both a remedy for our well-being, and a sign of your grace.'

But times have changed, clerical nerve has failed, and modern Catholicism appears to be in two minds about the spiritual potency of even sanctified matter. Palms are still blessed and carried each year, but the formula currently approved avoids any suggestion that blessing the branches has any objective effect on them, or on their bearers. So now the celebrant prays, 'Lord, sanctify these branches with your blessing, so that we who rejoice to follow Jesus as our King may attain through him to the heavenly Jerusalem.' In this account of what is going on, the palm branches are little more than a pious prop in a ceremony that is simply a metaphor for following Jesus, the blessing of the branches a ritual gesture that is assigned no instrumental value at all.

It is tempting to see the influence of the Protestant reformers in this novel Catholic coyness about the objective power of sanctified matter, for sixteenth-century Protestant leaders like Huldrych Zwingli and John Calvin rejected or minimized the spiritual value of material objects. But Caroline Walker Bynum has suggested that ambivalence about the notion of sanctified matter has much deeper roots: the issues highlighted by these changes in modern Catholic worship troubled also the Christianity of the Middle Ages.

Caroline Bynum is America's foremost scholar of medieval religion. In a stream of books characterized equally by eloquence and deep learning, she explored one aspect or another of the history of the human body and its religious significance in medieval Europe. This field has long been a happy hunting ground for those approaching the study of medieval history with a range of modern agendas, from militant feminism to economic or materialist readings of the past. So the writings or biographies of medieval nuns and female saints and mystics have been ransacked by historians for the evidence they yield of the oppression of women and the structural misogyny of medieval society, or for proof of Christianity's fundamental pessimism about the human condition, or its dualistic inability to come to terms with human and especially female sexuality. Bynum's work, by contrast, has been characterized by its consistent refusal of glibly anachronistic or reductivist readings, and by its determination to explain medieval people in their own terms, however strange or alien those terms may seem to modern sensibilities.

The title essay of the book that established Bynum as a major voice in medieval studies, *Jesus as Mother* (1982),[1] drew attention to the use of feminine and maternal imagery by medieval monks and clergy when addressing or talking about Christ and the divine, and challenged the widespread assumption that the use of such feminized language was a special characteristic of female piety. In *Holy Feast and Holy Fast* (1987),[2] she moved naturally on from such metaphors of mothering to consider the special significance for medieval women of food, nourishment and nurture, especially in relation to the Eucharist. *Holy Feast* included a characteristically sophisticated exploration of a well-known feature of the period, the abstinence by Saint Catherine of Siena and many other holy women from ordinary food, and their reliance for survival instead on the regular reception of holy communion.

Other historians had interpreted this bizarre and radical asceticism through modern medical categories, seeing in it a form of 'holy anorexia', evidence of a morbid and dysfunctional sensibility, driven by an internalized misogyny and self-loathing determination to punish the body and eliminate female sexual characteristics.[3] Bynum, while not altogether discounting such explanations, argued against the anachronistic reductionism of modern medical or psychoanalytical readings of complex medieval behaviours and beliefs. She emphasized the special links between these women and the Eucharist, and pointed to the many ways in which the manipulation of food in sacred settings gave them control and direction over their own lives and environments, and established a privileged space for them in an institution otherwise dominated by male concerns and male authority. She thereby restored agency and opportunism to women seen by other historians as passive victims of an oppressive patriarchal system.

This was much-admired but also controversial work: the suggestion that these holy women should be seen not as victims but as resourceful people in control of their own destinies outraged some readers, and Bynum was accused by less sophisticated feminists of displaying more respect for medieval than for modern women. Perhaps understandably, she has not confined herself to the history of femininity, sex and gender. She has cast her net widely, and drawn her subject matter from abstruse theological debates, manuals of devotion, alchemical treatises, even werewolf legends.

But all her writing has remained resolutely focused on aspects of the body and the meaning of corporeality for medieval society. Her study *The Resurrection of the Body in Western Christianity, 200–1336*[4] explored medieval thinking about the nature of death and resurrection, of the connections between the living and the dead body, and hence of self, identity and permanence. In 2007 a new book, *Wonderful Blood*, analysed theological reactions to a burgeoning fifteenth-century German phenomenon: pilgrimage to the shrines of miraculously bleeding Eucharistic wafers.[5] Bynum used this as the starting point for a wide-ranging exploration of the meaning of the macabre but ubiquitous 'blood piety' that loomed large in Western Christianity in the later Middle Ages.

Christian Materiality, the expanded text of three lectures given at the Hebrew University in Jerusalem in 2007, represented a distillation of the work Bynum had been pursuing over the previous fifteen years or so.[6] Anyone familiar with her writings could recognize the themes, the authors and the works discussed, and even many of the pictures used as illustrations, remaining firmly in the territory covered in *The Resurrection of the Body* and *Wonderful Blood*. The book's value, therefore, was as a synthesis of a great scholar's thinking about late medieval religion, and about medieval attitudes toward corporeality and the material world.

That subject matter was daunting, even gross: the medieval fascination with the remains – or relics – of the fragmented bodies of the saints, and the display of such relics from 1200 onward in reliquaries shaped like body parts; statues and paintings that move, weep, bleed, speak; congealed blood that liquefies on significant dates; communion wafers that spurt blood when broken or pierced, often, in late medieval anti-Semitic legend, as a result of attacks by Jews; pictures and crucifixes that imprint themselves on living bodies: visions in which the Eucharist is transformed into live babies on the altar, or gaping wounds, or bleeding hunks of flesh. All this is likely to strike modern secular readers as bizarre, and even repellent. A moment's reflection, however, on the popularity of the novels of Patricia Cornwell, of the Hannibal Lecter films, and of TV detective series like *Bones* and *Waking the Dead*, which exploit the more gruesome aspects of forensic science, might suggest that these medieval fascinations are not quite so remote from our own as might at first appear.

Bynum was concerned to rescue this material and the piety that surrounded it from modern 'incomprehension and condescension'. She mobilized the *disjecta membra* of her grisly materials in support of a broad and bold thesis that the period from about 1100 until about 1550 was the great age of 'Christian materiality'. Other historians had seen the early Middle Ages as the era of credulous, mechanistic and materialistic piety, and presented the later Middle Ages, by contrast, as reacting against all that, 'a turn to interiority on the part of spiritual writers and reform-minded church leaders'.[7]

The fourteenth and fifteenth centuries, Bynum agreed, were indeed the age of mystics and of writers like Thomas à Kempis or Nicholas of Cusa, who downplayed exterior piety and pilgrimage and called for a Christ-centred journey within. But she insisted on a paradox: that alongside this turn to interiority, there was a great burgeoning of fascination with the material, so that the piety of the four centuries before the Reformation might be characterized as a turn towards rather than away from the object.

Relics and other sacred objects had long held a place of importance in Christianity, but the period after 1100 was the age of 'living holy matter',[8] when sacred objects took on a new kind of animated vitality. These were the centuries in which miraculous 'hosts' (the Eucharistic wafer) began to bleed, in which saints first began to find the wounds of Jesus printed on their living flesh, when relics animated themselves and the blood of saints like the Neapolitan Saint Januarius first began to liquefy, and when wooden or stone images of Christ and the saints began to weep, bleed, or gaze with living eyes on the faithful.

Bynum related this new interest in the power of living and moving relics and images to parallel developments in the liturgy, like the life-sized statues of Christ on a donkey dragged through the streets on Palm Sunday in France and Germany, or the jointed wooden figures of the dead Christ buried and resurrected in ritual tombs during Holy Week, or raised into the roof of great churches on Ascension Day. But she saw the phenomenon as going far beyond liturgical mimesis, rooted rather in a new sense of the vitality and potential of brute matter, a vitality that made it both fascinating and dangerous. Theologians and reformers might warn against treating dead matter as if it were alive, or attempting to pin God down in the material, but late medieval Christian instinct eagerly embraced the paradox of dead matter that came alive. In a culture much possessed by transience and decay, 'miraculous matter' – bleeding wafers or moving statues or liquefying blood – fascinated and reassured, because these things 'manifested enduring life (continuity, existence) in death (discontinuity, rupture, change)'. They were simultaneously what the theologians said they were, 'the changeable stuff of not-God', but also, and paradoxically, 'the locus of a God revealed'.[9]

The late Bob Scribner characterized the late Middle Ages as a period in which the 'sacred gaze' became central to Christian practice.[10] There was a huge increase in imagery of all kinds in churches and in manuscript and printed devotional literature, and at many shrines images rather than relics became the focus of devotion. Even more significantly, from the twelfth century onwards, the elevation of the Host in the Mass – the raising of the communion wafer above the priest's head – became increasingly the centre of the celebration. At a time when most people received communion only once a year, gazing at the Host at the elevation replaced its consumption as the main form of lay communion. These moves, from relic to image, and from communion to disembodied gazing in the Mass, might both seem to tell against Bynum's theory of an increasingly insistent materiality, so she devoted a chapter to exploring the place of the visual in late medieval Christianity.

Here her central insistence was that medieval images were more like physical relics than modern portraits: 'a medieval image is an object in a way that a Renaissance or modern painting is not'.[11] Bynum emphasized the plasticity of medieval images, their three-dimensionality, their use as containers for relics or the Blessed Sacrament, their decking with real cloth or real gold and jewels, all of which material 'self-referentiality' drew attention to their corporeality. What was involved here was not realism or mimesis, she insisted, but 'disclosures of the sacred through material substance'. There were echoes here of the sharp distinction made by the art historian Hans Belting between the cult image and the work of art,[12] and Bynum insisted that while images do increasingly replace relics as the focus of veneration in late medieval piety, in the process those images often came to be treated as if they were themselves relics.

But at times Bynum's argument, like Belting's, seemed to be pushed too far. Her insistence on the plasticity and physicality of late medieval carved winged altarpieces, for example, obscured the fact that most such altarpieces were in fact painted two-dimensional objects, which were certainly not intended to be touched. Her discussion of late medieval depictions of the legendary Eucharistic miracle of the Mass of Pope Gregory – when the wounded Christ appeared before the congregation after the Pope had prayed for a sign to convince a non-believer of the presence of Christ in the Eucharist – emphasized its physicality, but ignored the fact that many depictions of the Gregory Mass include a portrait of the donor precisely as *spectator*, suggesting that the notion of vision had more importance than plasticity or touch for those who commissioned or created such images.[13] She was on stronger ground in her exploration of the paper and parchment images of the wounds of Christ that became so important in late medieval piety, for such depictions were often explicitly intended to be touched, kissed and carried around as a protective talisman, functioning as a powerful contact relic of Christ, rather than a mere pictorial reminder of his passion.

From images Bynum turned to other kinds of holy matter – relics, sacramentals (blessed objects) and the Eucharistic bread, both ordinary and miraculously bleeding. These sacred objects had all been important in early medieval Christianity, but after 1100, Bynum argued, take on a new vitality and fascination. Her discussion of the changing form of reliquaries was particularly interesting. In the early and high Middle Ages, relics were normally kept for veneration in closed containers – purses, caskets, coffins or ornate boxes, the latter often gabled to resemble a church. Such reliquaries both concealed the relic itself and stressed 'the collection or gathering together of their contents'. These increasingly gave way to crystal monstrances, designed to expose the relic to view, and to 'speaking reliquaries', containers often grotesquely fashioned in the shape of a body part – head, foot or arm – and often with a crystal window, designed to 'flaunt the fragments of bone' that they contained.[14] As the possession of relics became more important to churches and wealthy lay devotees, reliquaries displaying ranked rows of bone and other body fragments became increasingly common, their multiple open chambers similarly drawing attention to the fact of the dismemberment of the holy bodies from which the relics were derived, and thereby flaunting their materiality.

Bone fragments were relatively permanent, and were given even greater symbolic permanence by their being enshrined in gold and precious stones. But the period also saw attempts to give material permanence to visions and miraculous apparitions. Many medieval visionaries (often women) experienced visions of Christ in the Eucharist. The spread after 1200 of belief in miraculous bleeding hosts, whether preserved themselves, as at the German shrine of Wilsnack, or in the form of the bloodstains on the altar linen, as in the holy 'corporal', or altar cloth, of Bolsena in Orvieto Cathedral, offered a way of making such ephemeral and private experiences permanent and public.

This form of Christian materiality posed difficult questions, for Christ was risen, and for medieval theologians that meant that every fragment of his body – blood, fingernails, hair – was risen also and reunited with his glorified body in heaven. There could be no body relics of Christ. How then could his blood (or his foreskin, of which there was more than one alleged relic!) remain to be venerated on earth? Moreover, the doctrine of transubstantiation insisted on the intrinsic invisibility of Christ's presence in the Eucharist. The substance of bread and wine, their inner reality, was replaced by Christ's substance. But their accidental qualities – colour, weight, texture, taste, smell, nutritive value – remained. Hence, if you could *see* it, by definition, it wasn't Christ. Theologians and preachers from Saint Thomas Aquinas to Nicholas of Cusa laboured to preserve the theological niceties while leaving room for well-intentioned popular pieties, which they themselves sometimes shared; in the process, they could seem to be attempting to square the circle.

There were similar intellectual agonies over sacramentals. Did blessed objects possess intrinsic power, or were they merely eloquent pointers to spiritual realities? Theologians dithered, and their conclusions could seem arbitrary or *parti pris*. Dominican theologians howled down the use by the Franciscan revivalist preacher Saint Bernardino of painted and gilded wooden tablets bearing the Holy Name of Jesus. When Bernardino held up such verbal icons, crowds knelt in adoration. Was this the idolatrous worship of a material object or the legitimate veneration of the Name, at which Saint Paul said every knee should bow? Bynum argues that these tensions were not and could not be resolved, and that late medieval Christianity, both mainstream and deviant, was therefore caught in a radical ambivalence, living rather than resolving the paradoxes of materiality, simultaneously embracing and rejecting material religiosity.

This insistence on paradox is a characteristic of Bynum's work and of her rhetorical strategy as a historian, often both refreshing and illuminating. Not for her tidy simplicities that bulldoze flat the intractable strangeness of the past. But her insistence on unresolvable ambivalences can be vexing too, by appearing to refuse necessary distinctions. Bynum wanted to insist, for example, that all medieval Christians shared, whether they acknowledged it or not, a conception of matter as fluid, vital, animated. So even the heretical opponents of holy matter, on her account, demonstrate their immersion in these paradoxes by the very vehemence of their opposition. English Lollards, cooking their cabbage over a fire made out of a desecrated saint's statue, were triumphantly demonstrating that the torched fragments were incapable of tears or protest. But, says Bynum, they simultaneously indicated the opposite, for they did so with 'what feels to a modern reader like genuine surprise'.[15]

Here, alas, Bynum parted company with the evidence. It is true that at least one Lollard claimed that the statues in the churches were infested with fallen angels, and so had an evil life within them. But the specific Lollard iconoclasm she alluded to is known to us only through the not very circumstantial testimony of hostile orthodox opponents. The accounts contain not the slightest indication that the heretical cabbage-cookers were *surprised* that the burned statue remained stubbornly inert. Quite the contrary: they burned it to show that they knew it was just a piece of dead matter, and therefore unspiritual. Bynum read the conflicted sensibility, and tacit Lollard acquiescence in a vitalist understanding of materiality, *into* rather than out of the contemporary account. The rhetoric of paradox has here carried her into pure speculation.

And rhetoric could colour her arguments elsewhere. In her fascinating discussion of reliquaries, Bynum reflected on the meaning of body-part reliquaries in relation to medieval horror at decay and putrefaction. By clothing bone fragments in gold and jewels, she argued, their makers demonstrated that what they feared was not the division of bodies, but the fact that the dead rot. 'Reliquaries', she wrote, 'glorify and sublimate partition. What they deny is putrefaction'.[16] But that claim would surely be just as plausible if it were reversed: body-part reliquaries do indeed sublimate the dismemberment of the saints by mimicking the dismembered fragment in precious and imperishable materials. But they also display or signal the presence of shards of bone, and therefore celebrate and sublimate the fact of death and decay exactly as they do that of dismemberment.

Dry bones, of course, make better and more permanent relics than soft tissue, and the bodies of dead saints, like those of dead kings and queens, were often eviscerated and boiled down to procure clean bones. But bones, especially fragmented bones, also functioned in medieval devotional language as vivid emblems of the grave, death and decay, rather than of permanence or incorruption. In many a medieval crucifixion scene, the horror of death that Christ overcomes on the cross is symbolized by the bones of Adam, scattered at its base. Bynum's neatly polarized rhetoric here closed down areas of ambiguity that the objects themselves leave open.

12

Treasures of Heaven: Saints and their Relics

In November 1231 Elizabeth of Thuringia, daughter of the King of Hungary and widow of Louis IV, Landgrave of Thuringia, died in the city of Marburg, aged twenty-four. Married before she was fifteen, Elizabeth bore three children to Louis before his death while on crusade in 1227, when she was just twenty years old.[1]

Even during her affectionate marriage her piety had been characterized by midnight prayer vigils, lavish works of charity and acts of penance, of a scale and intensity unheard of in a high-status, sexually active wife and mother. She now took a vow of celibacy, adopted the coarse grey habit of the newly formed Franciscan Third Order, and placed herself under the spiritual direction of the appalling Conrad of Marburg, a sadistic former inquisitor, who separated her from her children, replaced her personal maids with brutal warders, and subjected her to a penitential regime that included severe beatings and public humiliations.[2]

Elizabeth survived Conrad's abuse for only four years. But the humility and charity of the smiling princess, who dressed like a pauper and personally ministered to the destitute and diseased in a hospital built with her own money, spectacularly embodied the ideals of her admirer Francis of Assisi. Her contemporaries took note. Within hours of her death her coffin was besieged by crowds of eager suppliants in search of healing or blessing. Pilgrims tore strips from her clothes, or cut the hair, nails and even the nipples from her body as relics, and miracles began. A papal commission, ironically headed by her guide and tormentor Conrad, investigated Elizabeth's miracles and virtues in 1232. Pope Gregory IX formally canonized her three years later.[3]

Elizabeth's radiant personality and the pathos of her short life make her one of the most endearing saints of the Middle Ages, while the course of her canonization highlights major shifts within the medieval cult of the saints. Her fame signalled the emergence of a new kind of female sanctity, active in the world rather than shut away in a cloister. Her canonization by the pope was equally novel, because for almost a millennium any bishop might proclaim someone a saint, and this right had been claimed as an exclusive papal prerogative only since the early 1200s: there were no known papal canonizations at all before AD 993. Once established, it was a monopoly that the medieval popes exercised very sparingly. The years between 1200 and 1250 witnessed an unprecedented blossoming of religious energy in Europe and the emergence of hugely successful new revival movements like the friars. Francis, the Poverello of Assisi, was merely the most famous of scores of notable Christian heroes and heroines. The century as a whole saw the local or popular veneration of more than 500 such people as 'saints'.[4]

Yet between 1200 and 1500 only forty new saints in all achieved canonization. The quasi-inquisitorial legal process preceding canonization by the pope was rigorous, expensive and increasingly long-drawn-out. By the late Middle Ages, a canonization process could take up to thirty years to reach a successful conclusion, and there was a very high failure rate. There were no fewer than six abortive attempts to secure the canonization of the English bishop Osmund of Salisbury between 1228 and 1452, before eventual success in 1457. The final campaign in the 1450s cost £731 13s, the equivalent of the annual income of a baron.[5] All this is in striking contrast to the prodigal record of the modern papacy, for in just twenty-seven years Pope John Paul II alone proclaimed no fewer than 482 new saints, more than all his predecessors put together.

Royal saints featured prominently in the early papal canonizations. In part this reflected the ability of the wealthy and powerful to pay the costs of the canonization process, in part the concern of the papacy to secure the loyalty of the ruling houses of Europe and thereby ensure their enforcement of Christian orthodoxy as Rome conceived it.[6] But it also reflected a widespread lay aspiration. In the Christian Middle Ages, the conviction that the social and political order did or should reflect the will of God himself found its focus in the person of the anointed king. The anointing of a new monarch by a bishop (borrowed from the Old Testament) was taken as the sign (some even said the sacrament) of divine endorsement of the king's authority. Monarchs were believed to be able by the mere touch of their hand to heal diseases like scrofula (tuberculosis of the lymph glands), known for that reason as 'the King's Evil'. Successive royal dynasties in both France and England practised this miraculous touching by the *roi thaumaturge* well into the age of the Enlightenment.

The most sacred kings of all were those who added to the intrinsic sanctity of monarchy the personal sanctity of a holy life. The saint-king was doubly blessed, a personal as well as political icon of Christ himself, ruling his people with justice and mercy, defending the poor, restraining the rich, mastering the perennial temptations to tyranny, luxury and lust that beset the powerful in every society.

Few medieval kings, of course, were even remotely plausible candidates for sainthood, but many medieval royal houses harnessed the reputation of saint-ancestors to validate monarchy in general and their own dynasties in particular. In twelfth-century Germany, Frederick Barbarossa promoted the royal cult of the Magi, the 'Three Kings of Cologne', and persuaded the anti-pope Paschal III to canonize Frederick's 'ancestor', the Emperor Charlemagne. In thirteenth-century England, King Henry III encouraged devotion to his predecessors among the Saxon royal saints, and rebuilt Westminster Abbey as a shrine for the greatest of them all, Saint Edward the Confessor. The abbey would serve a double function, as a royal shrine and a royal mausoleum, investing the Plantagenet dynasty buried there with the borrowed prestige of their holy forebear.[7]

The greatest of the medieval saint-kings, however, was Henry III's contemporary and brother-in-law, Louis IX of France. Louis succeeded to the French throne in 1226 when still a boy of twelve, and after a long regency shared with his formidable mother, Blanche of Castile, ruled till his death in 1270. In the intervening years he led two Crusades to the Holy Land, during the second of which he died of dysentery at Tunis. But long before his death, Louis had established a well-deserved reputation for personal integrity and just and compassionate rule. He had also presided over a cultural renaissance that saw the consolidation of the University of Paris as the intellectual powerhouse of Western Christendom, and the apotheosis of French Gothic art and architecture in the great churches of Chartres, Amiens and Rheims.[8]

The artistic vitality of France under Louis and the King's own ardent piety came together in the creation of the Sainte-Chapelle in Paris, the exquisite stone and glass shrine consecrated just months before he departed for his first Crusade. The building was designed to house the alleged relics of the passion of Christ – nails, lance, sponge and crown of thorns – that Louis had bought for a king's ransom from the bankrupt Latin emperor of Byzantium, Baldwin II. The Sainte-Chapelle and its relics therefore reflected the same ardent devotion to the Passion of Christ that lay behind crusading attempts to 'liberate' the Holy Places from their Muslim rulers.[9]

Louis's reputation for sanctity, well established in his own lifetime, depended, however, on far more than his very public devotional patronage. He dispensed justice without pomp, seeing plaintiffs informally, often in the open air, seated humbly on the ground. His charity to the poor was both lavish and highly personal. Like other grandees, he washed the feet of the poor on symbolic liturgical occasions. But Louis also routinely with his own hands fed the poor with food and drink from his own table.[10]

His scrupulous honesty was equally notable. Defeated and captured by Muslim forces at Fariskur in Egypt in 1250, he was ransomed for the immense sum of £200,000. His entourage managed to cheat his captors out of £20,000 of this ransom. When Louis heard of it, however, he insisted that the gold be paid in full, an example of honest dealing with the infidel that bewildered most of Christendom, and that was cited as a wonder at his canonization. His personal (and sometimes stern) discharge of justice, his attempted reform of corruption in royal administration, and his success in arbitration, both between his own barons and between foreign kings, earned him a reputation for righteousness and peace, *rex justus, rex pacificus*. In an age of relentless conflict between the popes and the German emperors, Louis managed to stay on good terms with both. He vindicated the French crown's claim to the title 'most Christian King' by collaborating with the papal Inquisition in enforcing religious orthodoxy in his realms. But he also resisted the more imperious demands of successive popes whenever he considered that they infringed the prerogatives and rights of the French monarchy.

Louis was widely recognized as a saint even before his death. When he died in 1270 at Tunis (lying stretched on a cross-shaped bed of ashes), his body was immediately boiled in wine and water to remove the flesh and entrails. Possession of the royal body was an important bargaining chip in the power vacuum that followed Louis's death. His son and heir, Philip III, was determined to take the bones back to France himself, to help establish his own authority. Philip's uncle, Louis's brother Charles d'Anjou, King of Sicily, wanted for similar reasons to take Louis's bones to Sicily. His determined nephew, however, fobbed Charles off with the gift of Louis's entrails, and took Louis's bones back to France for burial in the royal mausoleum of Saint-Denis.

But these secular manoeuvrings around the royal corpse were eclipsed by the popular feeling that the King's coffin housed the relics of a saint. Crowds flocked to see and touch the casket, and the long progress by sea and land would be marked by miracles, duly recorded as part of the canonization process (similar miracles attended the progress of the entrails through Sicily). The impression made by Louis's cortège was grotesquely enhanced by the fact that it was accompanied by a macabre and growing procession of lesser royal bodies. Along with Louis's relics went the bones of his son, Jean-Tristan, who had also died on the Crusade, and who had been similarly boiled down for ease of transport. To these were added en route the corpse of Louis's son-in-law Thibaud, King of

Navarre, who died on the return journey at Trapani, and then that of Isabelle of Aragon, wife and queen of Philip III, who fell from her horse as the royal cortège passed through Calabria and went prematurely into labour. The Queen's body and that of her stillborn child were duly added to the bizarre entourage trailing the relics of the saint-king through Italy into France.

Canonization procedures were inaugurated immediately. The first biography, by Louis's Dominican confessor, Geoffroy de Beaulieu, had been completed and sent to Rome within three years of the King's death, to provide the basis for the official process. In the event, though, high papal mortality meant that the canonization itself had to wait till 1297, when Boniface VIII, anxious to promote good relations with the French crown, completed a process that had staggered on through eight earlier pontificates. Saint Louis thereby became France's only canonized king, his role as an abiding icon of French identity and national pride marked in subsequent centuries not least by the bestowal of his name on cities and villages wherever France's writ ran.[11]

Both the process of making saints, therefore, and the kinds of people who achieved sanctity were changing during the high Middle Ages. The veneration of saints in itself, however, was a phenomenon almost as old as Christianity. One of the earliest Christian documents outside the New Testament is an eyewitness account of the martyrdom of Polycarp, the aged bishop of Smyrna said to have known Saint John the Evangelist, and who was burned in the arena for his Christian faith around AD 155. Polycarp's congregation later searched the pyre for his relics, gathering up 'his bones – more precious to us than jewels, and finer than pure gold'. These they buried 'in a spot suitable for the purpose' where they could gather annually to celebrate 'the birthday of his martyrdom'.[12]

In this narrative, the core elements of the cult of the saints – shrine, relics and annual feast day – are all already in evidence. Most of the earliest saints were martyrs like Polycarp, for their witness to Christ by the shedding of their blood made them powerful intercessors on behalf of weaker or more timid Christians. Those who had succumbed during persecution and offered sacrifice to the pagan gods flocked to the prisons to seek absolution and intercession from martyrs awaiting execution. The martyrs' prayers were considered even more powerful after their death. With the easing of persecution, and the establishment of Christianity as the religion of the Roman Empire, churches were built over the graves of the martyrs, and became magnets for pilgrims. The martyr's shrine and the remains of his shattered body were defiant affirmations of the central Christian belief that defeat in the cause of Christ was in fact a transcendent victory. The body brutalized by torture and death would shine one day in glory, as Christ's risen body shone, and was already a channel of divine healing and consolation. Christians flocked to the graves of the martyrs, and treasured oil or water or cloth which had come into contact with their blood or bones.

These shrine churches outside the city walls posed a problem for bishops seeking to unite the local churches around their own authority. The burial sites where the martyr-saints were sought out as heavenly patrons or physicians threatened to become rival centres of religious power and influence. The great fourth-century biblical translator Saint Jerome wrote, 'The city itself is moving; the people flood past the half-ruined temples and run to the tombs of the martyrs.'[13] The prestige of these shrines was so great that it seemed to threaten the institutional authority of the Church and its bishops, but the problem was solved by moving the bodies of the martyrs under the cathedral altars. The charisma of the saint was thereby united to the power of the institution, the grave of the martyr identified with the tomb of Christ, relic and Eucharist joined in a single overwhelming nexus of holiness.[14]

This 'translation' of a saint's bones from grave to altar or shrine would remain the act constituting canonization for almost a thousand years. And this public veneration of the saint's dead body marks a momentous divergence from Roman paganism and from Christianity's parent faith, Judaism, for both shunned the bodies of the dead as sources of pollution. By contrast, Christians looked to the ultimate resurrection of the whole person, body as well as soul, after death, not to mere survival of the spirit. They saw in the bodies of the saints, sanctified in life by the indwelling of the Holy Spirit, a pledge of that future resurrection, and a source of power and blessing in this world. The saint was believed to be present in his or her relics, as Christ was present in the Eucharist. To journey to a shrine, to touch the holy bones or the tomb in which they rested, to anoint withered limbs with oil from the lamps that burned before them, to drink water in which dust from the shrine had been dissolved – all this brought the devotee physically and concretely within the scope of the saint's power and patronage. *Brandea* – pieces of cloth that had touched a saint's bones – were believed to become heavier from the contact.[15]

At first saints were venerated only at their place of burial, and for centuries the Roman Church viewed with revulsion the Eastern custom of dismembering the saints so as to multiply their relics. When the Empress Constantina asked Pope Gregory the Great for the head of St Paul, he responded in June 594 with horror stories of workmen struck dead for accidentally disturbing the Apostle's rest and disapproving accounts of Greek monks as pious graverobbers, and sent her instead filings from the chains of St Paul.[16] But escalating demand made the division of the bodies of the saints necessary, and the dismemberment which the saints had endured in their martyrdoms may have made it seem symbolically appropriate. The Fifth Council of Carthage required every altar to have relics 'buried' within it, and as Christianity spread north and west, demand greatly exceeded supply. In the churches of Carolingian Europe and Anglo-Saxon England, the relics of the martyrs of the early Roman Church were prized above all, symbols of Christian triumph over the still potent forces of paganism, and at the same time a coveted link to the glories of ancient Rome. One ninth-century Roman deacon, Deusdona, ran a lucrative international trade in holy bodies, ransacking the Roman catacombs for the bones of 'saints', and sending them by mule train north and west to the kings, bishops and monasteries eager to acquire them. And those unable to afford or procure a whole body had to settle for a skull, a rib, a finger bone.[17]

So by the early Middle Ages, fragments of bone, hair, teeth or flesh, shrined in silver and gold, enamel and crystal, made the influence of the saints everywhere both visible and portable.[18] The process could be gruesome. Head relics were considered especially powerful, and head reliquaries were particularly striking. Often such reliquaries took the form of realistic metal or wooden busts, which enclosed the relic completely. But Elizabeth of Thuringia's head was separated from her body soon after her death, and displayed in a reliquary that exposed her skull to view. So that 'the sight of it should not strike horror into the onlookers,' the custodians peeled away the decaying flesh, skin and hair 'with a little knife', and the Emperor Frederick II himself donated a gold crown for the stripped and cleansed skull.[19]

Avidity for relics might take extreme forms. In 1190, Hugh, Bishop of Lincoln, himself destined to be canonized one day as a saint, visited the abbey of Fécamp in Normandy, to venerate the monastery's greatest treasure, an arm bone of St Mary Magdalene. The relic was duly produced, sheathed in silk, but Hugh sliced open the wrapping, to see and kiss the bone. Then, to the mounting horror of the monks, he tried to break off a piece and, when that failed, gnawed at it, first with his incisor and then with his molar teeth, at last snapping off and pocketing two splinters. The monks complained that he had profaned the relic 'like a dog', but Hugh would have none of it. What he had done, he declared defiantly, had honoured the saint, and was no more a profanation than when Christians honour their Lord by receiving his body and blood in communion, as he himself had done that day.[20]

St Hugh's startling behaviour was no one-off aberration: when he venerated the fingers of St John the Baptist at Bellay he took away part of the purple cloth in which they were wrapped, and at Peterborough he sliced and took away a sinew from the incorrupt arm of St Oswald. This was more than a collector's urge. Hugh's hunger for relics (he accumulated more than thirty) reflected a number of widely shared medieval convictions: the universal belief that the fragmented bodies of the saints were charged with holiness and power, worth journeying great distances to see; the prestige which ownership of such relics brought (the Burgundian Abbey of Vézelay was a rival claimant to Mary Magdalene's relics); ambiguity over whether the power of the relic could be tapped through its appearance – concealed in this instance by its silken cover – or by brute physical contact with its sanctified matter; the comparison between the holiness of the relics of the saints, and the holiness of the body and blood of Christ in the Mass; and finally the lengths to which someone might go to secure even tiny fragments of the relic for their own church or community.

Even inanimate objects might be relics, sanctified by contact with holy flesh and holy places, a belief reflected in the pious souvenirs – flasks of oil or water blessed by contact with the relics, and of course the pilgrim badges – which were sold at shrines. Inanimate relics might range from the stones or earth of the Holy Land, to the clothing or sandals of the Apostles and martyrs. In early Christian Ireland the gospel book, bell or staff of many saints mattered more than their bodily remains. The Emperor Constantine was believed to have made a bridle for his horse from one of the nails of the Crucifixion, as a protection in battle. In the later Middle Ages, the Kings of France gloried in their possession of Christ's Crown of Thorns. The supreme relic of this kind was the wood of Christ's cross, allegedly discovered by the Empress Helena in the late 320s, fragments of which were prized all over medieval Christendom.[21]

The enshrining of relics in precious materials was fundamental to the whole cult – ivory, silver, gold, coloured enamel, precious and semi-precious stones, even cameos and intaglios from pagan Rome, or rock-crystal perfume bottles from the Islamic East.[22] To the outward eye, relics might seem no more than the dust and residue of corruption and passibility, gruesome fragments of tortured flesh and broken bone. In God's eye, however, and eventually, at the last day, in the eyes of all humanity, the reality was and would be otherwise. Relics were the seeds of transcendence, trophies and tokens of the imperishable glory in store for all whom Christ had redeemed. As the Victorian Jesuit poet Gerard Manley Hopkins put it, though flesh might fade, and 'mortal trash/ Fall to the residuary worm', on judgement day 'In a flash, at a trumpet crash/ I am all at once what Christ is, since he is what I am, and/ This jack,

TREASURES OF HEAVEN: SAINTS AND THEIR RELICS   159

joke, poor potsherd, patch, matchwood, immortal diamond, / Is immortal diamond'.[23]

And so the lavish display of the reliquary was a glimpse of heaven: the concealment of the dust of death served to reveal a higher truth. Relics, like the bread and wine of the Eucharist, sheltered mortal eyes from the bloody and cruel events which had occasioned them, and pointed to the glory those events had earned. That was why, till relatively late in the history of relics, no one seemed to mind if the reliquary hid the relics from sight. One of the most fascinating exhibits in the British Museum's 2011 exhibition of relics and reliquaries, *Treasures of Heaven*, was an exquisite twelfth-century German portable altar, a foot or so square, made of porphyry bound in engraved and gilded copper, and sumptuously decorated with ivory and rock crystal. On its underside are the names of the forty or so saints whose relics it supposedly contains – Apostles like Peter and Andrew, Evangelists like Matthew and John, deacons like Stephen and Lawrence, martyr-bishops like Cornelius and Cyprian, bishops and monks like Blaise and Benedict. In comparison, the relics themselves, which were unpacked by the museum staff for display, seem drab and inconsequential chips and scraps of bone, hair and stone, each wrapped in a screw of cloth labeled with a vellum strip.

Such relics might be little more than a speck of dust or a single hair, and, as Julian Luxford has observed, 'The name as written in a list must often have been larger than the relic it stood for'.[24] Yet to the medieval believer these were the real treasures, each tiny fragment a guarantee of the invisible presence of the saint from whose body it had been taken. The collection was more than a souvenir or a metaphor. It was a quasi-sacramental embodiment of the company of heavenly protectors, who would be revealed in their glory at the end of time.[25] The idea that relics embodied the Church triumphant might be expressed visually, in reliquaries shaped like a miniature church, or in the reconstruction of Church buildings themselves as elaborate settings for multiple relics, enabling pilgrims to progress round them, enacting the journey of the Christian life towards the heavenly Jerusalem. And if the possession of a great relic often gave medieval communities their status, their local identity and often even their name, the pilgrim routes which criss-crossed Europe and the Middle East transcended locality, to map and bind the Christian world together, in a common set of beliefs, hopes and practices.

If many reliquaries concealed their contents, others proclaimed them. From the twelfth century onwards, 'speaking reliquaries' proliferated, shaped to represent the relics they contained: head and bust relics to contain skulls, feet reliquaries for foot bones or sandals and, perhaps most strikingly of all, arm relics, dramatic life-sized objects of silver and gold which brandished, beckoned or seemed to bless the pilgrim. In fact, not all such 'speaking reliquaries' contained arm bones: they might simply hold assorted collections of relics, but their dramatic form powerfully represented the dynamism believed to reside in the relics, and could be used to powerful effect in the liturgy and processions, manipulated to touch or bless.[26]

One of the most spectacular of such 'speaking relics' is the sensational life-sized gilded copper bust of the Auvergnais St Baudime which formed the mesmerizing centrepiece of the *Treasures of Heaven* exhibition. The saint's bust has a raised left hand holding the base of a phial which once contained his blood; the bust's magnificently curled and bearded head, with movable white and black eyes, may or may not once have contained his skull. The St Baudime reliquary makes no attempt at realism. It is a transcendent expression of the saint's glory, not the likeness of a living man.[27] By contrast, the sixteenth-century female bust-reliquary from the Netherlands which featured on the publicity material for the exhibition was disconcertingly realistic, the product of an age where statues were beginning to displace relics as the commonest focus of pilgrimage. The saint's skull (still present) is concealed in a hinged compartment within the head, and a circular glass brooch between her breasts displayed the fragmentary relics of other saints. Here the reliquary is indeed 'speaking', ringing the changes playfully, if not altogether comfortably, on realism and symbol, concealment and revelation.[28]

And everywhere, the veneration of the saints in their relics helped integrate the newly converted nations into an older Christian world through a common devotional culture. Relics and relic fragments were distributed by monasteries, bishops and popes as marks of favour or tokens of esteem; missionaries carried them with them into pagan territory to protect and overawe; soldiers bore them into battle as an army of heavenly auxiliaries. Churches, monasteries and cities gained power, wealth and prestige from the possession of notable relics, and fairs and markets to mark the saints' feast days became crucial to the prosperity of whole regions. In the words of the *Miracles of [St] Thecla*, God had 'sown' the world with saints, as 'ambassadors, intercessors, mediators, for nations, cities, races and peoples against plague, famine, war, drought, earthquake'. The saints of medieval Europe were both patrons and power brokers.[29]

Patronage carried responsibility as well as rights. If the saints could command the veneration of their devotees, those devotees in turn could demand results. Saints who failed to deliver might have their images or reliquaries 'humiliated' by being placed on the ground, or shrouded in sackcloth, or have access to their shrines blocked with nettles or thorns until prayer was answered. Ecclesiastical authorities protested against such superstition, and the second Council of Lyon banned all such practices in 1274, but in vain.[30] A saint might even be punished because he was working *too many* miracles. When the holy monk Stephen of Thiers died in 1124 in the isolated monastery of Grandmont in the Auvergne, the flood of pilgrims to his tomb disturbed the devotions of the monks. Miracles multiplied, as did the crowds, till at last the abbot berated Stephen at the tomb: 'We believe you are a saint without their proof. Please stop... If you don't, I'm warning you, we'll take your bones out of this place and throw them in the river.'[31]

Modern historians, like the Protestant reformers, have found this aspect of the cult of the saints deeply problematic. Robert Bartlett, in an otherwise invaluable recent survey of the cult of the saints, argued that Christianity in its origins 'was a radical revivalist cult' that rejected temple, cult, priesthood, sacrifice and other attributes of organized religions. The acceptance of all of these into third- and fourth-century Christianity represented the loss of its radical distinctiveness from other religions – 'A priest of Baal or of Isis or of Yahweh would certainly have recognized what kind of thing the Christianity of the late fourth century was.' Bartlett includes among these alien elements even the notion of a holy place, the root of pilgrimage, which was later absorbed by Christianity as it became established.[32]

But these are highly contestable claims. It is, for example, hard to see how a religious movement so deeply indebted to the Psalms for its prayers and liturgies could be intrinsically hostile to the notion of the holiness of Jerusalem, and hence of sacred places more generally. At the same time, the central Christian doctrine of Incarnation might be argued to entail of necessity the celebration of the material and not just the spiritual world, including the bodies of the saints.

And that emphasis on miraculous materiality, welcome or unwelcome, is fundamental to understanding the veneration of the saints. Since the sixteenth century, and partly in reaction to Protestant criticism, the Catholic Church has tended to locate the significance of the saints mainly in their value as exemplars. Evidence of 'heroic virtue', rather than the power to heal or help, is the dominant consideration in modern canonizations. But for most of Christian history, the emphasis has lain the other way. Three-quarters of the witnesses in canonization processes in the thirteenth and fourteenth centuries were there to give evidence about the miracles wrought by the saint rather than the holiness of their lives, and that proportion climbed to 90 per cent by the end of the fifteenth century.

This was no new development. The classic early saints' lives, such as Athanasius's life of Saint Anthony, Sulpicius Severus's life of Saint Martin of Tours, or Gregory the Great's life of Saint Benedict, are catalogues of wonders to which no ordinary Christian could ever aspire – visions, prophecies, healings, the exorcism of demons, the raising of the dead.[33] These early lives do indeed celebrate the saints' virtues, but in the form of monastic asceticism, spectacular fasting, and the renunciation of marriage and family – a call to heroism, not a pattern of living for average Christian men and women.

In a similar way, the 'Acts' of the early Christian martyrs were chronicles of heroic endurance in the face of horrifying sufferings.

What mattered about the saints was not their ordinariness, but the transcendent spiritual prowess that was the source of their ability to protect and heal, and which after death inhered in their physical remains. Princes, townsfolk, even Arab nomads flocked for healing, advice and the resolution of disputes to the fifteen-metres-high column on which the fifth-century Syrian ascetic Simeon the Stylite chose to live, half-starved, sleep-deprived, and exposed to freezing wind and scorching sun. Renunciation on this scale, it was believed, must make anyone capable of it a source of wisdom and blessing.

Sanctity is not a static notion, and new types of saint would overtake the old – Scandinavia and Eastern Europe, latecomers to Christianity, contributed a distinctive kind of sanctity, that of the ruler who suffered a violent death, like good King Wenceslas. Saints from the Italian city-states dominated late medieval canonizations, many of them from the new mendicant orders. But the impress of the earliest written lives marked the literature of sanctity throughout the Middle Ages. Hagiography was a highly formulaic activity, and the life of a new saint might even be composed simply by changing the names in an older narrative.[34]

For the literature of sanctity was deeply conservative. As we saw in Chapter 3, the most successful book of the Middle Ages was the collection of saints' lives compiled by a Dominican friar based in Lombardy, Jacobus de Voragine, in the 1260s. It took the form of a 'Legendary', a word derived from the Latin verb *legere*, to read, which carried no overtones of fiction or the far-fetched. Though probably intended primarily as a source book for the preaching clergy, Jacobus's *Legenda* became the most widely read book of the Middle Ages. By the end of the thirteenth century, hagiographers all over Europe were lifting material wholesale from it, earning it the nickname the *Golden Legend*. It was translated into most of the languages of Western Europe and survives in more than a thousand manuscripts, far eclipsing every other book from the Middle Ages. And with the advent of printing, Jacobus's text proved even more popular in the new medium. Between 1470 and 1500 an astonishing eighty-seven Latin editions of the *Legenda* were printed, as well as sixty-nine in various vernaculars, including four editions in English, considerably more than all the known printings of any book, even the Bible, during the same period.

So it is all the more striking that Jacobus's book should have been deeply conservative, containing almost no saints of his own or recent times. As we have seen, the canonizations by successive popes in the sixty or seventy years before Jacobus wrote publicized a wide spectrum of holiness and states of life, much of it new.[35] As a good member of the Order of Preachers Jacobus did include lengthy accounts of the mendicant founders Francis and Dominic, as well as a similarly extended treatment of the Dominican order's proto-martyr, Peter of Verona. He also included a life of the English martyr-archbishop Thomas Becket.

But above all, he focused on the martyr saints of the first four Christian centuries, and his accounts of them are marked, as the earliest saints' lives had been, by fearsome suffering, rejection of the world, and spectacular miracles. Writing hagiography for an age of warmly human and approachable saints like Francis of Assisi and Elizabeth of Thuringia, he turned to starker and more spectacular patterns of holiness, first portrayed in the earliest saints' lives centuries earlier, and represented in his own times by the thriving cult of relics, those jewel-clad fragments of brutalized mortality. The resulting narratives are two-dimensional, devoid of personality or depth. Yet they were well calculated to appeal to medieval taste for wonder and romance, excitement and pious entertainment. Their breathless pace and spectacular incident no doubt help to account for the *Golden Legend*'s popularity far beyond its original clerical target audience. They make clear to a modern reader how very recent is the notion of the saint, and the saint's life, as a pattern for ordinary living. And they remind us that beyond any message of moral improvement, the cult of the saints spoke of the hope of permanence, transfiguration and glory beyond the multitudinous ills of humanity – suffering, death, and descent into the dust.

13

St Erkenwald

THE MEDIEVAL CULT OF ERKENWALD

St Erkenwald was consecrated bishop of the East Saxons in 675 by Theodore of Tarsus, the reforming Greek who had been appointed archbishop of Canterbury by Pope Vitalian.[1] A monastic founder, he established a house for men at Chertsey in Middlesex, and for women, presided over by his sister Ethelburga, at Barking in Essex. We know very little else about him, except that he lived to an advanced age, had a reputation for sanctity in his own lifetime, and that the horse-drawn litter in which the ailing bishop travelled round his diocese became an object of veneration after his death, splinters of it being eagerly sought as apotropaic relics. The litter remained a prominent feature of his cult throughout the Anglo-Saxon period, generating its own miracle-stories: Bede noted that it was particularly effective as a cure for fevers. Bede is our main source for Erkenwald's life and early cult, but he seems to have been more interested in the bishop's sister and a series of miraculous events at the convent at Barking than in Erkenwald himself. Nevertheless, the presence of Erkenwald's feast day, 30 April, in more than a dozen surviving pre-Conquest calendars, indicates a widespread cult, which may have been centred on but was by no means confined to his burial-place in St Paul's.[2]

Erkenwald's relics underwent a catastrophic trial by fire during the burning of London in 1087, which razed St Paul's to the ground.

Erkenwald's litter was probably destroyed in this fire, but the saint's bones, enshrined on a tall plinth behind the high altar, survived unscathed, as did their wooden outer shrine and even the linen pall which covered it.[3] Understandably, this was taken to be a miracle, and almost certainly helped secure continuing Norman interest in this Saxon saint. The earliest surviving evidence of the promotion of the cult by the canons of the Norman cathedral is the Latin *Vita* composed early in the twelfth century, and a set of nineteen Miracles, composed in the early 1140s by Canon Arcoid, nephew of a former Bishop of London, Gilbert the Universal. The stimulus to this literary activity may well have been the campaign to secure the canonization of Edward the Confessor then being orchestrated up-river at Westminster Abbey, and the consequent pressing need for the clergy of the Eastminster, St Paul's, to promote the cult of their own rival saint.[4] The composition of the *Vita* and *Miracula* went alongside the construction of a magnificent new silver shrine for the saint. A number of the miracles centre on the temporary lodging of the saint's body in the crypt, and the long-drawn-out process of construction of the new shrine. The translation to the completed shrine behind the new high altar took place in 1148.

Both the *Vita* and the *Miracula* suggest, however, that the cult of Erkenwald at St Paul's was anything but secure and settled. By far the dominant element in the *Vita* is an elaborate and lengthy account of the angry contest between the monks of Chertsey, the nuns of Barking and the people of London led by the canons of St Paul's, for possession of Erkenwald's relics. According to the *Vita* the matter was settled, and the rights of St Paul's established, by direct divine intervention, as the Thames parted, just as Jordan had once done for the Ark of the Covenant, to provide a dry pathway for the funeral cart to journey to London. Behind this story must lie contested claims between the canons of St Paul's and the religious of the saint's own foundations for possession and management of Erkenwald's cult.[5]

The nineteen stories in the *Miracula* of Canon Arcoid provide even more striking evidence of the fraught and problematic nature of Erkenwald's cult in Norman England. 'Vengeance' miracles, in which saints punish those who desecrate their shrine or possessions, or who disregard their feast day or impugn their sanctity or power, are a commonplace feature of many medieval cults.[6] Such incidents are to be found in the cult stories of even the most genial and gentle saints, like St Francis or the Virgin herself, and they occur in the cults of other medieval English episcopal saints, as in the story of Julia of Hereford, struck blind for doubting the power of Thomas Cantilupe.[7] But Erkenwald's *Miracula* bristles with an exceptionally large number of such prickly and daunting stories: the labourer carrying timber outside St Paul's on St Erkenwald's feast day who stumbles over a half-buried skull in the graveyard and dies of concussion (Miracle 2); the man seized with agonizing stomach cramps because he prevented his wife making an offering for Erkenwald's shrine (Miracle 6); Eustace the silly silversmith, who jokingly lay down in the half-completed shrine of the saint and called out for offerings, and who was instantly seized with pains which carried him off a few days later (Miracle 10); Vitalis the London fletcher whose scraper-blade slipped and put out his eye as he was working on the saint's festival (Miracle 12); and Teodwin the painter, whose insistence on carrying on his work in the crypt of St Paul's hindered the faithful from approaching the saint on his festival, and who was beaten up by Erkenwald himself with his pastoral staff (Miracle 17).

These savage little revenge stories can be matched in other medieval English cults, but their sheer number is striking, and their prominence is underscored by the hectoring insistence of Arcoid's narrative on the ills which befall the 'impious and prophane' who neglect the saint's feast days. The miracle of the labourer who is brained by tripping over a skull, for example, contains a set-piece altercation between one of the cathedral clergy and the doomed man, in which the cleric attacks those who dishonour the pope and the 'priests serving God in the diocese of Erkenwald' by refusing to keep the festival. The labourer responds by denouncing the idleness of the clergy and their observances, contrasting them with the labour of the laity – 'the jobs we work at are useful … But you clerics, with your everlasting useless dirges, you despise the life we lead, and because our type of work is not like yours, you condemn it...'[8] There was, clearly, considerable resistance in twelfth-century London to the extension of the cathedral cult of Erkenwald into the wider community (intriguingly, Arcoid claims that the wealthy citizens neglected the saint's cult, but that the poor of London responded more generously).[9] Preoccupation with this resistance would remain a feature of the saint's cult for the rest of the Middle Ages. Though later versions of the saint's life and miracles would tone down the more strident aspects of Arcoid's narrative, and would present Erkenwald much more straightforwardly as the saint of the people of London, no fewer than four of the conflict-laden revenge miracles would continue to feature in the Matins readings of the Sarum Office for St Erkenwald to the end of the Middle Ages.[10]

The Sarum Office, like the earlier office devised for St Paul's Cathedral itself, did not in fact draw directly on the twelfth-century *Vita* and *Miracula,* but was extracted from John of Tynemouth's c. 1330 redaction of the earlier treatments in his *Sanctilogium Angliae*.[11] John added a cluster of stories which probably emanated from the convent at Barking, including a new miracle story, in which Erkenwald and his sister elongate a beam of wood cut too short by the builders working on the convent church. This eminently practical miracle featured in all subsequent versions of the saint's life, would be included in the London and Sarum Matins office, and would be cited with relish and approval by Thomas More in his *Dialogue Concerning Heresies*.[12]

John of Tynemouth's reworking of the legend of St Erkenwald coincided with the energetic elaboration of his cult and shrine within the rebuilt St Paul's. Between 1314 and 1326 the canons built an elaborate gothic shrine for Erkenwald in stone and alabaster, housing a coffin of precious metal, and the relics were translated to their new setting at Candlemas 1326. By now the cult was evidently a focus of considerable lay interest, the translation taking place at night because of fear of mass hysteria among the crowds of devotees. Seed donations of rings and jewels by the cathedral clergy were soon joined by the gifts of the well-to-do, including a donation of twelve nobles in 1340 from King John of France. Pilgrim offerings made the further elaboration of the shrine possible, and in 1339 three goldsmiths were set to work on the shrine for a whole year.[13] Despite these evident signs of cult at the shrine, however, there was still a problem in securing the wider observance of Erkenwald's feast days, and offerings were meagre both in London and in the diocese at large. In 1386 Bishop Braybrook of London complained that the four major patronal festivals of the cathedral – the two feasts of the Conversion and the Commemoration of St Paul and the two feasts of the Translation and Commemoration of Erkenwald '*ubique per nostras Civitatem et diocesin quasi ab omnibus prophenari*' ('profaned by almost everybody throughout our city and diocese'): it is difficult to know how seriously to take his conventional-sounding claim that this represented a decline from old decency, when these feast days had been properly observed.[14]

Braybrook's complaint of the recent neglect of these feast days has been accepted at face value by historians, and has even been seen by some as evidence of an episcopal response to the growth of Lollardy in London.[15] It seems more likely, however, that it is merely a mark of a gap between parochial and cathedral observance that has no such ideological overtones. Braybrook offered the routine inducement of forty days' indulgence for all the faithful who duly observed the four cathedral feasts. But his specific liturgical provisions for the four feasts suggest that he was attempting to step up the cult of Erkenwald to a new level, rather than to restore decayed observances. For the feasts of St Paul he required churches to use the services already in their books and *antiquitus ordinato* for those days. For the feasts of Erkenwald, by contrast, he was clearly making new provision. He stipulated the use of the common office for any confessor bishop, and provided a collect, offertory and post-communion prayer for use at Masses in honour of Saint Erkenwald; none of this would have been necessary had there been an established set of proper prayers already in parochial liturgical books.[16]

However that may be, the next twenty years show the steady promotion of Erkenwald's cult within cathedral and diocese. In August 1393 a solemn procession to the shrine of Erkenwald formed part of Richard II's ritual reconciliation with the city of London.[17] In the following year Braybrook himself required the parish clergy of London to take part, vested in copes, in the cathedral processions for the saint's feast days, and there is evidence of a stream of gifts to the shrine, newly fenced in with an elaborate metal railing, from London clergy and the wealthy city laity. In 1407 the dean, Thomas de Evere, bequeathed £100 to buy city property to maintain lights before the shrine, and to pay the stipend of a chaplain for the St Erkenwald guild which was now functioning within the cathedral, itself perhaps a sign of growing lay involvement in the cult. There seems to have been a special connection between the cult of St Erkenwald and the London legal profession, and in 1431 Erkenwald's Translation, on 14 November, was proclaimed as one of the four principal feasts kept annually at Lincoln's Inn. This connection is not hard to explain. Newly created serjeants-at-law, the cream of the legal profession, were each allocated a pillar in St Paul's as a place of consultation, and not surprisingly the inauguration ceremonies for fifteenth-century serjeants included a procession to and offering at the shrine of St Erkenwald, in whose cathedral the serjeants would conduct this aspect of their profession.[18]

ST ERKENWALD: THE ALLITERATIVE POEM

It is in the context of this late fourteenth- and early fifteenth-century promotion of the cult of St Erkenwald that we should probably locate the most intriguing literary expression of devotion to the saint, the 350-line alliterative poem, *St Erkenwald.* Surviving in a single manuscript compiled in the 1470s and containing catechetical material and a set of saints' lives from the South English Legendary, *St Erkenwald* is quite unlike any other versified saint's life from the English Middle Ages.[19] The poem, which probably dates from the first quarter of the fifteenth century,[20] displays no interest in and tells us nothing about Erkenwald's life, death, miracles or cult. It is devoted to a single incident, in which Erkenwald unravels by divine inspiration the spiritual mystery of an incorrupt body in a gold-lined stone coffin found by workmen while the foundations of St Paul's Cathedral are being excavated. The story has in fact no real connection with Erkenwald: it is a version of one of the best-known legends of the Middle Ages, the story of Gregory the Great and the Emperor Trajan, in which the compassionate tears and prayers of the holy pope secure the release of the soul of the pagan emperor from Hell.

The plot of *St Erkenwald* is as follows. After a time of pagan perversion under the Saxon ruler Hengyst, who had overrun and destroyed the British Church, England is reconverted to Christianity by Augustine, sent to England by the pope. The temples formerly dedicated to demons are cleansed and rededicated to the saints, idols replaced by the images of God's 'dere hallowes'. In London this process was presided over by Erkenwald, a bishop of 'Augustynes art'. The great metropolitan temple of the pagans was torn down and rebuilt as the New Work of St Paul's Cathedral. As teams of merry masons work, they discover deep below the earth a mysterious stone coffin, carved with crisply gilded but unintelligible writing. The citizens of London swarm to see this 'toumbe-wonder', the mayor and the cathedral sexton cordon off the area and the coffin is prised open, to disclose the radiant and incorrupt body of a judge, dressed in the standard medieval legal uniform of coif and furred mantle, but also wearing a crown and a jewelled girdle and carrying a sceptre. News of this discovery, which to a medieval audience would immediately indicate the presence of a saint,[21] is brought to Bishop Erkenwald, then on a visitation of an abbey in Essex (presumably, though this is not said, his own foundation at Barking). The bishop sends his beadle to warn the citizens of his return to the city, but instead of going to see the wonder, he proceeds straight to his palace and spends the night weeping and praying for the guidance and help of the Holy Spirit, to unravel the mystery and confirm the faith of the people. He weeps so persistently that his prayer is answered and, armed with visionary certainty, next morning he celebrates a votive High Mass of the Holy Spirit in the cathedral, before a packed congregation of dignitaries, and, still vested in his pontificals, goes to the tomb. There the dean of the cathedral pompously explains that a seven-day search in the cathedral archives has yielded no information about the mysterious burial, but is rebuked by the bishop for vain reliance on human speculation in a matter where it has no light to offer. In such a case only God can confirm faith and strengthen belief.

Erkenwald then turns to the corpse, and conjures him in the name of Jesus to speak and reveal how and when he was buried, why he is dressed as a king, and whether his soul is in heaven or hell. The corpse stirs, though with borrowed life, and speaks as if in a trance. He declares that he is neither king, caesar nor knight, but one of the unhappiest mortals ever to live. He was, he explained, a judge in New Troy (London) long before the time of Christ. Serving the legendary King Belinus, one of London's greatest builders, he was given absolute authority to administer the law over the false and fractious citizens. In the discharge of his office he was absolutely just and impartial, free of all covetousness and favouritism, 'rygtwis and reken and redy of the laghe', and so when he died the people had his corpse decked with regal tokens 'For the honour of myn honeste of highest enprise'. The bishop asks him if his incorrupt state is the result of embalming, but the judge replies that it is the work of God:

> ... the riche kyng of reson, that right ever alowes
> And loves al the lawes lely that longen to trouthe:
> and moste he menskes men for mynning of rightes
> Then for all the meritorie medes that men on molde usen,
> And if renkes for right thus me arayed has,
> he has lant me to last that loves ryght best. [22]

(The great king of reason, who always favours justice and loves wholeheartedly all the laws that make up the truth; and above all honours people more for conforming their minds to justice than for any of the meritorious deeds that men perform on earth; and if men have robed me as a justicer, he who loves justice best has allowed my [appearance] to last.)

This apparent token of God's favour moves Erkenwald once again to ask about the state of the judge's soul. If he has dealt so

ST ERKENWALD

justly then surely God, 'that rewardes vche a renke as he has right servyd', cannot withhold from him some portion of his grace. But the corpse now explains his earlier puzzling reference to being the most wretched of men. However just his actions, he was a pagan with no knowledge of Christ. Despite his virtue, was he not, he asks, addressing Christ,

> a paynym unpreste that never thi plite knewe,
> Ne the mesure of thi mercy ne thi mecul vertue,
> Bot ay a freke faithles that faylid thi laghes
> That ever thou, Lord, wos louyd in? Alias the harde stoundes
> I was non of the nombre that thou with noy boghtes
> With the blode of thi body vpon the blo rode.

(Was I not an ignorant pagan, who never knew your promise, nor the measure of your mercy, nor your great power, but was always one who lacked faith, who failed in the laws by which you were loved? Alas the hard fates: I was none of the number whom with suffering you bought with the blood of your body on the darkened cross.)

And so when Christ harrowed hell to release the souls of the patriarchs, the pagan judge was left in darkness. Unhealed from the poison of original sin, he is exiled from the banquet of the redeemed,

> that solempne fest
> Ther richely hit arne refeyted that after right hungride.[23]

(That solemn feast where those who hungered after justice are richly fed.)

At this terrible revelation of the righteous judge's eternal exclusion from the joys of heaven, all the bystanders begin to weep, and the bishop, also weeping, bends over the body. If only God would grant the judge a moment of real human life, he says, just long enough for the bishop to fetch water and to recite the words of baptism – 'I baptise thee in the name of the Father, Son and Holy Ghost' – then he, as bishop, would have discharged his duty, and it would not matter if the judge then dropped dead on the spot.

And now the poem reaches its climax. As Erkenwald speaks the words of baptism, his 'lavande teres' 'trill' into the coffin, and one falls on the corpse's face. At once the judge sighs in fulfilled longing, and cries out in joy, '*Oure* Sauvyoure be loved' – he *is* now, after all, one of those bought with Christ's blood. At the moment the tear fell on his face his soul was ushered into the heavenly banquet – words and water have washed him clean, and he praises God, and the bishop, for his deliverance. And immediately

> his swete chere swyndid and faylid
> And all the blee of his body wos blakke as the moldes,
> As roten as the rottok that rises in powdere,
>
> (his sweet countenance withered and vanished, and all the colour of his body became black as the earth, as rotten as the decay that rises in powder.)

for the soul which has entered into eternal life has no need for the passing vainglory of mortal beauty. The poem ends with the whole of London rejoicing in the love of God, as mourning and mirth are mixed together. Erkenwald and his attendants lead the people in procession through the cathedral, 'And all the belles of the burgh beryd at ones'.

THE LEGEND OF TRAJAN AND POPE GREGORY

Discussion of *St Erkenwald* has inevitably focused on the fact that the poem is a reworking of a venerable medieval legend, the release of Trajan from hell by the prayers of St Gregory the Great. This legend exists in many different versions, but first appeared in the earliest Life of Gregory the Great, written in the late seventh century by a monk of Whitby. In this version Gregory crosses the Forum, 'a magnificent piece of work for which Trajan is said to have been responsible'. He learns (we are not told how) that Trajan, though a pagan, 'had done a deed so charitable that it seemed more likely to have been the deed of a Christian than of a pagan'. While leading an army in haste to battle, he had been appealed to by the widowed mother of a murdered son for justice: halting the entire army, Trajan secured compensation for the woman. Gregory sees in this action the fulfilment of Isa. 1: 17–18, 'Judge the fatherless, plead for the widow,' and, dismayed at the thought that the unbaptised Trajan languishes in Hell, goes to St Peter's and, 'as was his custom', weeps floods of tears, until it is revealed to him that Trajan has been admitted to heaven in answer to his prayers, 'seeing that he had never presumed to ask this for any other pagan'.[24]

This extraordinary story was to have a long medieval afterlife, for it raised in an acute and embarrassing way a cluster of knotty theological problems – the fate of virtuous pagans, the necessity of faith for salvation, the efficacy and indispensability of the sacraments, the finality of damnation. The mid-ninth-century biographer of Gregory, John the Deacon, poured buckets of cold water on the whole incident as related by the Whitby monk, insisting that Gregory would never have prayed for a damned man, and that at best his prayers might have freed Trajan's soul from the torments of hell, but could not have admitted him to heaven. Scholastic discussions of the story, for example by St Thomas, solved the problem by suggesting that the pope's prayers might have brought Trajan briefly back to life, so that he could believe and be baptized, in the form of a spiritual baptism of desire even if not one of real water. For medieval 'humanists' the story became a vehicle for exploration of the fate of the just pagan, and the universal value of virtue, and in Dante's *Paradiso* Trajan is an emblematic figure of Justice. In England, the Trajan legend was employed by Langland to suggest that the just pagan might be saved without any explicit faith in Christ, and without the benefit of Church or sacraments. He insists on Trajan's paganism, and denies Gregory any role except that of the recognition of Trajan's virtue and hence of his salvation.[25]

St Erkenwald plainly repudiates any such view. The poem elaborates the picture of the pagan judge's virtue, and puts in Erkenwald's mouth the humanist expectation that such virtue must surely receive divine reward, only to dash any such hope in the judge's own lamentation over his lost and unregenerate state. The emotional and theological dilemmas of the poem are acutely felt, but are resolved not by stretching theological categories, but by an artistic *coup*: the convergence of human pity, moral bafflement and the demands of theological orthodoxy, in the sacramental efficacy of the bishop's words and tears. The priestly character of the saint is heavily emphasized throughout the poem, and the saint himself delivers a stinging rebuke to the human curiosity and rationalist presumption which might seek a solution to the problem of human salvation outside the orthodox framework of grace and revelation.[26]

Historical, textual and linguistic evidence suggests that the author of *St Erkenwald* came from the north-west of England, but it is nevertheless emphatically a London poem, and a cathedral poem.[27] Both the profane bustle of the citizenry and the religious centrality of St Paul's are fundamental elements of the texture of the poem – the mayor and beadles, the sexton and dean, the maces and the civic and religious processions all evoke the life of the capital. The poem's major symbol of secular value, the pagan judge, is clothed as a member of the 'order of the coif', like the London lawyers who functioned within the Cathedral.[28] Moreover, despite the fact that its central plot is lifted from the Gregory and Trajan legend, the poem has been shown to be saturated with *topoi* and images adapted from the legend and liturgy of St Erkenwald: the themes of building and conversion which dominate his liturgical office, the insistence of the poem on the centrality of the liturgical and sacral over against the secular which, as we have seen, dominate the *Miracula,* and the presence at the heart of the poem of the concealed hagiographical convention of the 'Inventio', the discovery and translation of holy relics.[29]

THE WHITBY 'LIFE OF GREGORY' AND THE 'BAPTISM OF TEARS'

Concern to locate the poem within the spectrum of late medieval discussion of the Trajan legend, however, has meant that the fundamental oddity of the conversion of the Trajan legend into a story about Erkenwald has gone largely unexplored. The Trajan story was in fact adapted in this way elsewhere – Gollancz printed a fifteenth-century German version of the legend (which may however be later than the Erkenwald poem) in which Gregory is replaced by the bishop of Vienna, and the role of Trajan is taken by an unnamed pagan judge whose skull is exhumed and found to contain a living and speaking tongue, preserved because the judge never pronounced an unjust sentence: the tongue asks for baptism and the judge is saved.[30]

But, however germane such late medieval parallels may be, they have obscured the presence of elements crucial to an understanding of *St Erkenwald* in the earliest source of the legend, the Whitby 'Life of Gregory'. Following the lead of Isaac Gollancz, who printed the Trajan incident from the Whitby life as an appendix to his edition of the poem,[31] commentators on St Erkenwald have focused narrowly on the story itself, ignoring the context in which the Whitby monk presents it, and indeed ignoring the detail of the Whitby monk's narrative. In doing so, they have missed vital clues to the meaning of the poem, and to the reasoning which allowed the poet to transfer to Erkenwald an incident from the life of Gregory.

The Whitby 'Life of Gregory' is very self-consciously an *English* life of the pope who was responsible for the reconversion of England to Christianity. It is concerned to present his greatness as teacher and apostle of the English, not primarily as a miracle worker. So, the author insists at the beginning of his book, miracles are not an end in themselves but 'are granted for the destruction of idols of unbelieving pagans, or sometimes to confirm the weak faith of believers: most of all, they are granted to those who instruct the pagans'.[32] Gregory, '*apostolicum nostrum sanctum*', is one of those saints who bring a whole people to God. In sending missionaries to Britain, 'he entered the house of the strong man whom Christ had bound, taking as spoil those goods,' that is, ourselves, who were 'sometimes darkness but now are light in the Lord'. Thus the marvels by which he is to be known are not conventional miracles, 'not only in the healing of the body or the raising from the dead, but as our own Gregory has explained, still more in the healing of souls, because it is in them that we are the image of God'.[33] The author then devotes eleven of the book's thirty modern chapter divisions to an account of incidents in the early history of the conversion of England, though the northern provenance of the work means that Paulinus, not Augustine, is the missionary founder focused on.

Though the author of *St Erkenwald* certainly drew on a range of other sources, notably Bede's *Ecclesiastical History,* for the account of the conversion of England which forms the thirty-two-line prologue to the poem, there is a very striking correspondence between this aspect of the Whitby monk's presentation of Gregory's work and the poem's distinctive preoccupation with the spoiling of the demons and the transformation of their temples into churches.

> Then prechyd he here the pure fayth and plantyd the trouthe,
> And converted all the communnates to Cristendome newe,
> He turnyd temples that tyme that temyd to the devell,
> and clensyd hom in Cristes nome and kyrkes hom callid.
> He hurlyd owt hor ydols and hade hym in sayntes,
> And chaungit cheuely hor nomes and chargit hom better.[34]

> (Then he preached the pure faith and planted the truth, and converted all the citizens to Christianity anew, turned temples that were then dedicated to the devil, and cleansed them in Christ's name and called them churches, he hurled out their idols and brought in saints, and changed their names and charged them to the better.)

The parallels become closer still in the account of the Trajan legend. It opens with a passage which has been bafflingly ignored by commentators on the *Erkenwald* poem.

> Some of our people also tell a story related by the Romans, of how the soul of the Emperor Trajan was refreshed and even baptised by St Gregory's tears, a story marvellous to tell and marvellous to hear. Let no one be surprised that we say he was baptised, for without baptism none will ever see God; and a third kind of baptism is by tears.[35]

No other medieval source insists in this way on the baptism of Trajan in tears: the pope's tears are normally equated simply with his prayers, and where the notion of a spiritual baptism is retained, it is dissociated from the tears – in Aquinas's commentary on the story, for example, it becomes a *baptismum flaminis* baptism of the spirit. In these two sentences from the Whitby 'Life', however, the central themes of *St Erkenwald* are set out, for the poem is not simply a poem about how the dead pagan is baptised, but how he is baptised *in tears,* and it is very pointedly designed to illustrate the theological conviction that 'without baptism none will ever see God'.

The notion of a 'baptism of tears' was in fact a theological peculiarity of the Anglo-Saxon Church. It derives ultimately from an insular misunderstanding of Rufinus's translation of Gregory of Nazianzus's sermon *De Luminibus*. There the phrase referred not literally to the sacrament of regeneration, the beginning of Christian life, but to penance, the forgiveness of post-baptismal sin, a new baptism. The phrase referred to the forgiveness of sin by tearful repentance – a 'baptism' of tears which restores the grace of one's original baptism. But in its transmission into England that original sense was lost. In one crucial text, a recension of the *Ludicia* of Archbishop Theodore, the phrase *baptismum lacrimarum* was dislodged from its place in a discussion of penance, and tacked on to a quite separate argument about the merit acquired from good works done before baptism, and which was not lost in baptism. In the process, the phrase took on a new but confused meaning, the notion that a virtuous pagan might somehow attain salvation, on the basis of good works done outside the order of grace, from some ill-defined and non-sacramental 'baptism of tears'.[36]

Whatever the origin of the phrase, and the theological misunderstandings it carried with it, it is clearly central to the Erkenwald poem. Here the 'baptism of tears' ceases to be a mere metaphor, and becomes a literal reality, which nevertheless perfectly catches the metaphor. Tears flow throughout the poem. In fifteenth-century devotional exegesis there was a direct link between tears and the Holy Ghost, reflected in the Sarum Mass for the gift of tears, and the notion that the salt water of weeping was the primordial water of chaos over which the Holy Ghost hovers in creation and in regeneration. It is thus the bishop's sustained weeping during his night vigil which secures the enlightenment of the Holy Spirit which comes like the rising of the sun as day breaks:

> so long he grette after grace that he graunte hade
> An ansuare of the Holy Goste, and afterward hit dawid.[37]

(So long he wept for grace that it was granted to him, an answer from the Holy Ghost: and then came the dawn.)

The crowd 'wepyd for woo' when they hear the judge's story, and the bishop himself approaches the coffin with the 'lavande tears' which will work the miracle of the judge's regeneration, in the literal baptism of tears which forms the poem's climax. Indeed, these sentences from the preamble to the Whitby monk's version of the legend, with their insistence that no one can see God without baptism, and their provision of a baptism of tears to supply this lack in the just pagan, supply the formal programme and the shaping dilemma of the poem.

A final element in the Whitby 'Life' links it strongly to *St Erkenwald*, by providing a theological rationale for the transfer of the story from the pope of Rome to the bishop of London. The Gregory–Trajan narrative is immediately followed in the Whitby 'Life' by a discussion of the historical reliability of the work as a whole. The monk pleads with his readers not to be hyper-critical of his work, 'which has been diligently twisted into shape by love rather than knowledge'. If the miracle-stories in particular have become confused, the reader must bear in mind that there are discrepancies even in the gospels. Indeed, 'let no one be disturbed even if these miracles [of Gregory] were in fact performed by some other one of the saints' (*si quid horum de alio quolibet sanctorum fuisset effectum*), since, according to Paul, 'we are all members one of another'. Therefore 'we know that all saints have everything in common through the love of Christ of whose bodies they are members. Hence if anything we have written did not concern this man ... yet in his case we have little doubt on the whole that they were true of him too'.[38]

This blasé doctrine of the interchangeability of the miracles of the saints seems to me uncannily relevant to the poet's procedure in *St Erkenwald*, not least in its occurrence immediately after the Trajan story, for it legitimizes the transfer of the Trajan story to London and St Erkenwald. Added to the Whitby 'Life"s insistence on the theme of the conversion of England, and its unique focus on the *baptismum lacrimarum*, it is clear that the Whitby 'Life of Gregory' and the Erkenwald poet share a remarkable cluster of preoccupations and assumptions: it is difficult to resist the suspicion that the Erkenwald poet may even have known the Whitby 'Life'. There are admittedly real difficulties in this suggestion, which include the Whitby 'Life"s silence about St Augustine, who features so prominently in the poem's prologue. Even more daunting is the fact that there is no other evidence of the circulation of the Whitby 'Life' in late medieval England: it seems to have disappeared from view early in the Middle Ages, and survives now in a single ninth-century manuscript in the monastery library of St Gall. At the very least, however, we need to note the centrality in the poem of many distinctive features shared with the Whitby 'Life'.

POEM AND AUDIENCE: A CATHEDRAL GUILD ENTERTAINMENT?

What was the poem *St Erkenwald* for? Why and for whom was it written? The most learned commentator on the poem, Gordon Whatley, sees it as a 'conservative and defensive' clericalist response to secularism and a growing laical spirit epitomized by Langland: it was, he thinks, designed to oppose an account of human worth that exalted secular virtue at the expense of the Church's authority and sacraments.[39] There is clearly a good deal in this, though it oversimplifies and flattens out Langland's complex relationship to the Church, its sacraments and its liturgy. Moreover, to characterize the poem's moving resolution of the tension between natural and supernatural justice – a tension which gives such pathos to the figure of Virgil in Dante's *Commedia* – as merely 'conservative and defensive', seems to me to beg a good many questions. The poem's central theological problem – the impossibility of salvation for even the most righteous pagan without faith and the grace of baptism – was that debated in the fourteenth century between a sternly Augustinian theological orthodoxy, represented by Archbishop Bradwardine, and the so-called 'New Pelagians', represented by William of Ockham, and it is a recurrent preoccupation in a good deal of fourteenth-century religious literature.[40]

Yet the poem seems to demand some more specific occasion than so generalized a concern. The centrality of London, St Paul's, and the saint of London and St Paul's within it, make a London audience almost certain. But who, and why?

It is tempting to place an early fifteenth-century poem insisting on the indispensable role of sacraments and priesthood for salvation in the context of the campaign against Lollardy which in 1401 produced the ferocious Act *De Heretico Comburendo*, and evoked the zeal of Archbishops Courtenay and Arundel. Yet if *St Erkenwald* is directed against Lollardy, it is the most oblique and unfocused of polemics. Its burlesqued portrayal of the London citizenry, and the judge's characterization of their pagan ancestors as folk 'felonse and fals and frowarde to reule', do perhaps indicate that the poet shared the suspicion of the laity which characterized the orthodox establishment in the age of Archbishop Arundel's anti-heretical *Constitutions*.[41] Yet none of the central features of Lollardy are targeted in the poem. Lollard attacks on baptism were confined to its extremist fringes, and focused in any case on the value of the sacrament to the children of Christians, or the place or manner of the rite,[42] while there is not even the most glancing reference to Eucharistic heresy, to the temporal possessions of the Church, to the unworthiness of the clergy, or to the links between error and sedition. The poem's reference in the prologue to Augustine's replacement of pagan idols with the images of the saints offers such hostages to Lollard polemic, and is so casual in its contrast between pagan idolatry and Christian veneration –

John Talbot, 1st Earl of Shrewsbury, presents a collection of chivalric romances to Margaret of Anjou and Henry VI, her husband. Illuminated in Rouen in the mid-1440s, at the height of the Hundred Years War, Shrewsbury's book, which contains a genealogy tracing Henry VI's pedigree back to St Louis of France, is one of the most splendid manuscripts in the Old Royal Library. [Chapter 2]

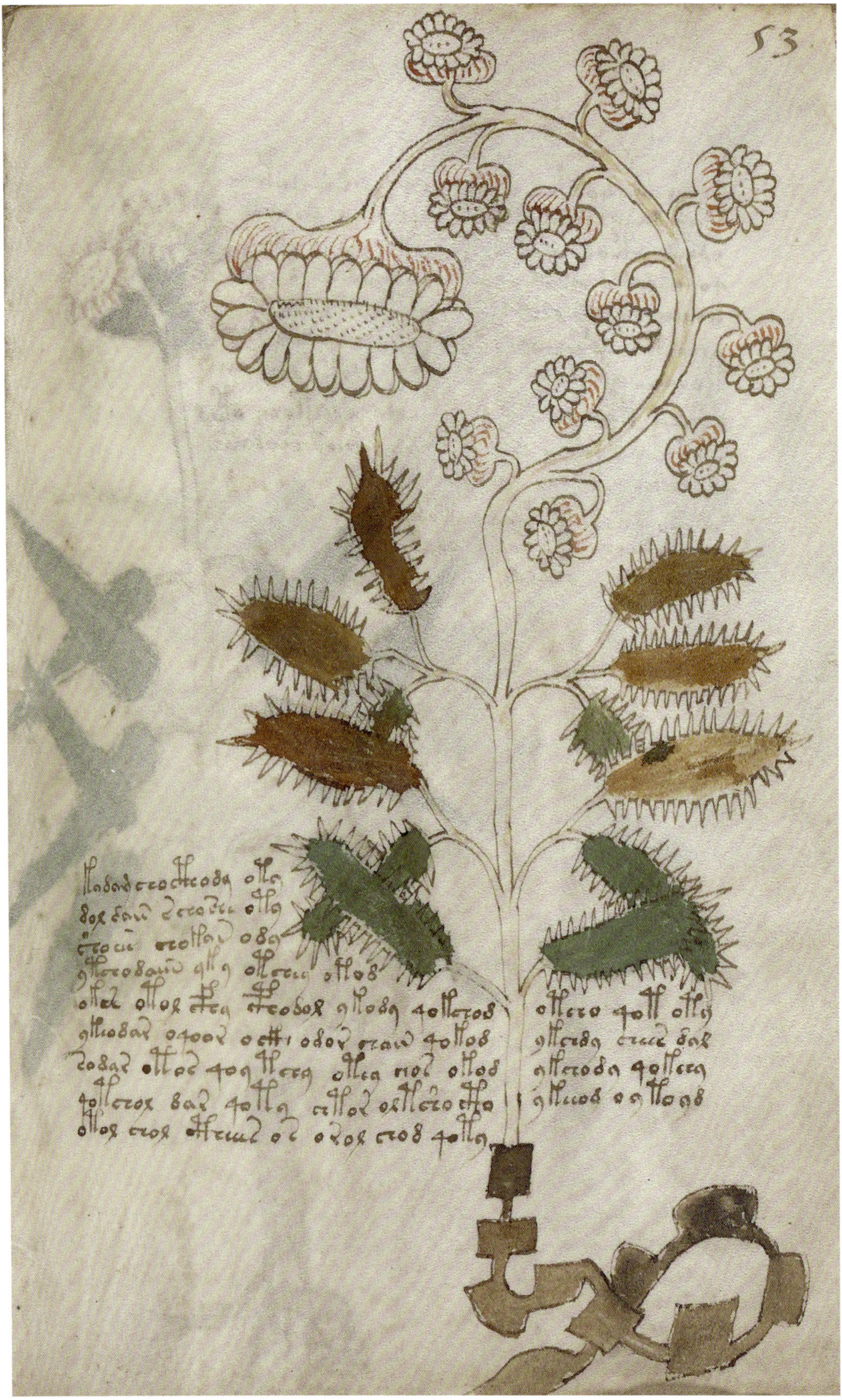
53

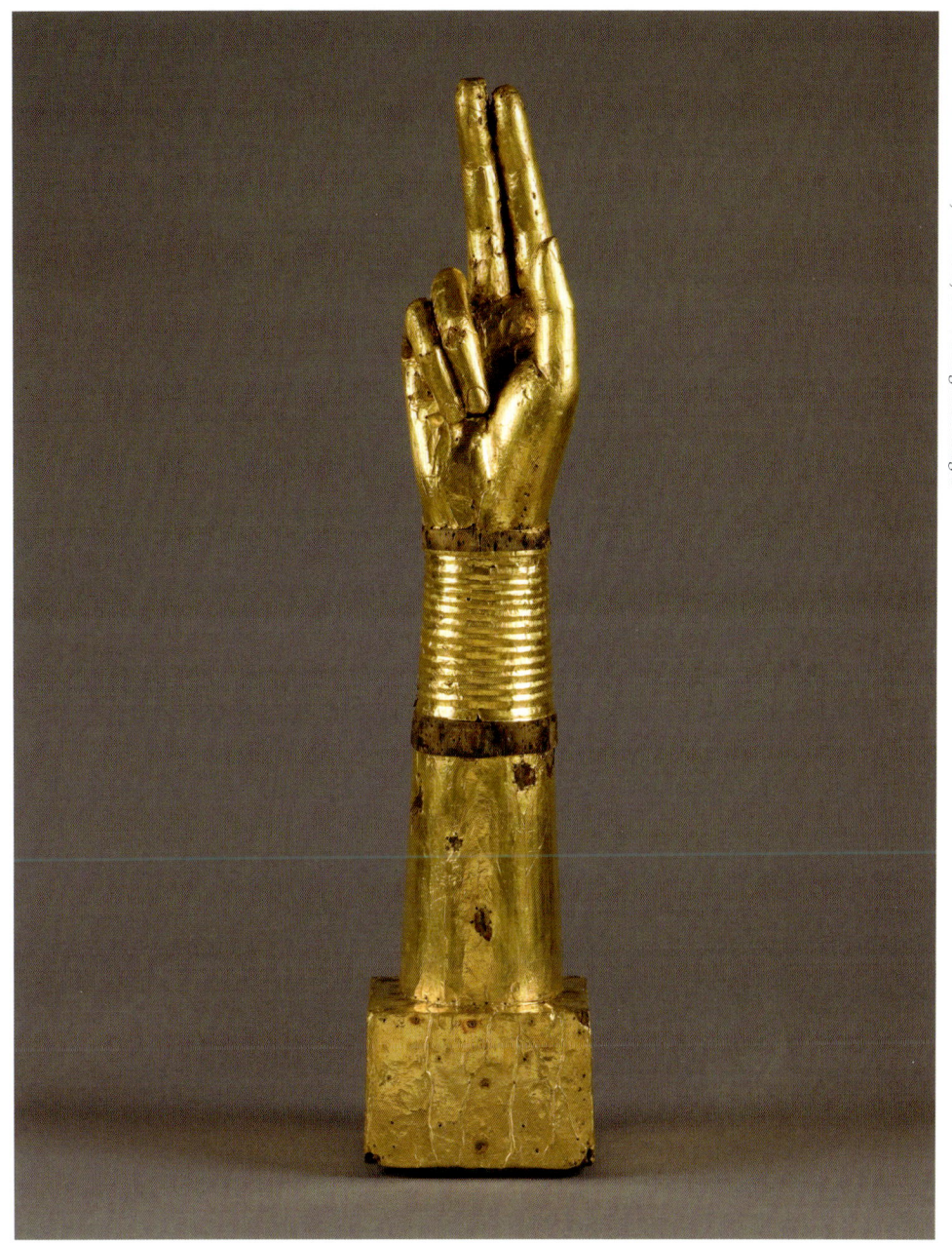

Saint Louis Art Museum, Missouri, USA / Bridgeman Images

Left: One of the many impossible plants illustrated in the mysterious – and probably fraudulent – 15th century Voynich Manuscript. [Chapter 4]

Above: Arm reliquaries, like this 11th century example from France, might contain any relic of the saint, and not necessarily bones from their arm: cast in the dynamic form of an arm raised in blessing, such reliquaries vividly symbolised the benign presence and power to heal and bless of the saint or saints whose relics were enshrined within. [Chapters 11 & 12]

Mike Dixon

The late 15th century figure of King Henry VI on the south aisle screen at Barton Turf in the Norfolk Broads, though painted in an unsubtle 'folk' idiom, reflects the standard iconography of the royal 'saint' – crowned, clean-shaven, ermine robed and carrying orb and sceptre. [Chapter 14]

The alabaster images of John De la Pole, Duke of Suffolk (d. 1491) and his wife Elizabeth Plantagenet (d. 1503), sister of Edward IV and Richard III, once highly coloured, dominate the chancel at Wingfield and back on to the De la Pole chantry chapel of the Holy Trinity (now the vestry), serving both as a reminder of the family's greatness, and a call to prayer for the repose of their souls. [Chapter 17]

The power of Mary's prayers: this 15th century Nottingham alabaster [Chapter 20] shows the Archangel Michael weighing souls. Demons seek to load the scales against the soul undergoing judgement, to drag it down to hell: the Virgin Mary, sheltering another suppliant beneath her mantle, lays her rosary on the scales, tipping the balance in favour of the sinner being weighed – a vivid illustration of medieval confidence in the power of her intercession, as in the final words of the Hail Mary – 'pray for us sinners, now, and at the hour of our death'. [Chapter 16]

Roundel 8 of the late 12th century Guthlac Roll depicts Guthlac at the gates of hell, being given a scourge to curb the demons by his patron saint, Bartholomew. The seventeen illustrations on the Roll were perhaps designs for stained glass roundels illustrating Saint Guthlac's legend in the shrine church. [Chapter 18]

Representations of wealthy parishioner John Baymunt or Baymonde (d. 1485) and his wife Agnes kneel before St Ambrose and St Jerome on the doors of the rood screen at Foxley in Norfolk, which they had paid for. The Latin inscriptions on the white banderoles appeal for prayers for their souls, while the depictions of the Four Latin Doctors – Pope, Cardinal, Archbishop and Bishop – present a strong image of ecclesiastical hierarchy. [Chapter 19]

This panel, now in the German National Museum, is one of Cranach's many schematic representations of the contrast between Law and Grace, proclaiming the Lutheran gospel of the centrality of faith in Christ's Cross as the only means of salvation: such images established an iconography taken up by other reformation artists, like Hans Holbein the Younger. [Chapter 21] German National Museum

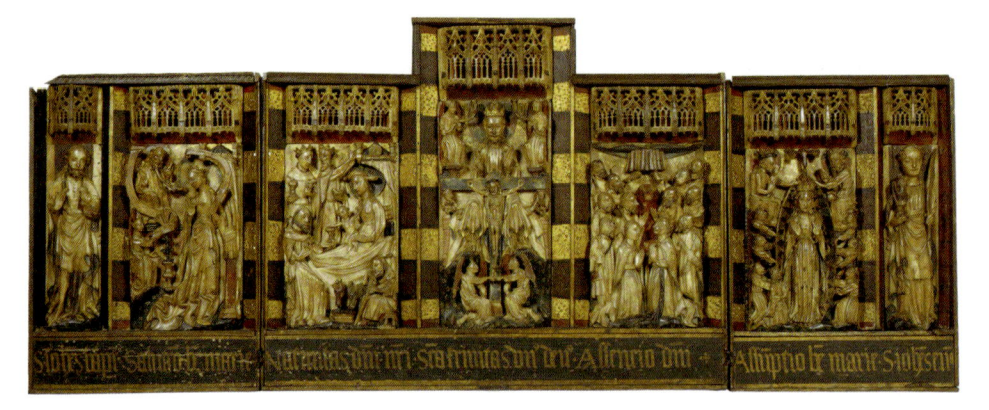

The late 15th century 'Swansea Altarpiece' has four panels depicting the 'Joys of the Virgin' (Annunciation, Adoration of the Magi, Ascension of Christ and Assumption of the Virgin) flanking the central image of the Trinity, in which Father and Holy Spirit support Christ on the cross. Thousands such altarpieces were smashed by English reformation iconoclasts, but Nottingham alabaster altarpieces had been a major pre-Reformation export, and many, like this one, survived in Catholic Europe. [Chapter 20]

He hurlyd owt hor ydols and hade hym in sayntes [43]

– that it seems impossible that the poet had Lollardy in view. Moreover, the only character in the poem rebuked for theological presumption is neither an 'urban secularist' of the type targeted in Canon Arcoid's *Miracula*,[44] nor an anticlerical Lollard, but the dean of St Paul's, whose pompous, finger-wagging exposition of the seven-day archival search for the meaning of the discovery of the coffin is slapped down by Erkenwald with a contrasting reference to the power of God, who

lettes hit hym ful litell to louse *wyt a fynger*
That all the hondes under heuen halde myght never.[45]

(it is little trouble to him to loose with a finger/ that which all the hands held under heaven could never do)

It has been argued persuasively that though the poem avoids direct use of the miracles and legends of St Erkenwald, it depends in fact for many of its effects on the audience's prior familiarity with them. The hearers of the poem knew who Erkenwald was and were familiar with his legend and miracles.[46] By 1401 there was an Erkenwald guild operating in the cathedral: elsewhere such guilds had saints' legends in verse read aloud to them at their feasts, and *St Erkenwald* is just about the right length for reading aloud on such an occasion.[47] We know nothing of the composition of the Erkenwald guild, except that it had its own chaplain, but it seems likely enough that it was made up of prominent city laity, including perhaps lawyers, a similar constituency to that catered for by the cathedral's Jesus guild later in the century. Such a group would of course be familiar with the Erkenwald legend, while the demands of a guild entertainment, with the challenge to bring to the annual celebration of the patron saint something fresh, would account for the composition of a poem saturated with allusions to the legend and liturgy of the patron saint, yet in which the central incident is a piece of pious adaptation. On all these scores, the cathedral's Erkenwald guild thus seems a plausible audience for the poem. The fact that the poem is written in a dialect of Middle English, and survives in a single manuscript, both of which associate the poem with the north-west of England, is a difficulty for this supposition, but does not by any means rule it out. Whoever wrote the poem was well acquainted with London and St Paul's, and makes 'insistent and expert reference' to the city. London and London's patron saint are integral to the poem, and the city is therefore more than a mere *mise en scène*.[48] There were hundreds of Cheshire gentry, yeomen and soldiers in the London of Richard II, and though specifically Cheshire names don't occur in the surviving membership lists of the guild, the guild did have many members from the Midlands and further afield, and a Cheshire-born priest-poet might well have been commissioned to write for it.[49]

However that may be, the debate with the New Pelagians, or speculation about the fate of the righteous pagan, might seem arcane matters for the pious entertainment of the London laity. In fact, the religious thrust of the poem is not so very remote from one of the main pastoral preoccupations of the fifteenth-century English Church, and one which once again would have had a direct appeal to guild members, whose shared functions involved participation in the obsequies of fellow members of the guild. It has not, I think, been remarked upon that the central episode of the poem is, among other things, a deathbed encounter between a priest and a penitent, and there are other aspects of the poem which evoke fairly directly the literary and religious conventions of deathbed and burial. The horrifying collapse of the judge's corpse at the end of the poem, for example, 'rotton as the rottok that rises in powdere', is more than a little reminiscent of the violent relish of decay and the dismissal of any pomp or funeral vanity around the testator's 'stinking carrion', which characterized the wills of K. B. MacFarlane's 'Lollard knights', but which have since been shown to have been by no means confined to the heterodox.[50]

More importantly, the conversation between the judge and the bishop in *Erkenwald* is, for all its miraculous character, a deathbed scene, in which a man poised between life and death is quizzed by a priest about his hope of salvation. In its essentials, that encounter was one which had pressing existential interest for every man and woman in late medieval England, and the handbooks of the early fifteenth-century Church provided quite explicit pastoral guidance about what the priest was to ask at this final moment – guidance which rapidly moved outside clerical circles to become a staple of the deathbed literature circulating among literate laypeople. At the centre of these deathbed scrutinies was an insistence that the dying person should renounce all reliance on their own works or merits, and place all their hope in the passion of Christ. According to one such fifteenth-century text, circulating widely from the second quarter of the century, the priest was to hold up the crucifix, and to ask the dying person if they believed in God, Father, Son and Holy Ghost. The quizzing went on,

> Leuyst thou that thou ne no man may be sauyd but through hys passioun and his mercy?
> [R] Ye...
> Therfore meddle thi thought with his passioun, and wrappe the as in a cloth yn his mercy, and trust stedfastliche ther-inne

> (Do you believe that no one may be saved but through his Passion and his mercy
> [R] Yes.
> Therefore fill your thoughts with his Passion, and wrap yourself in his mercy as in a cloth, and trust steadfastly therein.)

The dying person was to be encouraged to pray that

> I knowleche that i may not helpe my-selfe ne ayeyn-bugge me with my dedys; but stedfastliche i truste in thi passioun...I trust not to my dedys, but i despise to trusten in hem...[51]

> (I acknowledge that I cannot help myself nor ransom myself by my own works, but steadfastly I trust in thy passion ... I trust not in my works, but I despise to trust in them...)

The theological convictions embodied in these deathbed scrutinies came to shape a good deal of the lay piety focused on the *bona mors*, the good death, and they would certainly have been familiar to the elite laity of the city. They are prominent, for example, in the late fifteenth-century will of the successful Suffolk lawyer, Roger Townsend:

> First and principally I bequeth my soule and commend hit to allmyghty god my maker and the redemer of me and of all mankynde in the most humble wise that I canne besechyng him for the merytes of his bitter and gloriouse passion to have mercy oon me and to take me into his mercy which is above all works ... of the wych numbre of contrite synners I mekely and humbly besechith him that I may be oon and come of the number predestinate to be found. . .[52]

The same pattern is built into the structure of *St Erkenwald*: the bishop opens his questioning of the 'corce' with an evocation of Christ on his cross, and proceeds to demand from him an account of his soul's state, as every curate at every deathbed was required to do:

> Sythen Jesus has juggit today his joy to be schewyd,
> Be thou bone to his bode, I bydde in hys behalve,
> As he was bende on a beme quen he his blode schadde,
> As thou most wyterly and hit wele leuen,
> Ansuare here to my sawe, concele no treuthe![53]

To an audience schooled in such concerns, the judge's lament in *St Erkenwald* that

> I was non of the nombre that thou with noy boghtes
> With the blode of thi body vpon the blo rod

would have been no exotic abstraction about the righteous pagan, but a powerful literary expression of some of their own deepest anxieties, and the mode of his salvation, reliance on the blood of Christ and not his own merits, was the ending they hoped for themselves.

14

The Cult of 'St' Henry VI

Some time during the night of 21 May 1471, King Henry VI was done to death in the Tower of London, on the orders of Edward IV, who had usurped his throne.[1] The precise manner of Henry's death, just hours after Edward's triumphal entry into London after his defeat of Henry's queen at the battle of Tewkesbury, at which Henry's son and heir Prince Edward had been killed, is not known: on some accounts the king was bludgeoned to death, on others, stabbed: in the 1530s, the popular shrine of the Virgin at Caversham in Berkshire claimed to possess the 'holy dager that kylled kyng Henry', venerated there as a relic.[2]

Venerated, because within a matter of months of Henry's death, news had spread that heaven had shown that he was a saint. Miracles had begun to happen at his tomb, and pilgrims had begun to make their way there, in search of help and healing. Anxious to bury Henry's memory as well as his body, Edward IV had had his corpse displayed in an open coffin at St Paul's to establish that he really was dead. Inevitably it was rumoured that the body had bled, a sign of both his murder and his innocence. Edward then had him taken by night, without ceremony or royal honours, to the obscure abbey of Chertsey on the Thames, where he was privately buried. That decision was rapidly to transform Chertsey from one of the least distinguished monasteries in England into the centre of the fastest-growing saint's cult on the eve of the English Reformation.[3]

At first sight, this popular canonization of 'good King Harry' might seem baffling. The son of Henry V, arguably England's greatest king, Henry VI had equally arguably been England's feeblest king, his chaotic reign troubled by civil war, usurpation and his own recurrent bouts of madness. A subfusc king notably lacking in the essential royal virtue of magnificence, deposed by Edward in the 1460s, he had spent five years as a prisoner in the Tower, had been briefly restored in 1470, only to be deposed once more and murdered the following year. Alive, he had aroused little enthusiasm among his subjects: when during his brief restoration in 1470 he was paraded through the streets of London to elicit the loyalty of the city, his shambling figure, clad in a shabby blue velvet gown and cap, had not impressed. Paradoxically, this public display of the figure of a king, humbly dressed like a commoner, would burn itself into the popular memory of him, and would later become an important element in his cult. So how and why did Henry acquire a reputation for sanctity so soon after his death?

The nub of the matter, of course, is that Henry was a murdered king. There was a long tradition in medieval Christendom of veneration for the figure of the suffering leader, the innocent or just ruler struck down and in some sense bearing the sins and sufferings of his people.[4] In England even harsh and vindictive figures like Edward II had benefited from this tendency to venerate the ruler victim, and he too had been briefly venerated as a saint after his murder, as had other political victim figures, such as Edward's opponent Thomas Plantagenet, Earl of Lancaster, executed for treason in 1322, or Archbishop Richard Scrope, executed in 1405.[5] Henry VI was certainly a more plausible candidate for sanctity than many such figures. A gentle, pious soul, he was simple in manner, charitable, approachable. He had repeatedly forgiven his political enemies, even those who had planned his overthrow and murder, and his pious benefactions to the Church, in the form of his collegiate foundations at Eton and King's College Cambridge, established his credentials as a Christian ruler, careful for the souls as well as the bodies of his people.

Behind the figure of the innocent and righteous murdered king, of course, stands the figure of Christ himself, and the very circumstances which had made Henry a failure as a king emphasized his resemblance to Christ. His misfortunes – exile, defeat, public humiliation, imprisonment and, finally, his murder – became a sort of passion, all the more intense for being inflicted on the highest and noblest in the land. The deposed and murdered king's life of protracted suffering made him seem to the men and women of the late fifteenth century a sympathetic and empathic figure, who could be trusted to understand and have compassion on the sufferings of others.[6]

These aspects of Henry's personal sanctity feature large in the memoir of the king produced ten years or so after his death by the Carthusian John Blacman, formerly precentor of Eton College and Warden of King's Hall, Cambridge, who had known the king well during his time at Eton, often celebrating masses at which the king had acted as server.[7] Blacman had abandoned an academic career to enter the Charterhouse, and was a collector of books on contemplative spirituality. His portrait of the king turns him into an icon of the devout layman, but also explores the positive spiritual dimension of Henry's apparent failings as a king. His lamentable weaknesses as a ruler, for Blacman, were mirror images of his great virtues as a Christian. So he stressed Henry's intense concern for justice, his personal piety, his chastity and detestation of all lewd behaviour, his disdain for earthly riches and power, his humility and patience when 'he patiently endured hunger, thirst, mockings, derisions, abuse and many other hardships, and finally suffered a violent death of the body', his pity and compassion for others, and his forgiveness even of the enemies who had sought his life and his crown. The final chapter of the memoir culminates with a celebration of Henry's supernatural insight, his visions of Christ in the Eucharist and of the Virgin assumed into heaven, and especially of his foreknowledge of Edward's usurpation and his own murder. According to Blacman a mystical 'audible voice' had warned Henry 'how he should be delivered up by treachery, and brought to London without all honour like a thief or outlaw, and led through the midst of it, and endure many evils devised by the thoughts of wicked men'.[8] The echo of Christ's journey from Gethsemane to Calvary is unmistakable.[9]

Blacman seems to have died before his memoir received its final revision, and it remained unpublished for thirty years. It was almost certainly *not* intended as part of any formal canonization proceedings. But it *was* undoubtedly intended as a contribution to the growing cult of Henry as a saint, and Blacman pointed approvingly to the miracles at Henry's tomb at Chertsey as the clinching evidence that the deposed king had won a heavenly crown:

> his soul, as we piously believe upon the evidence of the long series of miracles done in the place where his body is buried, lives with God in the heavenly places, where after the troubles of this world he rejoices with the just in the eternal contemplation of God and in the stead of this earthly and transitory kingdom, whereof he patiently bore the loss, he now possesses one that endures for ever.[10]

Blacman may well have been writing in the final months of the reign of Edward IV, Henry's murderer, to whom sentiments of this sort were extremely unwelcome. Edward had been alarmed at the cult springing up around the deposed and murdered king, and had tried to suppress it. Already by 1473, just two years after Henry's death, offerings were being made to an image of the king in York Minster, and the Archbishop of York was mobilized to put a stop to these devotions, on the grounds that they were injurious to King Edward and disrespectful to the Pope, who had not approved the cult. In 1480, an ordinance of the Mercer's Company reminded its members that pilgrimage to Chertsey was forbidden. These attempts at suppression, however, proved futile: the stream of pilgrims continued to grow, and we can trace that growth in the semi-official Latin and English devotions to Henry as a saint which multiplied, and were copied into the prayer books of literate lay-people. Richard III, who succeeded Edward in 1483, was anxious to establish the legitimacy of his own reign by disparaging the evils of his brother's reign.[11] As part of that process of establishing clear blue water between himself and Edward, Richard decided to embrace and promote Henry's cult. In the summer of 1484, therefore, he had the king's body exhumed and removed from Chertsey to Windsor, where, with supreme irony, the martyr-king was enshrined in the choir of St George's Chapel, only a few feet across the chapel from the tomb of his murderer.

While Henry's body lay at Chertsey, we have only indirect evidence about the nature and extent of his cult. A Latin hymn to Henry written while his body was still at Chertsey celebrates the holy king as 'light of the English' and 'teacher of ecclesiastics', a reference no doubt to his foundations at Eton and Cambridge, and goes on to celebrate his lamb-like patience under suffering

Mitis ut Agnus patiens
Fuisti in Christo confidens
Mira diversa faciens   *brutis et hominis*

(You were meek as a suffering Lamb
Placing your trust in Christ
Performing various wonders,   for men and beasts)

And then the hymn provides an itemized list of the kinds of miracles happening at Chertsey where Henry lay '*fossus in diliculo*'.

Ave! per quem plures sanantur
Aegroti, caeci illuminantor,
Perigrinantes vero liberantor   *de magno periculo.*

Dementes etiam restiuuntur
Claudi, decrepit gradiuntur,
Paracliti consequuntur   *salutem in vehiculo.*

Ave, revelator carceratorum,
Pestis medicina, spes mestorum,
Maculas pellens desperatorum   *febribus fatigatis*

Resuscitator ter innocentis,
Vermes foeminae habentis
Sedecim purgans esto petentis   *protector in datis*[12]

(Hail, o thou by whom many sick are healed, the blind enlightened, pilgrims freed from great dangers. And also the restorer of the demented, the dumb, the lame, even paralytics who come in vehicles seeking health, hail liberator of captives, healer of the plague, hope of the depressed, and of those hopeless ones with pockmarked skin exhausted by fever. Hail three times reviver of executed innocents, purger of a woman afflicted with sixteen worms, in your goodness be a protector to all who petition you.)

This is a very generalized list, covering the full range of afflictions one might expect at any late medieval healing shrine: and the list of healings in these Latin devotions can be matched at other shrines, for example in Henry Bradshaw's verse accounts of the miracles at St Werburge's shrine in Chester, printed in 1513,

> To the dombe was gyuen / speche and language,
> To blynde theyr syght / to defe theyr herynge,
> To halte and lame people / helthe, in euery aege,
> By deuyne grace / and her ghostly lyuynge.
> The people approchynge / nygh to her in dwellynge,
> By cally[n]ge to her / in the name of Ihesu
> Had theyr petycyon / by her synguler vertu.
>
> Some other that were / fully possessed
> With wycked spyrytes / vexynge the mynde,
> Or with sekenes incurable / myserably greued . . .[13]

Much the same list is provided in Richard Pynson's verse account in 1520 of healings at Walsingham.

> Many seke ben *here* cured by Our Ladyes myghte,
> Dede agayne reuyued, of this is no dought,
> Lame made hole and blynde restored to syghte,
> Maryners vexed with tempest safe to porte brought,
> Defe, wounded and lunatyke that hyder haue sought,

And also lepers *here* recouered haue be
By Oure Ladyes grace of their infyrmyte.

Folke that of fendys haue had acombraunce
And of wicked spyrytes also moche vexacyon
Have here be delyuered from euery such chaunce[14]

But there is a startling specificity about the references in the last verse of the Latin hymn I have quoted: to Henry's resurrection of three innocent victims of miscarriages of justice, after their executions, and the healing of a woman purged from sixteen intestinal worms. These make it clear that the author of the hymn was not merely ticking boxes automatically, providing a round-up of the usual kind of miracles. The particularity of the numbers suggests that the author had access to the register of miracles kept at Chertsey, and he was in all probability a monk there. The Chertsey register has not in fact survived, but, as it happens, the register of miracles later kept at St George's, Windsor contains a detailed account of one of those executed innocents who came first to Chertsey. He was Thomas Fuller, a poor man who took casual work as a sheep-drover to what turned out to be a flock of stolen sheep: arrested with the sheep-stealer who had hired him, Fuller was hanged on Castle Hill in Cambridge. The real thief, however, could read, pleaded benefit of clergy, and escaped execution. When the unfortunate Fuller was turned off the ladder, he called for help to Henry, as he later testified, because he considered the dead king 'the most speedy succour of the oppressed, as the fame of his miracles showed'. He therefore 'commended to him his innocence and the great wrongs he suffered'.

Fuller was left for dead, but his body was cut down and taken down the hill in a cart to the graveyard of the Greyfriars (now the garden of Sidney Sussex College). There he revived, and claimed that Henry and the Virgin Mary had appeared during his execution and had supported his feet to save him. In due course, he made his way to the king's shrine at Chertsey, and testified to the monks there about the miracle. After the removal of Henry's body to Windsor,

Fuller went again on pilgrimage to the new shrine, to ensure the miracle would not be forgotten: Fuller was duly depicted kneeling with the halter round his neck before the image of the king in the official shrine poster.[15]

It's clear from Fuller's testimony that word of the miracles happening at Chertsey had become very widespread, and that Henry's reputation as a heavenly patron included a sense that he had a special care for the oppressed. That was what had led Fuller to make a direct link between his own innocent sufferings and those of the holy king, and to appeal to Henry for help. Similarly, another of Henry's supplicants, the priest William Edwardes, vicar of Hollington in Sussex, healed in 1488 from wounds inflicted on his eyes and tongue by hostile parishioners, appealed to the holy king as *'piissimo oppressorum suggragatori'*, 'most merciful helper of the oppressed'.[16]

There is an obvious appropriateness in these appeals to a murdered king by victims of legal miscarriage or oppressive acts of violence. A king's duties included the protection of the weak and the administration of true justice, and this was all the more fitting in a king who had himself been the victim of violence and injustice. But the majority of favours received at Henry's shrine were the standard late medieval aid in affliction which might be found at any healing shrine, the sorts of things listed in the Latin hymn we considered earlier, which might range from the cure of the fever to the purgation of a woman afflicted with tapeworms.

From 1484 we have a very clear picture of the range of miracles attributed to Henry's intercession, because the Canons of St George's kept a detailed register. Between 1484 and 1500 they recorded almost 400 miracles, some in brief and generalized entries, others in meticulous detail, giving the names, dates and places at which favours were received. This information was gathered at the shrine from the grateful pilgrims who came to give thanks at Windsor. Though there were some healings at the shrine itself, most of the alleged miracles took place in the beneficiaries' home towns or villages, usually in response to the afflicted person's promise to go to Windsor if they were healed. This promise was often sealed in the customary way, by bending a silver coin and promising to donate it to the shrine in due course. These miracle records were kept in English, sometimes recording the beneficiaries' own words. Under Henry VII, however, an official campaign was launched to have Henry VI canonized, and between 1497 and 1500 the Dean of Windsor, John Morgan, had a selection of 138 miracles, occurring in thirty-four English counties, translated into Latin, to form the basis for the official process at Rome. The sole surviving manuscript of this Latin text has annotations in the margins, which show that it was a working document of the canonization process, used as the basis for a formal investigation of just over half the alleged miracles, many of which had occurred twenty or thirty years earlier, of which in the end twenty-three were judged to be certainly genuine. Most of the alleged miracles were concentrated in the south and west, which might suggest that the king's cult was strongest there, but this apparent geographic bias may simply reflect the fact that it was easier for pilgrims to make their way to Windsor from the southern counties of England. There are recorded miracles from as far afield as Staffordshire, Cheshire, Lancashire, Westmorland and Durham. Interestingly, even though, as we have seen, there was a cult of Henry VI in York Minster in the 1470s, the collection includes no miracle stories from Yorkshire. This may well mean that Yorkshire recipients of Henry's favours didn't go to Windsor to give thanks, but instead went to a more accessible shrine in the Minster, from which no records survive. Unsurprisingly, with the single exception of a healing in the cathedral city of Durham, only miracles from the south of England were investigated by the canonization commission.[17]

These reports of miracles from thirty-four different counties, however, make it clear that by 1500 Henry's cult had become genuinely national in scope. Royal patronage had a lot to do with this, first from Richard III and the translation of the king's relics to Windsor, and then the even more enthusiastic support of Henry VII and his mother Lady Margaret Beaufort. Henry VII's wife, Elizabeth of York, daughter of Henry's murderer, was devoted to the shrine. Equally clearly, 'Good King Henry' exerted a strong popular appeal, even without this exalted encouragement. More than 400 pilgrim badges depicting Henry VI survive, a stupendous number, eclipsing those from all other English shrines except Canterbury, and Becket's shrine had of course been a centre of pilgrimage for four centuries, compared with the mere sixty-five years of Henry's cult from its beginnings in 1471 till Henry VIII's suppression of all pilgrimage in the 1530s.[18] Surviving images of the king, or documentary records of the existence of such images once upon a time, bear out the wide spread of devotion to the holy king. We know of altars and images of the king at which offerings were made in the 1490s at Alnwick parish church in Northumberland, in Durham Cathedral, York Minster, Ripon Minster, at Bradford and Terrington in Yorkshire, and in a scattering of churches in Lincolnshire, Northamptonshire and Worcestershire. The bridge chapel at Bridgnorth in Shropshire was a shrine to Henry where his coat was preserved as a relic, and there were altars and images dedicated to him in Hereford Cathedral and St Alban's Abbey. Images of 'Good King Harry' were very numerous in Kent and in East Anglia, and in Norfolk, in particular, a number survive to this day.[19]

Most of these surviving images are panel paintings on rood screens, and they survived because after the Reformation they were covered with whitewash. Carved statues of the holy king were certainly once numerous, but only three are known to have survived the Reformation, and none of them are undamaged. Images on rood screens are a very special kind of image: unlike statues, they were not the object of cult. They decorated the dado or lower part of the screen which divided the chancel from the nave in parish churches. The images on the lower part of the screen were not venerated; nobody lit candles in front of them or made offerings in their honour. Candles and lamps did burn in front of the carved images of Christ crucified, and Mary and John at the top of the rood screen, but the saints lower down were intended as pious decoration rather than the focus of veneration in their own right: that was normally reserved for free-standing statues, or single-panel paintings of saints placed as the reredos of altars. Nevertheless, the surviving East Anglian paintings of Saint Henry give us a clear sense of what the many statues which did receive lights and offerings must once have looked like. Though there is a fair amount of variety in detail, the overall pattern is carefully stereotyped. Henry is portrayed always as an unbearded and young king, crowned in an ermine robe and carrying orb and sceptre – sometimes a book replaces the orb, which might be a reference to his piety, or to his educational foundations at Eton and Cambridge.

At Barton Turf, in the Norfolk Broads, he appears as part of a set of four holy kings, the others being Ss. Olaf of Norway, Edmund the Martyr, of Bury, and Edward the Confessor.[20] He is paired again with St Edmund on the screen at Ludham, painted in 1493, and there and at Eye in Suffolk, his robe is blue.[21] All these images testify in a general way to the spreading awareness of the cult of King Henry in the last decade of the fifteenth century. They don't necessarily tell us much about whether Norfolk or Suffolk people went on pilgrimage to Windsor, and it should be noticed that most of the Norfolk images of Henry occur as parts of sets. The screen at Ludham has matched pairs of saints – holy doctors or theologians, holy virgins, holy kings, and so on – and at Barton Turf Henry appears as part of a set of four. It would be possible, therefore, to see the occurrence of his image in these places as almost accidental, part of a job lot of saints bought out of a painting workshop's pattern-book.

The representation of King Henry at Gateley in Norfolk, however, can't be treated in that way. The images on the screen in this small church, painted in or after 1485, are a mixed lot. On the north screen there are four panels, two depicting Mary and her cousin Elizabeth in the biblical scene of the Visitation, and two depicting female pilgrimage saints, St Etheldreda of Ely and the mysterious nun saint 'Puella Redybone', to whom a number of East Anglian testators left money in wills. On the south screen, two of the four panels depict two of the Four Latin Doctors, St Gregory and St Augustine. On the other two, are Henry and Master John Schorne.[22] Schorne was a fourteenth-century Buckinghamshire rector (North Marston), venerated as a healer after his death, and reputed to heal both the ague and gout. One of his boots was preserved at his shrine in North Marston for sufferers from gout to put their foot into, and he was normally depicted driving the Devil out of a boot by blessing it : his grave became a very popular pilgrimage site. Master John, however, was also to end up at Windsor. In 1478 the Dean and Chapter of St George's, who owned the advowson of North Marston, confiscated the body of this uncanonized priest-saint, and transferred the relics to Windsor. They were almost certainly acting at the instigation of King Edward IV, with the object of enhancing the religious attractions of the new Chapel Royal by transferring to it an established and popular saint's cult. The transfer of Henry's body there a few years later would complete this equipping of the Chapel Royal with miraculous attractions.[23]

The presence of both these unofficial Windsor saints on a screen painted soon after the translation of both sets of relics to Windsor must surely mean that the donor had been to Windsor on pilgrimage. It's even possible that commissioning these two images of Windsor saints may have been intended as a thanksgiving for favours received at the shrines there, though the presence of St Etheldreda and Puella Redybone on the other half of the screen may suggest that the donor was simply keen on pilgrimage in general. There are similar assemblies of pilgrimage saints on other Norfolk screens, notably North Burlingham, which has saints from half a dozen East Anglian and national shrines.[24]

The similarity of all these Norfolk images to the surviving statues of the king, and to the figure of the king in the official poster commissioned by the Dean and Chapter of Windsor, indicates that the painters were working within the limits of an established iconography, derived almost certainly from the main image of the king at his shrine, on which presumably the shrine poster is modelled.[25] This replication of a conventional or stereotyped image was important for any saint's cult. It enabled the saint's clients to identify images of the saint in the churches they visited, and in some cases to recognize the saint when he came to grant them a miraculous favour. The images of holy King Henry, however, raised especially difficult issues of iconography and recognition. In his images, Henry has no special saint's attribute – he is simply a king, in crown, ermine robe, carrying orb and sceptre. In the poster the Dean and Chapter of Windsor commissioned of Henry, presumably modelled on the shrine image, and in some other representations, a heraldic horned hart at his feet provides more specific identification.

But there is no dagger or club as the instrument of his martyrdom, and no miraculous attribute to parallel St Edmund King and martyr's arrow, or St Edward the Confessor's pilgrim ring. The regal figure of King Henry in these statues and paintings, therefore, relates only to his kingly status, and not to the distinctive emphasis in his cult on his meekness under unjust maltreatment, or his humility and lack of regard for worldly status and power. Yet those attributes do in fact form part of the popular perception of Saint Henry. I mentioned earlier that Henry's shabby appearance in a blue velvet robe when he paraded through London in 1470 had not impressed at the time, but it had subsequently entered popular folklore about him. John Blacman claimed in his memoir that Henry in his humility customarily wore round-toed boots and shoes like a farmer, and a long townsman's robe rather than richly decorated royal robes.[26] In several of the miracle accounts gathered at Windsor, that blue velvet robe reappears. In the record of the resurrection of Richard Beys, an innocent man hanged at Salisbury in 1488, the king appeared on the scaffold and put his hand between Bey's throat and the rope. According to the Latin account, 'He appeared even as he used to be, tall in body, his face full, his head covered with grey hairs ... he was dressed royally, a coat of blue velvet upon him, in which guise his appearance has been reported by many.' Beys could recognize his heavenly benefactor not only because he had called on him, but because the king appeared recognizably 'as he used to be', dressed 'as has been reported by many'.[27]

The role of images in establishing this recognizable set of signs is even clearer in the case of the healing of Henry Walter, a mariner in Richard III's navy who had a hole blown through his body by a cannonball: the wound was so large the food he ate was visible in the hole. Unsurprisingly, the wound festered, and Walter's shipmates, unable to cope with the stench, towed him behind their ship in a rowboat, where he lay at death's door for fifteen days. Eventually, he was healed by a double apparition of King Henry and St Erasmus, patron saint of sailors and of stomach and bowel ailments. Henry, had fifteen days' growth of stubble on his chin, presumably an act of solidarity with Walter's fifteen days' ordeal in the boat, and the king was dressed like a pilgrim in a blue velvet gown. He was also wearing a yellow cap: this may well be an allusion to the shrine at Windsor, where Henry's cap was placed on the head of pilgrims suffering from headaches. Walters claimed to have recognized Henry 'by his features'. He recognized St Erasmus because, as he said, he appeared 'as he is often represented in churches as being tortured by his executioners'. This was having his bowels wound out on a windlass, a form of suffering exactly appropriate to Walter's cannonball wound. Miraculously surviving gruesome surgery, Walter went to Windsor, and his wax *ex-voto*, a naked statuette of himself complete with circular cannonball hole in the stomach, is plainly visible in the Windsor print.[28]

Notice in this story the importance of the representations of saints in the churches, which enable Walter to identify his benefactors – Henry by his features, Erasmus by the manner of his torture. But clearly also oral tradition about Henry's appearance and his humility in dress plays a part in the story. The blue velvet gown may lie behind the fact that Henry's ermine robe is blue at Ludham and at Eye, but otherwise his statues and painted images reflect his royal status rather than his humility. But quite evidently there is in these miracle accounts a complex interplay between the king's story – how he was known to have been – and his visual representations – how he was depicted in the churches. The statues and paintings multiplying in early Tudor churches explicitly encoded Henry's royal status, but did not contain symbols of his leading characteristic as a holy man, his meekness and humility. Nevertheless, the images may well have served to evoke for the Tudor devotee those aspects of Henry's saintly persona as well, for the association of royal status and humility was evident in the iconography of another cult, which was expanding at much the same time as Henry's: the local East Anglian cult of St Walstan of Bawburgh.

The cult of Walstan was a largely local one, popular in early sixteenth-century Norfolk and Suffolk, with some outposts in Essex and the east Midlands. Walstan is a largely fictional Saxon saint. According to his legend, he was born in Blythburgh in Suffolk, a king's son: however, he renounced his royal status, and journeyed to Norfolk where he was unknown, and where he became a reaper. Walstan worked all his life as a labourer in total obedience to his master, in absolute humility and poverty. Going barefoot, he gave all he earned to the poor. But all his work is blessed, and his employers, at first exasperated by his eccentric asceticism, come to recognize his holiness and offer to make him their adopted son and heir: he accepts instead the gift of a single cow, which eventually bears two calves, destined to draw Walstan's funeral cart. After a recognition scene in which his royal status is revealed, Walstan dies an edifying death in the fields, first asking for the Sacraments from the parish priest, and making his will, like a good parishioner. His body is drawn away by the unguided oxen, and wells spring up where they pause for rest. Eventually arriving at Bawburgh, the oxen finally halt and Walstan is buried. The Bishop of Norwich canonizes him.[29]

Walstan's clientele were drawn mostly from East Anglian farming people, but his legend incorporated the fairy-tale themes of the prince in disguise, and of the rich and powerful one who renounces all for a life of humble service among the poor. Walstan's images, like those of Henry, were multiplying in early Tudor East Anglia, and they bear a striking resemblance to those of King Henry – Walstan also appears ermine-robed and crowned. In place of or as well as a sceptre he carries a scythe, and he is depicted barefoot: in some images, the two oxen who drew his funeral cart sit at his feet.[30]

The image of Walstan at Ludham has a particular relevance in the context of the cult of St Henry. I mentioned that the images on that screen are grouped in paired sets. At Ludham, Henry VI appears on the north screen, Walstan on the south. There are six saints on each screen, and the paired sets work inwards from left and right towards the chancel doors in the centre of the screen. So St Mary Magdalene and St Stephen the Deacon on the north match St Appolonia and St Lawrence the deacon on the south; then come St Edmund King and Martyr and St Henry on the north, and St Walstan and St Edward the Confessor on the south. The final pairings are St Augustine and St Ambrose on the north, St Jerome and St Gregory on the south, making the complete Four Latin Doctors. Walstan and Edward the Confessor, therefore, are paired with Henry and St Edmund of Bury. All four are pilgrimage saints popular with East Anglian people in the 1490s, when the screen was painted, and each pair is clearly seen as matching the other. Edmund and Edward are long-established icons of royal sanctity: they stand together behind Richard II on the Wilton Diptych: clearly for the parishioners of Ludham, Walstan and Henry made an equally natural pairing, Walstan's mythical royal humility and renunciation in some way corresponding to the actual story of the deposed King Henry, who, like Walstan, had hidden his status by dressing like a farmer.[31]

One should not build elaborate theories on a single piece of evidence, but the parallels in East Anglian devotion between the cult of these two humble royal saints is intriguing. As we shall see in chapter 15, Walstan's legend survives in a Latin prose form, but some time early in the reign of Henry VIII a verse life was produced which recited the legend of his life, related how his shrine came to be at Bawburgh, and gave an account of the miracles worked for pilgrims there. That verse legend was copied on to a pinnacled parchment triptych displayed for the information of pilgrims beside Walstan's shrine at Bawburgh: it survives in a seventeenth-century copy made from the triptych.[32] We don't know whether it was ever printed, but it resembles very closely a series of versified saints' lives and shrine legends produced between 1515 and 1520 by the London printer Richard Pynson, to promote a series of regional shrines – Walsingham, the Holy Blood of Hailes in Gloucester, and the shrine of Joseph of Arimathea at Glastonbury. It seems likely that the Walstan legend was produced by Pynson or in imitation of Pynson, early in the reign of Henry VIIII, and was designed to harness the latest advertising techniques to promote pilgrimage to the shrine at Bawburgh.

No comparable verse legend was produced to promote the cult of Henry VI, but it is interesting that it is at just this time that the Latin memoir by John Blacman was printed by Richard Copeland.[33] Printed saints' lives were in the air. In 1516, Caxton's successor Wynkyn de Worde had published in Latin a series of saints' lives, the *Nova Legenda Angliae* attributed to John Capgrave, providing legends for popular English saints omitted from the standard medieval hagiographical collection, the *Golden Legend*.[34] In the same year, Richard Pynson published a shortened English translation, so there was obviously a market.[35] The *Nova Legenda* is therefore a sort of rough guide to the saints popular in the first years of Henry VIII's reign. In addition to native English saints like Osmund of Salisbury, Hugh of Lincoln or John of Bridlington, the collection included some foreign saints like Erasmus or Brigid of Sweden whose cults were popular in England. Neither Henry nor Walstan were included, but it was almost certainly the publication of the *Nova Legenda*, and perhaps also the English verse legends which Pynson began producing in 1515, which suggested either to Copeland or to the Canons of Windsor that they might usefully print a life of Henry to encourage pilgrims to come to his shrine.

But the days of that shrine were numbered. With the death of Henry VII and his mother Margaret Beaufort, royal enthusiasm for Henry VI's canonization waned: the last approach to Rome on the subject was in 1507, and the projected transfer of Henry's relics to the new chapel in Westminster Abbey which Henry VII had built for them never took place. By the time Blacman's memoir of good king Harry appeared sometime in the 1520s, bad king Harry was already becoming fidgety about his Spanish wife's waning attractions and inability to produce a live male heir. By 1527 his eye had alighted on the saucy, Frenchified lady-in-waiting Anne Boleyn. Within seven years more, the idea of sacred kingship would have taken a radically different direction from the humble holy folly of Henry VI. The royal supremacy would assert itself subject to no limits or controls. The figure of brute royal power would displace the figure of the king who had submitted to his persecutors meekly as a lamb led to slaughter.

15

The Dynamics of Pilgrimage in the Late Middle Ages

In 1986 work to strengthen the south-east tower pier in Worcester Cathedral uncovered a shallow late medieval grave. It contained the skeleton of a stocky man who had died in his sixties, still clad in a lined woollen tunic and thigh-length walking boots. By his side was a stout metal-shod wooden staff, once painted bright red, and a pierced cockleshell, the conventional sign of a late medieval pilgrim.[1] The whole burial and not just the shell was clearly self-consciously symbolic: the expensive walking boots had been almost new when they were slit along their lengths to dress the corpse; the metal double-spike which shod the staff showed little sign of wear. The state of the skeleton's knee and hip joints, by contrast, suggested a man who had walked long and far, and archaeologists concluded that the boots, staff and shell represented a deliberate evocation of one or more pilgrimages that had retained deep significance for the dead man and those who buried him.

The symbolic language here is plain. Death itself is being presented as the last long pilgrimage, the culmination of the Christian life conceived as a journey away from the familiar towards the divine. Such symbolism had its biblical sources in Abraham's abandonment of his homeland at the command of God, in Israel's journeyings in the wilderness, in the biblical idealization of the holy city of Jerusalem, and in Christ's homeless wandering with nowhere to lay his head. All this was evoked in the liturgy of death itself – *Proficiscere anima Christiane, de hoc mundo* (Go forth Christian soul, go from this world), and in the very name given to the dying Christian's last communion – *viaticum*, journey-money.

Understandably, this is the set of resonances and associations that have found most favour in modern discussion of the symbolic meaning of late medieval pilgrimage, and that in fact were to survive the practice of pilgrimage in England to re-emerge as a literary metaphor in the hands of writers like Bunyan. The work of the social anthropologist Victor Turner in particular has encouraged historians to think of pilgrimage as a 'liminal' phenomenon: a religious rite that temporarily liberates pilgrims from the constraints and boundaries of the familiar by removing them physically and socially from their normal environments, across geographical and social thresholds, and that thereby creates a new and wider *communitas* in which social class, wealth and a convention give way to a wider common identity and equality. As Patrick Geary has written:

> Christians have gone out into the wilderness, that is they have left their familiar locales, their normal social positions and their accustomed activities in favour of the ambiguous, ill-defined liminality of the pilgrim in order to seek a variety of persons and things. For some, the life of the pilgrim itself was the goal: as the Christian is a stranger and a wanderer in this world until he reaches the heavenly kingdom of the next. . .[2]

Or, as the *Pilgrimage of the Lyfe of the Manhood* expressed it, 'alle, as seith Seynt Paul, be thei riche, be thei poore, be thei wise other fooles, be thei kynges other queens, alle thei ben pilgrimes.'[3]

Yet all this raises questions for the historian aware that the single most important energy in late medieval English religious practice was its drive towards localism. The defining institutions of fifteenth- and early sixteenth-century Christianity in England were the parish and the guild, and the English laity lavished their devotion and their excess wealth in the construction of local religious identities in the elaborate reconstruction and furnishing of their parish churches. There is, of course, no contradiction here: no religion is monovocal, and every religious system holds a range of often divergent energies in creative tension. So medieval people inhabited both their localities and a wider world. But they were not schizophrenic, and we need an account of the popularity of pilgrimage that brings it into some sort of intelligible relation with this drive towards the local.

In this chapter I do not want to challenge the value of the rich and suggestive notion of 'liminality' as a tool in teasing out the meaning of medieval pilgrimage in general: I do want to suggest, however, that there are crucial aspects of late medieval pilgrimage that the notion obscures rather than illuminates.[4] For many medieval Christians, going on pilgrimage was, it seems to me, not so much like launching on a journey to the ends of the earth, as of going to a local market town to sell or buy geese or chickens. Shrines were features by which medieval people mapped the familiar, as much as signposts to other worlds and other social realities. The shrine, and the journey to the shrine, might be a local as much as or more than a liminal phenomenon.

There were, of course, national shrines like Walsingham or Canterbury drawing visitors in their thousands from all over England, and a steady stream of English men and women made their way even further afield to Rocamadour and Compostela, Jerusalem and Rome. But most fifteenth-century pilgrimages were to sacred sites within one's own region: journeys that might take one no further than the next parish, and rarely further than the nearest market town.[5] When John Baylis of Rolvenden's wife went to her own parish church on Relic Sunday 1511 to gain the annual indulgence for venerating the parish's relics, she described herself as going on 'pilgrimage at the relics'. She applied the metaphor of journeying to her stroll to the parish church, recalling that 'the parson declarid and said for every foote that a man or a woman sett to the reliques he shal have great pardone.' Nevertheless, it makes very little sense to try to force Mistress Baylis's steps towards her parish church into a model emphasizing a perilous and disorienting venture into the unknown. It is this perception that I shall try to explore in this chapter, which will focus on the phenomenon of local pilgrimage.

The first thing to grasp about late medieval pilgrim centres is that they were legion, and that most of them were localized or regional in their appeal. Pressure of space means that I can look at just one such shrine, the pilgrimage to the East Anglian local saint St Walstan, whom we have already met in a previous chapter. His cult is unmentioned in any surviving liturgical book or calendar, and was initially confined, like so many of these popular cults, to the immediate hinterland of the saint's burial place at Bawburgh. Till the end of the fifteenth century none of the standard collections of *vitae* of British saints has any mention of Walstan. By 1516, however, Walstan's cult had become sufficiently important for a fairly full legend to be included in Wynkyn de Worde's printed edition of John Capgrave's *Nova Legenda Anglie*. This had thirteen new lives of saints not included in any of the manuscript versions, half of whom can be associated more or less directly with new or newly flourishing cults: a couple with fifteenth-century English canonisations – John of Bridlington and Osmund of Salisbury – the rest with popular English shrines, like that of Joseph of Arimathea at Glastonbury, or St William of Rochester, or the East Anglian shrine of the True Cross at Bromholm, with which I think the life of St Helena should be associated. The life of St Walstan falls into this cluster of shrine legends.[6] To recapitulate the account in the previous chapter, its outline is as follows.

Walstan is a Saxon prince, son of Benedict and Blida, born in 'the southern part of Great Britain'. At the age of twelve he renounces his right to royal succession, and with his parents' reluctant agreement leaves home, travelling north to Taverham in Norfolk, where he settles to a life of virtuous labour and poverty, working on the land as a paid man and giving away his food and even his shoes to the poor. His mistress, angered by such ostentatious goodness, spitefully sends him barefoot into the woods to load a cart with thorns and thistles, but Walstan is unharmed, and his mistress is converted by this miracle. His childless lord and lady offer to make him their son and heir: he refuses.

After a life of virtuous toil, Walstan is eventually warned by an angel of his imminent death – he dutifully seeks *viaticum* and anointing. On the Saturday before his death he throws his scythe away at the hour of noon, since work done after this hour profanes the Sabbath. Walstan duly dies while at work in the meadow on the following Monday, first asking that any labourer who comes to his shrine driven by any necessity may receive help and healing, and that his intercession will also be accepted for ailing farm animals. His body is taken in an ox cart to Bawburgh for burial: en route the oxen stop twice and where they stop miraculous wells spring up. The legend concludes by emphasizing the saint's chastity, self-mortification and charity to the poor, and his humility in renouncing royal authority to bind himself to 'simple rural people'. The reader is assured that Walstan's power is effective even for men and beasts who have actually lost organs, such as their eyes or genitals: he is declared to have died on 30 May 1016.

Two distinct elements seem to be combined in this Latin *vita*. At one level is the story of an aristocratic youth who renounces wealth and security to take up a life of self-denial and labour, whose life is attended both by persecution and by miraculous signs of divine favour, and who becomes an intercessor for farm labourers and sick animals – what André Vauchez calls 'a saint of charity and labour'. Overlaying these elements is a lightly priggish and decidedly clericalist picture of a pious and obedient parishioner anxious to make a good ending in devout penitence, concerned about Sabbath observance and the evil of servile work in the fields carried out on a Sunday.

The legend of St Walstan survives, however, in another greatly expanded form, which was printed in 1917 by M. R. James.[7] The original source was a pinnacled triptych panel made of wainscotting about 3 feet high, and covered with a verse legend written on parchment, formerly in Bawburgh Church. It is clear from internal evidence that it had hung near the shrine for the information and edification of pilgrims.

This Walstan verse legend is written in a rather spavined Rhyme Royal, made up of seven decasyllabic lines rhymed *ababbcc*. This was an established verse form for saints' lives, with a particular East Anglian pedigree established by Lydgate and others. The language of the Walstan legend suggests that it was written around the turn of the fifteenth and sixteenth centuries, and as it happens the first decades of the Tudor century saw a spate of such verse legends, most of them appearing under the auspices of the publisher Richard Pynson.[8]

Several of these early Tudor legends were clearly commissioned to promote pilgrimage to particular shrines, a fact which itself throws an interesting light on the management of pilgrimage in late medieval England, and the adaptation of new technologies to promote it. The legends all follow a common pattern, first narrating the story of the shrine's foundation or the life of the saint, then going on to give details of miracles performed there and encouraging the reader or hearer to come and test the power of the place for themselves. Pynson's legend of the Holy Blood of Hailes falls in this category,[9] as does his legend of Walsingham, published in the late 1490s and perhaps the most likely direct model for the Walstan poem,[10] and the Glastonbury legend of Joseph of Arimathea.[11]

The Walstan shrine legend is a thoroughly clericalized production. It begins with an elaborate theological reflection on the mystery of predestination.

> Almightie God in his eternall majestie
> disposing all things by his providence
> some he chooseth, some reproved be
> Scripture holy testifieth in sentence;
> Jacob elect was, Esau rejected by his power immense
> ye apostle called, not all chosen, I wys,
> some to damnation and some to eternal bliss.

The poem follows the basic pattern of the Latin *vita*, but incidental detail is elaborated – the harsh mistress is not only pierced with compunction on seeing Walstan's miracles, but also physically torn with the thorns she had hoped would pierce the saint; the theme of Walstan as a figure promoting fertility, hinted at in the *vita,* is spelled out in the verse legend. Holy Walstan

> goth forth to semination.
> The angell above his head by multiplication
> Corn in his seedlepe make to increase.

The poem also greatly elaborates the theme of Walstan's royal birth, and the account of Walstan's life closes with the arrival of the bishop of Norwich for the funeral: the people tell him of the dead man's miracles; the result is an official local canonization:

> The Bishop layd ear and harkened soore
> And allowed him a saint for ever more.

The second half of the poem is devoted to an account of eleven miracles performed at the shrine. They are a pretty standard set: a manacled lunatic restored to sanity, the cure of a woman wounded by an arrow, a priest with a perforated hernia restored by bathing in the holy water placed on the tomb, a drowned man raised to life after his body was laid before the shrine – and so on. Most of these miracles are local – four in Bawburgh itself, three for people from villages within a 10-mile radius. The only remote cure is that of a Canterbury weaver who had vainly gone to Becket's shrine on crutches and, on the advice of a Norfolk man whom he met there, had sought instead St Walstan, who succeeded where Becket had failed. But Sir Gregory Lovell, an identifiable person healed of 'bone ache' who died in 1507,[12] lived 30 miles from the shrine, and there is a miracle for labourers in the Flegge, 25 miles the other side of Norwich. The legend summarises many miracles

> done in this place
> of Men also women, wch to him will sue . . .
> Good folks cease not, devoutly seeke and pray
> yee shall be succoured and comforted ere yee gang away.

The author provides a prayer to Walstan to be recited even

> though ye be unlearned nor can read nor spell,

and the poem ends with another polysyllabic theological meditation on God's power and love:

> Omnipotent God and nature doth werke
> neither frustratory nor vainly, but to an end,
> as the Philosopher wch is called a Clerke
> testifieth ready is to defend;
> and yet could not the first cause perfectly comprehend
> which is the will of God and create all things,
> but stood and abideth in himself musing.

Even more than in the Latin *vita*, two divergent energies are evident in the Walstan verse legend. On the one hand there is the fairy-tale story of the secret prince, the king's son who makes himself humblest of the humble, and whose touch brings renewal, fruitfulness and healing. But this is framed within a theological grid in which a nervous desire to provide official episcopal credentials for the saint's status is in evidence, in which marvellous tales of atrocious wounds healed and the dead raised are topped and tailed by abstract meditation on the sovereignty of God. And as in the *vita*, the picture of the wonder-working prince is overlaid by the virtues of a good Tudor parishioner, elaborately respectful of a strict sabbatarianism, conscientiously performing the corporal works of mercy, seeking the last sacraments from his parish priest as death approaches. A popular saint's life has been pressed into a moralizing clerical mould and, more than that, the piety of pilgrimage is clearly being assimilated to the localized parochial piety that was the heart of late medieval religion.[13]

It seems clear that Walstan's cult was gathering momentum in the later fifteenth century. Badges of Edward IV on the nave roof at Bawburgh suggest that the body of the church was rebuilt in the 1460s or 1470s, and in 1460 Thomas Easthawe, a former vicar, left

20 shillings to the building of St Walstan's chapel. By the early 1470s parishioners were leaving bequests to this chapel; by 1496 there was a Walstan guild, which over the next decade was itself the recipient of small bequests ranging from 1 to 12 shillings, and the shrine had joined the list of local and national shrines – Walsingham, Woolpit, Master John Schorne and King Henry – to which routine mortuary benefactions might be left.[14]

The shrine was clearly booming by this stage. The Norfolk antiquary Francis Blomefield claimed that there were six chantry priests working at St Walstan's altar, a figure he seems to have plucked from the air.[15] But chantry chaplains there certainly were, and by the end of the fifteenth century the parochial incumbent was routinely a graduate, a sign of the prosperity that pilgrimage had brought to the parish. By the early years of the sixteenth century local clergy and lay people regularly bequeathed their souls not merely to God and the company of heaven, but in particular to St Walstan.

This evident growth of devotion and of devotional infrastructure in the parish was reflected in the appearance of devotional imagery further afield. Traces of nine images of Walstan appear on Norfolk screens, the best of them at Sparham, at Barnham Broom, at Ludham, at Litcham All Saints, and at Burlingham Saint Andrews. On several of these screens Walstan keeps company with other East Anglian pilgrimage saints, suggesting the location of his cult within a generally vigorous interest in the shrines of the region and beyond – at Ludham with St Edmund of Bury but also Henry VI, at Litcham with St Edmund, St William of Norwich and (probably) St Etheldreda of Ely.[16] St Etheldreda occurs again at Beeston, and both St Etheldreda and St Withburge of East Dereham at Burlingham St Andrews and at Barnham Broom: in both these cases St Withburge holds her shrine church in her hand.[17] The Burlingham screen also carries images of Edward the Confessor and Thomas Becket. The earliest datable of these images is the one at Ludham, painted in the mid-1490s or soon after; Litcham and Sparham probably date from about the same time; the screen at Barnham Broom probably dates from the second decade of the sixteenth century; while the latest is certainly that at Burlingham St Andrews, completed in 1536 after the break with Rome.[18] The geographical scatter of these images, contrary to my own earlier impressions, suggests a thriving cult of Walstan well outside the immediate area of his burial place, borne out by the statement of the East Anglian Protestant polemicist, John Bale, who declared that Walstan was 'after the maner of Priapus the God of theyr fieldes in Northfolke and gyde of theyr harvests, al mowers and scythe folowers sekyng hym once in the Yeare'.[19] Outside the county, there is a wall painting of Walstan with clients, which I have not seen, at Cavenham in Suffolk; he is carved on the hammerbeam roof at Earl Stonham, painted on the screen at Foxearth, Essex, and there was a chapel dedicated to him in St Mary's, Bury St Edmunds.[20]

I have dwelt at length on the cult of Walstan because it provides a comparatively full case study of one of late medieval England's myriad local shrines. But many, perhaps most, of these local shrines were centred not on a body, as at Bawburgh, but on an image, and it was the multiplication of images in the later Middle Ages that made possible the multiplication of shrines.[21] Image shrines could, of course, loom just as large and serve the same function as grave shrines: Rocamadour and Walsingham were image shrines. Below these great international image shrines were thousands of lesser images that themselves attracted local loyalty. The good rood of the North Door of St Paul's, or the Rood of Boxley, were matched by hundreds of lesser roods, niched or tabernacled above side altars in country churches – like the 'Good Rood upon the northseyde' of Blythburgh Church to which John Brown left 40 shillings in 1533 'to make hym a new cote', or the good rood on the north side of Bramfield Church whose decorated niche is still visible.[22] The cluster of shrines to which the early fifteenth-century Alice Cooke of Horstead declared 'I will have a man to go ... pilgremages' – Our Lady of Reepham, St Spirit of Elsing, St Parnell of Stratton, St Leonard without Norwich, St Wandred of Byskeley, St Margaret of Horstead, Our Lady of Pity of Horstead, St John's head at Trimingham, and the Holy Rood of Crostwight – were all local image shrines, some of them known only from this single mention.[23] All over late medieval England the local shrines of the Virgin were based on images, some of which achieved a regional status that put them on a par with more famous shrines.

Our Lady of Woolpit in Suffolk was an image in a chapel on the north side of Woolpit Church.[24] By the early thirteenth century the offerings of pilgrims were significant enough for Bury Abbey to demand a share: by 1286 a fair had sprung up, held on the main pilgrimage day, 8 September, the feast day of the Nativity of the Virgin. By the fifteenth century local people were lavishing gifts on the shrine, like the diamond ring bequeathed by Dame Elizabeth Andrews of Baylham in 1473, one of a pair, the other of which went to Our Lady of Walsingham, or the 'pair of beads of thrice sixty garnished with silver and three gold rings set thereto, with a cross and heart of silver' offered to the shrine by Robert Reydon of Creeting in 1505, on condition that they remained always round the neck of the image of Our Lady of Woolpit. From the 1450s to the late 1520s local wills from many of the surrounding villages and towns – Thorndon, Thurston, Otley, Gislingham, Wetheringsett, Kelsale, Fornham – make arrangements for pilgrimages on behalf of the dead to Our Lady of Woolpit, and the shrine had clearly become a focus of regional identity. Lord John Howard of Stoke-by-Nayland, future Duke of Norfolk, made several benefactions of money, lights and silver-gilt votive images to our Lady of Woolpit in the early 1480s, and Woolpit was one of the five East Anglian shrines (alongside our Lady of Walsingham, Ipswich, Sudbury and Stoke by Clare) to which Queen Elizabeth sent a pilgrim to pray for her in Lent 1502. As all this suggests, local shrines certainly helped focus and express the regional sensibility of lay elites. In the same year that Queen Elizabeth's pilgrims toured their shrines, the prosperous Norfolk grazier William Atereth commissioned a painting of St Helena for his parish church of Cawston: she is depicted holding the reliquary of the True Cross from the East Anglian shrine of Bromholm.[25] Twenty years or so earlier a replica of a pilgrimage souvenir card from Bromholm, containing an indulgenced hymn and prayers to the Cross, like the one pasted into the Lewkener Hours at Lambeth, was carefully bound into an East Anglian Book of Hours which shows other signs of a self-conscious interest in local shrines, such as St Edmund's at Bury. The devotions of the shrine were thus transplanted into the daily piety of the book's owner.[26]

Shrines might help define and sustain the boundaries of regional identity in other ways. In 1499 a group of parishioners from the village of Great Ashfield, 4 miles from Woolpit, were found guilty of magical practices. They were required to perform public penance not only in their parish church, but also at Norwich Cathedral, Bury St Edmunds' marketplace, and during the procession at the shrine of Our Lady of Woolpit, where they were required to offer candles to the image of St Mary in the chapel.[27] The shrine and its liturgy were therefore felt to provide a suitable and conspicuous regional forum for the exemplary punishment of religious deviants. Other shrines were used in this way throughout the late Middle Ages. In 1411 the bishop of Salisbury required the rector of Ramsbury, convicted of fornication, to make a pilgrimage to Salisbury to offer a pound of wax to the image of the Virgin.[28] In 1486 the bishop of Hereford required a group of parishioners from Bosbury who had attacked a local cleric to make a pilgrimage to the shrine of St Thomas Cantilupe in Hereford Cathedral.[29]

Salisbury is 25 miles from Ramsbury, Hereford is 15 miles from Bosbury: the penitential elements of distance, inconvenience and expense were clearly part of the point of these pilgrimages of reparation. But once again the notion of 'liminality' does not seem an altogether helpful analytical tool. These penitential pilgrimages were indeed part of the process by which deviants might be restored to the wider *communitas* of the Church. In many cases, however, and certainly that of the magicians of Great Ashfield, the penitents were sent to their regional shrines not to lose or submerge their individuality in a wider *communitas,* but precisely so that their specific misdemeanours might the better be made excruciatingly public. Their pilgrimage was designed to endorse and enforce rather than to dissolve the values of the local community.

In any case, the distance these reluctant pilgrims were obliged to travel mattered not because it sent them on a journey beyond the familiar, but because it put them to trouble. Pilgrimage was a labour, an arduous and expensive work – the Kentish Lollard John Franke considered that 'pilgrimages to holy and devoute places be not necessary nor meritorious for mannys soule, but that money and labor doon and spent therabout is all in vain.'[30] This emphasis on 'doing', 'labouring' and 'spending' was not the isolated perception of heretics. Testators making provision for surrogate pilgrimages to be undertaken on their behalf as a form of post-mortem intercession stipulated payments to those making the pilgrimages 'for their labours'.[31]

Provisions for these surrogate pilgrimages were extremely common, and they illustrate further the problematic character of the concept of liminality as a tool for interpreting late medieval local pilgrimage. The devotee who pays someone else to go on pilgrimage is clearly happy to dispense with the symbolic value of journeying, of abandoning the safe and familiar things of home, in favour of a transaction in which a transferable benefit is secured. The point of the pilgrimage is not the journeying but the pardon it secures, and the pilgrimage is simply one means among many of gaining a desired spiritual benefit. Even the pilgrimage to Rome might be viewed in this way. Thomas Herynge of Walsingham left money in 1504 so that 'as sone as my executor may know that any troste man that is a preste of this cuntre have any eryn to Rome, that he shall gyve unto him a certeyn money, to synge for my soule and for the soules of my good benefactors, v massys at Rome, at such places as moste mede is at'.[32] The priest here, we note, is to be chosen because he already has an errand at Rome. What Herynge wants is masses at powerfully privileged altars, for which the journey itself has no apparent significance. Even pilgrimage literature might present the benefits of pilgrimage in this resolutely sedentary and unadventurous way. William Brewyn's guide to the Roman pilgrimage, listing the indulgences available at the Lateran, made the conventional comment that 'if people only knew how great are the indulgences of the Lateran church, they would not think it necessary to go across the sea to the Holy Sepulchre.'[33]

The role of indulgences as a motive for pilgrimage in late medieval England hardly needs demonstration. The whole pilgrim-literature genre represented by *The Stacyons of Rome* turned on it – all such books were essentially trainspotter's guides to the best and most powerful relics and indulgences.[34] One of the spiritual privileges Christ granted Margery Kempe when she desired to go again to Jerusalem was a dispensation from the *need* to travel: 'Dowtyr, as oftyn-tymes as thu seyst or thynkyst "Worshepyed be alle tho holy placys in Ierusalem that Crist suffyrde bitter peyn and passyon in," thu schalt have the same pardon as gyf thu wer wyth thi bodily persens bothyn to thi-self & to alle tho that thu wylt gevyn it to.'[35] The same eagerness for indulgences motivated local pilgrimage. The episcopal registers of Edmund Lacy provide dozens of examples of indulgences granted to local chapels, hospitals and churches to help defray the costs of building or repair work: donors wanting the indulgence had to go to the parish in question '*devote causa perigrinacionis*', penitent, confessed and contrite, and make an offering.[36] 'Gostly helth'[37] rather than physical healing was the object of such pilgrimages (which perhaps formed the majority of pilgrimages in fifteenth- and sixteenth-century England). In them, pilgrims were primarily interested in the spiritual benefits of an indulgence, and the consequent reduction of time spent by the devotee in purgatory after death.

The association with indulgences was an important aspect of the integration of pilgrimage into the soteriology of late medieval Christianity, in which grace and obligation were finely balanced. The arrangements made by Henry VII's queen Elizabeth of York for pilgrimages to be made on her behalf in Lent 1502 to shrines all over the country have often been cited, and I have already mentioned them here. It is not usually noted, however, that the payments to the two pilgrims concerned are for exactly forty days' journeying in total – a *lent* of pilgrimages, carried out during Lent of that year, and a very clear signal of the assimilation of pilgrimage to other forms of penitential observance.[38]

The same processes of assimilation are evident in the management of vows of pilgrimage. Pilgrimages might be taken as the result of pure devotion, or as the consequence of a vow. Vows of pilgrimage were by and large treated very seriously, and promises of pilgrimage to the major shrines of Rome, Compostela and Jerusalem could be dispensed only by the pope himself.[39] Pilgrimage vows might be undertaken as an act of devotion to a saint or to secure help or healing in emergency. When the ship in which the Norfolk priest Sir Richard Torkyngton was travelling back from the Holy Land was caught in a January storm, the crew and passengers pledged themselves to pilgrimage, 'sum of us pylgrymages to or blyssed lady of Lorett in Ytalya, and sum to or Lady of Walsyngham and sum to Seynt Thomas of Caunterbury we that war Englyshmen'. The captain of the ship clinched all these vows by taking a collection to offer at the shrine of the three kings of Cologne, patron saints of travellers.[40] Vows of this sort had to be fulfilled one way or another, and if sickness or circumstances prevented it, then it had to be done by proxy. William Couper of Stone in Oxney asked his executors in 1517 to make provision for someone to perform four pilgrimages 'undone in my life'.[41] Agnes Parker of Keswick in Norfolk told her executors in 1507 that 'I owe a pilgrimage to Canterbury; another to St Tebbald of Hobbies, and another to St Albert of Cringleford.'[42] Margaret East, widow of the parish of St Martin in the Bailey, made arrangements for her executor, her 'right trusty and well beloved cosyn Thomas Thurkell, shoemake in Berstrete', to go on her behalf:

> steyn [certain] pylgremage, that is to scy, in my lyf to the holy St Wandrede, and after my dissease he xall go unto Seynt Thomas of Canterbury, and there to prey for me to release me of my vowe which I made thyrdyr myself. And from thens the same Thomas sall go for me on pylgrymage unto the Abbey of Chelkey [Chertsey] then as Kyng Henry lyth, yf my goodys wyll stretch so fer for his costs. And so be hys pylgrimages that I may be relesyd of myn avowes.[43]

The argument of this chapter has been a modest and simple one. Much of the most interesting recent work on late medieval religion has emphasized the central place of the local in it, and we have become intensely aware of the importance of community and community-formation in the religious priorities of the late medieval laity. Much recent discussion of pilgrimage, by contrast, has emphasized the solvent and 'liminal' character of the practice of pilgrimage, and its power to remove Christians from their local contexts and integrate them into a wider and more anonymous *communitas*. I have argued that in practice late medieval pilgrimage tended to be assimilated to the locality and to community-formation in the narrower and more specific sense. Going on pilgrimage might be a liminal phenomenon only if, and to much the same extent as, going to market was a liminal phenomenon. Pilgrimage *might* take one beyond the familiar, and might dissolve the ties that bound. But we should not be mesmerized by Margery Kempe. Most late medieval pilgrims were consolidating, not dissolving, their social and religious world.

16

'Lady, Pray Thy Son for Me': Prayer to the Virgin in the Late Middle Ages

On 19 January 1511 the young King Henry VIII came to the shrine of the Virgin at Walsingham to give thanks for the birth, three weeks earlier on New Year's Day, 1511, of a son, Henry Prince of Wales. He was the latest and, as it turned out, the last of a long line of English kings to come to the shrine. As he knelt in the Holy House he will have seen, close to the statue of the Virgin, the gilded image of his own father, Henry VII, and the line of royal devotees who came to kneel at the feet of the Virgin and leave their gifts stretched back through Henry VI in the 1440s to Henry III in 1226. Henry VIII would remain a pious client of our Lady of Walsingham for two-thirds of his reign. When the Royal Commissioners came to destroy the shrine twenty-six years on, they would find there a candle still burning which was maintained at the cost of the King, in perpetual intercession for the birth of a son and heir.[1] In fact, Henry's first-born son died just over a month after that first visit, on 22 February 1511. Had he survived, the medieval Holy House at Walsingham would almost certainly still be standing, and the history of England would have been unimaginably different.

Henry's gesture in travelling to give thanks to the Virgin was an absolutely characteristic medieval expression of devotion, for in the late Middle Ages almost anyone who prayed at all, prayed to Mary. Her cult had begun to blossom in England, as everywhere else in Europe, in the twelfth century, and the growth of the fame of the shrine at Walsingham was itself a symptom and expression of her growing centrality in the Christian imagination, a centrality to which painting, architecture, book production, music, all bore testimony. That cult showed itself at every level, not least in the evolution of elaborate Marian liturgy, housed in the Lady chapels added to many of the cathedrals and great churches of England from the late twelfth century onwards.[2] In those often very lavish spaces an increasingly elaborate musical liturgy developed in honour of the Virgin, and the daily Lady mass became in many places the main sung service, requiring teams of singers, musicians and clerks to staff it. In the same way, in many parish and collegiate churches as well as in the cathedrals, by the fifteenth century the daily singing of an evening anthem to the Virgin, generally referred to as the *Salve* (though in fact a range of texts were used), had become a popular focus of lay piety.[3] In late medieval London the wills of shopkeepers and merchants often contain bequests to provide clergy to assist at these musical services, leaving money for singers and lights to beautify them. The *Salve* guild of St Magnus the Martyr, London Bridge, employed chaplains and clerks to sing the Lady Mass and the antiphon to the Blessed Virgin Mary (usually sung each evening, but sometimes after the Lady Mass).[4]

In other churches, the *Salve* and other Marian anthems were sung only on certain weekday evenings – Friday and Saturday being the favourites. And the spread of musical services in honour of the Virgin wasn't confined to cathedrals and city churches. In fifteenth-century North Yorkshire, for example, 'Our Lady Service or Guild' was one of seven such guilds in Topcliffe, and was fairly typical of the 'services' maintained by parishioners in many places to augment the worship of their churches, in this case the votive offices and mass of the Blessed Virgin Mary. The guild chaplain was required not only 'to say masse and to pray for the prosperytie of the parochienns, lyvyng, and for the soules of them departed' but also 'to kepe the queyer with .vj. chyldren all haly and festyvall days; which .vj. chyldren the same incumbent is bounde to teche to syng, and to fynde song bokes for the servyce ther'. In 1522, the

Lincolnshire merchant John Robinson left money to the guild of our Lady in Boston to provide 'two honest priests' skilled both in plainsong and polyphony, to enhance the services of the guild in honour of our Lady.[5]

This elaboration of the services devoted to the Virgin – her Mass, her Offices and her anthems – was perhaps most famously expressed in the foundation of Eton College in 1440, where seventy poor scholars were to be educated and where a team of ten priest fellows, ten chaplains, ten clerks and sixteen choristers would maintain an elaborate round of musical services in honour of the Virgin. Eton rapidly became the centre of a blossoming cult of the Virgin, with a major pilgrimage there on the feast of the Assumption each year (the College organized a fair to coincide with the pilgrimage, which lasted for six days). Two astonishing monuments to this flourishing fifteenth-century cult of the Virgin at Eton survive to this day. One is the remarkable set of wall paintings commissioned for the north wall of the new College Chapel in 1480, painted in the latest Flemish style and depicting the miracles of the Virgin Mary. Miracles of the Virgin had been a popular theme in thirteenth- and fourteenth-century Books of Hours, and a magnificent sculptured cycle of the miracles of the Virgin was the chief decoration of the Lady Chapel at Ely.[6] But by the Tudor period a more scriptural emphasis was fashionable, and when the new windows at Eton's sister foundation at King's College were installed a generation later, they would illustrate the life of the Virgin and of her son Jesus, and not her posthumous miracles. All the same, the Eton miracle cycle was popular and impressive enough to be imitated in the Lady Chapel at Winchester Cathedral round about 1500.[7] The Eton miracle-cycle pictures are among the best surviving paintings of the English late Middle Ages.

But the most precious survival of the cult of the Virgin from Eton is the great choir book compiled between 1490 and 1510. The book, one of only a handful of surviving archives of fifteenth-century English choral music, and far and away the fullest of them, originally contained Mass, office and motet settings in honour of the Virgin by twenty-four different composers. It is now damaged and incomplete (ninety-eight pages or one third of the total are missing), but, even so, it contains nine different settings of the Magnificat for use at Vespers (out of an original fifteen), and it also contained forty motets and votive antiphons in honour of Mary.[8] Those which survive include settings of some of the most famous hymns and anthems in her honour, from the *Salve Regina* to the *Stabat Mater*, as well as settings of other texts immensely popular then but hardly known at all now, like the multiple settings of the anthem *Stella Coeli Extirpavit*, which invokes the virgin as protectress against the plague.[9]

The Eton music and paintings were created for a royal foundation: this was Marian piety for an educational and social elite. But the cult of Mary stretched all the way down the social scale, and the late Middle Ages saw the emergence of the most popular of all devotions to the Virgin, one that is still alive and well today, for the most familiar fifteenth-century prayer to the Virgin is the Rosary. Strings of beads or knots had been used for counting repetitious prayers for centuries, but it wasn't till quite late on in the Middle Ages that the prayer we know as the rosary took its familiar form. Early medieval prayer beads were known as Paternosters and, as that suggests, were used for counting multiple recitations of the Our Father.[10] It was common to repeat prayers in multiples of fifty or 150, in imitation of the monastic recitation of the 150 psalms of the Psalter, and circular strings of beads were sometimes called 'Psalters'. Multiple repetitions of the Hail Mary couldn't happen, of course, till the Hail Mary itself emerged as a separate prayer, and that seems not to have occurred before the twelfth century. Till the late sixteenth century the Hail Mary wasn't in fact a prayer at all, strictly speaking, but a salutation or greeting, consisting of the opening words of the Angel Gabriel to Mary at the Annunciation, and some of the words of Elizabeth to Mary at the Visitation – 'Hail Mary full of grace, the Lord is with thee' and 'Blessed art thou amongst women, and blessed is the fruit of thy womb.' The addition of the name Jesus, and the whole of the second half of the modern Hail Mary – 'Holy Mary Mother of God, pray for us sinners now and at the hour of our death,' wasn't added till the sixteenth century, and didn't become a routine part of the prayer till 1568.[11]

The words of the first half of the Hail Mary, forming the whole of the prayer throughout the later Middle Ages, had, so far as we know, first been brought together in the late sixth century in the offertory anthem for the mass for the fourth Sunday in Advent. They didn't float free as a separate prayer recited by lay people till the emergence in the eleventh century of the set of devotions known as the Little Hours of the Virgin Mary. This was a sort of mini-breviary, arranged like the breviary round the eight monastic Hours of prayer from Matins and Lauds to Vespers and Compline, and drawing on some of the most beautiful psalms in the Psalter. Round these were grouped hymns, prayers and antiphons in honour of the Virgin. Because it was relatively short, and didn't change much with the changing liturgical seasons, the Little Hours became immensely popular with well-to-do, literate lay people, women as much as or even more than men, and by the end of the Middle Ages Books of Hours would be the most popular of all books. [12]

The most often-recurring text throughout the Little Hours was the Angel's greeting, *'Ave Maria, Gratia Plena'*, used as an antiphon to top and tail the psalms, and it seems to have been the prominence given to this salutation in the Hours of the Virgin that set lay people using these words as a staple of daily prayer even when they weren't using the book. Inevitably, people who couldn't read began to use multiples of this short Hail Mary — fifty, 100, 150, in place of the psalms, and naturally the chaplets of psalters of Paternoster beads already in use to count Paternosters and other prayers were now used to count Hail Marys.

In the course of the fourteenth and early fifteenth centuries a lot of different people had the idea of attaching texts, stories or verses relating incidents from the life and passion of Jesus to these prayers, for people to meditate on while they recited the words of the Hail Mary as a sort of mantra. To begin with, in order to use any of these schemes you would have needed a book or sheet of paper in front of you, because there was often a single verse of scripture or a verse of a rhyme or hymn, for every single Hail Mary, so no one could have memorized them all, and of course they would have been no good at all to the majority of the population who were illiterate. But in the 1470s and 1480s Friars of the Dominican Observant Movement (to which Savonarola belonged) anxious to promote a biblical prayer-life among ordinary people, simplified these schemes down to the familiar fifteen joyful, sorrowful and glorious mysteries, and commissioned printed broadsheets, often arranged like chaplets of roses in three groups of five, depicting the mysteries, often without any text at all. These pictures helped make the mysteries easy to remember, and the Rosary now took off as the most popular of all schemes of prayer. Its spread was helped by the establishment of Dominican Rosary confraternities, offering well-publicized indulgences and other spiritual benefits to anyone who joined them.[13]

The Observant Movement was slow to catch on in England, and there isn't much evidence of the spread of Rosary confraternities here. But even so, in England as elsewhere the Rosary was a universal prayer. Everybody, rich or poor, said it, and everybody who was anybody owned a rosary. Rosaries suited all pockets, as well as all spiritual abilities. They might be as simple as ten dried beans on a piece of string, or they might be an elaborate chain strung with coral or amber, ivory or ebony, and images of them are everywhere in representations of late medieval and early Tudor people. Making and selling rosaries became big business, and in fifteenth-century London the workshops of the manufacturers of rosary beads clustered together in the streets to the north and west of St Paul's Cathedral, and street names there still commemorate the trade: Paternoster Row, Ave Maria Lane.[14]

The Hail Mary was of course said in smaller numbers than the ten or fifty of the rosary. Though the Angelus as we have it hadn't yet been invented, the custom was spreading of reciting three Hail Marys in honour of the Incarnation at the ringing of a bell called the Ave Bell, at six o'clock in the morning, at noon, and at nine in the evening. Henry VII's Queen Elizabeth of York petitioned Pope Sixtus IV for an indulgence of 300 days for the recitation of this form of the Angelus, and that papal grant was augmented in 1492 by other local indulgences of forty days for each time of recitation, granted by the Archbishops of Canterbury and York and nine other bishops, showing that repeating Hail Marys was something that royalty and the hierarchy were just as keen to promote as any village priest.[15]

The rosary grew out of the Book of Hours, and became in effect a sort of Book of Hours for those who couldn't read. But in the later Middle Ages more and more people, women included, *could* read, and the use of the Book of Hours was very widespread, especially once printing made such books widely and cheaply available. Books of Hours were scriptural prayer books, focused on the Incarnation, Mary's part in the Incarnation, and all that flowed from the Incarnation. They were also crammed, of course, with non-biblical material – suffrages to and images of the saints, litanies, indulgenced prayers to the wounds of Jesus, to the Blessed Sacrament, as well as to the Virgin Mary.

But overwhelmingly the prayers of the Hours were drawn from the Psalter, and the illustrations in most of those books which had any illustrations at all were predominantly scenes from the Bible, depicting the infancy of Jesus, or the incidents of his Passion. The core of the book was the Little Office of the Virgin, with its constant refrain of '*Ave Maria Gratia Plena*', the greeting of the Angel Gabriel. The hymns and lessons of the Hours returned again and again to the moment at which God took human flesh in the womb of the Virgin at the Annunciation.[16] Like the pictures which often preceded each of the Hours, they formed in effect a prolonged meditation on the mystery of the Incarnation, while the psalms these offices contained included many of the most tender and beautiful prayers of the Psalter – 'I will lift up mine eyes to the Mountains', 'I was glad when I heard them say', 'God be merciful unto us and bless us', 'When the Lord turned again the captivity of Sion'. The Hours also included some of the most beautiful and resonant of Marian prayers – antiphons like the *Salve Regina*, hymns like the exquisite '*Ave Maris Stella*'. These texts would have been familiar to any pious literate person wanting to say their prayers devoutly, and naturally they often provided the words which composers set to music for the *Salve* services which were so popular with lay people. So these prayers to Mary from the Book of Hours inspired some of the most sublime music ever written in England.

The core of Marian devotion in the Book of Hours focused on the Incarnation. But the range of prayers to and about Mary was very wide. Many of the hymns contained in these books celebrated in particular her joys and her sorrows. One of the most popular was the hymn 'Gaude Virgo Mater Christi' –

> Rejoice, O Virgin, Mother of Christ
> Who conceived through the ear
> At Gabriel's announcement
> Rejoice, for filled with the Godhead
> You gave birth without pain.
> With the Lily of purity
> Rejoice, because of him who was born of you
> And whose death you mourned
> The Resurrection shines forth.
> Rejoice at the ascension of Christ,
> Into the heavens while you looked on
> Carried upwards by his own power.
> Rejoice because you ascend there after him
> And that you have there great honour
> In the palace of high heaven.
> Where may it be granted to us
> To enjoy the fruit of your womb
> In unending rejoicing.[17]

These Latin prayers and hymns on Mary's joys were immensely popular: they were frequently set by composers, and lines from them, in Latin, were woven into the English devotional poems and carols which were multiplying throughout the fourteenth and fifteenth centuries. Richard Hill, a London grocer who copied devotional texts into his commonplace book in the early sixteenth century, includes one long devotional poem which is an expanded version of the *Gaude Virgo Mater Christi*: here is the first verse, with an excruciating rhyme for *Gabrielis Nuncio*.

Gaude Maria, Christe's Mother!
Mary mild, of thee I mean:
Thou bare my Lord, thou bare my brother,
Thou bare a lovely child and clean.
Thou stoodest full still without blyn,
When in thy ear that errand was done-so:
Thy gracious God the light within,
Gabrielis nuncio.[18]

The Joys of Mary provided one of the recurrent themes of Marian piety, but her Sorrows were equally central. By the end of the Middle Ages many Books of Hours included the *Stabat Mater*, a poem which dwelt on the tears and heartbreak of the Virgin under the Cross as she watches her son die, in order to evoke from the penitent tears of sorrow for the sins which had crucified him. The *Stabat Mater* is a text constantly set by medieval and early Tudor composers, a sure sign of its wide popularity, and prayers evoking the sorrows of Mary recur again and again in the devotions of the period.[19]

The fifteenth century was captivated by the power of Mary's sorrow, the grief of the mother lamenting her dead child, which rang so many bells with men and women for whom such bereavements were very common. This is the era, in England as elsewhere in Europe, in which the image of the Pietà, Our Lady of Pity, caught the lay religious imagination.[20] Statues of the Pietà appeared in many churches, and in the wills from Kent on the eve of the Reformation, for example, the most popular site requested for burial was in the church, near the statue of the Pietà. Images of the Pietà were often reproduced in prayer books and as separate devotional prints, and poems and prayers evoking Mary's sorrow as she cradles the dead Christ multiplied. We have a vivid eyewitness account of a pious East Anglian housewife's first encounter with the Pietà: Margery Kempe saw one in a Norwich church early in the fifteenth century and

> through the beholding of that pity her mind was all wholly occupied in the Passion of our Lord Jesus Christ and in the compassion of our Lady St Mary, by which she was compelled to cry full loud and weep full sore, as though she should have died. Then came to her a priest, saying, 'Damsel, Jesus is dead long since.' When her crying was ceased, she said to the priest, 'Sir, his death is as fresh to me as though he had died this day, and so I think it ought to be to you, and to all Christian people.'[21]

The Joys and the Sorrows might be prayed together. Books of Hours almost invariably included a long Latin prayer to the Virgin commemorating her Joys and her Sorrows together, which began, '*Obsecro te, Domina sancta Maria Mater Dei.*' It is too long to translate in its entirety here, but it is remarkable in the first place for the beautiful series of titles by which it invokes the Virgin, in effect, a sort of Litany of the Virgin:

> I implore you, holy Lady, Mother of God full of tender love, daughter of the High King, mother most glorious, mother of orphans, consolation of the desolate, right road for those who go astray, health and hope of all who hope in thee. Virgin before childbirth, virgin in childbirth, virgin after childbirth. Fountain of mercy, fountain of health and grace, fountain of tenderness and joy, fountain of consolation and gentleness.

The prayer then goes on to invoke Mary's help through the joy of the Incarnation.

> By that holy and inestimable joy which exalted your spirit in that hour when, through the Archangel Gabriel the Son of God was announced to you and conceived within you. And

'LADY, PRAY THY SON FOR ME'

by the holy and inestimable tender care, grace, mercy, love and humility by which the Son of God descended to take human flesh in your most venerable womb... And by those most holy fifteen joys which you had from Our Lord Jesus Christ.

The prayer then turns to invoke Mary by her sorrows

By that great and holy compassion and most bitter sorrow of heart which you had when Our Lord Jesus Christ was stripped naked before the Cross, and you saw him raised and hanging there, crucified, wounded, thirsting with bitter gall set before him, when you heard him cry out and saw him dying. And by your Son's Five Wounds, and the sorrow you had to see him wounded. And by the fountain of his Blood, and all his passion, and by all the sorrows of your heart, and by the fountains of your tears.[22]

The drift towards the creation of a Marian litany which can be detected in that prayer is present also in some of the pictures illustrating printed books of Hours from the late fifteenth century. Representations of the Virgin surrounded by emblems of the titles given to her in patristic and medieval theology and piety anticipate the titles of the Litany of Loreto. The Parisian publisher François Regnault, who dominated the market for Books of Hours for England in the reign of Henry VIII, regularly included such pictures, which he used on the title page of one of his bestselling lines, and the labels on the emblems make up a litany – Star of the Sea, Tower of David, Mirror without spot, garden enclosed, cedar of Lebanon, Gate of Heaven, and so on.[23] There were similar pictures of the Virgin's mother, St Anne, with the Virgin in her womb, an image encapsulating the doctrine of the Immaculate Conception.

So far I have been emphasizing aspects of late medieval Marian piety which we can readily understand, and which would not seem strange to a modern Roman Catholic or Anglo-Catholic. Marian pilgrimage flourished in late medieval England, most famously at the major English Marian shrine at Walsingham, but also in the many local shrines focused on Marian images like Our Lady of Woolpit which I discussed in Chapter 15. But it is also worth emphasizing that Marian piety might take rather less familiar forms. Prayers to the Virgin might be used in ways which would be likely to disconcert modern devotees. Many of the prayers to the Virgin found in Books of Hours and other devotional collections are prefaced by rubrics attaching not only spectacular indulgences to their use, but often miraculous promises – the devout user will not die a sudden death, or will be protected on their travels, or the Virgin will appear to them on their deathbed to take them to heaven.[24] There is a good example of such a prayer copied into a manuscript Book of Hours now in the Cambridge University Library.[25] The book was produced in the Netherlands for the English market in the early fifteenth century.[26] It was bought by a Suffolk family, and was used in East Anglia for at least two generations. Eventually it was sold or given away, and acquired by a gentry family at Neasden in Middlesex, the Roberts family. They copied many additional prayers into the book, and one of these prayers is an elaborate ten-day devotion which involved the recitation of a thousand Hail Marys. Here is what the book says about it.

> Ye shall say M [a thousand] tyme Ave Maria [Hail Mary] and ye shall sey them in X days, that is every day a hundreth, and ye shall say them standyn and goyng and knelyng or syttynge and ye shall have a certen almys in your hande while ye make your prayer, and after, say thys orison or prayer that followeth.

> O Adonai, Lord, great and wonderful God, who gave the salvation of human kind into the hands of the most glorious Virgin, your Mother Mary: through her womb and merits, and through that most holy body which you took from her, in your goodness hear my prayers and fulfil my desires for [my] good, to the praise and glory of your name. Liberate me from every tribulation and assailant, and from all the snares of my enemies who seek to harm me, and from lying lips and sharpened tongues, and change all my tribulation into rejoicing and gladness. Amen.

And when ye have seide thys orison kysse your almos, and after, geve it to a pore man or woman in honour of that blyssed joy that seynt Gabryel greeted our Lady [with], and for what thyng ye do thys ten days together, without doubt ye shall have that thynge ye pray for lawfully, with Goddes Grace.

Added in English in a later hand (1553):
I used this prayer well ten days, Edmund Roberts *inquit* [*says*].]

Other versions of this 'thousand *Aves*' charm are to be found in a number of surviving fifteenth-century Books of Hours. Like so many of the prayers I've been considering, the charm focuses on the story of the Annunciation, when the Angel Gabriel greeted Mary, the precise moment when Christ took human flesh and became a child in the Virgin's womb. It's a devotion which turned on a mixture of good intentions, multiple repetition, and the giving of money: the devotee is to recite a hundred Hail Marys (the equivalent of two rosaries) every day – the prayers can be recited while the devotee goes about their ordinary business, 'standing, going, kneeling or sitting', but is linked to the late medieval preoccupation with the works of mercy listed by Christ in the Parable of the Sheep and the Goats (Mt. 25) as a means of salvation. The success of the prayer is said to depend on its being accompanied by the relief of the poor, in honour of the Annunciation. But this edifying link is made in a quasi-magical way, which the Church authorities would certainly have condemned – holding money in the hand while the thousand *Aves* are recited, then kissing it before giving it to the poor recipient.

To the thousand *Aves* is added a Latin prayer which emphasizes the centrality in the salvation of mankind of the physical reality of the Incarnation at the Annunciation – Christ is invoked by his Mother's womb and by the flesh he himself took on in that womb. That flesh is declared to protect the user of the prayer especially from their enemies. Prayers against enemies – corporeal and incorporeal – were a very prominent feature of late medieval piety. Characteristically, the English instructions attached to the prayer display some awareness of the precarious line being trod between 'legitimate' prayer and forbidden 'magic': success is guaranteed if the prayer is rightly used (a guarantee theologians rejected as magical), but that guarantee is softened by the reference to praying 'lawfully, with God's grace'. Another version of this charm included in a Book of Hours now in Ushaw College, Durham declares that 'withoutttyn doute ye may noght fayle of that ye pray for and your desire be resonabyll.'

As I hope all this has suggested, prayer to the Virgin in late medieval England was very varied, and appealed to an enormously wide social spectrum. At one end of that spectrum were poor and illiterate people whose devotions perhaps never went much beyond reciting Hail Marys, with or without beads to help them count. At the other, there were the sophisticated glories of the Wilton Diptych,[27] and the exquisite and elaborate webs of music in her honour woven by composers like John Dunstaple, John Browne and William Cornysh.[28] People prayed to Mary using illuminated books worth a king's ransom, or by lighting a candle in front of the statue in their parish church, or by saying five Hail Marys on their fingers. In a religion dominated by men, her cult fostered gentleness and tenderness, and made a place for homely things to which ordinary men and women could relate – for the mysteries of birth and nurture, for hope and for tears. And it was a cult which linked rich and poor: the wealthy might pray from Latin books, but they also prayed on strings of beads; kings came on foot to her shrines; and it was a queen of England who persuaded the Pope to give Englishmen and women an indulgence for praying at the Angelus-bell.

And it was a king, in the end, who called a halt to her cult. The Prior and monks of Walsingham surrendered their priory and the shrine to the Crown in August 1538, and all over England pilgrimages came to an end. For a little while longer Englishmen and women would pray to the Virgin, but the reformers were increasingly hostile to a cult which they thought robbed the Virgin's son of his due honour. With the accession of King Edward VI, even rosary beads would be forbidden, and after the death of Edward's

Catholic sister Mary and a brief Catholic revival, those prohibitions would deepen. The Lady chapels were stripped of their imagery, and became redundant space, the books of music dedicated to her were dismembered and burned or used to wrap butter and cheese. Christianity, for the Protestant English, became a male religion.[29]

On the Eve of the Reformation

17

Provision Against Purgatory: Wingfield College, Suffolk

Wingfield College in north-east Suffolk, 7 miles east of the market town of Diss, was the product of an age of crisis. The foundation of Wingfield in 1362 is poised between the Black Death and the Peasants' Revolt.[1] Between the summer of 1348 and Christmas 1349, the Black Death wiped out anything up to half the population of England, and probably more than half the clergy. A generation on, the Peasants' Revolt of 1381 had its own bloody East Anglian climax in the Battle of North Walsham, when the local bishop, Henry Despenser, famously led his own troops in the slaughter of the rebellious peasantry of his diocese. So one could make a perfectly plausible case for seeing the later fourteenth century in England in general, and in East Anglia in particular, as very much an age of anxiety.

It used to be thought obvious that an event as devastating as the Black Death must have caused profound cultural upheavals and transformations – the art historian Millard Meiss famously argued that the Plague had caused a profound shift and darkening of the themes and iconography of Italian painting in the later fourteenth century.[2] According to the French religious historian Jean Delumeau, 'No civilization had ever attached so much importance to guilt and shame as did the Western world from the thirteenth to the eighteenth centuries.'[3] Delumeau thought that most late medieval people's minds were preoccupied with the fear of sin and its consequences, and he saw the Church as pursuing 'an Evangelism of Fear', which reinforced panic and pessimism about the human condition, a 'vast enterprise of guiltification' which originated in medieval monasteries and spread to the laity through theological writings, sermons, devotional literature, confessors' handbooks and iconography.[4] Delumeau thought that one reason for all this was the pessimism provoked by disasters like the Black Death.

The foundation at Wingfield was quite clearly an expression of dynastic ambition and the family pride of the Wingfields, the Staffords and the de la Poles, a symbol of stability, dynastic continuity, power and permanence. But in this essay I want to consider the religious context of the foundation of institutions like Wingfield, and to ask whether or not we should think of them rather differently, as monuments not to established power and status, but as institutions born out of the uncertainty and fear which Delumeau thought characterized late medieval culture.[5]

You might certainly be forgiven for seeing fear as one of the major motives for the creation of Wingfield, because of course death lay at the bottom of it all. It was a perpetual chantry foundation, and the main business of the nine priests and their master or provost provided for in the foundation charter was to say and sing prayers for the dead in the church which the Wingfields and then the de la Poles rebuilt, as a suitably glorious setting for the celebration of elaborate commemorative liturgies. Architecture, glass and wall painting, carving and music, not to mention the services of educated clergy and musically talented boys, were all directed here to the service of the dead. The urban historian Clive Burgess has described late medieval parish churches as anterooms of purgatory, because so many of them were built, furnished and staffed with money given so that the donors might avoid or at any rate shorten the torments they believed awaited all but the very holy after death, before they could be admitted to the presence of God.[6] And that, of course, was doubly true of a church like the one at Wingfield, which was rebuilt, staffed and furnished specifically as a chantry, a building devoted to the liturgy of the dead, and a very lavish and

PROVISION AGAINST PURGATORY 241

expensive witness to late medieval aristocratic belief in the reality of Purgatory.

So how far should we think of this place as haunted by death, and the fear of what might come after death?

Chantry colleges were one of the more elaborate forms of perpetual chantry, and the fourteenth century in East Anglia was the great age for the foundation of perpetual chantries – we know of 130 of them founded between 1300 and 1399, compared with just thirteen in the thirteenth century, and more than eighty in the fifteenth century. Historians used to link this fourteenth-century surge in the provision of permanent institutions to pray for the dead to the traumatic effect of the Black Death. In theory this seems plausible enough. You might well think that an epidemic that wiped out half the population in a matter of months would leave a permanent scar on the national psyche, as the famine did in nineteenth-century Ireland, and would focus people's thoughts on the reality of death, and give added urgency to beliefs about the afterlife. But if that was the case, there is little surviving evidence of it. In Suffolk as elsewhere in England, there was as much or slightly more provision for the dead in the fifty years before the Black Death as in the fifty years after it, and there was in fact a steep decline in the creation of permanent chantry institutions in the first half of the fifteenth century – exactly the opposite of what you might expect if the Black Death really had traumatized people and left a heightened fear of death, and what came after death. Permanent chantry provision begins to climb again in the second half of the fifteenth century, but so does every other kind of religious expenditure. There was more money about, and people were taking a more active interest in religion, so it looks as if intercession for the dead was just one of the many ways in which fifteenth-century people chose to display their piety and their prosperity: lay people were into devotional retail therapy in a big way in the later fifteenth century.

So counter-intuitively, in terms of chantry provision, the Black Death just doesn't seem to have been any kind of landmark. More than half the 130 fourteenth-century perpetual chantry foundations in the Norwich diocese were created before 1350, and the foundation of chantry colleges in particular was well under way even before the Plague arrived in England.[7] The establishment of Wingfield in 1362 might look superficially like a reaction to the great mortality, but it takes its place in a sequence of East Anglian foundations which straddles the arrival of the Black Death: Rushworth College near Thetford in 1342, Campsey Ash in 1346, Thompson College and Raveningham College in 1349 and 1350, then Wingfield in 1362; the sequence would go on with the establishment of St Gregory's College at Sudbury in 1375, and the relocation of Raveningham College to Mettingham in the early 1390s, and then on into the fifteenth century with the establishment of Mortimer College at Stoke-by-Clare in 1415 – and you find a broadly similar pattern in the more familiar pattern of the creation of colleges with chantry obligations at Cambridge, where the fourteenth-century sequence begins with Michaelhouse in 1324, Clare in 1326, Pembroke in 1347, Gonville Hall in 1348, and Trinity Hall in 1350.

Chantry colleges were a lavish way of providing the kind of mortuary liturgy once available only in monasteries. The Black Death may not have traumatized the national psyche, but it had shown people that an isolated chantry foundation – typically a single priest serving a side altar or chapel in a parish church – was very vulnerable to acts of God: specifically, to large-scale mortality. A lot of single-priest chantry foundations must have disappeared without trace as both their incumbents and the current generation of the families paying for them perished in the plague. So after 1350 a lot of the new chantry foundations were placed by their founders in local monasteries rather than parish churches, to improve their chances of survival in any future epidemic, and a supply of clergy to serve them (though even monastic chantries were more often than not staffed by secular priests).[8] The staffing of Chantry colleges in fact deliberately replicated the resources, and in theory at least the religious and moral standards, of a small monastery – Wingfield was to have up to nine priests living under the surveillance of a master, plus at least three choral scholars, with presumably a pool of other singers available from the other boys who were to be educated here. Music was central to Wingfield as it was in all these colleges. Of course, these intentions weren't always realized: the college at the priory at Campsea Ash established by the Ufford family in 1346 was moved to Bruisyard after ten years because it was felt it interfered with the nuns' choir, but eight years after that its patron, Lionel, Duke of Clarence, suppressed it altogether, because the priests were misbehaving themselves, living dissolute lives and neglecting their duties. Clarence diverted the resources instead to founding a house of Poor Clares, women being more reliable in the morals department, even if they couldn't celebrate mass.

The statutes of Mortimer College at Stoke are pretty representative of the staffing and regime such establishments provided.[9] There were to be eight vicars-choral and two senior clerks sworn to continual residence, and instructed in plainsong and part-song (*in plano cantu et discantu*); five choristers of good life to help in singing and to serve in quire; clergy or choristers absent from Matins, Mass or Evensong were fined. There were to be, in addition, two under-clerks, to act as keepers of the vestments, bell-ringers, lamp-trimmers, door-keepers, clock-winders, etc. The Matins bell was to be rung at 5, High Mass to be finished at 11 a.m. and Evensong at 5 p.m. The Mass of Our Lady was to be sung daily as well as the mass of the day, except when the mass of the day was of the Blessed Virgin, and then the second mass was to be of *Requiem*. Matins and Evensong were to be sung daily immediately after the ringing of the bell, save in Lent, when Evensong of Our Lady was to follow evensong of the day. The dress of the canons and vicars was regulated, and there was to be a schoolmaster to teach the boys reading, plainsong and polyphony. Every evening at eight the curfew bell was to be rung for a sufficient time to admit of walking from the church to the college, and when the bell finished every outer door was to be fastened, and no one of the household of the college, from canon to chorister, was to be outside the house. None of the personnel was to frequent taverns; they were not to hunt, nor were greyhounds or any kind of hunting dogs to be kept within the college, save by the dean, whose dogs were not to exceed four. No canon or minister of the college was to carry arms of any kind within the college. As I've said, there was an elaborate musical regime at all these foundations, so the Wingfield organ is probably a typical part of musical provision in colleges: there are references to the singing of elaborate polyphony at both Rushworth and Mortimer Colleges, and Mettingham not only had polyphonic music at its liturgy, but the canons also copied and sold musical manuscripts, and bought themselves an organ in 1414.

This liturgy was paid for by and intended to benefit the founders and the founder's kin, but of course it was an amenity for the parish within which it was located. Chantry colleges offered a range of additional benefits and amenities to the communities in which they were established, and these cumulatively constituted the incentive for allowing a parish church to be hijacked by a private patron, as Wingfield was. The parishioners gained from enhanced architecture, more elaborate and better-celebrated liturgy, from the charitable provisions and doles which were part of the intercessory regimes in the Colleges, from the guarantee of competent pastoral provision which a clerical community could offer, and from the schools and expert preaching and catechesis colleges provided.

And it was the guarantee of a supply of well-qualified clergy which Bishop Percy of Norwich emphasized when he granted the licence for the establishment of the college at Wingfield – too many parishes, he said, were in the hands of ignorant and mercenary curates, 'hirelings rather than shepherds', so God would greatly reward anyone who 'so increases the resources of his House that the necessities of Christ's family may be better provided for, and their numbers augmented', and therefore, considering 'that in this place the number of minsters of God's worship will be increased' by the College, the bishop granted permission to turn the parish church into a collegiate foundation, with the sacrist of the College as ex-officio parish priest.

Still, the declared purpose of a chantry college was intercession for the souls of the dead. Medieval Catholics believed that most ordinary Christians might be saved, but that few would die in a sufficient state of sanctity to be admitted at once to the beatific vision. All would have to undergo a process of painful purgation. Medieval people imagined Purgatory in a variety of ways, with

PROVISION AGAINST PURGATORY 245

Purgatory variously conceived as punishment or as therapy. In the most famous of all medieval evocations of Purgatory in Dante's *Commedia*, therapy is emphatically the central theme. Purgatory is a mountain rising by terraces towards Paradise: it is guarded by angels and no demons can enter it, and the souls who suffer there are eager participants in their own cleansing. The souls to whom Dante talks often end the conversation by saying they must return to their sufferings because by means of them they are on their way to God. So Dante's Purgatory is a place of hope and renewal: its theme colour is green.

But that, by and large, was *not* how medieval English people imagined it: in almost all the English literature on Purgatory, it is portrayed as a torture-house, a dungeon of ice or fire, or a kind of infernal concentration camp where the guards and torturers are gleeful demons, let loose to do whatever they fancy to the suffering souls. A fair example here is the early fifteenth-century vision attributed to an anonymous holy woman, which she is supposed to have had on 10 August 1422 and the days immediately following.[10] As in all Purgatory visions, the woman talked with one of the suffering souls in Purgatory, a former nun named Margaret. In this vision Purgatory was a pit filled with three great fires, one leading out of the other, the central fire

> so horrible and stynkande that all the creatures in the world might never tell the wicked smellynge thereof: for there was pykke and tarre, ledde and brymstone and oyle and alle manere of thynge that myghte brynne, and alle manere of paynes that mane couthe thynke, and alle manere of crystene mene and womene that hath lefed here in this werlde of what degree thay were.

Those in the horrible fire 'had so grete paynes that for drede I might not describe them', but they included having their hearts and bowels torn out by demons and raked with sharp irons, or being nailed up in barrels full of poisonous snakes. The nun Margaret was covered with bleeding wounds, and out of the wounds poured fire, and when first the visionary encounters her, the suffering soul of Margaret herself seems like a malevolent demon, and the visionary reports that 'me thought sche wolde have casten fyre upon me, and styrte to me to hafe slayen me.' Margaret cries out to the visionary, 'Cursed mote thou be and wo worth thee bot if thou haste thee to be my helpe.' In the end, it turns out that the point of the vision is to reveal an elaborate regime of masses and prayers absolutely guaranteed to release a soul from even the deepest torments of Purgatory – this regime included a hundred masses of the Trinity, a hundred of our Lady, fifty of St Peter and fifty of *Requiem*, together with three hundred recitations of the *Miserere mei Deus* psalm, and the *Veni Creator Spiritus* hymn – if these prayers and masses are procured for a soul in purgatory 'what manere of synne that he had done in his life, there shall no manner of pain in purgatory hold him that ne hastily he shall be delivered frae thayme, and many other saules be delivered for his sake.' But for those who can't afford such lavish provision, the same result will be achieved by thirteen masses: three of the Trinity, two of St Peter, two of the Holy Ghost, three of Our Lady and three of all saints will achieve the same effect.

Texts like the *Revelation shewed to a holy woman* indicate a widespread belief that certain kinds of sustained devotional regimes – particular sequences of masses, particular numbers or kinds of prayers – were especially effective in getting souls out of Purgatory, and the visions often provide expert guidance, as it were from the horse's mouth, because provided by a Purgatory soul. They also present a ferocious and terrifying picture of the fate which awaited, in the words of the *Revelation*, 'alle manere of crystene mene and womene that hath lefed here in this werlde of what degree thay were'.

So it would be surprising if late medieval men and women had not taken the prospect of Purgatory seriously. It was a preacher's commonplace that the agonies of purgatory were so intense that a few minutes there felt like years to those enduring them. In *The Stripping of the Altars*, I collected extracts from wills from all over England which suggested that some late medieval people were deeply affected by this kind of visionary horror, and so wanted intercession and good works done on their behalf to begin at the very moment of their death or even sooner, to minimize the torment they would have to suffer once they entered the other world. People making wills might ask for diriges, masses and doles to begin 'as hastily as possible after my departing from this world', or 'as soon as I am dead without any tarrying', or at the earliest moment 'as by mon erthly it may be perceived that my soule shuld be from my body separate', or 'when ye see me in the panges if death'. One Bedfordshire gentleman even asked for two friars to begin saying trentals, or sets of thirty masses, for him 'if tyme and season may be, when I lye in the article and point of death labouring towards the everlasting lyfe'.[11]

On the face of it, those sorts of requests lend some support to Delumeau's idea that the religion of fourteenth- and fifteenth-century men and women was driven by fear, and might seem to suggest that we should see a foundation like Wingfield as a reflection of a panic-stricken Christianity, a world view blighted by savage imaginings and terror of what awaited every soul after death. You'll have guessed that I don't myself believe this for a moment, but I thought it would be interesting to test it statistically, and two fat volumes of fifteenth-century wills edited for the Suffolk Record Society by the late Peter Northeast seemed to offer a rough and ready way of doing just that.[12]

Northeast edited 2,342 wills from the archdeaconry of Sudbury proved between 1439 and 1474. Every single one of them makes some kind of provision for post-mortem intercession, and some of that provision is very elaborate indeed, with some testators commissioning hundreds of masses from all the houses of friars in the region, sending pilgrims near and far to famous and not-so-famous shrines like Walsingham and Woolpit, Canterbury and Bury St Edmunds, Rome and Compostela, securing indulgences and arranging for doles to the poor and for elaborate funeral display: the wills demonstrate unequivocally the universal acceptance of belief in Purgatory and the attitudes towards death and the afterlife which make the huge outlay involved in an institution like

Wingfield intelligible: indeed, it's only in the context of that kind of universally accepted belief in the value of intercession that the vast proportion of family resources involved in creating and maintaining a college of priests and singing boys can be seen as a sensible investment.

But I wanted to use the wills specifically to explore whether or not the men and women of fifteenth-century Suffolk seemed specifically driven by *fear* in making these elaborate arrangements. What indications were there in these intimate deathbed documents that belief in Purgatory really was a source of anxiety or panic, or that might suggest that the driving force behind all these elaborate funeral and post-mortem arrangements, and so behind Wingfield, might be naked fear?

Sure enough, one can find in some of the wills definite hints that the prospect of Purgatory was viewed in some cases at least with something approaching panic. Several dozen of these fifteenth-century Suffolk testators specifically stressed the need for *hurry* in providing the masses, prayers and works of charity that would speed them out of the pains of Purgatory. As I've said, all the wills make provision for intercession and good works in some form or other, but many add clauses indicating the need to set the intercessory systems up within weeks or days or even hours of the testator's death. So there are many wills asking that the masses begin 'with all possible haste', 'as soon as possible after my death', 'in greatest haste'. Some wills show their makers trying to secure concentrated intercessory regimes that would blast them out of Purgatory on a tidal wave of prayer and good works, like the Lavenham testator who provided for 400 masses 'in the week of my death', or the Mildenhall testator who asked for 100 masses as soon as possible, if possible all on one and the same day, or the testator from Fornham All Saints, who left 4d apiece to 100 chaplains, stipulating they should all say mass for him on the same day, 'as soon after my decease as they can be provided', or the more modest Wattisham bequest for thirty masses to be said if possible within seven days, or the Sudbury request for a trental 'on one and the same day if possible'. The degree of organization required to honour the more elaborate of such requests must have been considerable, and one suspects that many were never fully achieved: so a good many testators left more realistic bequests for 10 shillings or more to go to the local houses of friars for funeral prayers and masses, where the concentration of clergy meant there was a better chance of the reasonably speedy fulfilment of requests for multiple masses and diriges.

Yet when one adds together all the wills containing such signs of anxiety about the speed of provision of post-mortem intercession, they are a drop in a bucket. The total number of wills with some hint of haste comes to forty-three out of more than 2,300 wills, or just under 2 per cent of testators. The vast majority of wills leave the timing of the masses and other good works they requested to their executors and families, and many clearly envisaged a regime of intercession which stretched out over time. Many particularly specify the distribution of the masses over a year or even longer, like the testator at Badwell Ash who requested the Dominicans at Thetford to celebrate a trental of masses 'at appropriate feasts, for a year',[13] or the Cambridgeshire testator who left £5 for a trental to be celebrated by a scholar of Cambridge University who would ride over to the testator's home village of Fordham at the major feasts, 'that is, the Nativity of our Lord, Easter, Pentecost and such like, to celebrate the masses in the parish church there'.[14] Some testators even delayed the establishment of chantry services or charitable activities till their widow had died and had no further need of their money or property, which might then be used for good works 'for the health of our souls'. For such testators, the religious symbolism of appropriate masses celebrated on the major feasts, in the Fordham case with the added enhancement of securing a learned and dignified priest-scholar from the University, mattered more than any urgency about hastening the soul out of its sufferings in the shortest possible time.

The most elaborate Suffolk example of opulent post-mortem religious provision was the remarkable will of John Baret, an immensely successful Bury St Edmunds cloth merchant who was also a gentleman of the chamber to the Abbot of Bury, and who established a lavish chantry in the Lady Chapel of St Mary's church in Bury.[15]

Baret's chantry employed only a single priest, but architecturally it was on a scale which rivalled all but the most sumptuous perpetual foundations in the county. Baret's will, made in 1463, runs to thirty closely printed pages in the nineteenth-century edition which made it famous, and its almost obsessively detailed provisions have struck a lot of modern readers as morbid, an impression strengthened by Baret's famously macabre grave effigy: the tomb, which he commissioned and installed in the Lady Chapel in the south aisle of St Mary's years before his death, portrays Baret himself as a rotting corpse, clutching at his shroud, the stretched skin on his grinning skull caught in the rictus of death, and the body hedged round with inscriptions pleading for prayers. Baret bought both papal and local episcopal indulgences to induce onlookers at the tomb to pray for him, and wanted these prominently placed in wooden display cases above the burial site, together with an English devotional ballad he had commissioned, presumably like the Purgatory poem by Lydgate painted on the roof of the Clopton Chapel at Long Melford. Baret called for the reconstruction and elaboration of the Lady Chapel in St Mary's round his burial place, with a new reredos on the theme of the Magnificat, which perhaps means that it portrayed the Annunciation; mirrors set in the ceiling above the tomb; and a new image of the Virgin commissioned from Robert Pyot, with elaborate candle holders before it. He paid for mechanical chimes in the steeple and in the Lady Chapel, which were to play the tune of *Requiem aeternam* at the elevation at both the Jesus and Lady Masses, as well as at the *Requiem*s celebrated for Baret himself, and to be rung also after the singing of the *Salve* at Compline on feast days and Sundays. Baret made careful provision for the manning and maintenance in perpetuity of the clock and chimes which were to be played in his memory. He also envisaged enlarging the Lady Chapel with a south aisle, and left money to lower the floor and raise the entrance arch to his chapel to encourage the parishioners to process through it with the parish cross and banners on Sundays. The funeral itself was to be spectacular: five poor men vested in black in memory of the wounds of Jesus, and five poor women clad in white for the joys of Mary were to carry torches round his hearse, the requiem masses were to be sung with both plainsong and polyphony, and there were special payments to the clergy, lay clerks and singing boys in surplices who attended. There was to be a dinner on the day of the funeral, for the aldermen, burgesses, gentlemen 'and other folks of worship', and doles to the local deserving poor and to the prisoners in Bury gaol. In the longer term, part of his spinning house was to be converted into a flat for his chantry priest to live in, and those priests were to call in perpetuity for prayers for Baret's repose whenever they were invited to say grace at public dinners in the town. His fellow servants in the abbot's household were all to receive silk and golden purses, and the senior monks of the abbey were given costly sets of rosary beads.

This meticulous attention to every last detail of his own funeral and post-mortem commemoration, stretching years into the future and involving a vast network of religious, business, social and kinship networks all harnessed to intercession for Baret's soul, might well be thought to be the direct result of a religion dominated by fear of punishment and a frantic desire to pre-empt or shorten that suffering. But that's not how Baret's will strikes one on an attentive reading. Here is an immensely rich man, a social arriviste buoyed up by new money made in trade, who has no children of his own, and so whose goods and business and memory will have to be carried by his brother William and his nieces and nephews, and by the various corporations and social and religious groups to which he belonged: Baret was undoubtedly a deeply devout man (though his will contained revealing provisions to compensate at least one business acquaintance whom he had diddled out of a substantial sum of silver). Equally clearly, his fantastically elaborate religious provisions represent a kind of displaced dynastic aspiration, a desire to perpetuate his memory and his influence through a kind of extended family. His centre of operations was one of the great ecclesiastical corporations of late medieval England: personal service in the household of the Abbot of Bury was the means by which Baret and his wealth gained entrée to aristocratic circles and lifestyle, and it strikes one that there is more social than religious anxiety in all his insistence that his emblems and motto (he doesn't seem to have had a coat of arms) should be emblazoned in his chapel and on the vestments of the priests who celebrated services there in his memory. His lavish commemorative gifts to the Abbot's household, to the more notable monks, to the parish, his erection of a processional cross with a wooden shelter round it before his house for use during rogation processions and so on – all these suggest a man determined to make and leave his mark on the community in which he had made good.

And that, I think, is true of late medieval preparation for death and the afterlife in general. Fourteenth- and fifteenth-century English people had distinctive and daunting beliefs about the afterlife. They thought God was both merciful and just, and they thought that the consequences of sin must be met before they could enter into God's bliss. But they viewed that formidable prospect as another of the facts of life: they provided for it, but only those prone to panic about everything seem to have panicked about this. For the most part, post-mortem provision was a way of extending the network of friendship and obligation which constituted the community of the living: intercession for the dead was less like fire insurance than the extension of the obligations of friendship and family and neighbourhood into the dark world of the dead. Purgatory provision helped domesticate death; it did not make it more terrible. A chantry like Wingfield was about many things besides remembrance of the souls of the faithful departed: it was important and worth spending lavishly on because it was also an expression of power, of wealth, of conspicuous consumption and lavish display: it continued de la Pole patronage of the local community into the world beyond.

Above all, perhaps, a chantry was about lineage and family. The English aristocracy of the late Middle Ages, like aristocracy everywhere, I suppose, were obsessed with pedigree and kin: prayers for the dead catered for that concern as well, for a perpetual chantry was designed to ensure the permanent commemoration of the ancestors. To put it like that, though, is maybe to empty the doctrine of Purgatory of its most attractive feature: its projection of the bond of charity and the obligation of care for friends and kin even beyond the grave. Prayer for the dead was the measure and last proof of our love for them. In the last of all late medieval English evocations of revelations from the souls in Purgatory, Thomas More's *Supplication of Souls*, published in 1529, this is the dimension of Purgatory most insisted upon. The dead depend upon us, the living, for relief and comfort: they are the beggars at our door, the Lazarus of the gospel story, on whom we must take pity if we in our turn hope for the pity of God beyond the grave. The first and sharpest pain of Purgatory, according to More, was the shame of meeting the loved ones we had neglected or for whom we had forgotten to pray, and according to More it is not fear, but the pathos of the dead and the demands of charity which the doctrine of Purgatory embodies. So let's leave the last word to More's souls in purgatory, beseeching us, their friends, for our prayers.

In most pytouse wyse continually calleth & cryeth vppon your devoute cherite & moste tender pyte / for helpe cumfort & relyefe / your late aqauyntaunce / kindred / spouses / companions / play felowes / & frendes / & now your humble & unacquainted & halfe forgotten supplyauntys / pore prysoners of god ye sely sowlys in purgatory / here abydyng & enduryng the grevouse paynys & hote clensyng fyre / that freteth & burneth oute the rustye & filthy spottes of oure synne/ tyll the mercy of almighty god the rather by your gode & cherytable meanes / vowchesaufe to delyver us hense.[16]

18

Monasticism and the Religion of the People: Crowland Abbey

There is always, more or less by definition, a gap between the religion of the monastery and the religion of the people. The deepest urge of monasticism, the energy at its root, is withdrawal from the *saeculum*, from the flux of life lived in the world, and the multiple distractions and fret involved in the getting of livings and the begetting of families. That is not to say that monasticism is escapist. The first monks were convinced that, like Christ, they fled to the desert not to run away from temptation, but to encounter it in its strongholds. The demons, they knew, were to be met everywhere, and most dangerously of all when the veneer of normality was removed, and men were left alone with their thoughts, with the time and the clarity of vision to see things as they really are. For medieval men and women, therefore, there was a sense in which popular religion was always a second-best, a makeshift approximation to the more demanding Christianity involved in living out the evangelical counsels in a life of poverty, chastity and obedience.

Crowland or Croyland Abbey is located in the South Holland district of Lincolnshire, just over a mile north-east of Peterborough, across the country boundary with Cambridgeshire. Yet even today it feels remote. Flat in the flood-plain of the river Welland, the parish, still vulnerable to flooding, is bordered by the drains and dykes which are physical testimony to the watery terrain in which the Abbey was founded. The modern parish church occupies only the north aisle of the Abbey Church, and the still dominant and dramatic ruins of the remainder of the original building, 'the shattered pile/Of this old abbey struggling still with time', excited romantic poets like John Clare, and painters like Turner, John Sell Cotman and Thomas Girtin.[1] That Romantic fascination with the mystique of Crowland was not entirely anachronistic. The stones of Crowland were raised in the first place as signposts of transcendence, a summons away from spiritual mediocrity and a call to something more demanding.

In the early Middle Ages, when Crowland was young, ordinary people, high and low, aristocrat and peasant, the men who fought and the men and women who toiled in the fields, by and large left religion to the monks, associating themselves with the holiness cherished in the cloister by gifts to the monasteries or burial in their precincts, or by mute attendance at the liturgy of the Church. By the end of the Middle Ages all that had changed. Lay people were far more active in religious matters, far more in charge of their own religious lives. They went on pilgrimage, wore and prayed on rosaries and, if they had money to spare and could spell a few words, on Books of Hours. They hired priests to say extra masses, they staged or watched religious plays, they joined religious guilds. Yet still the monastery remained a benchmark: the piety of laypeople was to some extent the poor cousin of monastic piety, just as the book of hours was a dumbed-down version of the monastic hours of prayer, and the religious regime recommended to devout laypeople an attempt to re-create in the home and the workplace some at least of the rhythms of the monastery.

That was the theory. In practice, of course, monasteries were often something less. Life in medieval Crowland certainly had its rigours. Winter and summer, its monks rose in the night to sing the office, and braved the raw fen weather seeping through a church built on an island in the largest swamp in England. But life here, whatever its drawbacks, was at least in the later Middle Ages more secure than the life of the peasants who worked the fields and marshes round about. The monks of Crowland could not marry;

they passed their names to no descendants. But they ate more regularly and slept more warmly than most of their contemporaries, and they were cushioned against the precariousness of everyday life by their membership of a great landed institution, whose mitred abbot was one of the most powerful men in the realm, a Lord of Parliament and the ruler of estates which, though depleted at the Norman Conquest, eventually ran the breadth of eastern England.[2]

There is another and special difficulty in speaking of popular religion and Crowland Abbey.[3] As it happens, one of the most famous and valuable historical documents of the English Middle Ages was written in the monastery, by a succession of monk chroniclers. *The Crowland Chronicle* is a precious evocation of the life of this region and the history of England stretching from the tenth to the fifteenth century. It is full of unforgetable detail, like the account of the fire that destroyed the monastery in 1091. Yet, considered as evidence for the religion of the monks of Crowland, it is a deeply depressing document. To start with, it is of course a complex tissue of forgeries, impossible in many cases to disentangle from the genuine historical material woven into it.[4] And above all, it is obsessively preoccupied with lands and possessions. From start to finish, the central aim of the Chronicle is to prove the rights of the monastery to contested property, and to demonstrate how God and his saints through the centuries had vindicated the abbey and struck down its enemies. A typical example is the story of the crooked bailiff Asford of Helieston, who had swindled the monks out of ten acres of meadow land, but whose guilt was demonstrated at his funeral in 1076, when his body was swept from its bier by a flash flood which rolled the corpse in filth, and terrified his friends and relatives into restoring the alienated lands.[5]

That preoccupation with the monastery and its rights inevitably affected Crowland's relationships with its neighbours and its tenants. If we are to judge by the *Chronicle*, those relations were often strained and even violent. Again and again the *Chronicle* recounts the monstrous turbulence of the men of the fenland, scoundrels and ravening beasts who poached the Abbey's fish and game, sabotaged the Abbey's dykes and waterways, cut the Abbey's thatching reed and woodlands, grazed their cattle on the Abbey's pastures, and withheld the Abbey's rents and rates. To judge by the *Chronicle*, the Abbey and the people were often at daggers drawn, and one wonders how many tears were shed for this community when the commissioners of Henry VIII silenced for ever the round of monastic prayers and stripped the lead from the roof. Of course, it would be unjust to judge by this one document the spirituality of a monastic community which flourished here for centuries, from Saxon times till the Tudor dissolutions. Yet it is the monastery's own creation, the way in which successive generations of Crowland monks chose to represent themselves, and it is hard for the historian, peering into the dark backward and abysm of time, to escape the nagging suspicion that the monks of Crowland had not altogether renounced the world they were supposed to have left at the monastery gate.

St Guthlac arrived at Crowland in what was then a boggy island in the 'wild places of a vast desert', the immense tract of fenland which reached from Cambridge to the Humber, a region, as Guthlac's first biographer wrote, 'now of marshes, now of bogs, sometimes of black waters overhung with fog, sometimes studded with wooded islands and traversed by the windings of tortuous streams'.[6] And the first thing to grasp about Guthlac's life as a hermit is that it was at one and the same time an expression of popular religion, and a rejection of the very idea of popular religion. Guthlac's religion was in one sense typical of its day, and the biography written by his younger contemporary Felix is closely modelled on some of the classical lives which helped to shape the piety of the Anglo-Saxon Church – the life of St Martin, the life of Anthony, the life of the Irish monk Fursy, and Bede's life of St Cuthbert. Guthlac's life is, in that sense, 'conventional', and indeed we can't be sure how much of what is said about him is simply borrowed from other holy lives. The deathbed of Guthlac, for example, seems to have been pasted together from passages from Bede's account of the death of Cuthbert, and so is probably not a reliable historical account.

But if Guthlac's religion is in that sense conventional and popular, it is in another and equally obvious way craggy, uncomfortable and uncompromising, very much of its time, but not a piety which a modern Christian, whatever his or her denomination, can easily come to terms with. Guthlac came to the wilderness of Crowland as a refugee twice over from the company of other men. At the age of twenty-six he had suddenly abandoned a career as a successful and bloodthirsty Mercian warlord, in favour of the life of a monk under the rule of the abbess Aelfryth in the monastery of Repton. In his two years at Repton he acquired the essential tool of the Anglo-Saxon monk – the ability to recite from memory all 150 psalms in Latin – but he had antagonized his more conventional monastic brethren by his spectacular asceticism – renouncing, for example, the taste of any alcohol except the chalice at communion. Guthlac had come to monastic life driven by an overwhelming sense of the transience and darkness of human existence. It was a common enough theme in Anglo-Saxon Christianity. There is a famous passage in Bede's *Ecclesiastical History of the English People*, in which one of the counsellors of the pagan King Edwin of Northumbria makes a comparison between the life of a man and the fleeting passage of a sparrow through a firelit banqueting hall in winter:

> inside all is warm, while outside the wintry storms of rain and snow are raging: the sparrow enters in at one door and quickly flies out through the other. For the few moments it is inside, the storm and wintry tempest cannot touch it, but after the briefest moment of calm, it flits from your sight, out of the wintry storm and into it again. So this life of man appears for a moment, what follows or indeed what went before we know nothing of at all. If this new doctrine of Christ brings us more information, it seems right that we should embrace it. [7]

And in fact, for Bede and his contemporaries, the storm and darkness were not just the great unknown before birth and after death: they surrounded every human life through all its phases. Guthlac's biographer tells us that the saint abandoned warfare because he found himself 'storm-tossed amid the gloomy clouds of life's darkness and amid the whirling waves of the world'.[8] He found no refuge from those storms within the monastery, however, and eventually he sought out the most desolate region in the England of his day, a watery desert haunted by nameless terrors and demons, where others had tried and failed to live a hermit's life. We are dealing here with a man self-consciously cast in the heroic role of dragon-slayer, setting out into a desert beyond human company or human help to wrestle, as Beowulf fought with Grendel, with the internal demons of his own sinfulness, and with those equally terrifying external demons whom Guthlac and his contemporaries believed haunted the wastes of the fen.

He became therefore a man outside human society, dressed in skins, living on barley bread and fen water, assaulted by devils who dragged him through the swamps to the mouth of hell itself, rescued by the heavenly protection of his patron St Bartholomew, on whose feast day he had first come to Crowland. The cult of Guthlac at Crowland would be inextricably linked to the cult of St Bartholomew, and indeed both elements of the Crowland coat of arms, the flesher's knife and the scourge, relate to Bartholomew more than to Guthlac, though the scourge is a distinctively Crowland invention. Monastic tradition here embellished the story in Felix's life of Guthlac in which Bartholomew rescues Guthlac from the fiends who have dragged him to hell, by adding the claim that Bartholomew handed Guthlac a whip with which he beat the demons. The story encodes, of course, the fiercely ascetical lifestyle by which Guthlac had brought his turbulent nature under control, but I think it almost certain that the scourge must have been a Crowland relic, which featured as an element in later pilgrimage to the shrine of the saint. On the magnificent rebuilding of the west front of the monastic church the monks set a quatrefoil with five scenes from the life of Guthlac, in two of which the scourge features prominently.[9]

Guthlac's cult was embraced by the royal house of Mercia. Fourteen churches in Mercian territory were dedicated to him, and the cult spread to St Albans, Westminster and Durham: Archbishop Ceolnith of Canterbury attributed his own cure from ague in 851 to

Guthlac.[10] A Latin life of Guthlac by a monk named Felix (though Orderic calls him 'bishop Felix') was commissioned some time after AD 713 and before 739 by Aelfwald, king of the East Angles (this East Anglian provenance itself perhaps a testimony to the spread of Guthlac's cult). The Latin life was in due course translated into Anglo-Saxon, and portions of it found their way into at least one vernacular sermon collection.[11] Two Anglo-Saxon poems preserved in the Exeter Book and written probably at the end of the ninth century celebrate Guthlac's ascetical prowess as a hermit and his triumph over demons, and were presumably monastic in origin or patronage.[12] Guthlac's feast day would duly find its way into the calendars of monastic churches in the West Country and even in France, but he emerges in all these early documents as a model of the eremitic or monastic life rather than a popular wonder-worker. His reputation seems to have spread largely through the material influence of the monastery founded on his shrine, rather than because of the pull of the saint himself in the form of a folk reputation for healing or powerful intercession. Despite its charming stories of Guthlac's troubled but benign relations with the local wildlife, especially the birds, and the colourful details of his hair-raising encounters with demons and voyage to the underworld, there is not much in Guthlac's legend to suggest or prompt popular attachment to him. It is probably significant, for example, that Felix's life records only one miracle at the shrine, the healing of a blind man through the application of salt water by Guthlac's sister Pega.

The origins of the Benedictine monastery of Crowland, and the precise nature of the continuity between the monastery and the hermit and his shrine, are lost beyond recall. The shrine of Guthlac was certainly one focus for the piety of the royal house of Mercia, and by the time the Danes established themselves in Eastern England there was an established monastery to be robbed and burnt, which they duly did. But the documented history of Crowland does not properly begin until the late tenth century, 250 years after the death of Guthlac, and in the early eleventh century he features in surviving sources essentially as the protector of the Abbey lands. Guthlac is presented not so much as a saint of the people, as the heavenly guardian and enforcer of the material well-being of his monks. Crowland was to lose much of its lands and influence during the Norman Conquest, but, with the help of St Guthlac and a series of determined and strong-minded abbots, it re-built its fortunes. It was never a large house – it probably never had more than four dozen monks – but the reclamation of the fenland for agriculture, and the exploitation of the natural wild resources of the region, from fish and game to reed for thatching, made it one of the wealthiest in Eastern England. The wealth was manifested in successive building projects from the twelfth century onwards, and the famous and beautiful twelfth-century Guthlac Roll in the British Library was probably intended as the set of drawings for an elaborate series of story windows, telling the legend of the saint for the Abbey Church, as part of one of these phases of expansion and rebuilding.[13]

The pattern for the medieval expansion of Crowland was set in the late eleventh and early twelfth centuries, under a series of enterprising and larger-than-life abbots, notably Ulfcytel, Ingulf and the first Norman French abbot, appointed by Henry I in 1110, Geoffrey of Orleans. These men were dedicated to the defence and extension of the estates of the monastery, on which the well-being and influence of the monks depended. We should not imagine that this preoccupation lacked a spiritual dimension, and I shall say something about that presently. Its most remarkable long-term expression, however, was the *Historia Croylandensis*. This is a fictionalized history of the monastery, which eventually ran from the time of Guthlac to the age of the Tudors, and which constructed an account of the life and times of the monks of Crowland mainly designed to document the monastery's right to its lands and possessions.

The security of any community in Norman England depended on the possession of documentary evidence of its endowments. A succession of fires destroyed much of Crowland's crucial archive, and from the time of Abbot Ingulf onwards the monastery was engaged in the creative recovery of much of this vital documentation. Not to put too fine a point on it, from the early 1100s onwards

Crowland began to produce a series of forged charters and other documents, which would eventually crystallize out into chronicle form, providing a largely fictional early history designed to back the claims of the monastery to often contested properties through the length and breadth of eastern England. In this activity, Crowland was by no means an isolated case. This was the great age of forged charters, bulls and decretals: early medieval men did not share our squeamish understanding of the nature of historical evidence. If the monks of St Guthlac were certain from their own traditions that they had been given a piece of land, but vital documentary evidence was sadly lacking, then what could be more natural or more just than to compose a document which translated dependable oral tradition into legally produceable parchment and ink?

But if such forgeries were an accepted fact of life in the Middle Ages, Crowland was to excel in the persistence and plausibility of its production. *The Chronicle of Crowland*, one of the most important surviving medieval sources, especially for the fifteenth century, was the outcome. It did not of course begin as deliberate forgery, but as the careful collection and expansion of remembered tradition. Early in the twelfth century the Abbot of Crowland commissioned one of the greatest historians of the day, Orderic Vitalis, to come to Crowland for a six-week visit and write up the Abbey's history from the documentation that survived. It is clear that Orderic made a serious attempt to get things right: he produced a simplified paraphrase of Felix's life of Guthlac which shows him as a reliable reader of his sources. Alongside his account of the life of Guthlac, however, he also provided an account of a new saint's cult at Crowland, which throws a sudden shaft of light on the relation between the monastery's not altogether attractive preoccupation with its possessions, and the religious life of the people of the region. This was Orderic's account of the cult which had taken root at the tomb of the earl Waltheof.[14]

Waltheof, Earl of Huntingdon, is one of the most interesting figures of the age of the Norman Conquest. Virtually the only Saxon layman retained in office by William the Conqueror, he was an immensely influential and respected political figure, and a major benefactor of the Church in the form of a series of monastic endowments. Oddly, in view of subsequent events, there is no securely documented connection between Crowland and Waltheof during his lifetime. The monastery would later claim that he had given to the monks the land at Barnack from which the beautiful stone for the rebuilding of the monastery was quarried. Unfortunately, what contemporary evidence there is contradicts the monastery's claim to the quarries, and we simply do not know what benefactions, if any, Waltheof gave to Crowland. In 1076, however, he was beheaded at Winchester for involvement in a plot against William, and Abbot Ulfkytel got permission to exhume his body and carry it to Crowland for honourable burial in the chapter house. Waltheof remained a martyred hero to many Saxons, the victim of an oppressive invader, and the Abbey's action in securing Waltheof's body may represent a deliberate act of identification with Saxon resistance. Ulfkytel, 'an Englishman hated by the Normans', was subsequently deposed, as Orderic says, 'by the malice of the Normans' and replaced by Ingulf, himself a Saxon, but a clerk who had worked in William's household and therefore considered safely Normanized.[15]

However that may be, in the passage of time the Saxon hero metamorphosed into the Christian saint. At some unspecified date Abbot Ingulf had the body moved from the chapter house into the church for reburial near the altar: this act of translation was the traditional equivalent of local canonization. Ingulf had ordered water to be heated to wash Waltheof's bones, as was customary before reburial. When the coffin was opened, however, the body was found to be whole and uncorrupt, the head joined still to the body with only a thin red line to mark the decapitation, all this another traditional sign of sanctity. In 1112, forty years after his execution and three years into the abbacy of the Frenchman Geoffrey of Orleans, miracles began to occur at Waltheof's tomb.

Details of twelve of these miracles survive attached to an anonymous 'Vita' or life of Waltheof produced at Crowland some time in the first two decades of the thirteenth century, but almost certainly drawing on one or more earlier miracle collections, which was clearly designed to attract pilgrims to the executed earl's tomb.[16] It relates twelve miracles at the shrine in the Abbey Church, and the miracle stories provide a fascinating glimpse into the religion of the fenland in the early twelfth century.[17] The miracles were mostly closely clustered together in May and June of 1112, though continuing on into mid-August of the same year, and it is clear that something approaching a religious revival had drawn pilgrims to the monastery that summer, as news of healings at Waltheof's grave spread. Several of those healed, we are told, were drawn to Crowland *'Crebescente ubique rumore sanctitatis beati Waldevi'*, 'by the spreading everywhere of the report of the holiness of Blessed Waltheof'.

We catch in the stories poignant glimpses of the procession of the afflicted pilgrims: Reginald, a deaf man from Lolworth in Cambridgeshire;[18] Radolfus, a blind teenager led by one of the monks from Loddington, in the north of the county, to healing at the shrine. Radolfus slept there all night and, as he drifted from sleep at dawn, woken by the mass bell, he thought he saw the shape of a man rising out of the tomb. He then discovered that he could see the candles round the tomb.[19] Then there was Egeleva, a blind woman from Sleaford, healed on the feast of St Alban 1112, or Sigiva,[20] the *'puellula clauda'*, the little lame girl from Leicester, who followed soon afterwards, having been afflicted for a long time with deformed knee joints, and whose lower legs were wasted so that she could barely walk, but came to the shrine leading her blind brother: ironically, it was the sister, not the blind brother, who went away healed.[21] Or there was the lunatic boy from Whaplode, brought by his distraught mother, or Osmund of Moulton in Holland, who brought his blind daughter to the tomb on the eve of the Assumption in August 1112. They lay together by the tomb all night till the monks began to sing the morning office, and the little girl, awakening, realized she could see the lamps burning around the shrine.[22] A five-year-old boy from Leicester was likewise laid to sleep by the tomb on the eve of the feast of Saints Peter and Paul: he too received his sight again at dawn, the time of day at which Waltheof had been executed.[23] Godric, an old man of Yaxley, lay night after night by the shrine for a week till his sight also was restored.[24]

Most of these were local people: six of them from Lincolnshire, three from neighbouring counties, two from Leicestershire. Only one, a dropsical woman named Ethel, came from a great distance, for she had heard of Waltheof in Normandy, and had made her way to Crowland in quest of healing.[25] What we see in the *Miracula* is the birth of a local cult, spreading by word of mouth through the region, especially to communities like Whaplode and Moulton where the abbey had lands. In some cases, the miracles seem directly linked to each other. On 4 July 1112 a blind woman from Stamford was healed; a week later, another blind woman, from Scottesgate, '*in eadem civitacula*', 'in the same little town', was healed.[26] Strikingly, nine of the twelve miracles were the healing of blind people, and you may recall that the only miracle recorded by Felix at the shrine of Guthlac was the healing of a blind man. It is possible that the *Miracula*, whose phrasing is often reminiscent of Felix's life of Guthlac, is similarly conforming to a Crowland theme in the type of healings the new saint specialized in. And these miracle stories give us a glimpse of the interaction of pilgrims and monks. The shrine is 'near the altar', presumably the high altar of the abbey church, yet male and female pilgrims sleep round it, for weeks at a time, they kiss its marble, they cluster beneath the lamps and candles that burn above and around it. Pilgrims are woken from sleep by the sounding of the mass bell or by the singing of the morning office.

Of course, we do not know exactly why miracles began to happen around the tomb of Waltheof in the summer of 1112. But it is clear that the monks had wanted something of the sort, since they had first brought the earl's body for burial in the chapter house in the first place. Abbot Ingulf's translation of the corpse from the chapter house, and his preparations for the washing of the bones, constituted a deliberate act of canonization, and William of Orleans invited both Orderic Vitalis and William of Malmesbury, the two best historians of their day, to come to Crowland and write up the story of the saint. It is tempting to see the cult as a political one: the veneration of a Saxon hero whose murdered body could bring healing – and indeed Orderic tells us that news of the miracles 'had gladdened the hearts of the English, and the common people flocked in great numbers to the tomb of their fellow countryman'. He follows this with the story of a visiting Norman, a monk of St Alban's Abbey, who had reviled Waltheof as a traitor, mocked the pilgrims, and denied his miracles, only to die horribly shortly after his return to his own monastery. As you might expect, most of the pilgrims healed at the shrine had English, not Norman, names. But that is not much of a surprise in the early twelfth-century fenland, so we should not lay too much emphasis on it, and the abbot who warned this doubter against mocking the works of God was himself a Norman, the Frenchman Geoffrey of Orleans.[27]

Abbot Geoffrey was certainly eager to recruit Waltheof as yet another powerful protector of the monastery's interests. On the night after he had received news of the death of the Norman doubter, he had a vision, in which St Guthlac and St Bartholomew had appeared in shining white, standing by the tomb of Waltheof, and recited a three-line verse on the new saint:

Acephalos non est
Comes hic fuit
At modo rex est

(He is no longer headless,
who once was a mere count
But now reigns as a king)[28]

– not great poetry, but celebrating the miracle of Waltheof's incorrupt body and the miraculous restoration of his head to his body, and establishing him as a member of a trinity of heavenly patrons for the monastery, alongside Guthlac and Bartholomew. Geoffrey also commissioned from Orderic a verse epitaph on Waltheof, which recorded his great generosity to the Church, and above all his special love for Crowland.

Waltheof was not the only saint Crowland tried to recruit to strengthen the devotional loyalty of the people of the region. The monks told Orderic that Abbot Oscytel had received from his sister the lady Leofgifu the gift of the relics of St Neot, formerly at the monastery of Eynesbury in Huntingdonshire, because Leofgifu thought the monks of Eynesbury were showing 'insufficient reverence to this great man'. She therefore summoned the monks of Crowland to Whittlesea, where she handed over the relics 'to the monks whom she believed to be more worthy'. According to Crowland tradition, the body of St Neot was enshrined on the north side of the church near the Lady altar where, Orderic tells us, 'it is reverently adored by the faithful to this day.'[29] This claim was denied by the monks of Eynesford, who insisted that they still had the relics, and all the surviving contemporary evidence suggests that they were telling the truth: St Anselm himself claimed to have seen the intact body of St Neot at Eynesbury in 1080, long after the date of the supposed translation to Crowland, but this only underlines the keenness of the Crowland monks to lay claim to as many heavenly protectors as possible, and to encourage the devout veneration of these patrons within the Abbey Church by the lay people of the region.

So the cult of Waltheof does to some extent look stage-managed by a monastic community single-mindedly intent on securing as many heavenly witnesses and supporters as possible. Yet the Waltheof miracle stories nevertheless do bear many of the marks of an authentic popular cult. The circumstantial detail of the pilgrimage routines, the custom of sleeping at the tomb, the geographical spread of the healings and their concentration within the summer months of 1112 all suggest a genuine upsurge of religious excitement and expectation.[30] And that is something all the stage-management in the world cannot supply. The Middle Ages are littered with evidence of cults that might have been, of holy corpses expensively enshrined and surrounded with liturgy, but which produced no miracles or pilgrimages, because the people did not come. What we see at Crowland is different: the coming together of the concerns of the monks with the instincts of the people: and the result was the cult of a new saint.

Like most of the local saints cults of the Middle Ages, of course, it did not last. In religion, as in everything else under the moon, there is a tide of fashion, which rises and then ebbs. Waltheof's cult flourished, or at any rate persisted, for a century or so, but by the end of the Middle Ages had been long forgotten. By the 1530s, when Henry VIII's ministers compiled the *Valor Ecclesiasticus*, the great register of clerical wealth, they included for Crowland an estimate of the annual income from pilgrim offerings at the shrines in the abbey church: 20/- in the collection box at the shrine of the Blessed Virgin, and another 13/4 in candles; 10/- at the shrine of St Alban; 8/- at the shrine of St Guthlac; eightpence at the shrine of St Bartholomew. There is no mention of any shrine of St Waltheof.[31]

That modest eightpence for St Bartholomew is possibly an indication of the friction between the monastery and the religion of the commons of the fenland. The cult of St Bartholomew had always been prominent here, and the feast of St Bartholomew was one of the great days in the Crowland calendar, drawing large crowds of pilgrims to the abbey. By the fifteenth century, it had become customary for the monks to distribute to the crowds on St Bartholomew's Day free souvenirs or pilgrim badges in the form of little knives, sometimes embossed with the scourge which Bartholomew had given to Guthlac to fight the demons. The large numbers involved made this custom a drain on monastery finances, and it was abolished in the 1470s by Abbot John de Wisbech. Abbot John was a formidable and enlightened man, whose lavish building of the monks' hostel at Cambridge, now Magdalene College's First Court, is a testimony to his commitment to academic standards and the improvement of the calibre of his monks. In his attack on the St Bartholomew's Day customs he may have had more in mind than the cost involved. *The Crowland Chronicle* records several ugly incidents on these St Bartholomew's Day gatherings, which seemed to have been occasions when local resentment against the monastery and its control of the region's resources might flare into violence. The abbot may have been trying to discourage such gatherings altogether, by abolishing the pilgrim badges, which were probably understood as having protective or healing powers, and hence which drew the crowds. Abbot de Wisbech had a reputation as a prudent and peaceable resolver of disputes, and he may have seen in the volatile gatherings on St Bartholomew's day a flashpoint better damped down.[32]

Those local resentments feature large for Crowland's chroniclers. But I think it would be a mistake to lay too much weight on them. The *Chronicle* is not a general history of the monastery and region: it is a piece of special pleading, focusing on disputed properties. No doubt the day-to-day relations of the monastery with the people of the fenland were less fraught than this one document suggests. But when all that has been said, there is no mistaking the undertow of unrest. In the fenland, the rights to graze geese or cattle, to cut willow or thatching reed, to hunt hare and rabbit, to catch fish, were fundamental to local prosperity and sometimes survival: the monastery's determined extension and defence of its rights over all these activities brought it at times into direct conflict with the common people, and there will certainly have been a religious consequence. The wills of late medieval Lincolnshire contain almost nothing in the way of bequests to the monastery, and the abbey's tenants were more likely to leave bequests to our Lady of Walsingham, or the good Rood of Boston, or to leave a few shillings to the Friars for a *Scala Coeli* mass in Boston.[33]

This may have nothing whatever to do with perceptions of Crowland in particular. The fifteenth century in religious terms is the age not of the monastery but of the parish church. The religious lives of ordinary men and women were focused there, not in the monastic enclosure. Monasteries were not always sensitive to this shift, and the fifteenth-century episcopal visitations of Crowland suggest, for example, that the monks were less than zealous in keeping the house of the priest who served as parish chaplain in good repair. But if they were marginal in the day-to-day devotion of the people, monasteries were often guardians of relics, images or altars valued by local people. One of the striking things about the lists of confiscated objects compiled by the commissioners for the dissolutions is how many monasteries had relics or blessed belts loaned out to local women for protection during childbirth, for example. The prominence of offering in money and in wax at the shrine of the Virgin in Crowland, specifically associated with the ceremony of the churching of women after childbirth, may well be associated with that sort of cult.

And in any case, it would be a great mistake to imagine some crude religious gulf between monastery and parishes. The monks of Crowland, too, for all their preoccupation with the lands and rights of St Guthlac, were men of the fenland, and shared the religious sentiments of the world and the church around them. The fifteenth-century Crowland chroniclers were men of their time, and they record with as much pious awe as the merest layman the signs and portents which foretold the calamities of the final stages of the Wars of the Roses: the appearance of three suns in the heavens, or the shower of blood which stained the washing on the lines; or the armed horsemen riding through the skies; or the unfortunate Huntingdonshire woman whose pregnancy was made terrible by the desolate weeping of the child in her womb.[34] In one of the most vivid sections of the later *Chronicle,* the chronicler celebrates the miracle of 1465 during the building of the west tower, when the beam that was to support the bell fell while it was being hauled into place, bringing tons of masonry down on the crowds below, despite which no one was killed or injured, so that multitudes of local people joined the monks in a *Te Deum* in honour of St Guthlac, who had once more protected his own.[35]

And another incident in the same section of the *Chronicle* demonstrates the extent to which the religion of the monastery and the parishes, for all the tensions between them, continued to be intimately interwoven. This was the story of how a local daylabourer named John Wayle, guilty of some shameful and mortal sin, concealed it in his annual confession made at Easter 1463. To this dishonest and sacrilegious confession he added the worse one of receiving the Body and Blood of Christ unworthily with the rest of his parish on Easter Day. Terrified and despairing at his own wickedness, he became mad, seized with violent trembling fits, ripping his clothes, a danger to his wife and children: in the end he had to be manacled with his feet in heavy fetters. News of his afflicted state spread through the region, and a party of Crowland monks came to investigate. Convinced that the Devil was at work, they decided to exorcize Wayle, sprinkling him with holy water and reading over him the opening verses of St John's Gospel. But Wayle's frenzy only increased, and he displayed terrifying demonic strength, particularly when the names of Christ or the saints were invoked, and when a crucifix was held before him. So next day his neighbours brought him to the abbey church, and there in the north aisle bound him to a pillar before the shrine of the Virgin, setting guards over him day and night: here he remained for several days, visited by the monks, exhausted from his own screaming and struggles. Gradually he became able to bear and even to reach out to the crucifix, but was unable to speak or to make his confession. At last the monk who had devoted himself specially to comforting Wayle suggested that he should be brought to the shrine of St Guthlac, who had himself overcome the demons. Eventually, pushed and dragged by his neighbours and friends, the possessed man was brought to kneel before St Guthlac, and there, at dawn next day after Lauds, he was able to respond to the sins named by one of the monks, and to acknowledge his sin. Reclothed and restored to his family, he was sent to his own curate for confession, but returned to the abbey and for seven days stayed there in thanksgiving to Guthlac and the other saints of Crowland. The chronicler ends the story with the information that Wayle returned annually to the abbey for the rest of his life in thanksgiving for his deliverance.[36]

This extraordinary incident allows us a vivid glimpse of the religious world of the fifteenth-century fenland, of the shared beliefs of monks and people, of the crowds of agitated neighbours dragging the demented man to the abbey, and of the continuing imaginative and religious power of the ancient story of Guthlac and the demons. The shrines of the Virgin and of Guthlac himself in the abbey church feature here as community resources, offering healing and hope when every other expedient had failed. The abbey itself, for all the frictions over marsh and meadow, continued to serve that role in times of stress. Notice, though, that Wayle's neighbours brought him first not to the special saints of the monastery, but to the shrine of the Virgin in the parish's part of the church. It was a monk, one of the sons of Guthlac, who suggested recourse to the monastery's patron. That sequence of appeal tells us a great deal about the different religious priorities of parish and monastery, even as it reminds us that in a time of crisis those different loyalties might converge and complement each other.

The abbey church, then, still had something to offer the parishioners of Crowland and the region at large, in the counsel and ministrations of its monks, and the powerful presence of its saints. Certainly the men and women of Lincolnshire valued the monasteries, and resented their destruction, as widespread Lincolnshire involvement in the Pilgrimage of Grace in 1536 would demonstrate. Equally clearly, if the pennies of pilgrims are a reliable indication, the saints whose intercession and prestige had once underpinned the spiritual and material authority of the monastery no longer loomed so large in the religious sensibilities of the men and women of the fenland as perhaps they had once done. But they remained powerful and hopeful presences, to be invoked in time of peril, capable still of serving as a source of strength and healing, and as signs of the risen life of Christ at work in the bodies as well as the souls of Christian men and women. At the end of the Middle Ages, the stones of Crowland were still landmarks in the religious landscape of the men and women of the fenland.

19
The Four Latin Doctors in the Late Middle Ages

This enquiry starts from two late medieval phenomena which are probably related, though, as I think will emerge, it is not easy to say precisely how. The point of considering them is to ask if anything sensible can be said about their interrelation. The first of these phenomena is what appears to be the emergence in fifteenth-century England of a new heretical tradition of animosity towards the Four Latin Doctors, Saints Ambrose, Augustine, Gregory and Jerome. The second is the proliferation of images of these saints in fifteenth- and early sixteenth-century England, and, more particularly, the occurrence of a number of overt gestures of special reverence towards the Doctors by lay donors: in particular, their self-portrayal in prayer before them.

The Four Latin Doctors had been a collective symbol of Christian learning and authoritative Church teaching since at least the time of Bede, whose *Epistola Hortatoria* to his commentary on Luke seems to have been the first grouping of the four. But their listing together as the principal teachers of Latin Christendom became routine from the ninth century onwards: they are compared to the four Evangelists, and to the four rivers of Paradise watering the whole Church. Later in the Middle Ages they would be associated with the four ways of interpreting scripture – literal, allegorical, tropological and anagogical – or would have allocated to them different areas of Catholic truth: Augustine was raised up to refute errors about the Trinity; Ambrose to deal with doubts about immortality and future rewards and punishments; Gregory to provide rules and guidance for upright living; and Jerome to translate and explain scripture.[1] Extracts from their writings form the backbone of most medieval *Florilegia* and collections of Sentences. One of the earliest of these, the seventh-century *Liber Scintillarum*, which has eighty-one chapters, begins with the gospels, then has extracts from the writings of Saints Peter and Paul, then the other apostolic writers, then Solomon, then the rest of the Bible, and then the Four Latin Doctors.[2] One of the *Florilegia* most used in late medieval England was the *Speculum Christiani*, a catechetical resource book for preachers and clergy arranged round the Commandments, Virtues, Vices and Sacraments. It is essentially a tissue of illustrative quotations attributed to major Christian authorities from the Bible to recent luminaries like Reginald Pecock and Richard Rolle of Hampole, but in which the four Latin Doctors, though cited individually rather than as a group, are easily the dominant authorities.[3]

Till the early fifteenth century this quasi-canonical standing of the Four Doctors was challenged by no one. Even the Wyclifite tradition invoked their authority in support of its distinctive teachings. Respect for the Doctors is explicit in the General Prologue to the Wyclifite Bible, and citations from Augustine, Jerome, Ambrose and Gregory dominate the material in the Lollard Glossed Gospels, made up of 'the opyn and schorte sentences of holy doctours both Grekis and Latyns' (but mainly Latin).[4] The doctors were specially invoked in support of the need for clergy to lead lives of evangelical simplicity, and to preach. Jerome, of course, provided a precedent for biblical translation, and a characteristic Lollard sermon in defence of 'simple prestes that prechon now Goddes lawe faste aboute, thorough grace of God' (i.e. the Wyclifite clergy) insisted that

> these pore prestes allege hem hooli Scripture of diverse
> prophetes of the Olde Lawe, and Cristes own words in the
> gospel, and his hooly apostles, and manie hooly auctorities of

the foure doctoures, how eche prest is bounde to the office of prechynge.[5]

Nevertheless, in due course this Lollard approval of the Doctors gave way, at least at popular level, to open animosity. In 1430, a young man named John Skyllan of Bergh Apton in southeast Norfolk was cited for heresy into the court of the bishop of Norwich. Skyllan was evidently a wag, with a vivid turn of disparaging phrase. Among the many heretical sayings he acknowledged were punning dismissals of pilgrimage to 'the Lefdy of Falsyngham, the Lefdy of Foulpette and to Thomme of Cankerbury'. He had also declared that 'the foure doctours, Augustyn, Ambrose, Gregory and Jerom, whiche the Churche of Roome hath aproved for seyntes, were heretikes and here doctrine, which Crisitis puple calleth doctours draght, bey opin heresies.'[6] In the same year, Thomas Bagley, vicar of Manuden in Essex, was burned at Smithfield after a five-day trial in convocation. Attempts had been made to save his life by persuading him to renounce his beliefs, but he had refused, saying that he would rather hold to the views of John Wyclif than to those of Jerome, Augustine, Gregory and Ambrose.[7]

These were the earliest but not the only attacks by Lollards on the central symbols of orthodox learning and teaching in the later Middle Ages, the Four Latin Doctors. Another heretical clerk, Thomas Bikenore of Bristol, who abjured at Wallingford in October 1453, acknowledged having taught that the scriptural glosses of the Four Doctors were of no repute.[8] And in October 1518 Bishop FitzJames of London handed the relapsed heretic John Stilman over to the secular arm to be burned, for having maintained, among other errors, that 'the doctours of the church have subverted the truth of holy scripture, expounding it after their own minds, and therefore their works be naught, and they in hell: but that Wickliff is a saint in heaven, and that the book called his Wicket is good, for therein he showeth the truth.'[9]

So much for heretical animosity: four examples spread over ninety years hardly make an overwhelming case, but it is evident that within grass-roots Lollardy, though not its academic matrix, the Latin Doctors sometimes at any rate served as a symbol of all that they objected to in official Church teaching: what a modern Roman Catholic might now call the *magisterium* of the Church, and that, accordingly, Lollards might express their rejection of that teaching by denouncing and abusing the Doctors.

The second and matching phenomenon with which I am here concerned is the multiplication in fifteenth-century English churches, in many media, of images of the Doctors. In the nature of things this proliferation can be documented only impressionistically, since many of these images have perished, Nevertheless, enough remain for us to have a sense of just how widespread they once were.

The major casualty, of course, has been images in glass. Sets of the Doctors survive, in whole or part, as you might expect, in a number of academic and collegiate contexts – St George's, Windsor; All Souls, Oxford (where the founder, Archbishop Henry Chichele, was indeed a determined anti-Lollard warrior, and where they may have been included in the College's iconography as a self-conscious gesture against the memory of Oxford Wyclifism);[10] and King's College, Cambridge (where we know they were the gift of Provost Hacomblen, who ruled the College for the first twenty years of Henry VIII's reign).[11] We know also of sets in a number of cathedral and monastic churches – Rochester, Durham, Malvern and Launde. G. McN. Rushforth considered that 'most churches of importance would have had a window of the Four Doctors.'[12] They were certainly often present also in parish settings, and there are surviving sets at (for example) Fairford in Gloucester, and at Methley in Yorkshire. It is impossible to say how common such representations were in parish-church glazing, however. Ann Nichols's survey of all the surviving medieval art work in churches for the county of Norfolk has come up with just nine churches which contain or were once known to contain images of the Four Doctors in painted glass.[13]

Surviving images of the doctors in other media are considerably more common. In 1297 Pope Urban VIII linked the veneration of the Doctors with that of the Evangelists: from then on any eight-compartmented sacred space, like the vault crossing in the first bay of the Basilica at Assisi, was liable to be decorated with the matching groups of Doctors and Evangelists. In fifteenth-century East Anglia this matching arrangement was commonest on the squared or octagonal face or stems of sculpted fonts, in which the Doctors were sometimes paired with tetramorphic symbols of the Evangelists or with representational carvings of the Gospel-writers themselves. For these fonts at least, nineteen of which survive for Norfolk, a more or less standard iconography evolved, in which the Doctors are robed in tippet over gown, and wearing an academic cap or pileus, though they can be represented in other ways, as at Great Witchingham, on a font from the 1490s, where angels hold their names on scrolls and the Doctors and Evangelists are represented by tetramorphic symbols.[14]

The image of the Doctor as seated teacher was the earliest form of representation of both evangelists and doctors – repeated, for example, in the mosaic at San Clemente in Rome, and canonized as the normal depiction of Gregory the Great, at his writing desk and with the dove of the Holy Spirit whispering inspiration.[15] The image of Jerome was similarly standardized in the early fourteenth century as a figure seated at a desk and wearing a cardinal's hat: he might or might not be accompanied by a lion.[16]

The Doctors are depicted as seated teachers in the set painted on paper and rather oddly pasted over four of the early sixteenth-century series of standing apostles on the screen formerly at Lessingham. They are similarly depicted on three fifteenth-century Norfolk pulpits.[17] The images at South Creake are now almost invisible, but the pulpit at Burnham Norton, presented to the church in 1450 by John and Katherine Goldall, shows the Doctors seated at elaborate desk-chairs, with their names inscribed in the arch above them. Ambrose is mitred, wearing a tippet and cape, and holds a rubricated scroll; Gregory is in cope and tiara, the latter, as you might expect, defaced at the command of Henry VIII. He writes on a scroll which hangs over the desk, and he is surrounded by the implements of the scholar – penknife, ink-pot, pen case. Jerome, robed as a cardinal, also sits writing at a desk over which the scroll uncurls itself. Augustine, robed and mitred as a bishop, also writes a scroll, pen in right hand, penknife in the left.

At Castle Acre, where the pulpit is undocumented but probably comes from the same period or a little earlier, the Doctors once again are seated on benches and named on scrolls above their heads. Augustine, robed in Doctor's scarlet and wearing a black Doctor's cap, holds a book in his left hand, his fingers between the pages. Gregory is robed as a mitred bishop with an archiepiscopal double cross. Jerome is dressed as a cardinal, holds a closed book, and has a cross stave in his right hand. Ambrose is robed in green with an academic hood and a flat cap. All four Doctors at Castle Acre have scrolls with a sentence or phrase, presumed to come from their writings. Augustine's is *Impleti spiritu sancto predicant veritatem* (filled with Holy Spirit they preached the truth); Gregory's is *Gloria predicantium est profectus audientium* (the improvement of the hearers is the glory of preaching); Jerome's is *Ne te decipiat sermonis pulchritudo* (don't be taken in by fine words); and Ambrose has *Evangelium mentes omnium rigat* (the Gospel refreshes the minds of all). Jonathan Alexander searched the *Patrologium Latina* for a paper for the Harlaxton conference some years ago but succeeded in identifying only the quotation from Ambrose. All the texts focus, appropriately for a pulpit, on one aspect or another of preaching the gospel: the quotation, if that is what it is, from Jerome, is perhaps intended to evoke the famous story of Jerome's dream, when he is scourged at the command of Christ for his excessive love of classical writing, as a result of which he vowed never again to read profane literature. But it would probably be a mistake to search too solemnly for exact correspondences here: given the culture of the *Florilegia*, these sentences, and the corresponding fragmentary sentences on the paintings of the Doctors recently uncovered at St Gregory's Norwich, were probably culled from some such compilation: the clearly legible phrase on the scroll being written by Gregory on the screen at Weasenham All Saints says, 'O Felix Culpa', which is in fact from St Augustine, and of course features most famously in the text of the *Exultet* on Easter Eve: its attribution to Gregory thus seems both arbitrary and mistaken.[18]

The depiction of the Four Doctors on pulpits is obviously appropriate – its best-known English occurrence is on the fifteenth-century carved pulpit at Trull in Somerset – but it can never have been common. By contrast, the portrayal of the Doctors on fifteenth- and early sixteenth-century painted rood screens was clearly very common indeed. The earliest of these surviving screens with the Doctors date from around 1450, the latest from the early-1530s, with the majority concentrated in the last quarter of the fifteenth century and the first decade or so of the sixteenth.[19] At Castle Acre the pulpit was part of a decorative scheme which included a magnificent set of slightly camp International Gothic Apostles, and the association of Doctors and Apostles was extremely popular. In Devon this grouping is to be found at Chivelston, Dartmouth, Holne (where the Evangelists are also included), Kenn, Widdicome and Manaton.[20] In Norfolk, where the Doctors occur on twenty-six screens,[21] they accompany or once accompanied the Apostles at North Elmham, Tunstead, Cawston, Gooderstone, Fritton and Salle. At Salle, as at Cawston, Gooderstone and North Elmham the Doctors were painted on the chancel doors, and were flanked by the Apostles on the screens: it is very likely that some of the surviving Apostle screens of East Anglia had the Doctors on now-disappeared doors. At Gooderstone and Salle the Apostles are each accompanied by the clause of the Apostles' Creed which they were believed to have composed, so the total programme of the screen is overwhelmingly didactic, an elaborate icon of the teaching church. Pairings of the Doctors with other groups, like the Four Evangelists, at Morston or Foulden or Weasenham All Saints, or at Potter Higham (where, however, the donor's devotion to St Eligius has replaced St Luke with St Loy, and interrupted an otherwise balanced scheme), similarly underlie the role of the Doctors as symbols of Christian teaching.

This emphasis on the teaching role of the Doctors certainly had a hierarchical element. In late medieval legend Jerome was anachronistically considered to have been a cardinal, Gregory was of course Pope, Ambrose an archbishop, and Augustine a bishop: the Doctors therefore combined the authority of Church Fathers with that of the full range of the highest echelons of the clergy as they were understood in the Middle Ages: pope, cardinal, archbishop,

bishop. This carefully graded dimension is represented in the glass at Methley, where Augustine carries a simple crozier, Ambrose an archiepiscopal cross, Gregory both cross and tiara, and Jerome is robed as a cardinal, and this ranking is present also in some of the screen paintings – for example, at Cawston, at Foxley and at Fritton, where Ambrose has a cross-stave and Augustine does not. At Ashton in Devon Augustine alone is dressed as a doctor, so that the hierarchical sequence is preserved. But this is not a fixed or dominant element in the iconography of the Doctors: Ambrose and Augustine are often not iconographically distinguished, both appearing simply as crozier-carrying bishops, as they are at Ludham, and there could be confusion. At Potter Higham Augustine, not Ambrose, wears the Pallium. And in some cases these two Doctors are presented, as on the sculpted fonts, primarily as teachers. Both Augustine and Ambrose appear in academic rather than hierarchical robes at Castle Acre. By contrast, Gregory and Jerome almost always appear as pope and cardinal respectively, but that, I think, is because there was an established iconography for these two saints unconnected with their corporate identity as members of the Four Latin Doctors. I shall return to this point shortly.

The majority of these painted representations were, of course, the product of lay donation (though the Evangelists and Doctors at Morston were the gift of a late-fifteenth-century rector), sometimes the gift of individuals or single families, sometimes the corporate benefaction of a parish or parochial subgroup like a guild. And some of these lay donors made a point of representing themselves kneeling in prayer before the Doctors. Four out of the five surviving East Anglian sets of panel paintings which represent the donors in prayer before saints have the Doctors as the saints in question. At Burnham Norton (1450), John and Kate Goldall kneel on the fifth and sixth panels of the pulpit. At Fritton (c. 1512), John Bacon and his family recite the rosary before the Doctors. At Foxley (c. 1485), John and Hillary Baymonde kneel at the feet of Ambrose and Jerome, and on the late-fifteenth-century screen at Houghton St Giles, where the Doctors on the south screen are matched unusually with the Holy Kindred on the north screen, the anonymous female donor kneels at the feet of one of the two holy popes who accompany the Doctors, St Sylvester and St Clement. She prays on a scroll to St Sylvester, but she faces towards the Doctors.

That image of a laywoman kneeling before Popes and Doctors seems a powerful representation of lay submission to clerical teaching, which looks to be the natural and obvious reading of all these donor images. Are we looking here at a self-conscious gesture of orthodoxy, maybe even designed to offset or repudiate the sort of Lollard rejection and abuse of the Doctors, and with them, of the Church's authority? Are we looking at a lay reaction to Lollardy?

Certainly, it is difficult to interpret these images straightforwardly as devotional gestures to much-loved saints, because there is no evidence, apart from these images, that anyone in late medieval England had the slightest devotion to the Four Latin Doctors as a group. There is a striking mismatch between the devotional world of the late medieval English laity as it is mirrored in devotional texts like the prayers of the *Horae*, and these painted panels. Of course, Gregory, Jerome, Augustine and, to a lesser extent, Ambrose occur again and again in the prayer books of the laity, as the recipients of prayers in their own right, and as the authors or guarantors of favourite prayers. Gregory is most commonly associated with devotions to the Five Wounds, and above all with the Image of Pity and the so-called Mass of St Gregory.[22] The Mass of St Gregory is everywhere in late fifteenth- and early sixteenth-century lay devotion, especially, though not exclusively, associated with the cult of intercession for the dead, probably because of the connection with St Gregory's trental, a sequence of masses arranged round the major feasts and believed to be specially efficacious in releasing souls from purgatory. Augustine was believed to have been the recipient by a special revelation of the prayer '*Deus propitius esto mihi peccatori et custos meus sis*,[23] one of the many prayers believed to protect against sudden death and other calamities. In fourteenth- and fifteenth-century Italy, devotion to Jerome was one of the fastest-growing cults of the fifteenth century. In the high Middle Ages he had been venerated as the biblical commentator par excellence, and his iconography was established: a seated or standing cardinal with a book, accompanied by the lion which he had tamed by removing a thorn from its paw, the one miracle normally attributed to him.

This image would be developed in the Renaissance into the cardinal scholar in his study, surrounded by books. In the course of the fifteenth century, however, he became above everything else the image of extreme asceticism, the desert hermit torturing his body with penitential fasting. He was adopted as the patron of some of the most severely penitential monastic groups of the period, and some of the most memorable renaissance images of Jerome show him in this role.[24]

All this seems to have passed England by. Jerome appears in English devotional illustrations always as the cardinal with his lion, not as the ascetic visionary.[25] The proper for his feast day, of course, highlights his role as teacher and interpreter of scripture, and that emphasis is replicated in the suffrages in the *Horae*, which are of course normally borrowed from the breviary, but otherwise at a devotional level that dimension is not particularly dominant. The commonest text associated with Jerome in the *Horae* is the so-called Psalter of St Jerome, a catena of 190 verses taken from the whole Psalter which was used as a shortened form of the daily office by ecclesiastics and religious obliged to say the breviary but pressed for time: it was usually preceded by a Latin rubric which explained the virtues and celestial origin of the shortened Psalter, and the circumstances (travel and the like) in which it might be used. The Psalter was usually prefaced by a full-page miniature of Jerome and his lion, so regular a feature of Books of Hours that the quality of the Jerome miniature can be used as a quick-reference guide to the quality of the illustrations in the book as a whole.[26] As might be expected, the Psalter of Jerome also occurs as an item in priests' books of one sort or another.[27]

Individual doctors, then, do feature within lay and clerical piety. But they hardly do so at all *as Doctors*, and I have encountered not a single example of a prayer in an English source directed to all Four Doctors. The suffrages and devotions addressed to them individually are sometimes clustered together in Books of Hours, at any rate those addressed to or associated with Jerome, Augustine and Gregory, and the Doctors normally, but by no means invariably, occur together in the litany of the saints in Sarum Books of Hours: by and large, however, they do not seem to have had a real collective identity.

It seems, then, that the very striking proliferation of pictures of the Four Doctors is a visual convention, without much in the way of resonance within private devotion. The essence of the matter appears to be that the Doctors come as a set, and so can be arranged in architectural and decorative schemes alongside other sets – Evangelists and Apostles, as we have seen, but also, as at Ludham, helper saints and holy kings. Above all, they served as a shorthand reminder of the Church as teacher, and so were an obvious element in decorative schemes which emphasized Christian teaching: hence their presence on fonts, with their creedal and initiatory character, and hence their appearance alongside Evangelists and Apostles, and their association with the creed. Thomas Habington, the Elizabethan antiquary who recorded the appearance of the catechetical sequences of glass on the north side of Malvern Priory, wrote

> the glasse whereof is a mirror wherein we may see how to beleeve, how to live, how to dye, how to passe through temporality to eternity ... there are set forth the Pater Noster, Ave Maria, the creede, the Commandments, the Masse, the Sacraments issuing out from the wounds of our saviour; my memory fainteth. But to conclude all in one, there is the whole Christian doctrine and the fower doctors of the Latine Church.[28]

The ubiquity of these sorts of decorative schemes suggests a high level of lay as well as clerical interest in the catechetical drive to instruct Christians 'how to beleeve, how to live, how to dye, how to passe through temporality to eternity'. To see this commitment as the consequence of Lollardy, however, is to let the tail wag the dog. It is not merely that evidence of widespread adherence to or concern about Lollardy is rare, and indeed for most of the country almost entirely lacking after 1450, when almost all the surviving images were commissioned.

Just as importantly, the multiplication of the imagery of the Doctors is emphatically not a uniquely English phenomenon. From the early fourteenth century the Latin Doctors appear regularly in Italian art – for example, in Giotto's Assisi entrance-vaulting paintings, matching Cimabue's Evangelists at the other end of the upper basilica, or on Ghiberti's Baptistry doors in Florence. North of the Alps they are a feature of Cathedral porches and doors, as at Rouen.[29] A renewed interest in catechesis and orthodoxy is a feature of the fifteenth-century Western European Church generally, associated in France with Gerson and the University of Paris: it triggered a flood of books of instruction and campaigns to encourage preaching and teaching, and there is a corresponding growth of representations of the Doctors in painting, sculpture and glass all over Europe at the same time. Emile Mâle commented on the spread of this phenomenon in fifteenth- and early sixteenth-century France, where the Doctors are usually matched with the Evangelists: he disparaged it as a novelty, which was more ingenious than profound.[30] In the late fifteenth century the Doctors provided a shorthand method for theologians and pastors to signal a commitment to informed orthodoxy. One of the earliest and crudest of Dürer's many woodcuts of St Jerome, which we have already seen, was a version of the conventional representation of the saint for inclusion in Locher's *Theologica Emphasis sive Dialogus super eminentia quatuor doctorum ecclesie Gregorii, Hieronimi, Augustini, Ambrosii*, which was published in Basle in 1496.[31]

Despite the conventional character of the representation of the Doctors as symbols of the teaching *magisterium*, however, there can be no doubt that some at least of this proliferating European imagery of the Doctors was associated in the early fifteenth century, both north and south of the Alps, with a specific concern to promulgate or endorse doctrines which were or had recently been denied by heretics. The so-called Norfolk triptych, which originated in the diocese of Liege c. 1415, has as its central image the *Imago Pietatis*, the dead Christ supported by angels above his tomb and displaying his wounds, from which blood pours. This image was certainly closely associated with the Eucharistic presence, and among the clusters of saints grouped in fours on the wings of the triptych are the Four Doctors. Here, though, there is no overt hint of a preoccupation with heresy: the Doctors are clearly invoked as witnesses to the teaching of Christ's presence in the Eucharist, and the origin of the altarpiece around the year of Hus's condemnation and execution by the Council of Constance is suggestive.[32]

A much more explicit concern with eucharistic orthodoxy and error is evident in Sassetta's now dispersed and incomplete Arte Della Lana altarpiece, painted in the late 1420s for the Sienese wool guild, who commissioned the altarpiece for the chapel of the Carmelites in association with the newly established celebrations for Corpus Christi. Here the Doctors, who are matched not with Evangelists but with four of the patron saints of Siena, flank the central image of a Monstrance containing the Host. The predella and lower sections of the lateral panels had scenes in which the themes of orthodoxy and error loom large, depicting the institution of the Eucharist, the teaching of Thomas Aquinas, a punishment miracle story in which an unbelieving monk is struck dead by a bleeding host at Mass, and the burning of a heretic.[33] The Carmelite provenance of Sassetta's picture is striking, since the Carmelite order in England played a leading role in the confutation of Lollardy.

What these examples establish is that in the first half of the fifteenth century, the Latin Doctors were routinely cited, visually as well as verbally, as witnesses to the Church's orthodox teaching in general, and her eucharistic teaching in particular. This role might indeed be explicitly linked to the defence of the Church's controverted teaching on the presence of Christ in the Eucharist, and to the struggle against heresy. It is important to note that this concern was not confined to worry about Lollardy, and was found as far afield as Siena, but it is certainly possible that the English images of lay devotion to the Latin Doctors which we have been considering are indeed to be read as a conscious response to heresy in its local guise. Nevertheless, I think it would be rash to do so. Though all our surviving English images postdate the incidents I have cited of

Lollard hostility to the Doctors, that heretical priority, and the consequent implication that the orthodox images are to be understood as a response to it, is just as likely to be an accident of survival as the outcome of design. The massive wave of parochial investment in pious decoration in fifteenth-century England means that our perception of the iconography of the late medieval parish church is skewed by the much higher survival-rate of mid- and late fifteenth-century decoration. More importantly, no significant geographic or temporal correspondence can be established between the surviving English iconography of the four Doctors and the incidence of or nervousness about Lollardy. To assume that every manifestation of deliberate orthodoxy is a response to the presence of heresy is to allow the tail to wag the dog.

Indeed, the matter is far more likely to be the other way about. What an early fifteenth-century North European pious artifact like the Norfolk Triptych demonstrates is that the Doctors could and did appear as part and parcel of early fifteenth-century devotional preoccupation with the Eucharistic presence. Given that association, it makes more sense to see popular Lollard hostility to the Doctors as a reaction to that dimension of Church teaching, and to the self-consciously 'correct' and orthodox character of English lay piety, rather than to take the imagery of the Doctors as a reaction to Lollardy. This 'correctness' was certainly fostered by the early fifteenth-century scare over heresy, but it was too ubiquitous a feature of fifteenth-century Catholic Christianity to have been dependent for its drive or direction on the numerically and geographically restricted Lollard movement. If in England, as elsewhere in the early fifteenth century, the Doctors were a recognized shorthand for orthodox doctrinal and devotional emphases, including the eucharistic presence, we can account more readily for the discrepancy between academic Wyclifism, which had respected and invoked the authority of the Doctors against scholastic sophistication of gospel truth, and popular Lollardy, whose attacks on the Doctors look in this perspective like a consequence, not a cause, of the emerging popularity of the Doctors as symbols of orthodoxy in the parishes.

20

The Reformation and the Alabastermen

The luxuriance of late medieval devotion to images had always evoked concern and criticism. Theologians and pastors anxiously insisted that the honour paid to the image passed straight to the sacred personages the images represented, that *Latreia*, the worship in its fullest sense which was due to God alone, was not compromised by the honour paid to images, that images were laymen's books, signposts raising the mind beyond the material to the things above. But critics were well aware of the gap between theory and practice. In the twelfth century St Bernard of Clairvaux denounced the cult of glamorous images, decorated with gold and precious stones. To devotees dazzled by such sacred bling, 'the saint [is] believed to be the more holy the more highly coloured the image is,' so that 'people rush to kiss it, they are invited to donate, and they admire the beautiful more than they venerate the sacred.'[1] Two and a half centuries later the author of *The Imitation of Christ* lamented the lust for novelty which sent hordes of laypeople on pilgrimage to shrines and images, 'with such levity and so little contrition of heart that little or no fruits of amendment are carried home'. They would do better to stay where they were, and make their prayers to Christ's own presence in the sacrament of the altar in their parish church.[2] The spiritualising tendency of Erasmus's Christian humanism privileged interior piety over the religion of external acts, and in the process downgraded visible expressions of religion, including images: as he wrote in his *Enchiridion Militis Christiani*,

> You can only establish perfect piety when you turn away from visible things, which are for the most part either imperfect or of themselves indifferent, and you seek instead the invisible, which corresponds to the highest part of human nature.[3]

And even the devout Thomas More, concerned to defend the veneration of images against its attackers, satirised the London wives who gazed so intently on a statue of Our Lady of the Tower that they persuaded themselves that the insensate statue had smiled upon them.[4]

In late medieval England, these entirely orthodox worries about the cult of images found more radical expression in the native heretical tradition, Lollardy. With considerable reservations, the movement's founder, John Wyclif, seems in fact to have allowed the legitimacy of unadorned images as laymen's books and aids to devotion. But his followers developed those reservations into a wholesale rejection of the cult. The carving of images, they insisted, was forbidden by the Ten Commandments: images diverted to dead wood and stone the worship due to the living God and his saints, and money spent on the cult of images robbed the poor of the alms which were their due.

> And hereby the rude puple tristus utterly in thes deade ymagis, and loven Gode and hese commandmentis the lesse, for men skateren there love in siche stokkkis and leeven precious werkis of mercy undone tile here pore neyghbouris, whiche ben Cristis ymagis.[5]

Lollard disapproval did not confine itself to denunciation: though never common, iconoclastic attacks on images, the breaking or burning of crucifixes and statues, remained a form of direct action resorted to by the more intrepid Lollards, for whom fire and axe were more eloquent weapons against 'dumb stocks' than mere words.[6]

Wooden statues were more often the target of such demonstrations than images of alabaster or stone. Though alabaster is ruined by fire, it does not burn. Nevertheless, alabaster images, often painted and gilded and presented in decorated wooden tabernacles, certainly came under the general Lollard condemnation of 'gay' images, 'ryaly tabernackled with kerviing and peyntid with gold and precious jewelis'. And occasionally the heretical critique focused on images which were specially strongly represented in alabaster. Lollards denounced, for example, all attempts to portray the Godhead itself, as forbidden in the Old Testament. They therefore specially detested images of the Trinity, in which God the Father holds the crucifix between his outstretched hands, 'peyntyng the Fadir as an olde man, and the son as a yonge man on a crosse, and the Holy Gost coming further of the Fadur moythe to the Son as white dowfe'. Such images were particularly common in alabaster, and very large numbers of them survive.[7]

Heretical denunciations and heretical direct actions against images recurred episodically from the 1380s to the 1520s. But despite their persistence, such protests and attacks almost certainly had little or no impact on the practice of the veneration of images among the Lollards' orthodox neighbours. With the advent of the Protestant Reformation, however, what had been an outlawed and dangerous fringe campaign moved to centre stage, and in England would eventually be adopted as official policy.

The removal and destruction of images had emerged very early in the Reformation movement as a specially vivid and concrete gesture of repudiation of papal Christianity. Andreas Karlstadt's drastic iconoclastic preaching during Luther's absence from Wittenberg in January and February 1522 led to an eruption of popular destruction, which was rapidly disowned and denounced by Luther. The following year, the Zurich town authorities ordered the official removal of all images from churches, to prevent similar disorders there. Increasingly, the repudiation of images by word and action became a defining mark of the Reformation.[8] Protestant objections to images replicated those of the medieval Lollards, but rested also on a rediscovered sense of the absolute prohibition of images, especially carved images, in the Mosaic law. The medieval Church had been well aware of the prohibition of images in the Decalogue in the books of Exodus and Deuteronomy, but had understood prohibition as being subsumed under the teaching of the first commandment, forbidding the worship of false gods. Since images of Christ and the saints were manifestly not images of false gods, they were not excluded by that prohibition. The Protestant reformers, by contrast, arranged the text of the Decalogue so that the prohibition of images was put as a separate, second, commandment, permanently binding in its own right: all who venerated images, whatever their intentions, therefore, committed the heinous sin of idolatry.[9]

During the 1520s, royal policy in England was resolutely opposed to all these Protestant objections to images. In the summer of 1528, Henry VIII himself praised and publicised the French king's participation in a ceremony of solemn reparation to the Virgin Mary after the sacrilegious desecration of an image by Huguenot protesters in Paris, denouncing 'that damnable ... demeanour of those worse than Jews that would do such despite to the blessed images where they cannot do it to the thing itself'.[10] In 1530, Thomas More devoted part of his most brilliant polemical work, the officially commissioned *Dialogue Concerning Heresies*, to a spirited defence of the cult of images.[11]

More's defence of images in itself, of course, represented an admission that iconoclastic sentiment was spreading in England. The early 1530s saw an outbreak of image-breaking in Essex and Suffolk, most notoriously the burning of the Rood of Dovercourt, for which three of the culprits were hanged. In October 1533 it was even being reported that in some places in London images were being cast out of the churches as useless 'stocks and stones', and that some of those responsible would even sacrilegiously 'prick them with their bodkins to see whether they will bleed or no'.[12]

Till Henry VIII's break with Rome, all such iconoclastic acts were treated with severity as manifestations of heresy. But as royal policy turned against Rome, and Henry became increasingly reliant on committed reformers for support for the Royal Supremacy, official policy towards iconoclasm changed. From 1535, protégés of Thomas Cromwell, the king's chief minister, were permitted to attack the veneration of images openly. That year saw the publication of an English translation of Martin Bucer's iconoclastic tract *Das einigberlei Bild*, written to justify the removal and destruction of the images in Strassburg in 1530: the translator was William Marshall, a client of Cromwell's.[13] For Bucer, 'to pluck down images ... is an holy thing,' and he had insisted that according to scripture, we should not only remove images, but 'we ought to break them, yea, and that all to powder, that they might never be made whole again.'[14]

Henry would never authorize the indiscriminate removal or destruction of all images, but the Visitation of the smaller monasteries which began in July 1535, and which marked the beginning of the destruction of monastic life in England, targeted the abuse of images, identifying as abuse the overt veneration of images and relics with lights, censing and other ritual gestures, especially pilgrimage. Over the next three years Royal Commissioners would strip and remove all the major shrine images in England.[15] Royal policy manifestly radicalized as the dissolution of the monasteries progressed. The Royal Injunctions issued by Cromwell in 1536, in order to banish 'superstition and hypocrisy', forbade the clergy to 'set forth or extol any images' or 'entice' their people into pilgrimage: they were to discourage any offerings to or adornment of images, and to direct parishioners instead to give alms to the poor.[16] In the following year, the so-called Bishops Book offered a fundamentally hostile and grudging account of the place of images in church, conceding that they might be suffered as books of instruction, to encourage imitation of the virtues of Christ and the saints. But images were dangerous: they had constantly led Israel into idolatry, and they had been first admitted into the Church, the Book declared, only as a concession to 'the dullness of man's wits, and partly yielding to the customs of gentility' (i.e. paganism). Images of God the Father, the Book declared, were specially misleading, and it would be far better for Christians 'to be without all such images ...'.[17] By the autumn of 1538 when Henry's (and Cromwell's) second set of Royal Injunctions were issued, the 1536 prohibition of the abuse of images had sharpened and hardened into an all-out attack on the cult of images itself. According to the new Injunctions, all veneration of images 'in wandering to pilgrimages, offerings of money, candles or tapers to images or relics, or kissing or licking the same', were mere 'phantasies', unwarranted by scripture, and incurring 'great threats and maledictions of God, as things tending to idolatry and superstition, which of all offences God almighty doth detest and abhor'. The clergy therefore were to 'take down and delay' all 'feigned' images which had been 'abused' by 'pilgrimages or offerings of anything made thereunto'. From henceforth, they were to permit no 'candles, tapers or images of wax' to be set before any image or picture, with the exception of the great crucifix above the chancel, the sacrament, and the Easter Sepulchre. And in an ominous indication of the likely direction of future royal policy, the Injunctions promised that the king would 'more hereafter travail for the abolishing of such images as might be an occasion of ... offence to God'.[18]

The 1538 instructions to remove all 'abused' images proved in the event profoundly ambiguous. Radical reformers invoked the injunctions as a weapon against any image whatsoever, since almost all images had candles burning somewhere near them, and most were at least occasionally censed in the course of the liturgy. By contrast, conservatives insisted that only pilgrimage images had been abused, and most of the images in churches did not fall under the condemnations of the Injunctions. In the late 1530s and early 1540s conservatives and radicals with profoundly different attitudes to images found themselves locked in sometimes bitter conflict, which remained essentially unresolved.[19] The images of Christ and the saints would therefore remain technically legitimate for the remainder of Henry's reign, provided they were not the object of pilgrimage or other acts of veneration. Though committed Protestants like Archbishop Cranmer used the Injunctions as an excuse to remove even images which had never been so venerated,

Henry himself remained ambivalent, angrily suppressing all shrines, yet refusing to outlaw the liturgical veneration of the Cross in Holy Week , despite pressure from Cranmer and others to abolish it.

But despite these ambiguities, the Injunctions had struck a mortal blow at the cult of images all the same. The ban on the lighting of lamps and candles before the images of the saints outlawed the most overt and visible sign of devotion to them. In the conservative West Country parish of Morebath, which had a vigorous and expanding cult of the saints throughout the 1530s, the Injunctions of 1538 had an immediate and devastating effect. Throughout the 1530s, Morebath had been busy revamping old images in the church, and commissioning new: with the Injunctions of 1538, all such activities ceased. The parish wound up all the village 'stores' which had financed the lights before the images of the saints. Till 1538 the priest, a devout conservative with an ardent devotion to the saints, had invariably spoken of the images by their names, as if they were people – 'for dressing St Anne, for gilding St Sidwell, for a light before St George'. After 1538, he routinely referred to the images collectively as mere objects – 'the imagery of the church'. With the extinguishing of the lights, the images had ceased to have personalities, and became so many items of furniture.[20]

It seems likely that the drying-up of devotional activity focused on images at Morebath was replicated in other English parishes. Though the existing images might remain in place, they ceased to be venerated. Though a Passion altarpiece now in Afferden, Holland, was reputedly carved in 1542 and exported in the reign of Henry,[21] there can have been few altarpieces and fewer still new devotional images commissioned in England after 1538, in alabaster or any other medium. Images were on their way to becoming devotional fossils, dislodged from their central place in the practice of traditional religion.

And other royal measures of the late 1530s may have affected the production specifically of *alabaster* images in unexpected ways. After the break with Rome, all honourable mention of the Pope had been forbidden, and in 1535 the Pope's name and title were ordered to be removed from all liturgical books. That ban had been extended to papal imagery as well, and papal insignia, such as the papal tiara or even cardinals' hats, were routinely scraped out of panel paintings and book illuminations.[22] In November 1538, Henry added a new prohibition, ordering the destruction of all prayers to and images of St Thomas Becket, whose cult symbolised for the king the Church's age-old defiance of royal power. Once again, this instruction seems to have been very widely observed, even in prayer books designed for private use, and most surviving English images of Becket appear to have been defaced in obedience to this instruction.[23]

These twin prohibitions, of papal insignia and images of Becket, must certainly have impacted directly on the single most popular devotional image in alabaster, the mysterious one of the decapitated head of John the Baptist. Such images, with their allusions to the eucharistic 'Lamb of God', seem to have functioned as a symbol of the eucharistic presence of Jesus, and the carving of St John's heads was a specialty of the Nottingham alabastermen.[24] Often displayed in elaborately painted tabernacles, they were among the commonest domestic devotional objects in early Tudor England. Some examples of the image present the saint's head unadorned or on a disc-shaped plate. But in most of the surviving examples, the head of St John is flanked by miniature figures of two standing saints – St Peter, often with a papal tiara and keys, on one side, and St Thomas Becket, with his archiepiscopal cross, on the other. It seems inconceivable that images of this kind went on being produced after 1538, or even after the prohibition of papal imagery in 1535, and one can only speculate about whether the Tudor laity went on venerating even in private images potentially so obnoxious to royal policy.

It seems likely, therefore, that royal religious policy between 1536 and 1538 drastically reduced business for all the workshops producing devotional and liturgical images in whatever medium, the alabastermen among the rest. But the *coup de grâce* to the whole industry was administered in the next reign, with the accession of the boy king Edward VI.

From the start of his reign, Edward was cast by his Protestant Council as a radical reformer in the mould of King Josiah, the young King of Israel who had rediscovered the written law of God and purged Israel of its idols, an identification which underlies Tudor pictorial representations of Edward's reign, like the illustrated title page of the Edwardine section of John Foxe's *Acts and Monuments*, where Edward hands the bible to his subjects while in the background the churches are purged of idolatrous images, the 'papist's paltrie'.[25] Here was a reform agenda with drastic potential, and over the six years of Edward's reign that agenda was pushed relentlessly forward. A new set of Injunctions were issued in the summer of 1547, as the basis of a Royal Visitation of all the parishes of England. These injunctions theoretically permitted the continuing use of images 'only to put them in remembrance of the godly and virtuous lives of them that they do represent', but Injunction 28 was in fact a manifesto for the total destruction of all religious imagery, requiring that parishes 'shall take away, utterly extinct and destroy all shrines ... pictures, paintings and all other monuments of feigned miracles, pictures, idolatry, and superstition: so that there remain no memory of the same in walls, glass-windows, or elsewhere within their churches or houses', and specified that all such images should be removed from private dwellings as well as public spaces.[26] Though the regime dithered for a time over the retention in churches of the crucifix, worried by the potential for disorder in unauthorised iconoclasm, there was no mistaking the radical thrust of these instructions. All over England, the Visitation became a signal for systematic iconoclasm. In February 1548 the Council followed the logic of the Injunctions, using the excuse of dissent over images in the parishes as an excuse to order the total destruction of all images whatsoever. Despite riots in Yorkshire and the West Country, the policy was pushed through, leaving beleaguered conservatives no recourse except, where they could, to conceal specially loved images.[27] There is no doubt that many images, especially small portable ones like alabasters, were 'rescued' by being concealed in people's homes. In the wake of the prayer-book rebellions of 1549, the Council sought to close this loophole by issuing a proclamation on Christmas Day 1549 requiring the destruction of all Catholic cultic objects and books, and imposing swingeing penalties on all who concealed them. A statute in January 1550 explicitly extended these penalties to anyone who had in their possession 'any images of stone, timber, alabaster, or earth, graven, carved or painted ... and do not before the last day of June next ensuing deface and destroy or cause to be defaced and destroyed the same images and every one of them'.[28]

The devastation which these Edwardine iconoclastic orders might leave behind in the parishes is eloquently attested by the two dozen shattered alabaster fragments now preserved in the Cambridgeshire parish of Whittlesford. Alabaster images were cheap and readily available, and late medieval Whittlesford had clearly made the most of it. The remaining fragments reveal that till Edward's reign the parish church had contained three alabaster altarpieces with narrative scenes, a large image of the Virgin breast-feeding the child Jesus, which stood in the chancel and had been donated in 1519 by the widow Joanne Webbe, an image of the Trinity which Mistress Webbe had paid to have regilded, an image of the Pietà which stood on its own altar and to which other women of the parish had donated items of clothing, an image of the Nativity ('Our Lady in Gesyn'), an image of St Anne teaching the Virgin to read, and images of St Zita of Lucca, St Paul and St Loy. One can only speculate about the feelings of the parishioners when this crowded pantheon was cleared and smashed by Edward's Commissioners. A similar holocaust in another Cambridge parish of Toft has left fragments of images of a bishop saint, St Christopher, St Loy, and King Henry VI, uncanonized, but whose cult had been growing fast on the eve of the Reformation.[29]

The parishioners of Whittlesford and Toft clearly obeyed the Edwardine injunctions to the letter, and destroyed their images. But this requirement was certainly often flouted. Most large-scale images probably were destroyed, but smaller, portable items might not only be hidden by the devout, but also be secreted away and sold abroad by the financially enterprising. The drastic ritual changes ordered by the reformers brought on to the mid-Tudor market a tidal wave of precious and semi-precious materials: silk and velvet vestments, gold and silver chalices and ornaments, metal thuribles and crosses, even the brass images of the dead judged to have 'superstitious' inscriptions – and hordes of entrepreneurial traders and craftsmen hastened to cash in on this bonanza.[30] Alabaster altarpieces were certainly among these saleable commodities, and though many perished, alabaster images probably formed a high proportion of the images whose sale was complained about by the English ambassador in France, Sir John Mason, in September 1550. He reported to the Council that three or four ships laden with such images had recently come from England, and their cargoes were being eagerly bought in Paris, Rouen and elsewhere. But the sales had given the ignorant people there 'occasion to talk according to their notions', that is, to disparage the English as godless and irreligious for banishing the images of Christ and his saints. This, as Mason pointed out, 'needed not, had their Lordship's command for defacing them been observed'.[31]

This Edwardine diaspora of images to continental Europe helps explain the survival of so many examples of English alabaster work there, though many must have been the product of peaceful trade in the pre-Reformation period.[32] And though some of the alabasters concealed would survive to be safely exhumed once Protestant England had outlived its iconophobia, most of what remained in England was doomed to destruction.[33] The death of Edward in 1553 called a halt to the campaign against imagery, and Queen Mary's Catholic regime provided a five-year respite. Her Church required once again the installation of images in the parish churches of England. But after the massive destruction of Edward's reign, the iconographic objectives of the Marian regime were necessarily modest, amounting to no more than the replacement of the main rood image over the chancel arch, the provision of an altar cross, an image of the Virgin, and an image of the church's patron saint. Every church was required to have a side altar as well as a high altar, but few of these can have been provided with the carved reredoses which were probably the pre-Reformation norm. Most of this basic programme of replacement must have been carried out in painted or carved wood, and painted cloth. Even so, there was a shortage of available craftsmen, and long waiting lists for images.[34]

It is doubtful therefore that England's alabastermen benefited much from the Marian restoration. No doubt some of the alabaster workshops which had once catered for the booming demand for altarpieces and devotional images in early Tudor England had survived by diverting their output to secular purposes like the carving of tombs. But the drying-up of demand which almost certainly followed the Henrician enactments of the late 1530s and, more devastatingly, the locust years of Edward's reign, would prove fatal. A generation on, a later Elizabethan commentator would look back on that Edwardian watershed, when the Idols were 'pulled downe, and the church, as nere as they could, cleansed from the dregges of such an Antichrist', not just as the revealing of the Protestant gospel, but the end of a benighted industry:

> whereupon the painters that livde with such trashe, as trimming of shrines and of roodes, alters and saints, and the carvers that made such images, were fain, with Alexander the Coppersmith, to cry out against Paul and his doctrine, having so little woork, that they almost forgot their occupation.[35]

As Lawrence Stone has observed. 'The history of English medieval sculpture does not draw quietly to a close; it is cut off sharp.'[36]

21

Brush for Hire: Lucas Cranach the Elder

There seems to be something paradoxical, even self-contradictory, in the very notion of a Reformation image. The movement of religious protest inaugurated by Martin Luther in Wittenberg in 1517 quickly targeted the veneration of images as a damnable superstition, the idolatrous confusion of gross matter with an invisible God who was pure and eternal spirit. The fifteenth century had seen a great flowering of the visual arts all over Europe, and in Luther's Germany painters provided an astonishing flow of emotionally charged ultra-Catholic art, devotional or liturgical images for veneration or meditation in church and home.

But with the appearance of Luther, the age of the cult image in much of north-eastern Europe came to an end. Art, it seemed, was about to be eliminated by the word of God. The Kingdom of Christ, Luther declared, 'is a hearing kingdom, not a seeing kingdom: for the eyes do not lead and guide us to where we know and find Christ, but rather the ears do this.'[1] He was inclined to think at first that religion would be better off with no images at all. Great painters, Dürer among them, welcomed the new teaching as a God-given liberation of the spirit, but they trembled for their livelihood. As the Strasbourg painter Heinrich Vogtherr observed, throughout Germany the gospel had brought the 'diminution and arrest of all subtle and liberal arts', so that 'in a few years, there will scarcely be found anyone working as painter or sculptor.'[2] In 1522, one of Luther's closest collaborators, the priest Andreas Karlstadt, supervised the removal and destruction of all the images in the churches of Wittenberg, with the connivance of the city authorities – the first significant officially sanctioned iconoclasm of the Reformation era. As the new teaching spread outside Germany – to Switzerland, the Low Countries, eventually to England and Scotland – the public destruction of images would become a standard rite of purification, the concrete symbol of the overthrow of the Roman antichrist and the establishment of a gospel worship in spirit and in truth.

But not in Luther's Germany: alarmed by the extremism of the iconoclasts, Luther shifted from indifference to pictures, to positive approval of them. The human soul, he taught, was itself an image-making mechanism. When he heard of the Passion of Christ, he declared, 'it is impossible for me not to make images of this within my heart ... when I hear the word Christ, there delineates itself in my heart the picture of a man who hangs on the cross.' And if every hearer of the gospel has the image of Christ in his heart, 'why then should it be sinful to have it before my eyes?'[3] Images might therefore be usefully retained in church, so long as it was clear that they were not sacred in themselves, but served as mere reminders or teachers of gospel truths. To a papist, Luther thought, the crucifix was indeed an idol, something to be venerated and bowed down to. To the good Lutheran, by contrast, the same image was a message from heaven, a signpost directing the believer's gaze beyond the sign to the invisible signified.

As it happened, Wittenberg had in Luther's friend Lucas Cranach not only an ardently committed Protestant, but one of the most successful painters of his generation. Cranach and his highly commercialized factory-studio poured out images which decisively shaped the official visual propaganda for the new movement, creating not only dozens of bible illustrations or woodcuts idealizing Luther and lampooning the old religion, but also a series of elaborate painted altarpieces designed to adorn and explain the worship of the flagship churches of the new movement.[4]

BRUSH FOR HIRE: LUCAS CRANACH THE ELDER   303

Since the Romantic era, we have lived with the cliché that any artist worth his salt must be an unruly individualist, in rebellion against the moral and aesthetic constraints of a philistine world – a William Blake, a Toulouse-Lautrec, a Francis Bacon. In that perspective, the notion of the painter as tradesman-entrepreneur, successful, respectable, organizing his output on production-line principles and adapting both subject matter and style to the taste of the highest bidder, seems all wrong. But Lucas Cranach the elder, the great mythopoeic painter of the German Reformation, was just such a shopkeeping genius.

Cranach more or less singlehandedly invented the visual vocabulary for Luther's rebellion against the Catholic Church. Cranach charted his friend's evolution from wild-eyed monk to magisterial reformer in a stream of portrait prints and panel paintings. His mass-produced images made Luther's the most familiar face in sixteenth-century Europe, and became the definitive icons of the new religion.[5] And yet, at the height of his activity as Luther's publicist, he was working equally hard on lucrative commissions from the most powerful Catholic ecclesiastic in Germany: Cardinal Albrecht of Brandenburg, the very man whose blatant sale of indulgences had driven Luther to protest in the first place. Friendship, art and ideological purity were all very well, but for Cranach, business was business.

Nothing is known about his early life, though his background is suggested by his family name: Mahler, 'painter'. He was born in Kronach, in Saxony, and adopted the name of his home town to distinguish himself from other jobbing craftsmen. His early style would in any case have marked him out as special. When he first surfaces around 1500 in Vienna, Cranach was already a mature artist in his late twenties, whose work belonged to the same disturbing, imaginative world as Grünewald's Eisenheim altarpiece. Tormented figures drawn with rapid, agitated strokes inhabit landscapes whose vivid natural features mimic the emotions of the human characters. Crucified bodies seem to emerge out of the wood of the crosses on which they writhe. Cranach's intense colouring and detailed landscape backgrounds would inspire a new school of painters in the Danube region, but he moved away from this early work. While at Vienna, he also established himself as a portraitist, with a series of luminous paintings of distinguished Viennese academics and their wives. His sitters pose in idyllic landscapes filled with astrological symbolism, showing that the artist was absorbing the fashionable humanist learning then making its mark in the German universities.[6]

In 1505, however, Cranach left the imperial capital to become court painter to the elector of Saxony, Prince Frederick the Wise. After Vienna, Frederick's capital at Wittenberg must have seemed a provincial backwater, its 2,000 citizens squeezed into 400 houses within the city walls. But Wittenberg was on the up. A few years earlier, Frederick had founded a new university there and begun recruiting distinguished academic staff; he now recruited this talented young metropolitan painter to proclaim the wealth and sophistication of the Saxon court.

The work of a court painter was varied, but not always glamorous. Cranach and, soon, an extensive workshop of studio assistants were kept busy producing devotional paintings for the homes of the nobility, altarpieces and images of the saints for local parish churches, and portraits of the electoral family and principal courtiers, many of them designed as gifts for Frederick's friends and allies. Cranach rapidly evolved stereotyped likenesses of the elector and his family, which could be endlessly replicated by his assistants. But portraiture also produced some of his best work, especially his exquisitely sensitive portraits of the royal children, in which he captured with sympathy and affection their patent unease under the weight of their stiff court robes, and their nervous uncertainty about where to put their hands.

His daily bread, though, was a kind of work we associate with interior decorators rather than creative artists: heraldic devices for tournaments and hunts, table ornaments for banquets, shields and logos for the ducal coaches, house signs and banners. Frederick was passionate about jousting and hunting. To publicize these prestigious court events, Cranach produced a series of intricate woodcuts depicting the incidents of the hunt, or the jumble of lances, armour and horses at jousts. Frederick also owned one of Europe's most spectacular collections of relics: holy skulls, bones and teeth in their hundreds, a hair from the beard of Christ, threads from Our Lady's veil, a twig from the burning bush. Displayed in the castle church in eight aisles, the 5,000 relics and their precious containers were a major tourist draw. In 1509, Cranach provided 108 woodcuts for a lavishly illustrated printed catalogue, designed to advertise the indulgences granted for venerating the relics, and to be sold as a pilgrim souvenir.

His sketchbooks were filled with all he saw around him at court: a brace of pheasants in the castle larder, racing herds of deer, the head of a stag shot through the eye with an arrow, or the rugged face of an elderly peasant, maybe a gamekeeper or beater, caught in a rapid watercolour sketch and easily the most memorable of all his portraits. But he also responded to widening acquaintance with art and artists. There were wary personal encounters at Nuremberg with Dürer, whose work he admired, envied, imitated and occasionally parodied. A diplomatic mission to the Netherlands in 1509 triggered a series of paintings heavily influenced by Flemish models, including a deeply moving pietà and a candlelit nativity. A series of Italianate panels of the Madonna and Child from the mid-1510s onwards strongly recalls Perugino and Francesco Francia, and suggests that Cranach may have ventured south of the Alps at least once.

To these influences were added the special demands on a successful court painter – perhaps, most of all, the need to evolve a style that allowed him to delegate the more mechanical side of his commissions. The agitated individuality of his Viennese period gave way to a sweeter, blander manner. He established a successful workshop in the town, where mass-production techniques prevailed. His pictures were now routinely painted on birch-wood panels cut to standard sizes by a team of carpenters, often to the precise dimensions of the paper sheets and cover boards used in the bookbinding and printing business he was also running. He accumulated pattern drawings of heads, hands, limbs, as well as incidental birds and beasts, for use in different contexts. It became difficult to distinguish the hand of the master from that of his assistants. Cranach's own skills were undiminished, but the resulting stylistic smoothing-out can be gauged from two versions of the same subject, ten years apart. In an altarpiece depicting the martyrdom of Saint Catherine, painted in 1505 and now in Budapest, fire and brimstone cascade down from the stormy heavens, the torturer's toothed wheel explodes spectacularly, sending horses and riders tumbling in confusion (the falling figures were lifted from a print by Dürer), while in the foreground an orc-like executioner with a grotesquely bulging codpiece wrenches at the saint's décolletage and prepares to behead her. In the later version, painted for the ultra-Catholic bishop of Olmutz, all is decorous and calm. The exploding wheel and the brimstone appear scaled down in the remote distance, the horses and their riders stand calmly by, while a timid and elderly executioner, Private Godfrey in tights, apologetically moves aside the saint's hair so as not to harm it.

Brimstone and exploding wheels, however, were nothing to the upheaval that Cranach's friend Martin Luther was about to unleash on Christendom. The Augustinian monk had been sent by his order to Wittenberg in 1508 to teach scripture in the university. In 1517, fresh from an intense conversion experience after years of religious anxiety, Luther publicly challenged the scandal of the sale of indulgences. (The sale was being pushed in Germany to repay debts that Cardinal Albrecht had accumulated to buy his archbishopric; the Vatican's cut went to rebuilding St Peter's in Rome.) This protest against an obvious abuse soon spiralled into a wholesale rejection of the authority of the Catholic Church, and little Wittenberg leapt to prominence as the headquarters of the new movement.

From the outset, Cranach was crucial to its success. Through the early 1520s his printing house pumped out Luther's pamphlets, with handsome decorated title pages designed by Cranach himself. It was Cranach's press that issued Luther's German New Testament in 1522. His portraits of the Wittenberg reformer, available as painted panels or more cheaply as paper prints, had an honoured place in thousands of homes. In 1521, he collaborated with Luther's lieutenant, Philip Melancthon, to produce the most devastating pamphlet of the sixteenth century, *The Passional of Christ and Antichrist*. In this little booklet, twenty-six paired woodcuts with captions contrasted the evangelical Christ of Luther's preaching with the abuses of the papacy: Christ and his followers humbly trudging the roads while the Pope is carried in a litter; Christ washing his disciples' feet while the Pope's foot is kissed by kings and emperors; Christ crowned with thorns while the Pope is crowned with the triple tiara. Cranach's eloquent little woodcuts transformed Melancthon's rather undistinguished prose into a polemical Exocet. Sold in vast numbers for a few pennies each, it burned into the consciousness of Protestant Europe the conviction that the Pope was indeed the antichrist.

Cranach went on to devise a new pictorial language for Protestantism, including an ingenious schematic illustration of the relationship between law and gospel. This was eagerly copied by other painters, including the younger Holbein, though it is hard to imagine anyone warming to its stiff and preachy didacticism. More attractive were a series of cartoon-like gospel paintings illustrating the free gift of salvation: Christ blessing the little children, Christ with the woman taken in adultery. For Luther's own church in the 1540s, he created a great altarpiece depicting the reformer himself celebrating the communion, Last-Supper-style, flanked by side panels in which Melancthon baptizes a baby, and another colleague, Johannes Bugenhagen, hears confessions. In a smaller panel below, Luther preaches on the crucifix to his Wittenberg congregation, and the whole ensemble provided the new church with a powerful self-image. But perhaps the oddest of these pictorial renderings of Lutheran teaching was a series of small panels portraying the virtue of Charity as a naked and smiling young woman, surrounded by babies, with whom she suckles, cuddles or plays. The intended message here was that charity was a gift to the believer, as natural as motherhood and apple pie, not some duty-bound regime of good works. This theme embodied Cranach's growing interest in the classical nude. Gospel teaching here shades into a charming human idyll whose religious 'message' is easily missed, perhaps because, in the end, it was superfluous.[7]

Despite superficial resemblances to their medieval predecessors, these Lutheran altarpieces share a number of striking new features. Relentlessly didactic rather than devotional, often heavily encrusted with explanatory text and biblical quotations, they ring the changes on a small repertoire of images officially approved by Luther as elucidating the meaning of Christ's death: Adam and Eve and the tree of temptation, the brazen serpent which Moses raised in the wilderness and which prefigures the cross, the Last Supper, the lamb of God, the pointing finger of John the Baptist, the resurrected Christ trampling the dragon or skeleton of sin and death. Many of them also depict the new Church, in representations of Protestant celebration of the gospel sacraments of baptism and communion, and in portraits of its leaders or secular supporters. The Weimar altarpiece begun by Cranach in the 1550s but finished after his death by his son deploys almost all of this repertoire of official Lutheran imagery in an extended allegory of salvation, while in the foreground of the picture Luther and Cranach himself stand alongside John the Baptist under the cross. Luther points to a text in his Bible, 'The blood of Jesus Christ cleanses us of all sins,' while a jet of Christ's blood arcs spectacularly from his wounded side through the air to fall on Cranach's head, vividly if unsubtly imaging a direct salvation unmediated by priest or ceremonial, and reiterating in pictorial code the literal sense of Luther's text.

The dispiriting didacticism of this Lutheran art has often been commented on. Nineteenth-century Romantics blamed Luther for the death of art for art's sake, and its replacement with mere propaganda. Hegel thought that the Reformation inaugurated a tragic but necessary shift towards interiority which had robbed art of its intrinsic holiness, a disjunction between the beautiful and the true. The material world, fetishized by medieval Christianity in the cult of relics, the Eucharist and holy images, was now disenchanted, and from that point onwards, however skilfully God, Christ or the saints might be portrayed by painters, 'it is no help, we bow the knee no longer.' Art was no longer sacred, immediate, an encounter with the ultimate: instead, it offered an alternative form of textuality, mere food for thought.

In a scintillating, learned and eloquent book the art historian Joseph Koerner explored this shift by an extended investigation of the method and meaning of Cranach's Lutheran paintings. In particular, he focused on the monumental altarpiece Cranach painted for Luther's own church, the Stadtkirche at Wittenberg, installed there in 1547 as a memorial to the first and greatest of the reformers. Koerner saw in this altarpiece the key to a new aesthetic, which preserved art by turning it into a form of pious self-effacement, enacting its own theological redundancy by presenting itself as a mere system of useful signs, not so much an alternative as a supplement to text, a vehicle for information and affirmation of the new gospel. Emptied of emotion and of claims to transcendence, Lutheran art represented the sacred not by confronting the visible Church with images of the invisible Church, a company of the saints caught up in a heavenly worship (as in Catholic altarpieces such as Duccio's *Maestà* or van Eyck's Ghent *Adoration of the Lamb*), but by depicting the quotidian activities of the visible Church itself. For the first time, altarpieces included pictures of routine church services. Lutheran communions were therefore celebrated in front of pictures of Lutheran communion services, in a self-referential and resolute refusal of transcendence. Interestingly, while medieval high altarpieces almost never feature the Last Supper (a subject normally reserved for relic altars or monastery refectories), the overwhelming majority of Lutheran altarpieces include a picture of the Last Supper, as historical warrant for the contemporary Church's celebration. Even Lutheran representations of the crucifix strive to display the cross in the mundane setting and neutral space of the church building, not the sacred space of Calvary, thereby rendering it 'an emotional blank', not an object of worship but a sermon in paint. As Koerner, in a characteristically striking phrase, writes, 'Christ dies in the dead air of a schoolroom.'[8] This new 'mortification of painting through text' helped ensure Protestant art's survival and continuing use as a didactic and propagandist tool, but at the price of the aesthetic collapse for which traditional art historians have berated it.

Koerner's readings of Cranach's art are unfailingly arresting and inventive, but perhaps because of rather than despite their brilliance, the reader sometimes wonders if he doesn't over-read the evidence. What if the 'emotional blankness' of so much of Cranach's religious painting springs not from a 'new aesthetic', but from imaginative exhaustion, or from the routinization and decline of quality inevitable given the use of assistants and of mass-production methods in his money-spinning studio? And can one then claim that an ideological hiatus divides Cranach's pre- and post-Lutheran art, from Catholic expression to Protestant didacticism?

There is a wider issue here: it is perfectly true that early mid-sixteenth-century Lutherans, while retaining images, were wary of the danger of idolatry, a wariness that inform the sometimes leaden didacticism Koerner discerned in Lutheran art. But many overtly affective medieval devotional images survived in Lutheran churches, and by the late sixteenth century the conflict with Calvinism made the retention of older images and the creation of new a distinctive confessional 'marker' of militant Lutheranism. Lutheran altarpieces might incorporate late medieval devotional images, and newly commissioned Lutheran religious paintings and sculpture often deployed the same affective Baroque appeal to the heart of the onlooker as their Catholic counterparts. Lutheran clergy might comment on, and deplore, the renewed 'thirst for images' among their people, but the search for a more deeply internalized and affective piety led devotional writers like Jacob Arndt to plunder the mystical and devotional literature of the late Middle Ages. And the desire for a more ardent religion of the heart led Arndt to place a high value on the affective power of devotional art. In his 1597 treatise *Ikonographia* he wrote that 'Just as a figurative speech ... paints an image in the heart through hearing, and forms it so that it remains in the mind, so looking at a beautiful image and painting forms in a person's heart in a spiritual manner that which it signifies.' Such sentiments ensured that the Lutheran art of the Baroque era would often be hard to distinguish from its Catholic counterparts.[9]

But in any case, whatever the theological difficulties, financial considerations ensured that for Cranach, the break between his Catholic and his Protestant painting was never absolute. Cranach was undoubtedly a convinced Protestant. He and Luther were close friends, and personal friendship, as well as conscientious conviction and a shrewd eye to the main chance, lay behind his work on behalf of the Reformation. When Luther took the dramatic and scandalous step of marrying a former nun in 1525, the timid Melancthon stayed away, but Cranach was Luther's best man. He sold mass-produced sets of paired wedding portraits of the couple, a defiant proclamation of the reformer's evangelical freedom from monkish vows. Painter and preacher were godfathers to each other's children, and in 1527 Cranach painted tender portraits of Luther's aged father and mother.[10] The insight into character and obvious affection of these great pictures were another testimony to the painter's love for Luther and his family.

But religion and friendship were personal, business was business. When it came to winning a profitable commission, Cranach was a spiritual whore, a brush for hire to the highest bidder. A court painter who basked in the patronage of the great and the not-so-good, he was far from fastidious about his subject-matter: he specialized, for example, in soft-porn cabinet paintings of naked nymphs and goddesses, simpering alluringly at their aristocratic patrons.[11] And long after the Lutheran movement broke decisively from the old Church, Cranach repeatedly accepted commissions from its fiercest enemies. The 'new aesthetic' is nowhere in evidence in the work he produced for those clients. In 1534, Cranach produced a major Catholic work, the epitaph triptych for the ardently Catholic Prince George the Bearded of Saxony (now in Meissen Cathedral). In it the prince and his Polish wife, Barbara, kneel surrounded by (male) patron saints. The biblical texts that Koerner sees as the bane of Lutheran art are in evidence here, too, inscribed above the heads of the prince and his wife. The texts (in the Latin of the Catholic Vulgate Bible) are of a kind more often associated with Protestantism than Catholicism: above the prince's head are a series of Pauline passages commanding women to be subservient to their husbands, and above his wife is the epistle of St Peter's injunction to obedience to one's prince.

But the central panel of the triptych is utterly traditional: Christ as the Man of Sorrows displaying his wounds, supported by the

Virgin and St John, while a host of attendant angels carry the instruments of his Passion. It is before this image, traditionally associated both with intercession for the dead and with the sacrifice of the Mass, that George the Bearded and Princess Barbara kneel, the veneration of a cult image if ever there was one.

And during these same years, Cranach's workshop was turning out scores of Catholic pictures for Catholic patrons, including Luther's bête noire, Cardinal Albrecht, the Archbishop of Mainz. These included altarpieces for Albrecht's cathedral, devotional panels of Christ as the Man of Sorrows (an image closely associated with the doctrine of transubstantiation), images of favourite Catholic saints, or of Mary assumed into heaven. Cranach and his assistants painted Cardinal Albrecht himself as Saint Jerome in his study (in a composition borrowed from a famous print by Dürer), and as witness to the miraculous Mass of Saint Gregory, a subject associated not only with transubstantiation and the sacrifice of the mass, but also with the release of souls from purgatory, and so absolute anathema to Luther. Characteristically, however, Cranach never drew Albrecht from the life, and probably never met him: instead, he copied Albrecht's features from Dürer's 1519 portrait.[12]

These Catholic pictures are disconcerting to anyone who sees inner conviction as essential to the integrity of great art. It is as if Saatchi & Saatchi had hired David Hockney to design PR portfolios for both Margaret Thatcher and Arthur Scargill at the same time. It is true that divisions between Catholic and Protestant had not yet hardened irrevocably – Cardinal Albrecht had even sent Luther's bride a wedding gift. Yet the mood and devotional purpose of these pictures were deeply alien to the new doctrines to which Cranach subscribed. A tradesman, of course, cannot afford to be too choosy about his customers, but the power and tenderness that he and his assistants infused into many of these Catholic pictures speaks of art's ability to transcend ideology, however much Cranach's more conscientiously didactic works might seek to deny it.

This is perhaps merely to demonstrate the chameleon adaptability of a commercial painter. But it does suggest that the decisive aesthetic break which Koerner associates with Cranach's work from the 1520s to the 1550s can hardly be as absolute as he maintains. And it is certainly true that he often exaggerates, or at any rate mis describes, some of the contrasts he discerns between medieval and Lutheran religious sensibility. This Lutheran aesthetic, Koerner believes, broke decisively with the past in transforming art from a direct encounter with the sacred into a cognitive instrument, a didactic device in which understanding was everything, veneration banished. He therefore insists on the corresponding absence of this cognitive priority in medieval religion. At the heart of his argument lies a sharp distinction between the materiality and objectivity of medieval conceptions of the sacred, and the contrasting subjectivity of Lutheran approaches to the reception of the sacrament of the altar. In medieval Catholic ritual, he tells us, 'it counted for nothing whether a lay person entered or even understood the goings on. The Mass was effective *ex opere operato*, "from the work done", whenever and wherever a priest celebrated it.' In the Lutheran world view, by contrast, 'universal priesthood ... held each person responsible for making sacrament efficacious for them[selves].'[13]

Koerner here effectively articulates a modern version of an accusation often made by Lutherans at the time of the Reformation. Catholicism was external, magical and mechanical; Protestantism was interior and rooted in personal responsibility. Reformation polemic is thus recycled as considered historical generalization. As a description of medieval sacramental belief, however, it is quite simply mistaken. The medieval Church's insistence that the sacraments worked *ex opere operato* was a claim about the dependable availability of God's grace, but emphatically not a guarantee that grace would be effective for the recipient regardless of interior disposition. Essentially, the doctrine guaranteed the spiritual lives of ordinary people against wicked or inadequate priests. Mass might be celebrated by a saint, or by a clerical philanderer still reeking from his mistress's or his boyfriend's bed: but provided both had been duly ordained, and used the correct prayers, Christ would be just as truly present at the sinner's Mass as at the saint's. However, that presence, stupendous mystery as it was, was in itself no guarantee of benefit, either to celebrant or congregation. Medieval Catholics, just like sixteenth-century Protestants, thought that an unworthy or inattentive communicant not only received no blessing from the Eucharist, but on the contrary ate and drank damnation. Christ was objectively present even to the wicked; but the inner spiritual power and healing of the sacrament were available only to devout penitence and faith.

That indispensable condition is spelled out in one of the central communion devotions of the Middle Ages, the so-called Prayer of St Thomas Aquinas, routinely included in both medieval and modern missals as part of devout preparation for receiving the Host. Emphasizing the communicant's personal unworthiness, the prayer asks for the interior gifts of reverence and humility, contrition and devotion, purity and faith, and hence for a right disposition in taking communion, so that 'I may receive not merely the sacrament of the body and blood of the Lord, but also its reality and power' (*non solum sacramentum ... sed etiam rem et virtutem sacramentum*).

On this point, then, the theological contrast between externality and interiority which Koerner thinks contributes to so sharp a divide between a Protestant and a Catholic aesthetic is largely illusory. On the need for devout inwardness, medieval Catholics and early modern Lutherans were at one. We may therefore question the readings of pictures which Koerner deduces from that contrast. In the imagined objectivity of medieval worship, he tells us, '*understanding* was but an ornament to action,' and 'whatever thoughts the laity entertained affected the *ex opere operato* of sacrament only marginally.'[14] And this, he thinks, had direct consequences for painting: the marginality of lay people in the central mysteries of religion was reflected in medieval depictions of their presence at those mysteries. Sure enough, he carries these convictions into the gallery, and they colour what he thinks he sees there. Among the pictures Koerner offers in support of this contention are two which may be familiar to visitors to the Sainsbury Wing of the National Gallery in London, *The Exhumation of St Hubert*, painted around 1437 in the workshop of Rogier van der Weyden, and the anonymous *Mass of Saint Giles* of about 1500. In each case, Koerner's a priori conviction of the theological marginality of the medieval laity is so strong that it causes him to misread what is plainly before him on the painted surface.

Van der Weyden's *Exhumation of St Hubert* presents an idealized version of a historical event, the exhumation and enshrinement of the body of the saint in the church of St Pierre in Liège. The saint's perfectly preserved body, uncoffined in the foreground, is being raised from its grave by a group of robed clerics. They in turn are surrounded by a crowd of well-dressed laypeople, and the whole action takes place before an altar on which rests a large reliquary casket. Behind the altar is a slatted wooden screen, through which peer crowds of would-be spectators. 'Their access barred by a wooden grille ... their vision blocked by altar, altarpiece and clergy, the common folk ... cannot behold the uncorrupted flesh that the painter places front and centre.' This, Koerner insists, is because the holy place before the altar was meant to be inaccessible. Paradoxically, he thinks, even though 'the Church orchestrated an image-based piety', in practice 'it also restricted sight, exiling lay folk from what they yearned to behold.'[15]

To sustain this account of the picture, however, Koerner is obliged to ignore the presence of the large group of laypeople who stand in the foreground, crowding the sacred space between the body of the saint and the altar with its images and relics. The six clergy in the foreground – two bishops, two priests, and two clerks in minor orders – are outnumbered by fifteen laypeople, men, women and children, who cluster round them and enjoy an unhindered view of the saint's 'uncorrupted flesh'. The larger crowd of laypeople corralled behind the screen, therefore, are excluded not, as Koerner says, because they are the laity, but because they are the plebs, the many-headed multitude. The divisions the picture displays are not theological – between clerical and lay – but social, between rich and poor. And, as Koerner himself argues elsewhere in the book, that distinction would persist, even in sacred things, and would if anything deepen, after the Reformation. Luther's colleague Philip Melancthon, the great theorist of confessional Lutheranism, wrote dismissively of the 'stupid people', the 'mad riff-raff', 'Mr Everybody', 'the vulgar folks'. At Luther's insistence, social distinctions were preserved in the conduct of Protestant worship, and Lutheran church seating and proximity to sacred space, in the form of closeness to the altar, were carefully regulated according to social status.

Koerner projects the same polarities into his readings of other pictures of the medieval Mass. In the National Gallery's *Mass of Saint Giles*, for example, the saint elevates the Host at the moment of consecration. Behind him, two attendants kneel, laymen to judge by the long-sleeved gown and lack of tonsure of the one in front, who holds a tall torch aloft in honour of the sacrament. In the left foreground the emperor Charlemagne kneels to the side of the curtained altar, while his entourage, men and women, stand behind. The king's eyes are lifted to the Host, his hands raised and open in the conventional gesture of adoration and welcome which laypeople were expected to adopt at this point in the Mass (Richard II adopts the same posture in the Wilton Diptych). But both Charlemagne and the painting's viewer are distracted by the appearance of an angel, who descends from the top of the frame towards the altar, holding a letter of absolution for the secret sins which the emperor had been too ashamed to confess, but pardon for which St Giles's prayers and the virtue of the Mass had procured.

Once again, Koerner interprets this painting as a portrayal of lay exclusion from sight of the sacred. 'Meanwhile,' he tells us, 'blocked as usual from the proceedings … by a green curtain … stand the people … Able to glance surreptitiously from the ritual's periphery, they struggle to get a look at its centre, that white disc in which there is nothing to behold.' In fact, no one in the picture except the emperor struggles to look at the Host. The servers at the Mass could see it if they wished, but instead they focus on the penitent Charlemagne, who, himself a layman, has a ringside seat. The mixed entourage behind the curtain, understandably for courtiers in attendance on their master's routine devotions, look bored or abstracted. Far from struggling to see the Host, they face anywhere except towards the altar. One of them, a woman, has indeed pushed the altar curtain aside and holds it back, but she does this not so that she can see, but so that the emperor at his prayer-desk can see. She herself gazes calmly out of the picture, at the spectator.

Curtains, screens, archways and barriers of one sort or another certainly feature in several of the pictures of the Mass which Koerner discusses, but they function as emblems of proprietorship – enclosures symbolizing the availability of the Mass to some laypeople rather than others – rather than as excluders of laypeople as such. Contrary to Koerner's reiterated claim, laypeople do inhabit these sacred spaces, but usually with the best of rights to do so, because they are the patrons who have paid for the priest, and the Mass is being celebrated, and, in some cases, a picture of it painted, for their specific benefit. These pictures therefore reflect an aspect of medieval Christianity against which Luther was to protest: the fact that the Mass could be bought, celebrated at family or guild altars to which outsiders had restricted access. Here was indeed a profound difference between Catholic and Protestant, but it is not the one Koerner claims to discern, and I doubt whether it will sustain the stark and simple aesthetic divergence which even his brilliant advocacy seeks to discover there.

Perhaps fortunately, religion was never Cranach's only inspiration. Like many of his contemporaries, he was fascinated by classical representations of the human body. The devout Dürer had channelled this risqué interest mainly into statuesque representations of Adam and Eve, but Cranach was equally attracted by pagan mythology. Unlike Dürer, there is no evidence that he drew much from the human nude. Instead, he wove the stuff of fantasies – nymphs and fauns, heroes and goddesses, the judgment of Paris, Venus comforting Cupid stung by bees, the three graces, the people of the golden age gambolling naked in a garden of delights.[16] In these jewel-like idylls, Dürer's beefy Amazons have been replaced by impossibly nubile and lynx-eyed temptresses, Venus gazing slyly at the viewer, drowsy nymphs dozing under Latin inscriptions forbidding anyone to disturb, but whose inviting posture suggests something entirely different. These sixteenth-century Lolitas were quite new in German art. Their sly eroticism and elegant stylization fascinated twentieth-century artists, from Picasso to Giacometti, but are perhaps the flip side of the conventional misogyny reflected in another profitable line from Cranach's studio, his genre pictures of women deceiving men – the pickpocket prostitute, the adulterous wife swearing her innocence, Judith with the head of Holofernes, Salome with the head of Saint John. Yet Cranach's smiling seductresses have a more benign aspect as well. They are images of that nostalgia for an idealized and innocent human sexuality that fascinates precisely because it always eludes us. When in 2008 the Royal Academy staged a major exhibition of Cranach's work, the publicity material displaying one of these alluring Venuses was banned from the London Underground as unacceptably sexy, only for the ban to be lifted a few days later.[17] Across the centuries, Wittenberg's stolidly prosperous evangelical craftsman seemed suddenly to wink.

Acknowledgements

Chapter 1 is a revised version of an essay which first appeared in the *New York Review of Books* on 29 March 2007.

Chapter 2 is a revised version of an essay which first appeared in the *New York Review of Books* on 7 June 2012.

Chapter 3 is a revised version of the Introduction to *The Golden Legend: Readings on the Saints, by Jacobus de Voragine*, translated by William Granger Ryan, Princeton University Press, 2012.

Chapter 4 first appeared in the *New York Review of Books* on 20 April 2017.

Chapter 5 first appeared in the *Bodleian Library Record*, 21, 1 (April 2008).

Chapter 6 incorporates material which first appeared in the *New York Review of Books* on 23 May 2002 and 29 May 2008.

Chapter 7 is a revised version of an essay which first appeared in the *New York Review of Books* on 12 January 2012.

Chapter 8 is a revised version of an essay which first appeared in the *New York Review of Books* on 19 October 2006.

Chapter 9 is a revised version of an essay which first appeared in the *New York Review of Books* on 19 December 2002.

Chapter 10 is a revised version of an essay which first appeared in the *New York Review of Books* on 27 October 2016.

Chapter 11 is a revised version of an essay which first appeared in the *New York Review of Books* on 18 August 2011.

Chapter 12 incorporates material which first appeared in the *New York Review of Books* on 8 April 2010 and 19 June 2014, and in the *Guardian* newspaper, 24 June 2011.

Chapter 13 is a revised version of an essay which first appeared in *The Medieval English Cathedral, Papers in Honour of Pamela Tudor-Craig*, edited by J. Backhouse, Donington, 2003.

Chapter 14 is a revised version of the Bond lecture given at St George's Chapel, Windsor, 7 October 2009.

Chapter 15 is a revised version of an essay which first appeared in *Pilgrimage, the English Experience from Becket to Bunyan*, edited by Peter Roberts, Cambridge, 2002.

Chapter 16 is a revised version of an essay which first appeared in *Sacred Space: House of God, Gate of Heaven*, edited by P. North and J. North, London, 2007.

Chapter 17 is a revised version of an essay which first appeared in *Wingfield College and its Patrons: Piety and Prestige in Medieval Suffolk*, edited by Peter Bloore and Edward Martin, Woodbridge, 2015.

Chapter 18 is a revised version of a lecture given in Crowland Abbey in 2005.

Chapter 19 first appeared in *Tributes to Nigel Morgan: Contexts of Medieval Art: Images, Objects and Ideas*, edited by Julian M. Luxford and M. A. Michael, London/Turnhout 2010.

Chapter 20 is a revised version of an essay which first appeared in *Object of Devotion: Medieval English Alabaster Sculpture from the Victoria and Albert Museum*, edited by Paul Williamson, London, Art Services International, 2010.

Chapter 21 expands material which first appeared in the *London Review of Books*, 19 August 2004, and the *Guardian*, 1 March 2008.

Notes

INTRODUCTION

1 Womersley, David (ed.) (1995), *Edward Gibbon, The Decline and Fall of the Roman Empire Volume II*. Harmondsworth: Penguin (vol. 3, chapter 28 of the first edition of 1781), 92.
2 For a magisterial exposition of these newer perceptions, Brown, Peter (10th Anniversary Edition 2013), *The Rise of Western Christendom: Triumph and Diversity AD 200–1000*. John Wiley and Sons: xi–xlvii and 1–34.

CHAPTER 1

1 Grafton, Anthony, and Williams, Megan (2008), *Christianity and the Transformation of the Book: Origen, Eusebius, and the Library of Caesarea*. Harvard University Press.
2 For the many complex problems surrounding the nature and content of the Hexapla, see the essays in Salvesen, Alison (ed.) (1998), *Origen's Hexapla and Fragments*. Tübingen: Mohr Siebeck (Texte und Studien zum Antiken Judentum, 58).
3 *Christianity and the Transformation of the Book*, 178.
4 For a recent discussion, Skeat, Theodore (October 1999), 'The Codex Sinaiticus, the Codex Vaticanus, and Constantine', *Journal of Theological Studies*, New Series, vol. 50, no. 2, centenary Issue 1899–1999, 583–625.
5 *Christianity and the Transformation of the Book*, 169–70.
6 Williams, Megan Hale (2006), *The Monk and the Book: Jerome and the Making of Christian Scholarship*. Chicago: University of Chicago Press.
7 For more on the iconography of St Jerome, see Chapter 19 below.

CHAPTER 2

1 McKendrick, Scot, Lowden, John, & Doyle, Kathleen with Fronska, Joanna, and Jackson, Deirdre (eds.) (2011), *Royal Manuscripts: the Genius of Illumination*. British Library Publications.
2 *Royal Manuscripts*, 96–7.
3 *Royal Manuscripts*, 272–5.
4 *Royal Manuscripts*, 56–9.
5 *Royal Manuscripts*, 70–3 : for a vivid exploration of all aspects of Henry VIII's library, Carley, James (2004), *The Books of King Henry VIII and his Wives*. British Library Publications.
6 *Royal Manuscripts*, 81–3.
7 *Royal Manuscripts*, 130–1.
8 Duffy, Eamon (2006), *Marking the Hours: English People and Their Prayers*. Yale University Press, 49–52.
9 Starkey, David (2009), *Henry, Virtuous Prince*. Harper Perennial, 199–205.

CHAPTER 3

1 All citations of the *Golden Legend* refer to the one-volume reissue of the translation by Ryan, William Granger (2012), *The Golden Legend: Readings on the Saints*. Princeton, NJ: Princeton University Press.
2 The only full-length study is Monleone, G. (1941), *Jacopo de Voragine e la sua Cronaca de Genoa*. Rome: Istituto storico italiano per il Medio Evo.
3 For both, see Reames, Sherry L. (1985), *The Legenda Aurea: A Reexamination of Its Paradoxical History*. Madison: University of Wisconsin Press, 164ff.
4 Gorlach, Manfred (1974), *The Textual Tradition of the South English Legendary*. Leeds: University of Leeds. However, Gorlach is inclined to minimize the influence of Jacobus.
5 Seybolt, Robert Francis (July 1946), 'Fifteenth-century editions of the *Legenda Aurea*', *Speculum* 21:3, 327–38; brief discussion by Boureau, Alain (2000) in André Vauchez (ed.), *Encyclopaedia of the Middle Ages*. Chicago, London: Fitzroy Dearborn Publishers; Paris: Editions du Cerf; Rome: Città nuova), 620–1, and sources there cited.
6 *Golden Legend*, 53ff.

7 For Mirk's dependence on Jacobus, see Powell, Susan (ed.) (2009), *John Mirk's Festial*, vol. 1. Oxford: Early English Text Society O.S. 339, xxxii–xxxvii.
8 For these developments, see Vauchez, André (1997), *Sainthood in the Later Middle Ages*. Cambridge: Cambridge University Press, 33–84.
9 See the table of canonizations in Vauchez, *Sainthood*, 252–6.
10 Chapters 113, 149, 63.
11 *Golden Legend*, 24ff.
12 The compact discussion by J. P. Kirsch of the elaboration of the legend in the early sources, in his article on Saint Agnes in the *Catholic Encyclopedia*, retains its value, despite its venerable age. It is available online at *www.ewtn.com/library/MARY/CEAGNES.HTM*.
13 Boureau, Alain (1984), *La Légende dorée: Le système narratif de Jacques de Voragine*. Paris: Cerf, 118–20.
14 Cf. Boureau, *Légende dorée*, 101.
15 Boureau, *Légende dorée*, 75–108; Reames, *Legenda Aurea*, passim.
16 This is the central argument of Reames's *Legenda Aurea*.
17 Cited in Reames, *Legenda Aurea*, 52.

CHAPTER 4

1 This discussion is based on the facsimile version of the manuscript with an ancillary collection of essays edited by Clemens, Raymond (2016), *The Voynich Manuscript*. New Haven and London: Yale University Press.
2 The following discussion of Voynich as owner and the manuscript's recent provenance is indebted to the essay by Arnold Hunt in *The Voynich Manuscript*, 11–21.
3 The most comprehensive treatment of Kircher is Fletcher, John Edward, edited by Elizabeth Fletcher (2011), *A Study of the Life and Works of Athanasius Kircher, 'Germanus incredibilis': With a Selection of His Unpublished Correspondence and an Annotated Translation of His Autobiography*. Leiden: Brill. Aries Book Series: Texts and Studies in Western Esotericism 12.
4 Marci's letter is reproduced in facsimile in, *The Voynich Manuscript*, 4.
5 Bolton, Henry Carrington (1904), *The Follies of Science at the Court of Rudolph II, 1576–1612*. Milwaukee.
6 On attempts to decrypt the manuscript, see the essay by Sherman, William (2016), 'Cryptographic attempts', in *The Voynich Manuscript*,

39–43: D'Imperio, M. E. (1978), *The Voynich Manuscript, an Elegant Enigma*. Fort George G. Meade, MD: National Security Agency.

CHAPTER 5

1 De Hamel, Christopher (2001), *The Book: A History of the Bible*. London: Phaidon, 128–9.
2 For the Psalter divisions, see Taft, Robert (1986), *The Liturgy of the Hours in East and West*. Collegeville: Liturgical Press, 136; and Hughes, Andrew (1982), *Medieval Manuscripts for Mass and Office*. Toronto: University of Toronto Press, 873–85.
3 The standard contents are discussed in Wieck, Roger S. (1988), *The Book of Hours in Medieval Art and Life*. London: Sotheby's Publications.
4 Duffy, Eamon (2006), *Marking the Hours, English People and their Prayers*. New Haven and London: Yale University Press, 3–22.
5 I have based these calculations on the text of the Sarum *Horae* printed in STC 15973 (Regnault, 1531).
6 I have used the text in Cambridge University Library Ms Kk II 7 fols 11–12.
7 Duffy, *Marking the Hours*, 17.
8 Text in Hoskins, E. (ed.) (1901), *Horae Beatae Mariae Virginis, or, Sarum and York Primers*. London, 147–8.
9 Fisher, John, edited by J. B. Mayor (1876), *English Works*. Early English Texts Society, 292.
10 Savage, Anne, and Watson, Nicholas (eds) (1991), *Anchoritic Spirituality*. New Jersey: Paulist Press, 64.
11 Gascoigne, Thomas (1530), *Here after folowith the boke callyd the myrroure of Oure Lady very necessary for all relygyous persones*. STC 17542, London sig aii (v) – A iii.
12 De Hamel, *The Book*, 166–89.
13 I have used the texts in CUL Mss. Dd VIII 18 fols 8–9 and CUL Kk II 7 fols 11–12.
14 *English Writings of Richard Rolle*, ed. Hope Emily Allen (1931). Oxford UP, 7.
15 *English Writings of Richard Rolle*, 4–5.
16 *Horae Eboracenses*, Surtees Society, 1920, 116–23: another text of the Psalter of St Jerome with a translation, identifying the psalms from which the prayer is constructed, will be found online at

NOTES 325

<http://www.preces-latinae.org/thesaurus/Confessio/PsalterJerome.html>. For the standard accompanying rubric, Hoskins, *Horae Beatae Mariae Virginis*, 115.
17 Wieck, *The Book of Hours in Medieval Art and Life*, 108
18 Gascoigne, *Myrroure of Oure Lady*, fol. xv.
19 Beinecke Library, Yale, Ms Vault More: Martz, Louis L., and Sylvester, Richard R. (eds) (1969), *Thomas More's Prayer Book, a Facsimile reproduction of the annotated pages*. New Haven and London: Yale University Press.
20 Fisher, John (1508), *This treatise concernynge the fruytfull saynges of Davyd in the seven penytencyall psalms*. London: STC 10902-8.
21 For what follows, Duffy, *Marking the Hours*, 108–17.
22 *Marking the Hours*, 111–12.
23 *Marking the Hours*, 102.
24 Duffy, Eamon (2012), 'The spirituality of John Fisher' in *Saints, Sacrilege and Sedition: Religion and Conflict in the Tudor Reformations*. London: Bloomsbury, 155–8.
25 *Thomas More's Prayer Book*, 194.

CHAPTER 6

1 Little, Lester K. (ed.) (2006), *Plague and the End of Antiquity: The Pandemic of 541–750*. Cambridge and Rome: Cambridge University Press, American Academy in Rome.
2 The ancient Syrian sources for information about the plague are surveyed and vividly illustrated by Morony, Michael G., in *Plague and the End of Antiquity*, 59ff. See also the essay by Hordern, Peregrine (2004), 'Mediterranean plague in the Age of Justinian', in *The Cambridge Companion to the Age of Justinian*, ed. M. Maas. Cambridge: Cambridge University Press, 134–60.
3 Procopius's account of the plague is conveniently available at https://sourcebooks.fordham.edu/source/542procopius-plague.asp.
4 For Evagrius and his work, Allen, Pauline (1981), *Evagrius Scholasticus the Church Historian*. Leuven: Spicilegium Sacrum Lovaniense. Etudes et Documents, 41.
5 For Evagrius's account of the plague, Whitby Michael (trans. and ed.) (2000), *The Ecclesiastical History of Evagrius Scholasticus*. Liverpool: Liverpool University Press, 230–2.
6 *Plague and the End of Antiquity*, 59–86.
7 *Plague and the End of Antiquity*, 12.

8 For a discussion of the plague in Anglo-Saxon England, and Becle's account in particular, J R Maddicott, (1997) 'Plague in Seventh century England', *Past and Present* No. 156, 7–54.
9 *Plague and the End of Antiquity*, 204.
10 *Plague and the End of Antiquity*, 150.
11 *Plague and the End of Antiquity*, 99–118.
12 See the essay by Michael McCormick, 'Toward a Molecular History of the Justiniac Pandemic' in *Plague and the End of Antiquity*, 290–312.
13 The bibliography on the Black Death is immense, and contested: worthwhile recent studies include Aberth, John (2000), *From the Brink of the Apocalypse: Confronting Famine, War, Plague and Death in the Later Middle Ages*. London: Routledge; Benedictow, Ole Jørgen (2004), *Black Death 1346–1353: The Complete History*. Woodbridge: Boydell; Byrne, J. P. (2002), *The Black Death*. London; Cohn, Samuel K., Jr (2002), *The Black Death Transformed: Disease and Culture in Early Renaissance Europe*. London: Arnold; Herlihy, Daniel (1997), *The Black Death and the Transformation of the West*, Harvard: Harvard University Press; Horrox, Rosemary (1994), *The Black Death* (sources). Manchester: Manchester University Press; Twigg, G. (1984), *The Black Death: A Biological Reappraisal*. London: Batsford.

CHAPTER 7

1 Page, Christopher (2012), *The Christian West and its Singers: the first thousand years*. New Haven and London: Yale University Press.
2 Page, *Christian West*, 467, 362.
3 Page, *Christian West*, 459.
4 Page, *Christian West*, 458.
5 Page, *Christian West*, 52, 99–100, 161–2, 221.
6 Page, *Christian West*, 221, 161–2.
7 Page, *Christian West*, 229.
8 Page, *Christian West*, 248.
9 Page, *Christian West*, ch. 15 *passim*.
10 Page, *Christian West*, 400.

CHAPTER 8

1 Runciman, Steven (1954), *The Kingdom of Acre* (*History of the Crusades*, vol. 3). Cambridge: Cambridge University Press, 480.

2 Constable's essays on Crusade are collected in Constable, G. (2008), *Crusaders and Crusading in the Twelfth Century*. Ashgate.
3 Succinct summaries of Riley-Smith's influential ideas in his *The First Crusade and the Idea of Crusading*. University of Pennsylvania Press, 1991; and in his brilliant inaugural lecture 'Crusading as an act of love', in *History*, 65:214 (1980), 177–192.
4 Tyerman, Christopher (2006), *God's War: A New History of the Crusades*. Harvard: Harvard University Press,
5 For an admiring biography which nevertheless throws much light on Runciman's limitations, Dinshaw, Minoo (2016), *Outlandish Knight: The Byzantine Life of Steven Runciman*. London: Allen Lane.
6 *God's War*, 553.
7 The quotation is from Robert of Rheims, recollection of Urban II's Crusade speech at Clermont in 1095, in Philips, Jonathan (2012), *The Crusades 1095–1204*, 2nd edition. London: Routledge, 210–11.
8 *God's War*, 104.
9 Riley-Smith, Jonathan (1990), *The Crusades, A Short History*. London: Continuum, 130.
10 *God's War*, 560.
11 Vincent, Nicholas (2008), *The Holy Blood: Henry III and the Westminster Blood Relic*. Cambridge: Cambridge University Press.
12 *God's War*, 921.

CHAPTER 9

1 Ariès, Philippe, translated by Robert Baldick (1962), *Centuries of Childhood: A Social History of Family Life*. New York: Vintage.
2 For a critique of Ariès's views, Wilson, Adrian, 'The infancy of the history of childhood: an appraisal of Philippe Ariès', *History and Theory*, 19: 2 (February 1980), 132–53.
3 Kertzer, David I., and Barbagli, Marzio (eds) (2001), *The History of the European Family*, vol. 1, *Family Life in Early Modern Times, 1500–1789*. New Haven and London: Yale University Press.
4 Kertzer & Barbagli, *History of the European Family*, 219.
5 Ozment, Steven (2001), *Ancestors: The Loving Family in Old Europe*. Harvard: Harvard University Press.
6 *Ancestors*, 112.
7 Orme, Nicholas (2003), *Medieval Children*. New Haven and London: Yale University Press.

8 *Medieval Children*, 9.
9 *Medieval Children*, 284.

CHAPTER 10

1 For a recent discussion of this aspect of the Prioress's Tale, Bale, Anthony (2006), *The Jew in the Medieval Book: English Antisemitism 1350–1500*. Cambridge: Cambridge University Press, 56–88.
2 Biale, David (2007), *Blood and Belief: The Circulation of a Symbol between Jews and Christians*. Berkeley: University of California Press; Johnson, Hannah R. (2012), *Blood Libel: Ritual Murder Accusation at the Limit of Jewish History*. Ann Arbor: University of Michigan Press.
3 Statistics from the table printed in the *Jewish Encyclopedia*, 1901–6 (vol. 3, available online), 266–7.
4 News item reported, for example at http://www.ynetnews.com/articles/0,7340,L-3067416,00.html and also at http://www.orthodoxchristianity.net/forum/index.php?topic=5773.0.
5 Rubin, Miri (ed. and trans.) (2014), *Thomas of Monmouth, Life and Passion of William of Norwich*. London: Penguin Classics, 29.
6 Langmuir, Gavin I., in 'Thomas of Monmouth: detector of ritual murder', *Speculum* 59:4 (October 1984), 820–46, argues for the centrality of Thomas of Monmouth's narrative for the spread of the blood libel: this is challenged by McCulloh, John M., in 'Jewish ritual murder: William of Norwich, Thomas of Monmouth, and the early dissemination of the myth', *Speculum*, 72:3 (July 1997), 698–740, which argues that Thomas reworked ideas which originated in continental Europe, and that his text had little subsequent influence.
7 Rose, Emily (2015), *The Murder of William of Norwich: The Origin of the Blood Libel in Medieval Europe*. Oxford: Oxford University Press. Rose's book won the Phi Beta Kappa 2016 Ralph Waldo Emerson Prize for outstanding scholarship.
8 Rose, *Murder*, 45ff.
9 *Life and Passion*, 70; Rose, *Murder*, 67ff.
10 Bill, C. Harper, entry for William Turbe in *Oxford Dictionary of National Biography*. http://www.oxforddnb.com/view/article/29466.
11 Rose, *Murder*, 98.
12 *Life and Passion*, 81, 83, 108.
13 *Life and Passion*, 39–42, 56–63.
14 *Life and Passion*, 80, 114.
15 McCulloh, 'Jewish ritual murder', 740.

16 Rose, *Murder*, 152 and note 7, 304.

CHAPTER 11

1 Bynum, Caroline Walker (1982), *Jesus as Mother: Studies in the Spirituality of the High Middle Ages*. Center for Medieval and Renaissance Studies, UCLA.
2 Bynum, Caroline Walker (1987), *Holy Feast and Holy Fast: The Religious Significance of Food to Medieval Women*. University of California Press, The New Historicism: Studies in Cultural Poetics.
3 Notably, Bell, Rudolf M. (1987), *Holy Anorexia*. Chicago: University of Chicago Press.
4 Bynum, Caroline Walker (1995), *The Resurrection of the Body in Western Christianity, 200–1336*. Columbia University Press.
5 Bynum, Caroline Walker (2007), *Wonderful Blood: Theology and Practice in Late Medieval Northern Germany and Beyond*. University of Pennsylvania Press.
6 Bynum, Caroline Walker (2015), *Christian Materiality: An Essay on Religion in Late Medieval Europe*. New York: Zone Books.
7 *Christian Materiality*, 18.
8 Ibid., 20.
9 Ibid., 35.
10 Scribner, Bob, 'Popular piety and modes of visual perception in late-medieval and Reformation Germany', *Journal of Religious History*, 15: 4 (December 1989), 448–69.
11 *Christian Materiality*, 58.
12 Belting, Hans (1994), *Likeness and Presence: A History of the Image before the Era of Art*. Chicago: University of Chicago Press. Bynum was however aware of some of the limitations of Belting's approach – *Christian Materiality*, 323.
13 *Christian Materiality*, 66ff.
14 Ibid., 131.
15 Ibid., 240.
16 Ibid., 185.

CHAPTER 12

1 The fullest collection of source material in English is Wolf, Kenneth Baxter (2001), *The Life and Afterlife of St Elizabeth of Hungary: Testimony from her Canonisation Hearings*. Oxford University Press, with a useful essay on her life, pp. 43ff; Bartlett,

Robert (2013), *Why Can the Dead Do Such Great Things: Saints and Worshippers from the Martyrs to the Reformation*. Princeton and Oxford University, pp. 72–6.
2 Useful and judicious if old-fashioned short account in Thurston, Herbert, and Attwater, Donald (1956), (editors) *Butler's Lives of the Saints*. London: Burns Oates, vol. IV, 386–91.
3 For the canonization, Wolf, *Life and Afterlife*, pp. 3ff.
4 Bartlett, *Why Can the Dead*, pp. 57–64: Kemp, E. W. (1948), *Canonisation and Authority in the Western Church*. Oxford University Press; Vauchez, André (1997), *Sainthood in the Later Middle Ages*. Cambridge University Press, 22–58.
5 Malden, Arthur Russell (1901), *The Canonization of Saint Osmund, from the Manuscript Records in the Muniment Room of Salisbury Cathedral*, Salisbury; Farmer, David Hugh (1992), *Oxford Dictionary of the Saints*. Oxford University Press, 368.
6 Goodrich, Michael (1983), 'The Politics of Canonisation in the thirteenth century', in Wilson, Stephen (ed.), *Saints and their Cults*. Cambridge University Press, 169–87.
7 On the Abbey and its significance for Henry III, Binski, Paul (1995), *Westminster Abbey and the Plantagenets*. New Haven and London: Yale University Press.
8 Details of Louis's life are drawn from Le Goff, Jacques (2009), *St Louis*. University of Notre Dame Press.
9 For the Sainte-Chapelle see the essays gathered in Hediger, Christine (ed.) (2007), *La Sainte-Chapelle de Paris: Royaume de France ou Jérusalem céleste? Actes du colloque Paris, Collège de France, 2001*. Turnhout Brepols; for the importance of the Sainte-Chapelle for non-royal pilgrims, Cohen, Meredith, 'An Indulgence for the Visitor: The Public at the Sainte-Chapelle of Paris'. *Speculum*, Vol. 83, No. 4 (Oct. 2008), 840–83.
10 Shaw, M. R. B. (translator) (1963), *Joinville and Villehardouin, Chronicles of the Crusades*. Harmondsworth: Penguin, 177, 342.
11 Gaposchkin, M. Cecilia, & Field, Sean L. (eds) and L. F. Field (translator) (2013), *The Sanctity of Louis IX: Early Lives of Saint Louis by Geoffrey of Beaulieu and William of Chartres*. Cornell University Press.
12 Staniforth, Maxwell (translator) (1987), *Early Christian Writings*. Harmondsworth: Penguin, p. 131.
13 Bartlett, *Why Can the Dead*, p. 10.

14 Brown, Peter (1981), *The Cult of the Saints: Its Rise and Function in Latin Christianity*. London: SCM Press, 23–49.
15 Brief survey in Arnold Angenot, 'Relics and their veneration', in Bagnoli, Martina, and Klein, Holger A. (eds) (2011), *Treasures of Heaven: Saints, Relics, and Devotion in Medieval Europe*. British Museum Press, 19–28.
16 McCulloh, J. M., 'The Cult of Relics in the Letters and Dialogues of St Gregory the Great'. *Traditio* 32 (1976), pp. 145–84; Ewald, P., and Hartmann, L. M., *Gregorii Papae Registrum Epistolarum*. Berlin 1887–91, 4.30.
17 For Deusdona, Geary, Patrick J. (1978), *Furta Sacra: Thefts of Relics in the Central Middle Ages*. Princeton University Press, 44–9, and for the spread of the cult of relics more generally, 3–43.
18 Hahn, Cynthia, 'What Do Reliquaries Do for Relics?', *Numen*, Vol. 57, No. 3/4, Relics in Comparative Perspective (2010), pp. 284–316; Hahn, Cynthia (2017), *The Reliquary Effect: Enshrining the Sacred Object*. London: Reaktion Books.
19 Bartlett, *Why Can the Dead*, pp. 269–70.
20 Farmer, David Hugh (1985), *St Hugh of Lincoln*. London SCM Press, 89.
21 Drijvers, J. W. (1992), *Helena Augusta, the Mother of Constantine the Great and the Legend of her Finding of the True Cross*. Leiden, Brill.
22 For the importance of reliquaries, see Hahn, Cynthia (2012), *Strange Beauty: Issues in the Making and Meaning of Reliquaries, 400–circa 1204*. University Park, PA: Penn State University Press; and the same author's *The Reliquary Effect: Enshrining the Sacred Object*. London, Reaktion Books, 2017.
23 'That Nature is a Heraclitean Fire and of the Comfort of the Resurrection', Phillips, Catherine (editor) (1986), *Gerard Manley Hopkins*. Oxford University Press, 181.
24 Luxford, Julian, 'The Nature and Purpose of medieval Relic Lists', in Powell, Susan (editor) (2017), *Saints and Cults in Medieval England*. Donington. Sean Tyas, 65.
25 Bagnoli and Klein, *Treasures of Heaven*, 127 (no. 66).
26 Hahn, Cynthia, 'The Spectacle of the Charismatic Body', in *Treasures of Heaven*, pp. 163–72, and exhibits nos 104–112.
27 Bagnoli and Klein, *Treasures of Heaven*, pp. 191–3, no. 105.

28 Bagnoli and Klein, *Treasures of Heaven*, pp. 194–5, nos 107, 108.
29 Bartlett, *Why Can the Dead*, p. 103.
30 Geary, Patrick, 'Humiliation of Saints', in Wilson, *Saints and their Cults*, pp. 123–40.
31 Cited in Van Os, Henk (2001), *The Way to Heaven: Relic Veneration in the Middle Ages*. Amsterdam: De Prom, 17.
32 Bartlett, *Why Can the Dead*, p. 7.
33 All three lives are included in White, Carolinne (ed.) (1998), *Early Christian Lives*. Harmondsworth: Penguin.
34 Bartlett, *Why Can the Dead*, p. 521.
35 See above, chapter 3 pp. 29–42.

CHAPTER 13

1 Bede, ed. J. McClure and R. Collins (1994), *The Ecclesiastical History of the English People*. Oxford: Oxford University Press, 183–4; Farmer, D. H. (1992), *The Oxford Dictionary of the Saints*, 3rd edition. Oxford: Oxford University Press, 160–1.
2 Good outline account of the Saxon and Norman cult in Whatley, E. G. (ed.) (1989), *The Saint of London, The Life and Miracles of St Erkenwald*. Binghamton, New York: Medieval and Renaissance Texts and Studies, 58, 57–70 (hereafter cited as *Life and Miracles*).
3 For Erkenwald's shrine, Wilson, Christopher, 'The Shrine of St Erkenwald on paper and in reality', in Susan Powell (ed.), *Saints and Cults in Medieval England, Proceedings of the Harlaxton Symposium 2015*. Donington, 2017, 217–36.
4 This is the suggestion of Scholz, B. W., 'The canonisation of Edward the Confessor', *Speculum*, 26 (1961), 40ff; Thacker, Alan, 'The cult of the saints and the liturgy', in Derek Keene, Arthur Burns and Andrew Saint (eds), *St Paul's: The Cathedral Church of London 604–2004*. New Haven and London: Yale University Press, 2004, 113–22.
5 *Life and Miracles*, 91–7.
6 Ward, B. (1987), *Miracles and the Medieval Mind*. Aldershot: Scolar Press, 38, 49, 68–9, 139–49, 157.
7 Finucane, R. C. (1982), 'Cantilupe as thaumaturge', in M. Jancey (ed.), *St Thomas Cantilupe Bishop of Hereford: Essays in his Honour*. Hereford: Friends of Hereford Cathedral, 139.
8 *Life and Miracles*, 112–13.
9 Ibid., 132–3.

NOTES 333

10 Proctor, F., and Wordsworth, C. (eds), *Breviarium ad Usum Insignis Ecclesiae Sarum*. Cambridge, 1886, vol. 3, cols 1036–48.
11 Whatley, G., 'A Symple Wrecche at work: the life and miracles of St Erkenwald in the Gilte Legende', BL Add 35298, in B. Dunn-Lardeau (ed.), *Legenda Aurea: sept siècles de diffusion*. Montreal and Paris, 1986, 335: Horstmann, C. (ed.), *Nova Legenda Angliae*. Oxford, 1901, vol. 1, 391–405.
12 Lawler, T. M. C., Marc'hadour, G., and Marius, R. C. (eds), *The Complete Works of St Thomas More*, vol. 6, pt 1. New Haven and London: Yale University Press, 1981, 71, 81.
13 *Life and Miracles*, 67.
14 Sparrow Simpson, W. (ed.), *Registrum Statutorum et Consuetudinam Ecclesiae Cathedralis Sancti Pauli Londiniensis*. London, 1873, 393–4. For fourteenth-century Londoners' lack of enthusiasm for Erkenwald's cult, and Bishop Braybrook's efforts to promote it, Barron, Caroline, 'London and St Paul's Cathedral', in Janet Backhouse (ed.), *The Medieval English Cathedral*. Donington, 2003, 143–5.
15 *Life and Miracles*, 67, 204.
16 *Registrum*, 394: the Mass texts are also printed, along with the St Paul's Office for St Erkenwald, which unfortunately cannot be dated since it survives only in an eighteenth-century transcription by William Cole, in Sparrow Simpson, W. (ed.), *Documents Illustrating the History of St Paul's Cathedral*. Camden Society, n.s. XXVI. London, 1880, 15–24.
17 Wright, T. (ed.), *Political Poems and Songs Relating to English History...*, 2 vols, Rolls Series. London, 1859–61, vol. 1, 293.
18 Dugdale, W. (1716), *The History of St Paul's Cathedral in London*. London, 22–4; Baker, J. (1984), *The Order of Serjeants at Law*. Selden Society Supplementary Series, 101–4, though Baker is (unnecessarily) sceptical of any special connection.
19 I have consulted six editions of the poem: Horstmann, C. (ed.), *Altenglische Legenden: neue folge*. Heilbronn, 1881, 265–74; Gollancz, I., *Select Early English Poems*, IV. London, 1922; Savage, H. L., *St Erkenwald*. New Haven, 1926; Peterson, C., *Saint Erkenwald*. University of Pennsylvania Press, 1977; Morse, R., *St Erkenwald*. Cambridge, 1975; Turville-Petre, T., *Alliterative Poetry of the Later Middle Ages*. London, 1989, 101–19. Except where otherwise stated, all citations are from the Turville-Petre edition.
20 Best discussion of the dating in Peterson, *Saint Erkenwald*, 11–15, 21–3.

21 Vauchez, A. (1997), *Sainthood in the Later Middle Ages.* Cambridge: Cambridge University Press, 432.
22 Lines 267–72.
23 Lines 285–304.
24 Colgrave B. (trans. and ed.), *The Earliest Life of Gregory the Great.* Cambridge: Cambridge University Press, 1968, 126–9.
25 The evolution of the story is surveyed in Paris, Gaston, 'La Légende de Trajan', in *Mélanges de l'Ecole des Hautes Etudes,* 35 (1878), 261–298, and, more usefully, in Whatley, G., 'The use of hagiography: the legend of Pope Gregory and the Emperor Trajan in the Middle Ages', *Viator,* 15 (1984), 25–63.
26 For readings of *St Erkenwald* as endorsing a position similar to Langland's, Gollancz, ed. cit., xxxiv–lv; Morse, *St Erkenwald,* 15–31; for a definitive rebuttal, Whatley, G., 'Heathens and saints: *St Erkenwald* in its legendary context', *Speculum,* 61 (1986), 330–63.
27 Gollancz argued, not altogether convincingly, for a connection with the Booth family of Dunham Massey in Cheshire, one of whom was dean of St Paul's in the mid-fifteenth century, and who had many city and legal connections – ed. cit., v–vii.
28 On the 'order of the coif', see Baker, *Serjeants at Law, passim.*
29 Whatley, 'Heathens and Saints', op. cit., 330–63; Cairns, S., 'Fact and Fiction in the Middle English De Erkenwaldo', *Neuphilologische Mitteilungen,* 83 (1982), 430–8.
30 Ed. cit., 54–5. The skull in which a spark of life has been miraculously preserved until priestly absolution can be obtained for the dead man is a theme found in the Miracles of the Virgin: cf. Whatley, 'Uses of Hagiography', 38 n.
31 Ed. cit., 49.
32 Colgrave, *Earliest Life of Gregory the Great,* 78–9.
33 Ibid., 82–3.
34 Lines 13–17.
35 *Earliest Life of Gregory the Great,* 126–7.
36 The historical and theological tangle is expertly unravelled in O'Loughlin, T., and Conrad O'Brian, H., 'The Baptism of Tears in Early Anglo-Saxon Sources', *Anglo-Saxon England,* 22 (1993), 65–83.
37 Lines 125–6: for tears and the Spirit, see Duffy, E., 'The spirituality of John Fisher', in B. Bradshaw and E. Duffy (eds), *Humanism, Reform and the Reformation: The Career of John Fisher.* Cambridge University Press, 1989, 210.

38 Colgrave, *Earliest Life of Gregory the Great*, 128–33 (translation modified).
39 Whatley, 'Heathens and Saints', *passim*.
40 Leff, G. (1957), *Bradwardine and the Pelagians*. Cambridge University Press; and Whatley, 'Uses of Hagiography', *passim*.
41 Watson, N., 'Censorship and Cultural Change in Late Medieval England', *Speculum*, 70 (1995), 842–3.
42 Hudson, A. (1988), *The Premature Reformation*. Oxford University Press, 229.
43 Line 17.
44 Whatley, 'Heathens and Saints', 361.
45 Lines 144–46; my emphasis.
46 Cairns, S., 'Fact and Fiction in the Middle English De Erkenwaldo', *Neuphilologische Mitteilungen*, 83 (1982), 430–8.
47 The version of the Trinubium of St Anne preserved in the commonplace book of Robert Reynes of Acle (Bod Tanner MS 407) was explicitly designed to be read aloud to a St Anne Guild.
48 Salter, Elizabeth (1983), *Fourteenth-Century English Poetry*. Oxford University Press, 74–6; Scattergood, John, '*St Erkenwald* and its literary relations', in Powell, *Saints and Cults*, 339–41.
49 For the St Paul's Jesus Guild, New, Elizabeth, 'Fraternities: a case study of the Jesus Guild', in Keene et al., *St Paul's*, 162–3.
50 McFarlane, K. B. (1998), *Lancastrian Kings and Lollard Knights*. Oxford University Press reprint, 207–20; Thompson, J. A. F., 'Knightly piety and the margins of Lollardy', in M. Aston and C. Richmond (eds), *Lollardy and the Gentry in the Later Middle Ages*. Stroud: History Press, 1997, 95–111.
51 Horstmann, C. (ed.) (1896), *Yorkshire Writers: Richard Rolle of Hampole and His Followers*. London, II, 452–3; for the wide dissemination of this text, not only among clergy but as a devotional aid for the literate laity, see Joliffe, P. S. (1974), *A Check-list of Middle English Prose Writings of Spiritual Advice*. Toronto, 124–5; Doyle, A. I., 'A survey of the origins and circulation of theological writings in English in the fourteenth, fifteenth and early sixteenth centuries'. Unpublished Cambridge PhD thesis, 2001, I, 219–24.
52 Richmond, C., *John Hopton*. Cambridge University Press, 1981, 244.
53 Lines 180–4.

CHAPTER 14

1 For the reign of Henry VI and its end, Wolffe, Bertram (1981), *Henry VI*. New Haven and London: Yale University Press; Watts, John Lovett (1996), *Henry VI and the Politics of Kingship*. Cambridge: Cambridge University Press; Griffiths, Ralph A. (1981), *The Reign of King Henry VI: The Exercise of Royal Authority, 1422–1461*. London: Ernest Benn; Gross, Anthony (1996), *The Dissolution of the Lancastrian Kingship: Sir John Fortescue and the Crisis of Monarchy in Fifteenth-Century Englan*d. Stamford: Paul Watkins Publishing.
2 Wright, Thomas (ed.) (1843), *Three Chapters of Letters Relating to the Suppression of the Monasteries*. London: Camden Society, 222.
3 All the known contemporary accounts of the burial were published in Grosjean, Paul (1935), *Henrici VI Regis Miracula Postuma*. Brussels: Subsidia Hagiographica, Société des Bollandistes, 129*–151*.
4 Vauchez, André (1997), *Sainthood in the Later Middle Ages*. Cambridge: Cambridge University Press, 158–67; McKenna, John W., 'Piety and propaganda: the cult of Henry VI', in Beryl Rowland (ed.), *Chaucer and Middle English Studies in Honour of Russell Hope Robbins*. London, 1974; Walker, Simon, 'Political saints in later medieval England', in Richard H. Britnell and Anthony J. Pollard (eds), *The MacFarlane Legacy: Studies in Late Medieval Politics and Society*. New York, 1995; Piroyansky, Danna (2008), *Martyrs in the Making: Political Martyrdom in Late Medieval England*. Basingstoke: Palgrave.
5 McKenna, John W., 'Popular canonisation as political propaganda: the cult of Archbishop Scrope', *Speculum* 45 (1970), 608–23.
6 Craig, Leigh Ann, 'Royalty, virtue, and adversity: the cult of King Henry VI', *Albion: A Quarterly Journal Concerned with British Studies*, 35:2 (Summer, 2003), 187–209
7 Lovatt, Roger, 'A collector of apocryphal anecdotes: John Blacman revisited', in Anthony Pollard (ed.), *Property and Politics: Essays in Later Medieval English History*. New York, 1984, 172–97; Lovatt, Roger, 'John Blacman, biographer of Henry VI', in R. H. C. Davies & J. M. Wallace Hadrill (eds), *The Writing of History in the Middle Ages*. Oxford University Press, 1981, 417–29.
8 James, M. R. (ed. and trans.) (1919), *Henry the Sixth: A Reprint of John Blacman's Memoir with translation and notes*. Cambridge University Press, 43.

9 For an account of Blacman's memoir arguing that it was intended for an elite audience and presented Henry as a model for gentlemen, Freeman, Thomas, '*Ut verus Christi Sequestor*: John Blacman and the cult of Henry VI', *The Fifteenth Century* 5 (2005), 127–42.
10 James (ed. and trans.), *Blacman's Memoir*, 41.
11 These devotions in prose and verse are printed in Grosjean, *Henrici VI Regis Miracula Postuma*, 234*–262*: selection in Ronald Knox and Shane Leslie (eds and trans.), *The Miracles of King Henry VI*. Cambridge, 1923, 7–16.
12 Latin text in Knox and Leslie, *Miracles*, 8. Translation by E. D.
13 *Here begynneth the holy lyfe and history of saynt Werburge / very frutefull for all christen people to rede*: Carl Horstmann, *The Life of Saint Werburge of Chester, by Henry Bradshaw*. London, 1887, EETS o.s. 88, lines 2835–44.
14 [*Of this chapell se here the fundacyon*] London: Richard Pynson [1496?] (STC 25001), lines 94–101.
15 Knox and Leslie, *Miracles*, 89–98.
16 Knox and Leslie, *Miracles*, 41–9.
17 The entire register was edited in Grosjean, *Henrici VI Regis Miracula Postuma*, and Grosjean provided a thorough analysis of the contents, in Latin, 1–128*: brief summary in English in Knox and Leslie, *Miracles*, 16–29.
18 Spencer, Brian, 'King Henry VI and the London pilgrim', in J. Bird, H. Chapman and J. Clark (eds), *Collectanea Londiniensia*. London 1978; idem, 'Pilgrim badges of King Henry VI', *Henry VI Society newsletter* (December 1972), 10–13.
19 Marks, Richard, 'Images of Henry VI', in Jenny Stratford (ed.), *The Lancastrian Court*. Donington, 2008, 111–24; republished in Marks, *Studies in the Art and Imagery of the Middle Ages*. London: Pindar Press, 2012, 607–31.
20 List in Baker, Audrey, Ballantyne, Ann, and Plummer, Pauline (2011), *English Panel Paintings 1400–1558*. London: Archetype Publications, 120; photograph in Marks, *Art and Imagery*, 618.
21 Ibid., 138–60; Marks, *Art and Imagery*, 619.
22 Ibid., 142; Marks, *Art and Imagery*, 620.
23 Marks, Richard, 'A late medieval pilgrimage cult: Master John Schorn of North Marston and Windsor', in *Art and Imagery*, 583–606.
24 Baker *et al.*, *English Panel Paintings*, 163–4.

25 The Windsor poster, which survives only in a damaged copy now in the Bodleian Library, is reproduced in Marks, *Art and Imagery*, 615.
26 James (ed. and trans.) *Blacman's Memoir*, 36.
27 Knox and Leslie, *Miracles*, 149–56
28 Knox and Leslie, *Miracles*, 77–84.
29 For a fuller discussion of the cult of St Walstan, and his verse legend, see above, ch. 15.
30 For images of St Walstan, Baker *et al.*, *English Panel Paintings*, 36, 88, 89, 118, 121, 124, 135, 140, 157, 160, 164, 170, 189, 232, 238.
31 Baker *et al.*, *English Panel Paintings*, 159–62.
32 James, M.R. (ed.), 'Lives of St Walstan', Proceedings of the Norfolk and Norwich Archaeological Society, 19 (1917); 238–67.
33 But it should be noted that the case made in Freeman, *'Ut verus Christi Sequestor'* (above, note 9), perhaps militates against this association of the Blacman memoir with popular trends in the cult of the saints.
34 Scholarly edition by Horstmann, Carl (1901), *Nova Legenda Anglie as collected by John of Tynemouth, John Capgrave, and others, and first printed, with new lives, by Wynkyn de Worde 1516*. Oxford: Clarendon Press.
35 Scholarly edition by Görlach, Manfred (1994), *The Kalendre of the Newe Legende of Englande*. Heidelberg: Middle English Texts series, no. 27.

CHAPTER 15

1 Lubin, Helen, *The Worcester Pilgrim*. Worcester, 1990.
2 Geary, Patrick, 'The saint and the shrine: the pilgrim's goal in the Middle Ages', in L. Kriss-Rettenbeck and G. Mohler (eds), *Wallfahrt kennt keine Grenzen*. Zurich, 1984, 265. For a discussion of the specific applicability of Turner's model to late medieval English pilgrimage, see Theilmann, J. M., 'Communitas among fifteenth-century pilgrims', *Historical Reflections*, XI (1984), 253–70.
3 Henry, A. (ed.), *The Pilgrimage of the Lyfe of the Manhood*. EETS, 1985, 1.
4 For criticism of the 'liminality' account of pilgrimage from alternative anthropological perspectives, see Eade, J., and Sallnow, M. J. (eds), (1991), *Contesting the Sacred: The Anthropology of Christian Pilgrimage*. London and New York: Wipf and Stok.
5 For some other accounts of late medieval English pilgrimage, see Finucane, R., *Miracles and Pilgrims: Popular Beliefs in Medieval England*. London, 1977; Duffy, E., *The Stripping of the Altars, Traditional*

Religion in England c. 1400–1580. New Haven, CT and London: Yale University Press, 1992, 155–205; Whiting, R. (1989), *The Blind Devotion of the People: Popular Religion and the English Reformation*. Cambridge: Cambridge University Press, 54–9; Nilson, B. (1998), *Cathedral Shrines of Medieval England*. Woodbridge: Boydell and Brewer; Bernard, G. W., 'Vitality and vulnerability in the late-medieval Church: pilgrimage on the eve of the break with Rome', in J. L. Watts (ed.) (1998), *The End of the Middle Ages*. Stroud: History Press, 199–233; Webb, Diana (2000), *Pilgrimage in Medieval England*. London: Hambledon Continuum.
6 Horstmann, *Nova Legenda Anglie*, vol. II, 412–15.
7 James, M. R. (ed.), 'Lives of St Walstan', *Norfolk Archaeology*, 19 (1917), 238–67.
8 Duffy, *Stripping of the Altars*, 78–9.
9 The sole surviving copy of the Holy Blood poem is missing from the Gloucester Public Library, where it was on deposit: we now rely on the account in Oats, J. C. T., 'Richard Pynson and the Holy Blood of Hayles', *The Library*, 5th series, 13 (1958), 269–77.
10 Printed in Dickinson, J. C. (1956), *The Shrine of Our Lady of Walsingham*. Cambridge University Press, 124–30.
11 Robinson, J. A. (1926), *Two Glastonbury Legends*. Cambridge: Cambridge University Press; Traherne, R. F. (1967), *The Glastonbury Legends*. London: Cresset Press.
12 His will is in PCC Adeane 23, PRO Prob 11/15 LH 187: there is no mention of Bawburgh or St Walstan.
13 Duffy, *Stripping of the Altars*, 204.
14 These details are from: Blomefield, F., and Parkin, C., *An Essay towards a Topographical History of the Country of Norfolk*. London, 1805, vol. II, pp. 387–90; Gill, M., 'The Saint with a Scythe', *Proceedings of the Suffolk Institute of Archaeology*, 38 (1993), 245–54; Richmond, Colin, 'Religion', in R. Horrox (ed.) (1994), *Fifteenth-Century Attitudes*. Cambridge: Cambridge University Press, 187.
15 Blomefield and Parkin, loc. cit.
16 Baker, Audrey, Ballantyne, Ann, and Plummer, Pauline (2011), *English Panel Paintings 1400–1558: a Survey of Figure Paintings on East Anglian Rood Screens*. London: Archetype, 160 (Ludham), 156–7 (Litcham).
17 Baker *et al.*, *English Panel Paintings*, 118 (Barnham Broom), 120–1 (Beeston), 163–4 (Burlingham).
18 Baker *et al.*, *English Panel Paintings*, 159–60, 223 (Ludham), 156, 223 (Litcham), 189 (Sparham), 118 (Barnham Broom).

19 Blomefield and Parkin, loc. cit.
20 Gill, 'The Saint with a Scythe', 248.
21 On the proliferation of images in late medieval parish churches, Marks, Richard (2004), *Image and Devotion in Late Medieval England*. Stroud: The History Press.
22 NCC Punting 311r.
23 Hart, R., 'Shrines and pilgrimages of the county of Norfolk', *Norfolk Archaeology*, 6 (1864), 277.
24 For what follows on Woolpit, Paine, C., 'The chapel and image of Our Lady of Woolpit', *Proceedings of the Suffolk Institute of Archaeology*, 38 (1996), 8–12.
25 For the Cawston screen, Duffy, E., 'The Parish, piety and patronage in late medieval East Anglia', in Duffy, *Saints, Sacrilege and Sedition*, 66–7 and figs 4 and colour plate 3; Baker *et al.*, *English Panel Paintings*, 132–4.
26 Fitzwilliam Museum Mss 5, Horae *c* .1480, fol. 57b. Such gestures are extensions of the devotional vogue for pilgrim badges and tokens. These were widely believed to retain and transmit some of the power of the shrine itself, so that even bulky lead badges were sometimes pinned or glued into Books of Hours: see pl. 1, 148 in Spencer, B. W., 'Medieval Pilgrim Badges', in *Rotterdam Papers: A Contribution to Medieval Archaeology*. Rotterdam, 1968. (Replicas of pilgrim badges painted in the margins of a Flemish Book of Hours in Sir John Soane's Museum, Ms 4 fol. 122v.)
27 Northeast, P., 'Superstition and belief: a Suffolk case of the fifteenth century', *Suffolk Review*, n.s., 20 (1993), 44–6.
28 Horn J. M. (ed.), *Register of Robert Hallam, Bishop of Salisbury 1407–17* (Torquay, 1982), 215.
29 Bannister A. T. (ed.), *Registrum Thome Myllyng, Episcopi Herefordiensis 1474–92*. London, 1920, 107.
30 Tanner N. (ed.), *Kent Heresy Proceedings, 1511–12*. Kent Records, 1997, 4, 90; Wright D. P. (ed.), *The Register of Thomas Langton, Bishop of Salisbury, 1485–93*. Canterbury and York Society, 72.
31 Duncan L. L. (ed.), *Testamenta Cantiana: West Kent*. London, 1906, 271, 348.
32 Harrod, H. (ed.), 'Extracts from Early Norfolk Wills', *Norfolk Archaeology*, 1 (1847), 257.
33 Woodruff, C. E. (ed.), *A XVth Century Guide-Book to the Principal Churches of Rome Compiled c. 1470 by William Brewyn*. London, 1933, 25.

NOTES   341

34 Furnivall, F. J. (ed.), *The Stacyons of Rome*. London, 1867.
35 Meech, S. B., and Allen, E. H. (eds), *The Book of Margery Kempe*. EETS 212 (1940), 75.
36 Parry, J. H. (ed.), *Register of Edmund Lacy, Bishop of Hereford, 1417–20*. London, 1918, 21, 24, 28; Dunstan, G. R. (ed.), *The Register of Edmund Lacy, Bishop of Exeter 1420–1455*. Torquay, 1963, vol. I: 51, 107, 300, 306, 315; vol. II: 25, 314, 403; vol. III: 14, 38, 39, 136, 210.
37 Meech and Allen (eds), *Book of Margery Kempe*, 22.
38 Nicholas N. H. (ed.), *Privy Purse Expenses of Elizabeth of York*. London, 1830, 3–4.
39 The faculties given to private chaplains licensed at Rome routinely specify the power to dispense all pilgrimage vows except those to these greater sites: e.g., Twemlow J. A. (ed.), *Calendar of Entries in the Papal Registers Relating to Great Britain and Ireland: Paper Letters, vol. XIV*. London, 1960, 189, 255.
40 Wheeler, R. B. (ed.), 'Torkington's Pilgrimage to Jerusalem in 1517', *Gentleman's Magazine*, 82 (1812), 313.
41 Duncan (ed.), *Testamenta Cantiana: West Kent*, 326.
42 Hart, 'Pilgrimages of the County of Norfolk', 277.
43 Harrod, H. (ed.), 'Early Norfolk Wills', *Norfolk Archaeology*, 4 (1855), 338.

CHAPTER 16

1 For the offerings of the Tudor kings at Walsingham, and of royal devotion more generally, Dickenson, J. C. (1956), *The Shrine of Our Lady of Walsingham*. Cambridge: Cambridge University Press, 38–47.
2 Morgan, Nigel, 'Marian Liturgy in Salisbury Cathedral', in Backhouse, J. (ed.) (2003), *The Medieval English Cathedral* (Donington: Harlaxton Medieval Studies X), 89–111.
3 Harrison, F. L. (1963), *Music in Medieval Britain*. London: Routledge, 81–8.
4 Williamson, Magnus, 'Liturgical music in the late medieval parish', in C. Burgess and E. Duffy (eds), *The Parish in Late Medieval England*. Donington, 2006, 232.
5 Williamson, 'Liturgical Music', 190, 225, 240.
6 James, M. R., 'The Sculptures in the Lady Chapel at Ely', *Archaeological Journal* 49 (1892), 345–62.
7 James, M. R., and Tristram, E. W., 'The wall paintings in Eton College Chapel and the Lady Chapel of Winchester Cathedral', *Walpole*

Society 17, 1929, 1–44; Howe, Emily, McBurney, Henrietta, and Park, David (2012), *Wall Paintings of Eton College*. London: Scala; for the Winchester paintings, see the discussion by Julie Adams available at http://www.winchester-cathedral.org.uk/wp-content/uploads/The-Wall-Paintings-of-the-Lady-Chapel.pdf.

8 James, Montague Rhodes (1895), *A Descriptive Catalogue of the Manuscripts in the Library of Eton College*. Cambridge, 108–12; Harrison, *Music in Medieval Britain*, 307–29, idem, 'The Eton Choirbook: its background and contents (Eton College Library ms. 178)', *Annales Musicologiques I* (1953), 151–75; Curtis, Gareth, and Wathey, Andrew, 'Fifteenth-century English liturgical music: a list of the surviving repertory', *RMA Research Chronicle* 27 (1994), 1–69; Williamson, Magnus (2010), *The Eton Choirbook, Facsimile with introductory study*. Oxford: DIAMM Publications.

9 For the text of *Stella Coeli Extirpavit*, see *Horae Eboracenses* (Surtees Society, 1920), p. 69.

10 On rosary beads, the best study remains Wilkins, Eithne (1969), *The Rose Garden Game*. London: Victor Gollancz; on the evolution and content of rosary devotions, Winston-Allen, Anne (1997), *Stories of the Rose: The Making of the Rosary in the Middle Ages*. Pennsylvania: Pennsylvania University Press; brief treatment of the rosary in Rubin, Miri (2009), *Mother of God, A History of the Virgin Mary*. London: Penguin, 332–8.

11 Thurston, Herbert (1953), *Familiar Prayers*. London: Burns Oates, 90–114.

12 On the Book of Hours in lay piety, Wieck, Roger S. (1988), *The Book of Hours in Medieval Art and Life*. London: Sotheby's Publications; Duffy, E. (2006), *Marking the Hours, English People and their Prayers 1240–1570*. New Haven and London: Yale University Press; de Hamel, Christopher (1994), *A History of Illuminated Manuscripts*. London: Phaidon Press, ch. 6; Smyth, Kathryn A. (2003), *Art, Identity and Devotion in Fourteenth-Century England: Three Women and their Books of Hours*. London and Toronto: British Library Publications.

13 Winston-Allen, *Stories of the Rose*, 65–80.

14 Wilkins, *Rose-Garden Game*, 40.

15 Details in Duffy, *The Stripping of the Altars*, 289.

16 There is no accessible study-edition of the text of a standard medieval Book of Hours: the contents of such books in England in the late Middle Ages, allowing for the regional variations, can be gathered

NOTES 343

from the Surtees Society edition of *Horae Eboracenses*, cited in note 9 above.
17 I have translated the text from *Horae Eboracenses*, 63–4.
18 Duffy, *Stripping of the Altars*, 258.
19 For a discussion of some of the issues raised by devotion to the sorrows of Mary, Duffy, E., 'Mater Dolorosa, Mater Misericordiae: theological dimensions of late-medieval popular devotion to Mary, the Mother of God', *New Blackfriars* (May 1988), 210–227.
20 The fullest discussion of the European background of devotion to the Pietà is Ziegler, Joanna E. (1992), *Sculpture of Compassion: the Pietà and the Beguines in the Southern Low Countries c. 1300–c. 1600*. Brussels and Rome: Institut. Historique Belge de Rome.
21 *Stripping of the Altars*, 260–1.
22 I have translated from the text in *Horae Eboracenses*, 66–7.
23 See the title page reproduced in Duffy, *Marking the Hours*, 143.
24 Duffy, *Stripping of the Altars*, 266–98.
25 Cambridge University Library, MS Ii. 6.2.
26 For the Roberts book and the discussion which follows, Duffy, *Marking the Hours*, 81–96.
27 Gordon, Dillian (ed.) (1993), *Making and Meaning: the Wilton Diptych*. London; Gordon, Dillian, Monnas, Lisa, and Elam Caroline, (eds) (1997), *The Regal Image of Richard II and the Wilton Diptych*. London: Brepols.
28 Skinner, David, 'William Cornysh: clerk or courtier?', *Musical Times*, 138: 1851 (May 1997), 5–12; Bent, Margaret (1981), *Dunstaple*. Oxford: Oxford University Press; Fitch, Fabrice, 'Hearing John Browne's motets: registral space in the music of the Eton Choirbook', *Early Music*, 36:1 (February 2008), 19–40.
29 For the post-Reformation afterlife of Walsingham, and the revival of the shrine(s) in modern times, Waller, Gary (2011), *Walsingham and the English Imagination*. Farnham: Routledge.

CHAPTER 17

1 For Wingfield, see the collection of essays gathered in Bloore, Peter, and Martin, Edward (eds) (2015), *Wingfield College and its Patrons*. Woodbridge: The Boydell Press.
2 Meiss, Millard (1978), *Painting in Florence and Siena After the Black Death: The Arts, Religion, and Society in the Mid-Fourteenth Century*. Princeton, NJ: Princeton University Press.

3 Delumeau, Jean (1990), *Sin and Fear: The Emergence of the Western Guilt Culture, 13th–18th Centuries*. London: Palgrave Macmillan, 3.
4 Delumeau, *Sin and Fear*, 475.
5 For an outstanding study of the other great de la Pole mortuary foundation, Goodall, John A. A. (2001), *God's House at Ewelme: Life, Devotion and Architecture in a Fifteenth-Century Almshouse*. Aldershot: Routledge.
6 Burgess, Clive, 'A fond thing vainly invented: an essay on Purgatory and pious motive in late-medieval England', in S. J. Wright (ed.) (1988) *Parish, Church and People: Local Studies in Lay Religion, 1350–1750*. London: Hutchinson.
7 Figures from the 1998 Cambridge PhD dissertation by Rachel Elizabeth Ward, 'The foundation and functions of perpetual Chantries in the Diocese of Norwich c.1250–1547'.
8 Burgess, Clive, 'An Institution for all seasons: the late medieval English college', in Clive Burgess and Martin Heale (eds) (2008), *The Late Medieval English College and its Context*. Woodbridge: Boydell and Brewer, 3–27, at 19–20; and for a discussion of the relationship between monasteries and collegiate churches more generally, Martin Heale, 'Colleges and monasteries in late medieval England' in the same collection, 67–86.
9 Matthew Parker's transcription of the Statutes of Mortimer College is in Corpus Christi College Cambridge, Parker Library, Ms 108, item 8, fols 75–82, 117–24.
10 I have used the text in Horstman, Carl, *Yorkshire Writers*, 2 vols. London, 1895, vol. 1, 383–92; there is a modern scholarly edition by Harley, Marta Powell, *A Revelation of Purgatory by an Unknown Fifteenth-Century Woman Visionary: Introduction, Critical Text, and Translation*, Studies in Women and Religion 18. Lewiston: NY, 1985; for the context and early distribution of the vision, Erler, Mary, 'A revelation of Purgatory (1422): reform and the politics of female visions', *Viator* 38:1 (2007), 312–383.
11 Duffy, Eamon, *The Stripping of the Altars*. New Haven and London: Yale University Press, 1992, 346.
12 Northeast, Peter (ed.), *Wills of the Archdeaconry of Sudbury, 1439–1474: wills from the register 'Baldwyne'*, Part 1. Woodbridge, Suffolk Record Society, 2001; Northeast, Peter, and Falvey, Heather, *Wills of the Archdeaconry of Sudbury, 1439–1474*, Part II: 1461–74. Woodbridge, 2009.

NOTES   345

13 Northeast, *Wills*, Part I, 842.
14 Northeast, *Wills*, Part II, 187.
15 The will is printed in Tymms, Samuel (ed.), *Wills and Inventories from the Registers of the Commissary of Bury St Edmunds, and the Archdeacon of Sudbury*. Camden Society 1850, 15–44.
16 Manley, Frank, Marc'adour, Germain, Marius, Richard, and Miller, Clarence (eds), *Complete Works of St Thomas More*, Vol. 7. New Haven and London: Yale University Press, 111.

CHAPTER 18

1 The quotation is from Clare's sonnet 'Crowland Abbey', in John Clare, *The Midsummer Cushion*, ed. Kelsey Thornton and Anne Tibble. Ashington: Carcanet, 1990, 394; two of Cotman's watercolours of the Abbey are available online at http://poulwebb.blogspot.co.uk/2013/02/john-sell-cotman-part-1.html.
2 For the Abbey's finances, Page, F. M. (1934), *The Estates of Crowland Abbey: A Study in Manorial Organisation*. Cambridge: Cambridge University Press; Raban, Sandra (1977), *The Estates of Thorney and Crowland: A Study in Medieval Monastic Land Tenure*. Cambridge: Cambridge University Press.
3 For the Abbey's history, Gough, R., *The History and Antiquities of Croyland-Abbey in the County of Lincoln* (London, 1783 [recte 1784]), with *A Second Appendix to the History of Croyland* (London, 1797) and, for a modern overview, *A History of the County of Lincoln*, vol. 2 (originally published by Victoria County History, London, 1906), 105–18.
4 The literature on the 'Historia Croylandensis' and its various continuations is immense: a start can be made with Searle, W. G., *Ingulf and the Historia Croylandensis*. Cambridge, 1894; Williams D. (ed.), 'The Crowland Chronicles 615–1500', *England in the Fifteenth Century*. Woodbridge, 1987, 371–90; Roffe, David, 'The Historia Croylandensis: a plea for reassessment', *English Historical Review*, 110:435 (February 1995), 93–108; Hicks, Michael, 'The second anonymous continuation of the Crowland Abbey Chronicle 1459–86 revisited', *English Historical Review*, 122:496 (April 2007), 349–370: Pronay, N., and Cox, J. (ed.), *The Crowland Chronicle Continuations 1459–86*. Richard III and Yorkist History Trust, London, 1986; Hiatt, Alfred, *The Making of Medieval Forgeries: False Documents in Fifteenth-Century England*. London, 2004, esp. 36–69; Ispir, Christian Nicolae,

'A Critical Edition of the Crowland Chronicle', King's College London, PhD dissertation, 2015.
5 Fulman, William (ed.), *Rerum Anglicarum Scriptorum Veterum*, Tom 1. Oxford 1684, 77; Riley, Henry T. (trans.), *Ingulph's Chronicle of the Abbey of Croyland, with the continuations of Peter of Blois and anonymous writers*. London: George Bell and Sons, 1908, 155.
6 Colgrave, Bertram, trans. (1956), *Felix's Life of St. Guthlac*. Cambridge: Cambridge University Press, 87: Darby, H. C. (1940), *The Medieval Fenland*. Cambridge: Cambridge University Press; Oosthuizen, Susan, 'Culture and identity in the early medieval Fenland', *Landscape History*, 37:1 (2016), 5–24.
7 McClure, Judith, and Collins, Roger (eds) (1994), *Bede, The Ecclesiastical History of the English People*. Oxford: Oxford University Press, 95–6.
8 *Felix's Life of Saint Guthlac*, 81–3.
9 Henderson, George D. S., 'The imagery of St Guthlac of Crowland', in Ormerod, W. M. (ed.), *England in the Thirteenth Century: Proceedings of the 1984 Harlaxton Symposium*. Grantham, UK: Harlaxton College, 1985, 76–94, some points of which are corrected in Alexander, Jennifer S., 'Guthlac and Company ... on the west front of Croyland Abbey Church', in Susan Powell (ed.), *Saints and Cults in Medieval England*. Donington: Harlaxton Studies, 2017, 249–64; Bolton, W. F., 'The Croyland quatrefoil and Polychronicon', *Journal of the Warburg and Courtauld Institutes* 21 (1958), 295–6.
10 Farmer, David High (1992), *Oxford Dictionary of the Saints*. Oxford: Oxford University Press, 221.
11 Szarmach, Paul E. (ed.) (1981), *Vercelli Homiles ix–xxiii*. Toronto: University of Toronto Press. Survey of early material on Guthlac in Black, John, 'Tradition and transformation in the cult of St Guthlac in early medieval England', *The Heroic Age: A Journal of Early Medieval Northwestern Europe*, 10 (2007).
12 Roberts, Jane (ed.) (1979), *The Guthlac Poems of the Exeter Book*. Oxford: Oxford University Press; Roberts, J., 'An inventory of early Guthlac materials', *Mediaeval Studies*, 32 (1970), 193–233; Sharma, Manish, 'A reconsideration of the structure of "Guthlac A": the extremes of saintliness', *Journal of English and Germanic Philology*, 101:2 (April 2002), 185–200.

NOTES 347

13 Warner, G. F. (1928), *The Guthlac Roll*. London: Roxburghe Club (facsimile); discussion in Henderson, note 7 above.
14 Chibnall, Marjorie (ed.) (1968), *The Ecclesiastical History of Orderic Vitalis*, vol. II. Oxford: Oxford University Press, xxiv–xxix, 332–50.
15 Lewis, C. P., 'Waltheof, earl of Northumbria (*c.* 1050–1076)', *Oxford Dictionary of National Biography*. Oxford: Oxford University Press, 2004; Scott, F. S., 'Earl Waltheof of Northumbria', *Archaeologia Aeliana*, 4th ser., 30 (1952), 149–215.
16 Latin text of the *Vita Waldevi* in Michel F. (ed.), *Chroniques anglo-normandes*, Tome 2. Rouen 1836, 99ff: the text of the account of the twelve miracles 131–42; discussion of authorship and provenance, Watkins, C. S., 'The cult of Earl Waltheof at Crowland', *Hagiographica*, 3 (1996), 96–112 at 97–8.
17 For what follows, Watkins, 'Cult of Earl Waltheof', and Scott, 'Earl Waltheof of Northumbria', 149–215; Mason, Emma, 'Invoking Earl Waltheof', in David Roffe (ed.), *The English and Their Legacy, 900–1200: Essays in Honour of Ann Williams*. Woodbridge: The Boydell Press, 185–203.
18 *Vita Waldevi*, 131–2.
19 *Vita Waldevi*, 132–3.
20 *Vita Waldevi*, 133–4.
21 *Vita Waldevi*, 134–5.
22 *Vita Waldevi*, 135–6, 138–9.
23 *Vita Waldevi*, 140–1.
24 *Vita Waldevi*, 139.
25 *Vita Waldevi*, 141–2.
26 *Vita Waldevi*, 136, 137.
27 See the remarks in Watkins, 'Cult of Earl Waltheof', 105–6.
28 Chibnall, *Orderic Vitalis*, 348.
29 Chibnall, *Orderic Vitalis*, 342.
30 I diverge here from the conclusions of Dr Watkins, 'Cult of Earl Waltheof', 111.
31 Caley, J., and Hunter, J. (eds), *Valor Ecclesiasticus Temp. Henrici VIII: Auctoritate Regia Institutus; printed by command in pursuance of an address of the House of Commons of Great Britain*, vol. 4. London, 1821, 85.
32 Riley, *Ingulph's Chronicle*, 476; Fulman, *Anglicarum Scriptorum Veterum*, 560.

33 This was a mass celebrated by priests employed by the Boston guild of the Blessed Virgin, which carried the same religious benefits as a mass celebrated at the Scala Coeli shrine in Rome, a privilege negotiated on the guild's behalf by, of all people, the young Thomas Cromwell.
34 Riley, *Ingulph's Chronicle*, 444; Fulman, *Anglicarum Scriptorum Veterum*, 541.
35 Fulman, *Anglicarum Scriptorum Veterum*, 540–1; Riley, *Ingulph's Chronicle*, 442.
36 Riley, *Ingulph's* Chronicle, 434–9; Fulman, *Rerum Anglicarum Scriptorum Veterum*, 537–9.

CHAPTER 19

1 H. Leclercq in Cabrol, F., and Leclercq, H. (eds) (1920), *Dictionnaire d'Archéologie Chrétienne et de Liturgie*. Paris: Letouzey et Ane, Editeurs, iv (i), cols 1260–1 ('Docteurs de l'Eglise'); Rice, Eugene F. (1988), *Saint Jerome in the Renaissance*. Baltimore: Johns Hopkins University Press, 89–90.
2 Rouse, R. H. and M. A., '*Ordinatio* and *Compilatio* Revisited' in M. D. Jordan and K. Emery (eds), *Ad Litteram: Authoritative Texts and their Medieval Readers*. University of Notre Dame Press, 1992, 120–1.
3 Holmstedt, G. (ed.), *Speculum Christiani, A Middle English Religious Treatise of the 14th Century*. EETS, 1933.
4 BL Add Ms 28026 f 2r; Bodley Ms 243 f 115v (from which the quotation in the text comes). I am indebted to Professor Anne Hudson for these references and for guidance on this general point.
5 Cigman, G. (ed.) (1989), *Lollard Sermons*. Oxford: Oxford University Press, xlvii, 51; cf Matthew, F. D. (ed.), *The English Works of Wyclif hitherto unprinted*. London 1880, 58, 118, 258, 429.
6 Tanner, Norman P. (ed.) (1977), *Heresy Trials in the Diocese of Norwich 1428–31*. London: Camden Society, Fourth Series, vol. 20, 148.
7 Thompson, J. A. F. (1965), *The Later Lollards 1414–1520*. Oxford: Oxford University Press, 66.
8 Ibid., 65–6.
9 Townsend, George, and Cattley, S. R. (eds), *The Acts and Monuments of John Foxe*, vol. iv. London 1837, 207–8.
10 Where they were originally in the Library – Hutchinson, F. E. (1949), *Medieval Glass at All Souls College*. London, 38, 43, 49 and plates xxviii and xxix.

11 Wayment, Hilary, *King's College Chapel Cambridge: the Side-Chapel Glass*. Cambridge 1988, 194–5, illustrated 196.
12 Rushforth, G. McN. (1936), *Medieval Christian Imagery as Illustrated by the Painted Windows of Great Malvern Priory Church*. Oxford: Oxford University Press, 253–4, 316–20.
13 Nichols, Ann Eljenholm (2002), *The Early Art of Norfolk*. Kalamazoo, MI: Medieval Institute Publications, 153–7.
14 Nichols, *Early Art of Norfolk*, 159
15 Lasko, Peter (1994), *Ars Sacra 800–1200*, 2nd ed. New Haven and London: Yale University Press, pl. 149.
16 Rice, *Jerome*, 64–5.
17 Lucy Wrapson dates the seated figures of the Doctors on the Lessingham screen to c.1508–1520: Lucy Wrapson (2017) 'Towards a new methodological approach for interpreting workshop activity and dating medieval church screens', in Spike Bucklow, Richard Marks and Lucy Wrapson (eds), *The Arts and Science of the church screen in Medieval Europe*, Woodbridge the Boydell Press, 69. As Wrapson argues, my own earlier conjecture that the superimposed figures date from the Marian restoration now seems unlikely, given similarities in their workmanship to early Tudor screens at Fritton and elsewhere.
18 Jonathan Alexander, 'The pulpit with the Four Doctors', in N. Rogers (ed.), *England in the Fifteenth Century*. Stamford: Harlaxton Medieval Studies, 1994, 198–206, the Latin tags cited in note 9, 200; Nichols, *Early Art of Norfolk*, p. 154.
19 For a general discussion of these screens, Duffy, E., 'The parish, piety and patronage in late medieval East Anglia: the evidence of roodscreens', in B. Kumin and K. L. French (eds) (1997), *The Parish in English Life 1400–1700*. Manchester: Manchester University Press, 133–62.
20 For the presence of the Doctors on Devon screens I have relied on personal inspection and on the (alphabetically arranged by parish) listings in Bond, F. B., and Camm, Bede (1909), *Roodscreens and Roodlofts*, vol. 2. London: Pitman and Sons. Fuller bibliography in Duffy, 'Parish, piety and patronage', 133, note 2.
21 Listed in Williamson, W. W., 'Saints on Norfolk rood-Screens and pulpits', *Norfolk Archaeology* XXXI (1955–7), 229–46; approximate dates for many of the screens are provided in Cotton, S., 'Medieval roodscreens in Norfolk – their construction and painting dates', *Norfolk Archaeology*, XL (1987), 44–54. A fuller list of datings, based in part on Cotton's work, is printed in Wrapson, 'Towards a new methodological approach', 49–51.

22 This is discussed more fully in *The Stripping of the Altars: Traditional Religion in England c. 1400–1580*. New Haven and London: Yale University Press, 1992, 238ff, and see plate 49, reproducing the Mass of St Gregory and the opening of a prayer to the Trinity usually attributed to St Gregory.
23 Hoskins, Edgar, *Horae Beatae Mariae Virginis or Sarum and York Primers with Kindred Books*. London, 1901, 124; for this and other prayers with apotropaic powers attributed to St Augustine, see also Leroquais, V., *Les Livres d'Heures Manuscrits de la Bibliothèque Nationale*, vol. 1. Paris, 1927, xxv, 274, 280, 329.
24 Rice, Jerome, passim.
25 For a representative example, see the illuminated page from a Sarum book of hours of c. 1430 (made in Bruges) reproduced in Arnould, Alain, and Massing, Jean Michel (1993), *Splendours of Flanders*. Cambridge: Cambridge University Press, 103 (catalogue item 33).
26 An observation for which I am indebted to Mr Nicholas Rogers. For some examples of the conjunction of image and psalter, CUL Mss Ii.vi.14, f 164v–176v: Dd.6.1., f 130v: Kk.6.10, f 148v.
27 For a priest's book with Jerome's psalter, CUL Ms Ee.5.13 fol. 3ff.
28 Amphlett, J. (ed.), *A Survey of Worcestershire by Thomas Habington*, vol. 2. Oxford: Worcester Historical Society, 1895, 177.
29 Kirschbaum, Engelbert (ed.), *Lexikon der Christlichen Ikonographie*, vol. 2. Herder, 1970, cols 529–38.
30 Mâle, Emile (1986), *Religious Art in France: the Late Middle Ages*. Princeton, NJ: Princeton University Press, 212–13 and plates 122–3.
31 Kurth Willi (ed.) (1963), *The Complete Woodcuts of Albrecht Dürer*. Toronto, 14 and plate 69.
32 Van Os, Henk (1994), *The Art of Devotion in the Late Middle Ages in Europe 1300–1500*. Amsterdam, 118–22.
33 Christiansen, Keith, et al. (1988), *Painting in Renaissance Siena 1420–1500*. New York, 63–77.

CHAPTER 20

1 Cited in Webb, Diana (1999), *Pilgrims and Pilgrimage in the Medieval West*. London, 240.
2 Maine G. (trans.), *The Imitation of Christ*. London, 1957, 236 (Book 4, ch. 1).

NOTES

3 Cited in Eire, Carlos (1986), *War Against the Idols: the Reformation of Worship from Erasmus to Calvin*. Cambridge: Cambridge University Press, 34.
4 Aston, Margaret (1988), *England's Iconoclasts*. Oxford: Oxford University Press, 107.
5 Hudson, Anne (ed.) (1978), *Selections from English Wycliffite Writings*. Cambridge: Cambridge University Press, 87.
6 Aston, *England's Iconoclasts*, 133–43.
7 Hudson, *English Wycliffite Writings*, 83, 84; for the frequency of this subject in Alabaster, Cheetham, Francis (1984), *English Medieval Alabasters*. Oxford: Oxford University Press, 296; and for a listing of almost 130 surviving alabaster images of the Trinity, Cheetham (2003), *Alabaster Images of Medieval England*. Woodbridge: Boydell, 147–53.
8 Eire, *War Against the Idols*, esp. chs 3 and 4.
9 Atson, *England's Iconoclasts*, 408–45.
10 Cited in Aston, *England's Iconoclasts*, 210–11.
11 *A Dialogue concerning Heresies*, in Lawlor, Thomas M. C., Marc'hadour, Germain, and Marius, Richard C. (eds) (1981), *Complete Works of Sir Thomas More*, vol. 6, pt 1. New Haven and London: Yale University Press, 35–70.
12 Duffy, E. (1992), *Stripping of the Altars*. New Haven and London: Yale University Press, 380–1; for the attack on the rood of Dovercourt, Aston, Margaret (1993), *Faith and Fire*. London, 263–5.
13 For which see Aston, *England's Iconoclasts*, 201–10: the translation was *A Treatise Declaryng and Shewing Dyvers Causes that Pyctures and Other Ymages ... are in no Wise to be Suffred in the Temples or Churches of Cristen Men*. London 1535.
14 Aston, *Faith and Fire*, 296.
15 *Stripping of the Altars*, 383–5.
16 Frere, W. H., and Kennedy, W. M. (eds), *Visitation Articles and Injunctions of the Period of the Reformation*, vol. II. London 1910, 5–6.
17 *Formularies of Faith Put forth by Authority in the reign of Henry VIII*. Oxford, 1825, 134–8.
18 *Visitation Articles and Injunctions*, II, 37–9.
19 *Stripping of the Altars*, 408–20.
20 Duffy, E. (2001), *The Voices of Morebath*. New Haven and London: Yale University Press, 34–5.

21 Cheetham, *Medieval English Alabasters*, 53.
22 Hughes, P. L., and Larkin, J. F. (eds) (1964), *Tudor Royal Proclamations 1485–1553*. New Haven and London: Yale University Press, 229–32: Duffy, E. (2006), *Marking the Hours*. New Haven and London: Yale University Press, 29, fig. 17.
23 *Tudor Royal Proclamations*, 275–6; examples of the defacement of images and prayers relating to Becket in books of hours in Duffy, *Marking the Hours*, 152, 153, 154, 164.
24 Cheetham, *English Medieval Alabasters*, 317–32: *Alabaster Images*, 156–60.
25 Bradshaw, C. (1996), 'David or Josiah? Old Testament kings as exemplars in Edwardian religious polemic', in B. Gordon (ed.), *Protestant History and Identity in Sixteenth-Century Europe*. Aldershot, 77–90; for a fascinating exploration of another 'Josian' representation of Edward's reign, Aston, Margaret (1995), *The King's Bedpost: Reformation and Iconography in a Tudor Group Portrait*. Cambridge: Cambridge University Press.
26 *Visitation Articles and Injunctions*, 169.
27 *Stripping of the Altars*, 453–60.
28 Aston, *England's Iconoclasts*, 267.
29 Marks, Richard (2004), *Image and Devotion in Late Medieval England*. Stroud: History Press, 4, 251, 314 (note 116).
30 For a general discussion of the disposal of Church goods in Edward's reign, Duffy, E., 'The end of it all: the material culture of the late medieval English parish and the 1552 Inventories of Church Goods', in *Saints, Sacrilege and Sedition: Religion and Conflict in the Tudor Reformations*. London: Bloomsbury, 2012, 109–29.
31 Turnbull, William (ed.), *Calendar of State Papers, Foreign Series, of the Reign of Edward VI*. London 1861, vol. 1, 54–5.
32 An alabaster retable in the chapel of the Château de Grandmont bears an inscription, 'Ex dono M I Baille Huius Ecclesiae rectoris, 1551', making it likely to be a product of these Edwardian sales: Cheetham, *Medieval English Alabasters*, 53.
33 Examples of survival in Cheetham, *Medieval English Alabasters*, 53.
34 *Stripping of the Altars*, 543–559.
35 Halliwell, James Orchard (ed.), *Tarlton's Jests and News out of Purgatory*. London, 1844, 86–7; Marks, *Image and Devotion*, 268.
36 Stone, Lawrence, *Sculpture in Britain: the Middle Ages*. Harmondsworth: Penguin, 1972, 233.

NOTES 353

CHAPTER 21

1 Christensen, Carl C. (1979), *Art and the Reformation in Germany*. Athens, OH: Ohio University Press, 64; Koerner, Joseph Lee (2004), *The Reformation of the Image*. London: Reaktion, 2004, 38.
2 Koerner, Joseph Lee (2004), *The Reformation of the Image*, London, Reaktion, 38.
3 Koerner, *Reformation of the Image*, 160
4 The most comprehensive introduction in English to Cranach and his work is the catalogue to the Royal Academy of Art's 2008 exhibition, Brinkmann, Brodo (ed.), *Cranach*. London, 2008; for an overview of Cranach's career, ibid., 17–27.
5 Brinkmann, *Cranach*, plates 37–44.
6 Evans, Mark, 'Lucas Cranach and the art of humanism', in Brinkmann, *Cranach*, 49–62.
7 Koepplin, Dieter, 'Cranach's paintings of Charity', in Brinkmann, *Cranach*, 63–80.
8 Koerner, *Reformation of the Image*, 226.
9 For a fascinating discussion of the evolution of Lutheran attitudes to devotional art, which significantly modifies Koerner's thesis, Heal, Bridget (2017), *A Magnificent Faith: Art and Identity in Lutheran Germany*. Oxford: Oxford University Press.
10 Brinkmann, *Cranach*, plates 72–3.
11 Brinkmann, *Cranach*, plates 103, 111, 112, 113, 114.
12 Tacke, Andreas, 'With Cranach's help: counter-Reformation Art before the Council of Trent', in Brinkmann, *Cranach*, 81–90.
13 Koerner, *Reformation of the Image*, 303.
14 Koerner, *Reformation of the Image*, 352.
15 Koerner, *Reformation of the Image*, 358.
16 Brinkmann, *Cranach*, plates 101, 104, 105, 110, 111.
17 Brinkmann, *Cranach*, plate 114. Under the headline 'Venus banned from London underworld', Maev Kennedy in the *Guardian* of 13 February 2008 wrote: 'Wearing nothing but her best necklace, a wisp of gauze and a foxy expression, Venus has been delighting connoisseurs for almost 500 years – but she has been banned from the underworld, as London Underground has decided she is likely to offend rather than enchant the capital's weary commuters.'

Index

Abbreviatio in gestis et miraculis sanctorum (Jean de Mailly) 29
Abrahamic religions 3
Acts and Monuments (Foxe) 297
Aelfwald, king of the East Angles 261
African Christianity 91–2
Agnes, Saint 35
alabaster images 291, 295–6, 297–9
alabaster workshops 300
Albrecht of Brandenburg, Cardinal 303, 306, 312
Alexander, Jonathan 280
Alexios I Comnenos, Byzantine emperor 102
Alexius IV Angelus 106
Ambrose, Saint 202, 276
  De Virginitate 35, 37, 40
  images of 278–83, 284–8
Ancrene Wisse 59, 60–1
Andrew, Saint 38
Andrews, Dame Elizabeth 215
Anthony, Saint 34, 162
anti-Semitism 100, 104, 105–6
Apostolic Tradition 90
Appolonia, Saint 201–2
Aquila (Jewish convert) 11
Aquinas, Thomas 32, 33, 179, 287
Arcoid, Canon 166–8

Ariès, Philippe 111–14
Arndt, Jacob 310
Arte Della Lana altarpiece (Sassetta) 287
Arundel, Archbishop Thomas 182
Arundel, Earl of (Henry Fitzalan) 25–6
Asford of Helieston (bailiff) 257
Atereth, William 215
Athanasius 162
Augustine of Hippo, Saint 34, 38, 40, 101, 197, 202, 276
  images of 278–83, 284–8
avian (bird) flu 73–4

Bacon, John 282
Bacon, Roger 45, 46, 47, 50
Bagley, Thomas, vicar of Manuden 277
Bale, John 214
baptism of tears 174, 178–80
Barbagli, Marzio 115
Baret, John 249–52
Barnham Broom 213
Barschius, Georgius 46
Bartholomew, Saint 260, 267, 269
Bartholomew of Trent 29
Bartlett, Robert 161–2
Baudime, Saint 160
Baylis, Mistress 207

Baymonde, John and Hillary 282
Beaufort, Lady Margaret 59–60, 65, 195
Becket, Thomas 34, 133, 134, 164, 196, 213, 296
Bede, Venerable 77, 78, 94, 165
　Ecclesiastical History of the English People 178, 259
　Epistola Hortatoria 275
Belting, Hans 143
Bencheikh, Soheib (Grand Mufti of Marseilles) 97
Benedict, Saint 34, 162
Bennett, Alan 20
Bernard of Clairvaux, Saint 289
Bernardino, Saint 145
Beys, Richard 199
bibles
　Codex Sinaiticus 14
　Codex Vaticanus 14
　division into chapters 53
　earliest surviving biblical texts 8
　Hebrew Bible 7, 16
　Jerome's translation 16–17, 18
　lectern bibles 14
　Origen and 11–13
　translations of 16–17, 18, 61–2
　Vulgate 61
　Wycliffe Bible 61, 276
　see also Origen of Alexandria
biblical references
　Isa. 1: 17–18: 175
　Isa. 7:14: 11
Bikenore, Thomas (heretical clerk) 277
bird (avian) flu 73–4
Biscop, Benedict 94
Bishops Book 293–4
Black Death 74, 78, 83–6, 239, 240, 241–2
Blacman, John 189–90, 199, 203
Blois, France: blood libels 126, 133, 134

Blomefield, Francis 213
blood libels 125–35
Boccaccio, Giovanni 84
Boland, Jean 42
Bolton, Henry Carrington 46
Boniface VIII, Pope 154
books 7–9
　book rolls 7–8, 27–8, 262
　codices 8–9, 12
books of hours 22–3, 56–69, 256
　Henry VI: 27
　miracles of the Virgin 223
　organization/contents of 57–9
　production history of 56
　psalms omitted 58–9
　Psalter-Hours 53
　Psalter of Saint Jerome 63, 284
　St Bernard's Verses 63–4
　Sarum Books of Hours 57–9, 65, 285
　transition from psalters 53, 55
　Virgin Mary in 225, 227–8, 230–1, 232–4
Bora, Katherina von 117
Boureau, Alain 39
Bradshaw, Henry 192
Bradwardine, Thomas 182
Braybrook, Robert, Bishop of London 169, 170
Brewyn, William 217
British Library 27–8
　book rolls 28, 262
　Guthlac Roll 262
　illuminated books exhibition 21, 22
　King's Collection 19
　Treasures of Heaven relics/reliquaries exhibition 159, 160
bubonic plague 78–9, 81, 85
Bucer, Martin 293
Bugenhagen, Johannes 307
Burgess, Clive 240
Burlingham Saint Andrews 213–14

INDEX

Bush, George W. 97
Bynum, Caroline Walker 138–41, 142–4, 145–6, 147

Campsea Ash College 242, 243
canonization 150–4
Cantilupe, Thomas 167
Capgrave, John 203, 208
Carthage, Fifth Council of 156
Castle Acre priory 129, 280, 281
Catherine of Siena, Saint 139
Ceolnith, Archbishop of Canterbury 260–1
chantry colleges 240–4, 252–3
Charlemagne, Emperor 94, 95, 101, 151, 316–17
Charles II, King 20, 26
Charles d'Anjou, King of Sicily 153
Chaucer, Geoffrey 125
Chertsey Abbey 187, 190, 193, 194
Chichele, Henry, Archbishop 278
childhood 111–21
    early modern children 115–16
    histories of 111–21
    Holy Family 113
    medieval children 112, 117–21
    nuclear families 113–14
    17th century children 112–13
Christianity: materiality of 137–47
chronicles 89
    The Crowland Chronicle 257–8, 262, 263, 269–70, 271–2
    Eusebius 14–15
    Jacobus de Voragine 40
Chrysostom, Saint John 39
Church History (Eusebius) 13
Clare, John 256
Clement VI, Pope 83, 86
Clynn, John 84
Cobham, Lady 59–60
Codex Sinaiticus 14
Codex Vaticanus 14

codices 8–9, 14
Commedia (*Divina Commedia*, Dante) 175, 181–2, 245
Conrad of Marburg 149–50
Constable, Giles 98
Constantina, Empress 156
Constantine, Emperor 13, 14, 158
Copeland, Richard 203
Couper, William 219
Cranach, Lucas, the Elder 302–13, 317–18
    altarpieces 304, 306, 307–8, 309
    banned from London Underground 318
    The Passional of Christ and Antichrist 306–7
    portraits 304, 306, 311, 312
    triptychs 311–12
Cranmer, Thomas 26, 294–5
Cromwell, Thomas 293, 294, 348n33
Crowland (Croyland) Abbey 255–8, 261–73
    pilgrimages to 260, 264–6, 267, 268–9
    shrine of the Virgin 270–1, 272–3
Crowland Chronicle, The 257–8, 262, 263, 269–70, 271–2
crusades 97–100, 102–9, 152–3
    anti-Semitism 100, 104, 105–6
    crusade tax 105
    First Crusade 102–4, 105
    Fourth Crusade 100, 106, 108
    as pilgrimage 103, 205–20
    relics 107–8
    Second Crusade 129–30
Cuthbert of Lindisfarne, Saint 77, 78

Damasus, Pope 16, 35
Dante Alighieri 175, 181–2, 245
de Hamel, Christopher 61
De laude dei super psalterium (Jerome, attrib.) 59

De Laude Psalmorum (Augustine, attrib.) 61–2, 64
De Luminibus (Gregory of Nazianzus) 179
De Musica 88
De Virginitate (Ambrose) 35, 37, 40
de Worde, Wynkyn 203, 208
death
  as pilgrimage 205–6
  see also Purgatory; wills
Decline and Fall of the Roman Empire (Gibbon) 1–2
Dee, John 46–7
Delumeau, Jean 239–40
Despenser, Henry 239
Deulesalt/Deus Adjuvet (Norwich moneylender) 130, 131
Deusdona (Roman deacon) 156
Dialogue Concerning Heresies (More) 168, 292
D'Imperio, Mary 49
Divina Commedia (Dante) 175, 181–2, 245
Dominic, Saint 34, 164
Dürer, Albrecht 286, 301, 305, 312, 317

East, Margaret 219
Easthawe, Thomas 212–13
Ecclesiastical History of the English People (Bede) 178, 259
Eco, Umberto 50
Edmund the Martyr, Saint 197, 201–2, 213
Edward the Confessor, Saint 151, 166, 197, 201–2, 213
Edward II, King 188
Edward IV, King 198
  library 20, 24
  usurpation of throne 187, 188, 189, 190
Edward VI, King 22, 296–7

Edwardes, William 194
einigberlei Bild, Das (Bucer) 293
Elias, Prior 132
Elisabeth of Hungary 34
Elizabeth I, Queen 215
Elizabeth of Thuringia 149–50, 157
Elizabeth of York 195, 218, 226
Ely Cathedral: Lady Chapel 223
Enchiridion Militis Christiani (Erasmus) 289–90
Epilogus in gesta sanctorum (Bartholomew of Trent) 29
Epistola Hortatoria (Bede) 275
Erasmus, Desiderius 289–90
Erasmus, Saint 200
Erkenwald, Saint
  cult of 165–70
  miracles 166–8
  relics 165–6
  St Erkenwald (alliterative poem) 170–81
Erkenwald guild 170, 183–4
Ethelburga (sister of Erkenwald) 165
Etheldreda of Ely, Saint 197, 198, 213
Eton College 188, 191, 197, 223–4
Etymologiae (Isidore of Seville) 38
Eusebius of Caesarea 10, 13–15
Evagrius Scholasticus 75–6
Exeter Book 261
Exhumation of St Hubert, The 314–15

Fabyan, George 48
Felix: life of Guthlac 258, 260, 261, 266
Festial (Mirk) 33
Fisher, John 60, 65
Fitzalan, Henry, Earl of Arundel 25–6
FitzJames, Richard, Bishop of London 277
Flandrin, Jean-Louis 114
Florilegia 276, 280
flu epidemic (1918–19) 74

INDEX

forgeries 263
Four Latin Doctors, *see* Latin Doctors
Foxe, John 297
Francis of Assisi, Saint 34, 149, 150, 164
Franke, John 217
Frederick II, Holy Roman Emperor 157
Frederick Barbarossa 151
Frederick the Wise, Elector of Saxony 304–5
Friedman, William F. 48–9
Fuller, Thomas 193–4

Gallup, Elizabeth Wells 48
Garnett, Richard 44
Gascoigne, Thomas (monk of Syon) 61, 64
Geary, Patrick 206
Geoffrey of Orleans, abbot of Crowland 262, 264, 267
Geoffroy de Beaulieu 154
George II, King 20
George III, King 19–20
George IV, King 19
George the Bearded, Duke of Saxony 311–12
Gibbon, Edward 1–2, 3
Gilbert the Universal, Bishop of London 166
Gilson, Étienne 47
Godwin Sturt 128
Goldall, John and Katherine 279, 282
Gollancz, Isaac 177, 334n27
Grafton, Anthony 9, 12, 15
Grand Mufti of Marseilles (Soheib Bencheikh) 97
Gregory I, Pope (Gregory the Great, Saint) 34, 77, 91, 156, 162, 197, 202, 276
  images of 278–83, 284–8
  Mass of St Gregory 143, 283
  and Trajan, legend of 171, 174–7
  Whitby 'Life of Gregory' 174–5, 176–81
Gregory IX, Pope 150
Gregory of Nazianzus 179
Gregory of Tours 76–7
Guido of Arezzo 87, 88–9
Guthlac, Saint 258–62, 267, 271, 272
  cult of 260–1
  Felix's life of 258, 260, 261, 266
Guthlac Roll 262

Habington, Thomas 285
Hacomblen, Robert, Provost 278
hagiography 29, 162, 163–4: see also *Legenda Aurea* (Jacobus de Voragine)
Hakim, Fatimid caliph 103
Harper-Bill, Christopher 131, 134
Hebrew Bible 7, 16
Hegel, Georg Wilhelm Friedrich 308
Helena, Saint 158, 208, 215
Henry III, King 108, 151
Henry VI, King 27, 213
  book of hours 27
  cult of 187–203
  hymns to 191–2, 193
  images of 196–9, 201–2, 213
  miracles of 187, 190, 191–2, 193–5, 199–200
  murder of 187, 188, 189, 190
  and pilgrimages 200
  psalter 27
Henry VII, King 195
Henry VIII, King 28, 196, 221
  and iconoclasm 292–3, 294–5
  libraries 20, 24–5
Henry Frederick, Prince 20, 25
heresy 277: *see also* Lollards
Herynge, Thomas 217
Hexapla 11–13
Hilary, Saint 38, 39

Hill, Richard 228–9
Historia Croylandensis, see *Crowland Chronicle, The*
Historia Scholastica (Peter Comestor) 32, 38
History of the Franks (Gregory of Tours) 76–7
Holy Blood of Hailes 202, 210
holy war
    Christianity and 97, 100, 101–2, 103
    Islam and 100–1
Hopkins, Gerard Manley 158–9
Hořčický de Tepenec, Jacobus 46
Howard, John, Duke of Norfolk 215
Hugh, Saint, Bishop of Lincoln 157
Hugh of Lincoln 125
Hughes, Jonathan 67–8
Huguenots 292
hymns 215, 227
    to Henry VI: 191–2, 193
    to Virgin Mary 224, 225–6, 227

iconoclasm 297–8, 302
    Henry VIII and 292–3, 294–5
    Lollard 146, 290–1
idolatry 41, 292, 301, 310
Ignatius of Antioch 90
Ikonographia (Arndt) 310
images 289–300
    alabaster 291, 295–6, 297–9
    in glass 278
    Gregory the Great 278–83, 284–8
    Henry VI: 196–9, 201–2, 213
    iconoclastic attacks on 290–1, 292–3, 297–8
    Latin Doctors 278–88
    medieval 142–4
    Reformation repudiation of 291–2
    veneration of 289–90, 291, 301
Imitation of Christ, The (Kempis) 289
indulgences 102, 217–18, 226–7, 234, 250, 306

Ingulf, abbot of Crowland 262, 264, 266
Innocent III, Pope 106
Isabelle of Aragon 154
Isidore of Seville 38

Jacobus de Voragine 29–42, 163–4, 203
James, M. R. 209
Jean de Mailly 29
Jean-Tristan, son of Louis IX 153
Jerome, Saint 15–18, 39–40, 155, 202, 276
    images of 16–17, 278–88
    on singing in church 90–1
    translation of Bible 16–17, 18
Jews
    anti-Semitism 100, 104, 105–6
    blood libel 125–35
John II, King of France 168
John XIX, Pope (Romanus of Tusculum) 87, 88
John de Chesney 128–9, 130
John de Wisbech, Abbot of Crowland 269–70
John, Duke of Bedford 27
John of Bridlington 203, 208
John of Ephesus 76
John of Salisbury 20
John of Tynemouth 168
John Paul II, Pope 108, 150
John the Baptist 157
John the Deacon 175
Joseph of Arimathea 202, 208, 210
Julia of Hereford 167
Jurnet the Jew (moneylender) 126
just wars 101, 102–3
Justinianic plague 73–83

Karlstadt, Andreas 291, 302
Kempe, Margery 218, 229–30
Kempis, Thomas à 141, 289

INDEX

Kennedy, Maev 353n17
Kertzer, David 115
King's College, Cambridge 223, 278
Kircher, Athanasius 45, 46
Koerner, Joseph 309–10, 311, 312–13, 314–17
Kraus, Hans Peter 43, 44, 49
Kravchinsky, Sergei 'Stepniak' 44
Kulikowski, Michael 80
Kyrkby, Margaret 61

Lacy, Edmund 218
Langland, William 175, 181
Latin Doctors 202, 275–88
 in European art 286–7
 images of 278–88
 Lollards and 276–8
 see also Ambrose, Saint; Augustine of Hippo, Saint; Gregory, Saint; Jerome, Saint
Lawrence, Saint 201–2
lay people
 and literacy 55, 56
 and psalms 53–69
Legenda Aurea/Golden Legend (Jacobus de Voragine) 29–42, 203
 account of Saint Agnes 35–8
 conflicting accounts in 38–9
 Corpus Christi, omission of 33
 extant copies 29–30
 organization of 30–2
 printed editions 30, 163–4
 saints included in 33–40
 as source of sermon material 32–3
 sources 29, 35, 39
 translations 30, 163–4
Leland, John 25
Leo III, Pope 101
Leofgifu, lady 268
Leviva (Godwin Sturt's wife) 128
Liber Scintillarum 276
Liberius, Pope 91

libraries 10, 13
 British Library 19, 21, 22, 27–8
 Charles II: 20, 26
 Collegio Romano, Rome 45
 of Earls of Oxford 23
 Edward IV 20, 24
 Eusebius 14
 George III: 19–29
 Hampton Court Library 25
 Henry VIII: 20, 24–5
 Henry Frederick 20, 25
 Old Royal Library 19–21, 22–3, 24, 25, 26, 27
 Pamphilius 13
 royal libraries 19–28, 45
 Rudolf II: 45
 Vatican Library 45
Lincoln's Inn: and Erkenwald's Translation 170
Lingua Aegyptiaca Restituta (Kircher) 46
Lionel, Duke of Clarence 243
Litcham 213
literacy 55, 56
Little, Lester K. 74, 82
Locher, Jakob 286
Lollard Glossed Gospels 276
Lollards 182–3, 217, 285–6, 287–8
 and Four Latin Doctors 276–8
 iconoclasm 146, 290–1
London Underground: Cranach exhibition publicity material 318
Losinga, Herbert 132
Louis IV, Landgrave of Thuringia 149
Louis IX, King of France 151–4
Lovell, Gregory 211
Ludham 197, 200, 201–2, 213
Ludicia (Theodore of Tarsus) 179
Lumley, John, Lord Lumley 25–6
Luther, Martin 117, 291, 301, 302, 306, 308, 310–11, 312
 and social distinctions 315–16

Luxford, Julian 159
Lyon, Second Council of 161

McCulloh, John 133
MacFarlane, K. B. 184
McKinnon, James 93
Maddicott, John 79, 82
Mâle, Emile 286
Mallard, Jean 25
Manly, John Matthews 47, 48
Manners, Henry, Earl of Rutland 23
manuscripts
  book rolls 7–8, 27–8, 262
  illuminated 21–2
  Voynich manuscript (Beinecke MS 408) 43–4, 45–52
Marci, Johannes Marcus 45–6
Margaret, Saint 38
Marshall, William 293
Martin of Tours, Saint 162
Martyr, Peter 40
martyrdom 154–5
Mary I, Queen 23, 299
Mary, mother of Jesus
  in books of hours 225, 227–8, 230–1, 232–4
  cult of 221–35
  Gaude Virgo Mater Christi 228–9
  guilds 222–3
  musical liturgy 222
  Pietà image 229–30
  prayer to 234
  in psalters 225, 227–8, 230–1, 232–4
  rosary beads (Hail Marys) 224–7, 232–3
  shrines 270–1, 272
  Stabat Mater 224, 229
Mary Magdalene, Saint 34, 157, 201–2
Mason, John 299
Mass of Saint Giles 314–15, 316–17
materiality of Christianity 137–47
Meiss, Millard 239

Melancthon, Philip 306–7, 311, 315–16
mendicant friars 29
Mettingham College 242, 244
Michaud, J. F. 108
miracles 36–7, 92, 161, 166–8
  Elizabeth of Thuringia 149–50
  Eton College miracle cycle 223–4
  Henry VI and 187, 190, 191–2, 193–5, 199–200
  punishment miracles 287
  revenge/vengeance miracles 38, 166–8
  at Waltheof's tomb 264–6, 268
  Walstan 211
  at Werburge's shrine 192
  William of Norwich and 129, 131
Miracles of [St] Thecla 161
Miracula (Arcoid) 166–7
Mirk, John 33
monasticism 255
More, Thomas 65–8, 168, 253, 290, 292
Morgan, John, Dean of Windsor 195
Mortimer College 242, 243, 244
music
  in chantry colleges 242–4
  Eton choir book 223–4
  in honour of Virgin Mary 223, 227–8, 234
  notation, reform of 88–9
  sacred songs 87–96
  singing in church 90–1
  song schools 92–4
Myrroure of our Lady (Gascoigne) 61, 64

Neot, Saint 268
New Pelagians 182
Newbold, William Romaine 47–8
Nicholas of Cusa 141
Nichols, Ann 278
Nill, Anne 44

INDEX

Northeast, Peter 247
Nova Legenda Angliae (Capgrave, attrib.) 203, 208

Observant Movement 226
Ockham, William of 182
Olaf of Norway, Saint 197
Old Royal Library 19–21, 22–3, 24, 25, 26, 27
    Lindisfarne gospel book 22
Orderic Vitalis 263, 264, 266, 267–8
Origen of Alexandria 9–13
    Hexapla 11–13
    Septuagint 11–12
Orme, Nicholas 117–21
Oscytel, Abbot of Crowland 268
Osmund of Salisbury 150, 208
Oswald, Saint 157
Ozment, Steven 116–17

Page, Christopher 87, 88, 89–91, 92–3, 94, 95, 96
Pamphilius 13
pandemics 73–86
    avian flu 73–4
    Black Death 74, 78, 83–6, 239, 241
    bubonic plague 78–9, 81, 85
    flu epidemic (1918–19) 74
    Justinianic plague 74–83
    pneumonic plague 78–9, 85
    rats and 78, 79–80, 85
Panofsky, Erwin 50
Parker, Agnes 219
Paschal III, anti-pope 151
Passional of Christ and Antichrist, The 306–7
patronage 161, 195, 252
Paul VI, Pope 113–14
Paul, Saint 39, 90
Paul the Deacon 77
Paula, Saint 39–40
Pelagius II, Pope 77

Percy, Thomas, Bishop of Norwich 244
perpetual chantries 241, 252
Peter Comestor 32, 38
Peter of Verona 34, 164
Peter the Hermit 103, 105
Philip III, King of France 153
Pilgrimage of Grace 273
Pilgrimage of the Lyfe of the Manhood, The 206
pilgrimages 63, 68, 102, 162
    to Crowland Abbey 260, 264–6, 267, 268–9
    crusades as 103, 205–20
    death as pilgrimage 205–6
    female pilgrimage saints 197
    Henry VI and 200
    images of pilgrimage saints 197–8, 213–14
    and indulgences 217–18
    to Marian shrines 231–2
    penitential 216–17
    pilgrim badges 158, 196, 269, 340n26
    pilgrimage literature 217–18
    Pilgrimage of Grace 273
    pilgrimage saints 202
    relics as focus of 108, 159–60, 207
    shrines as focus of 140, 156, 158, 168–9, 194, 202, 203
    suppression of 196
    surrogate pilgrimages 215, 217, 218, 219
    symbolism of 205–6
    tombs as focus of 131, 161, 187, 190, 198
    vows of pilgrimage 218–19
Pippin the Short, King of the Franks 94, 95
plague 224
    bubonic plague 78–9, 81, 85
    Justinianic plague 74–83
    pneumonic plague 78–9, 85
    rats and 78, 79–80, 85

pneumonic plague 78–9, 85
Pollock, Linda 116
Polycarp: martyrdom of 154
Prayer of St Thomas Aquinas 314
Procopius 75
Prudentius (Aurelius Prudentius
    Clemens) 35
psalms
    lay people and 53–69
    penitential psalms 56, 58, 65–6
    psalms of the Passion 58, 66
    see also sacred songs
Psalter of Saint Jerome 63, 284
psalters 22–3, 53
    Henry VI: 27
    layout of 53–5
    for Louis of Guyenne/Henry
        VI: 27
    for Prince Alphonso and Margaret
        of Holland and Zeeland 26–7
    Psalter-Hours 53
    Psalter of Saint Jerome 63, 284
    Queen Mary Psalter 23
    transition to books of hours 53, 55
Puella Redybone, saint 197, 198
punishment miracles 287
Purgatory 244–8, 252–3
    Purgatory visions 245–6
Pynson, Richard 192–3, 202, 203, 210

Queen Mary Psalter 23

Radolphus the Cistercian 130
Reames, Sherry 39
Redemptus (4th-century deacon) 91
Redwald 77–8
Regnault, François 231
relics 140–2, 144–5, 146–7, 270
    crusades and 107–8
    Erkenwald 165–6
    as focus of pilgrimage 108,
        159–60, 207

Frankish 94–5
Frederick the Wise and 305
Henry VI: 187, 196, 203
Holy Blood of Hailes 202, 210
Louis IX 153
and patronage 161, 195
Polycarp 154
Sainte-Chapelle, Paris 152
of saints 153, 154, 155–61, 165–6
Treasures of Heaven exhibition
    159, 160
William of Norwich 133, 134
reliquaries 144, 146–7, 160, 161
Treasures of Heaven exhibition
    159, 160
Remedius, bishop of Rouen 95
Reydon, Robert, of Creeting 215
Revelation shewed to a holy
    woman 245–6
revenge miracles 38, 166–8
Richard II, King 169–70
Richard III, King 190–1, 195
Riley-Smith, Jonathan 98
Robert the Wise of Anjou, king of
    Naples 23–4
Robinson, John 222–3
Roger Bacon Cipher Manuscript, *see*
    Voynich manuscript (Beinecke
    MS 408)
Rolle, Richard 61, 62
rosaries 224–7, 323–3, 234
Rose, Emily 129–31, 132, 133, 134
Rudolf II, Holy Roman Emperor 45–6
Rudolf of Moutier-sur-Sambre 89
Rufinus of Aquileia 179
Runciman, Steven 98, 99, 106–7
Rushforth, G. McN. 278
Rushworth College 242, 244

sacramentals 137–8, 145
sacred songs 87–96
    reform of musical notation 88–9

song schools 92–4
see also psalms
St Bernard's Verses 63–4
St Erkenwald (alliterative poem) 170–81
 audience for 181–6
 deathbed scene 184–6
 and legend of Trajan and Pope Gregory 174–6
 and Whitby 'Life of Gregory' 176–81
Sainte-Chapelle, Paris 152
saints: cult of 149–64
Saladin 100, 104–5, 108
Salve guild, St Magnus the Martyr 222
Sanctilogium Angliae (John of Tynemouth) 168
Sarum Books of Hours 57–9, 65, 285
 psalms included 57–8
 psalms omitted 58–9
Sassetta (Stefano di Giovanni di Consolo) 287
Savonarola, Girolamo 65, 226
Schorne, John 197–8, 213
schola cantorum 92–3, 95
Scott, Walter 100
Scribner, Bob 142
Scrope, Archbishop Richard 188
Septuagint 11–12, 16
Sheppey, John, Bishop of Rochester 59
Shorter, Edward 114
shrines 155–6, 215–16
 Bromholm 108, 208, 215–16
 Canterbury 207
 Compostela 207, 219
 as focus of pilgrimage 140, 156, 158, 168–9, 194, 202, 203
 grave shrines 214
 image shrines 213–15
 Jerusalem 207, 219
 Joseph of Arimathea, Glastonbury 208
 Marian 231–2, 270–1, 272
 Rocamadour 207, 214

Rome 207, 219
Saint Werburge, Chester 192
Walsingham 192–3, 202, 207, 210, 213, 214, 215, 221, 222, 231–2
Sighere, king of the East Saxons 77–8
Simeon (Roman singer) 95
Simeon the Stylite 163
Simon de Novers 129–30, 131
Sint Truiden monastery 89
Skyllan, John, of Bergh Apton 277
song schools 92–4, 95
South English Legendary 30, 170
Sparham 213
Speculum Christiani 276
Stacyons of Rome, The 218
Starkey, David 28
Stathakopoulos, Dionysios 80–1
Stephen II, Pope 94
Stephen of Thiers 161
Stephen the Deacon, Saint 201–2
Stilman, John 277
Stone, Lawrence 114, 300
Strack, Hermann 126
Suetonius (Gaius Suetonius Tranquillus) 8
Sulpicius Severus 162
Supplication of Souls (More) 253
surrogate pilgrimages 215, 217, 218, 219
Symmachus (Greek Jew) 11

Talisman, The (Scott) 100
Thomas Plantagenet, Earl of Lancaster 188
Theodore of Tarsus 165, 179
Theodotion 11
Theyer, John 26
Thibaud, King of Navarre 153–4
Thibaut V, Count of Blois 126, 134
Thomas de Evere 170
Thomas of Monmouth 129, 130, 131–3, 134–5
Thomas, William 28

Thurkell, Thomas 219
Tiltman, John 49
Torkyngton, Richard 219
Townsend, Roger 186
Trajan, Emperor: and Gregory the Great, legend of 171, 174–7
transubstantiation 145
Turbe, William 130, 131, 134
Turner, Victor 206
Twigg, Graham 85
Tyerman, Christopher 99–100, 107, 108–9

Ulfcytel, Abbot of Crowland 262, 264
Urban II, Pope 102, 103
Urban VIII, Pope 278

van der Weyden, Rogier 314–15
Vatican Library 45
Vauchez, André 209
vengeance miracles 38, 166–8
Virgin Mary, *see* Mary, mother of Jesus
Vita (Arcoid) 166
Vitalian, Pope 165
Vives, Luis de 41
Vogtherr, Heinrich 301–2
Voynich, Wilfrid Michael 44–5, 46–7, 48
Voynich manuscript (Beinecke MS 408) 43–4, 45–52
Vulgate Bible 61

Walstan of Bawburgh, Saint 200–2, 208–14
  cult of 208
  images of 213–14
  legend 202, 209–12
Walsingham 192–3, 202, 207, 210, 213, 214, 215, 221, 222, 231–2
Walter, Henry 199–200
Waltheof, Earl of Huntingdon 263–6, 268–9
  cult of 264–7, 268–9
  miracles at tomb of 264–6, 268
war
  holy wars 100–2, 103
  just wars 101, 102–3
Wayle, John (day-labourer) 271–2
Webbe, Joanne 298
Werburge, Saint 192
Wesley, Charles 3, 137
Westminster Abbey 108
Whatley, Gordon 181–2
Whitby 'Life of Gregory' 174–5, 176–81
William de Warenne 129
William of Malmesbury 266
William of Norwich, Saint 127–35, 213
William of Rochester, Saint 208
Williams, Megan 9, 12, 15, 17–18
wills 186, 247–52
Wilton Diptych 202, 234
Windsor 191, 193–5, 197, 198
Wingfield College, Suffolk 239, 240–1, 242
Withburge, Saint 213
Woolpit Church, Suffolk 213, 215
Worcester Cathedral: pilgrim's grave 205
Wordsworth, William 111
Wrapson, Lucy 349n17
Wrigley, E.A. 115
Wyclif, John 290
Wyclifite Bible 61, 276

A Note on the Author

Professor Eamon Duffy is Emeritus Professor of the History of Christianity at the University of Cambridge, and a fellow and former President of Magdalene College. His previous books include *Reformation Divided, Saints, Sacrilege and Sedition* and *The Stripping of the Altars*.

A Note on the Type

The text of this book is set in Adobe Garamond. It is one of several versions of Garamond based on the designs of Claude Garamond. It is thought that Garamond based his font on Bembo, cut in 1495 by Francesco Griffo in collaboration with the Italian printer Aldus Manutius. Garamond types were first used in books printed in Paris around 1532. Many of the present-day versions of this type are based on the *Typi Academiae* of Jean Jannon cut in Sedan in 1615.

Claude Garamond was born in Paris in 1480. He learned how to cut type from his father and by the age of fifteen he was able to fashion steel punches the size of a pica with great precision. At the age of sixty he was commissioned by King Francis I to design a Greek alphabet, and for this he was given the honourable title of royal type founder. He died in 1561.